Managing Protected Areas in the Tropics

Managing Protected Areas in the Tropics

Compiled by

JOHN and KATHY MACKINNON, Environmental Conservationists, based
in UK; GRAHAM CHILD, former Director of National Parks and
Wildlife Management, Zimbabwe; and JIM THORSELL, Executive
Officer, Commission on National Parks and Protected Areas,
IUCN, Switzerland

Based on the Workshops on Managing Protected Areas in the Tropics
World Congress on National Parks, Bali, Indonesia, October 1982
Organised by the IUCN Commission on National Parks and Protected Areas

INTERNATIONAL UNION FOR CONSERVATION OF NATURE AND NATURAL RESOURCES
and the
UNITED NATIONS ENVIRONMENT PROGRAMME

INTERNATIONAL UNION FOR CONSERVATION OF NATURE AND NATURAL RESOURCES,
GLAND, SWITZERLAND
1986

IUCN – THE WORLD CONSERVATION UNION

Founded in 1948, IUCN – the World Conservation Union – is a membership organisation comprising governments, non-governmental organisations (NGOs), research institutions, and conservation agencies in 120 countries. The Union's objective is to promote and encourage the protection and sustainable utilisation of living resources.

Several thousand scientists and experts from all continents form part of a network supporting the work of its six Commissions: threatened species, protected areas, ecology, sustainable development, environmental law, and environmental education and training. Its thematic programmes include tropical forests, wetlands, marine ecosystems, plants, the Sahel, Antarctica, population and sustainable development, and women in conservation. These activities enable IUCN and its members to develop sound policies and programmes for the conservation of biological diversity and sustainable development of natural resources.

Published by: IUCN, Gland, Switzerland and Cambridge, UK in collaboration with the United Nations Environment Programme.
A contribution to GEMS – the Global Environment Monitoring System.

ISBN: 2-88032-808-X

Cover photos: Neotropical Realm: Education display in Tortuguero
   National Park, Costa Rica. IUCN photo: P. Dugan
Afrotropical Realm: Park rangers on patrol in Lake Manyara National Park,
   Tanzania. IUCN/WWF photo: Iain Douglas-Hamilton
Oceanian Realm: Parks staff conducting boundary survey.
   Irian Jaya, Indonesia. IUCN/WWF photo: J.B. Ratcliffe
Indomalayan Realm: Research on Axis deer. Royal Chitwan National Park,
   Nepal. IUCN/WWF photo: Peter Jackson.

Book design: James Butler

Printed by: Page Bros (Norwich) Limited, UK

Available from: IUCN Publications Services Unit,
   219c Huntingdon Road, Cambridge, CB3 0DL, UK

The designations of geographical entities in this book, and the presentation of the material, do not imply the expression of any opinion whatsoever on the part of IUCN or UNEP concerning the legal status of any country, territory, or area, or of its authorities, or concerning the delimitation of its frontiers or boundaries.

Reprinted 1989

Contents

List of examples

List of figures

Participants: Workshops on managing protected areas in the tropics

Workshop Coordinator: Jeffrey McNeely
Convenors: Graham Child, William Deshler
Session Leaders and Rapporteurs:

Managing Protected Natural Areas to Contribute to Social and Economic Development: Policies to Meet Expanding Needs – David Munro

The Biogeographical Basis for Protected Areas Systems – Miklos Udvardy and John MacKinnon

The Legal and Administrative Basis for Management: Organization Design – Barbara Lausche and Bruce Davis

Protected Areas and Regional Planning – Keith Garratt

Socio-economic Factors in Managing Protected Areas – John Newby and Roger Morales

Management Planning – James Thorsell and Jeff Kennedy

Implementing Management – Harold Roth

Determining Effective Management – Leslie Molloy and William Deshler

International Cooperation in Management of Protected Areas – Gary Wetterberg and Arne Dalfelt

Communication: Ensuring that the Right Message Reaches the Right Audience – James Butler

Preface

This handbook is one of a series of publications resulting from the World Congress on National Parks and Protected Areas held in Bali in October 1982. It draws on the papers presented at the various specialist workshops and in the plenary sessions of Congress. The companion volumes include the Congress proceedings (McNeely and Miller, 1984) and a specialist handbook on the management of marine and coastal reserves (Salm and Clark, 1984).

There are several reasons why this handbook focusses on protected areas in the tropics. In recent years, there has been a rapid growth in the number of protected area systems in the tropics. While professional expertise in the development of protected areas has spread from the temperate regions to the tropics, the methodology of management as developed in the temperate regions is not always appropriate for tropical countries where the needs for protection, the nature of the ecosystems to be managed and the soci-economic climate are so different. The delegates of the Bali Congress felt strongly that there was a need for a handbook specific to the management of protected areas in the tropics. New techniques developed in the tropics have resulted in many successes – and admittedly some failures – from which we can learn valuable lessons for wider application. Moreover, many delegates felt that, far from needing to borrow techniques from the more developed temperate countries, some tropical nations have enough experience and expertise to be able to teach a few lessons to the rest of the world.

For the purpose of this handbook the term 'tropical' is taken to cover only four of the major biographic regions as defined by Udvardy (1975) – the Neotropical, Afrotropical, Indomalayan and Oceanian Realms. Since this area includes most of the world's tropical rain forests – a resource that is vanishing at an alarming rate – some emphasis has been given to the problems of managing and protecting rain forest ecosystems.

This handbook is a guide to help those concerned with the planning and management of natural protected areas in tropical countires. It covers a broad spectrum of activities involved in selection, legislation, administration, planning, managing and evaluating management of reserves. It is aimed at senior management at the park planner, park supervisor and senior warden level, but it would also be useful for university-level classes on the subject.

Since this readership seeks practical rather than theoretical guidelines, theory is presented only to the extent it affects the taking of practical decisions and actions. Terminology has been kept to a minimum and long technical arguments avoided whenever possible. Descriptive examples are shown in boxes and diagrams.

To faciliate its use as a reference source, the handbook has been divided into three sections. Part A, 'The Basis for Establishing Protected Areas', describes the prerequisites for the development of a national protected area system. Chapter 2 explains the need to have a number of different complementary categories of protected areas if countries are to get full benefit from their living resources, and why it is helpful if these catagories conform to standard international criteria. Chapter 3 outlines principles for the selection of sites for protection and Chapter 4 describes the administrative and legal needs for the effective implementation of a policy to establish a system of protected areas.

Part B, 'Winning Suport for Protected Areas', discusses how to generate wide support for the principles of protected area management by better integration with regional development. Chapter 5 concentrates on the need to integrate protected area planning into wider patterns of land use, Chapter 6 deals with the challenge of getting the local people to appreciate the real benefits derived from protected areas, and Chapter 7 presents the needs for protected area managers to communicate with their visitors, users and sponsors to build the public support on which the success of protected areas depends.

Part C, 'Managing Protected Areas', deals more specifically with the principles and techniques of managing reserves to achieve certain objectives. Chapter 8 presents a discussion on the biophysical principles of protected area management. Chapter 9 details the need for clear planning on the basis of well-formulated objectives, and describes in some length the preparation of management plans which form the basis for all subsequent management activities and decision-making. Chapter 10 tackles the problems of implementation of plans – the actual operation of protected areas. Chapter 11 rounds off this Part with emphasis on the need to monitor constantly and evaluate the effects of management with a view to improving effectiveness.

The final chapter, Chapter 12, places protected area management in a more global perspective by discussing the need for international assistance in the development of protected areas and the role played by aid agencies and international programmes including IUCN itself.

The selected bibliography refers not only to the principles and examples cited in the following chapters but also lists other key works of value to the protected area manager in the tropics.

The handbook relies on a variety of sources, including the papers presented at the 1982 Bali Workshop on Managing Protected Areas and summary reports of workshop sessions. Each participant in the workshop has thus contributed to this book. Extra material from other reference sources has been included as the editors felt appropriate. In choosing the examples to highlight specific management topics we have tried to select appropriate examples from the various tropical realms to which the book is directed. Sometimes these examples may be appropriate to only one region but more often they can be applied or adapted to fit situations elsewhere in the tropics.

Compilation of the text of this handbook from the broad range of contributions was a difficult and time-consuming task. Overall responsibility was given to John MacKinnon with assistance from Graham Child and Jim Thorsell. In the final stages, important comments were provided by Norman Myers and Barbara Lausche (Chapter 4). John Blower, Dennis Glick and Jeffrey McNeely made valued substantive reviews of the final draft. Kathy MacKinnon took overall responsibility for editing and refining the text. CNPPA secretary Sue Rallo performed valiantly on the word processor to produce many drafts as well as the final copy. The production to printing stages were handled by Morag White, Lissie Wright, and Barbara Lambert.

Foreword

Protected areas in the tropical realms now number 1420 and conserve 174 million ha of land and water. It is in these regions, where the world's biological diversity is concentrated, that we have a special responsibility in ensuring maintenance of this rich natural heritage.

It is in the tropical realms too that most of the world's human population is to be found and where man's use of the land is intensive and longstanding. Management of protected areas under these circumstances is especially challenging and requires innovative approaches which cannot always be borrowed from the temperate world.

With these conditions in mind, participants at the management workshop, held at the World Congress on National Parks in Bali in 1982, began the deliberations which have led to this publication. The compilers of this volume have blended the results of the workshop with additional written materials and with their own experiences in some 30 tropical countries. The handbook illustrates the advances that have been made, many of which will have relevance to our colleagues in other protected areas of the world.

But protected area management is a relatively new field and one which involves a wide range of subjects from law and administration to public relations, ethics, sociology, and all of the biological sciences. Few managers can be expected to be both generalists and specialists in all of these fields. The value of this book is thus in its use as a reference for those dealing with the great variety of considerations that are involved in the task of ensuring effective management of protected areas in the tropics.

Readers of this handbook will note a particular theme: the integration of protected areas into regional land-use programmes and the concern for local people within the vicinity of protected areas. As the *World Conservation Strategy* notes, and as the *Bali Action Plan* prepared at the Parks Congress underlines, protected areas cannot be viewed as islands, they must be managed within the context of their regional settings.

As the tropical realm Vice-Chairmen of IUCN's Commission on National Parks and Protected Areas, we hope that the principles, guidelines and case studies provided in this volume will assist individual managers in ensuring that their protected areas will contribute to sustaining the natural features and processes on which human populations depend.

Marc Dourojeanni, Neotropical Realm (Peru)

Samar Singh, Indomalayan Realm (India)

Birandra Singh, Oceanian Realm (Fiji)

Walter Lusigi, Afrotropical Realm (Kenya)

1

Introduction

Modern concepts of protected areas

In the year 252 B.C. the Emperor Asoka of India passed an edict for the protection of animals, fish and forests. This may be the earliest documented instance of the deliberate establishment of what we today call protected areas, but the practice of setting aside sacred areas as religious sanctuaries or exclusive hunting reserves is much older and the tradition has been continued in many widely different cultures to the present day. In 1084 A.D., for instance, King William I of England ordered the preparation of the Domesday Book – an inventory of all the lands, forests, fishing areas, agricultural areas, hunting preserves and productive resources of his kingdom – as the basis for making rational plans for the country's management and development.

The modern concept of conservation – the wise maintenance and utilisation of the earth's resources – is no more than the combination of these two ancient principles: the need to plan resource management on the basis of accurate inventory; and the need to take protective measures to ensure that resources do not become exhausted.

Conservation has sometimes been thought of as a protective 'locking away' of resources by a powerful elite who have time to enjoy the beauty of nature, an essentially selfish and anti-development activity. On the contrary, protected areas, when designed and managed appropriately, are now recognised as offering major sustainable benefits to society. They play a central role in the social and economic development of rural environments and contribute to the economic well-being of urban centres and the quality of life of their inhabitants.

The establishment and management of protected areas is one of the most important ways of ensuring that the world's natural resources are conserved so that they can better meet the material and cultural needs of mankind now and in the future. It is only on Earth that we know that life can be sustained. Yet human activities are progressively reducing this planet's life-supporting capacity, while rising human numbers and consumption make increasing demands on it. The combined destructive impacts of a poor majority struggling to survive and an affluent minority consuming a disproportionately large share of the world's resources are undermining the very means by which all people can survive and flourish.

Humanity's relationship with the biosphere (the thin covering of the planet that contains and sustains life) will continue to deteriorate until a new environmental ethic is adopted and sustainable modes of development become the rule rather than the exception. The *World Conservation Strategy* (WCS) prepared by four of the world's leading conservation agencies – the International Union for Conservation of Nature and Natural Resources (IUCN), World Wildlife Fund (WWF), Food and Agriculture Organisation of the United Nations (FAO), and the United Nations Environment Programme (UNEP) – and launched in 1981 demonstrates how the conservation of living resources is essential for sustaining development by:

- maintaining the essential ecological processes and life-support systems on which human survival and development depend;
- preserving genetic diversity on which depend

1. Clear linkage of conservation with its development benefits is essential if protected areas are to gain wider high level support. The principles of the World Conservation Strategy are expounded at a press conference in Washington.
   Photo: WWF-US/Mort Broffman

the breeding programmes necessary for the protection and improvement of cultivated plants and domesticated animals, as well as much scientific advance, technical innovation, and the security of the many industries that use living resources;

• ensuring that man's utilisation of species and ecosystems, which support millions of rural people as well as major industries, is sustainable.

These objectives can only be met if governments, industry and the public support this strategy of protecting species and ecosystems within an overall programme for development. In general terms,

the maintenance of species and ecosystems requires that the use of living resources within a healthy environment must be done on a sustainable basis. Among other more specific actions, it requires the establishment of networks of natural protected areas for the conservation of species and ecosystems in wild environments.

Protected natural areas are essential for the conservation of a nation's living resources thus ensuring that:

• representative samples of important natural regions are retained in perpetuity;
• biological and physical diversity is maintained;
• wild genetic materials are conserved.

Protected areas also contribute to the conservation of living resources and to sustainable development by:

- maintaining the environment stability of the surrounding region and thereby reducing the intensity of floods and droughts, protecting the soil from erosion and limiting the extremes of local climates;
- maintaining the productive capacity of ecosystems, thus ensuring the continuing availability of water and plant and animal products;
- providing opportunities for research and monitoring of wild species and ecosystems and their relationship to human development;
- providing opportunities for conservation education for the general public and for policy makers;
- providing opportunities for complementary

rural development and the rational use of marginal lands;
- providing a base for recreation and tourism.

In view of rapid development and population increases in many tropical areas of the world, and the great speed with which natural resources are being depleted, there is considerable urgency in establishing adequate protected areas if we are to achieve the objectives of the World Conservation Strategy. In addition, the increasing pressure for land for agriculture and other uses forces conservation managers to review existing protected areas; clarify the justifications and objectives for each reserve; increase management efficiency to use these natural resources wisely for conservation; and make increasing efforts to accommodate other forms of utilisation if these are compatible with the protection requirements.

The road to Bali

The first national park – Yellowstone, in the United States – was established in 1872. This was a milestone in the evolution of the concept of national parks as we know them today. At this point parks became 'for people' rather than the preserve of elitist groups, as, for example, royal hunting grounds had been. Since Yellowstone's establishment, most governments have recognised the value of protected areas to their people. To date, there are more than 2600 protected areas in the world, covering nearly four million sq. km, established by 124 countries. During the 1970s, the number of protected areas increased by 46 per cent and the total area protected increased by over 80 per cent (Harrison *et al.*, 1984). Many of these recently created protected areas lie in newly-independent and tropical countries.

For most countries, the subject of protected area management is still new. The first contemporary international conference on the subject was held as recently as 1962 in Seattle. The second conference was held in 1972, appropriately in Yellowstone National Park on the occasion of its Hundredth Anniversary. The third, the World Congress on National Parks and Protected Areas was held on the island of Bali, Indonesia in October, 1982. It was the first of these congresses to be held in a tropical country, in itself a significant tribute to the role of many developing countries in allocating land for protection.

Most tropical countries have established protected areas. The exceptions include several small island nations: Comoros, Grenada, Maldives, Nauru, Niue, Tuvalu, and Vanuatu; and a few larger mainland countries: Bahrain, Burundi, Iraq, Lao People's Democratic Republic, Qatar, and both Yemens (data from IUCN 1984b). Even the most densely populated parts of the tropics have significant areas under protection. Java, for example, an island the size of Greece or the state of New York and inhabited by 90 million people, has more than 100 protected areas which cover over 650,000 ha; large mammals such as Javan rhinoceros (*Rhinoceros sondaicus*) and leopard (*Panthera pardus*) still survive there although the Javan tiger (*P. tigris javanicus*) has become extinct in the past few years.

A brief summary of protected areas in the major tropical realms is presented in Table 1. The total of 174 million hectares – the size of Iran and nearly twice the size of Venezuela, Pakistan, or Tanzania – seems quite respectable, especially since virtually all major countries are represented. But is this area really adequate to conserve the species, ecosystems, and ecosystem functions that the areas are established to protect? Leaving aside the question of how effectively the existing areas are managed, biogeography and population genetics suggest that the answer is still a clear 'no'.

How much land should nations allocate for pro-

2. Yellowstone National Park, USA. – the first 'park for the people'.
   Photo: WWF/Milada Leiska

Example 1.1. *Coverage of protected areas in the tropics*

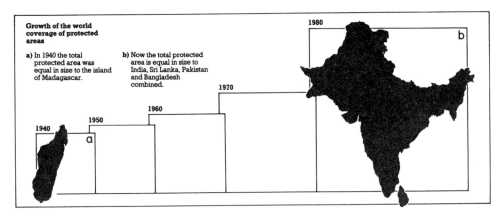

Growth of the world coverage of protected areas

a) In 1940 the total protected area was equal in size to the island of Madagascar.

b) Now the total protected area is equal in size to India, Sri Lanka, Pakistan and Bangladesh combined.

Realm	Number of Units	Area protected (ha)
Afrotropical	426	88,166,096
Indomalayan	572	27,568,406
Oceanian	51	4,108,584
Neotropical	296	43,503,474
Australian	75	10,752,012
Totals	1,420 Units	174,098,572 ha

Source: IUCN, 1985b

tected areas? This is a vital question. Allocating too much may deprive the nation of urgently needed production, but not protecting enough could ultimately mean a lowered capacity to produce at all. For many countries 10 per cent of the total land area would seem a realistic target figure, but even this figure is regarded as too low to protect some habitats. Some scientists have suggested that countries should aim to protect 20 per cent of rain forest, 10 per cent of savanna and 5 per cent of boreal ecosystems (Myers, 1979). Nine countries of over 20,000 sq km (including seven new African nations) already have over 10 per cent of their land area established as national parks or other reserves. But less than half of the countries listed by the United Nations as 'developing', most of which lie in the tropics, have properly established protected area systems.

It is of little use stressing the importance of nature conservation and the need for protected areas in developing countries without understanding the problems facing their governments. The international community must be prepared to provide effective assistance where needed. Many countries, including some in the lowest *per capita* income group, are expanding their protected area systems at a rapid rate and will need appropriate resources to finance this expansion. Areas which are really worthy of establishment as protected areas are part of the heritage of the whole world as well as of the country concerned. Many of the countries most urgently in need of protected areas to conserve their rich and unique natural resources are among those least equipped with manpower, expertise, or cash to do so. This handbook aims to offer some realistic solutions to these problems by drawing on present scientific knowledge and practical experiences relating to protected areas.

Challenges of managing tropical ecosystems

There are a number of major biophysical differences between temperate and tropical regions which dictate different management approaches.

a) Climatic conditions

Although the ranges of diurnal and annual temperatures found in tropical habitats are generally less than experienced in temperate regions, overall climatic conditions are more severe. Rainfall in the tropics is much heavier (when it does rain), while the tropical sun makes conditions hotter and drier. These factors make tropical soils highly prone to erosion and the vegetation susceptible to wildfire. Tropical soils are far more fragile than temperate soils and generally far less fertile.

b) Susceptibility to degradation

Natural tropical ecosystems are often very susceptible to degradation. Fire, overgrazing, and cultivation make it difficult for the original vegetation ever to return. The weakness of tropical soils and their inability to support intensive agriculture causes people to adopt destructive and unstable forms of agriculture and pastoralism which further threaten remaining natural areas. Shifting agriculture is practised in many parts of the tropics not only because fertility drops fast on newly-cleared lands, but because weeds choke out the fields to the point that the labour needed to keep them open is intolerable. The land is soon abandoned and left to return to its natural state but the period of agriculture leaves a permanent scar. Topsoil is lost and under some conditions (e.g. lateritic soils) the exposed soils become a hard pan which cannot easily be recolonised by desirable natural vegetation.

c) Species richness

Most tropical ecosystems are very species-rich, particularly those in rain forests and savannas. This means that most species occur only at very low density so that the area needed to conserve viable populations is large. In temperate regions, forest reserves of a few thousand hectares can be highly species-stable and even a stand of a few hectares may be a valuable wildlife refuge. This is rarely so in the tropics where such island patches would quickly lose most of their constituent species, as indeed occurred on Barro Colorado Island in Panama, where over 20 per cent of breeding bird species had vanished within 50 years of the reserve's creation (Willis, 1974).

d) Management factors

Effective management of protected areas in the tropics is also limited by our state of knowledge and the complexity of tropical ecosystems. As we have far less understanding of tropical rather than temperate ecology (even basic resource inventories are often not available), the manager is often faced with management decisions that have not been tested previously or are subject to considerable uncertainty.

It follows that the protected area manager in the tropics must be a generalist. Compared to the well-developed and intensively-managed systems in most temperate countries where a park staff may include specialists in various fields of management (e.g. planners, interpreters, law enforcement officers), the tropical reserve manager rarely has sufficient trained staff to allot to specific duties. Instead, he or she must be more of a multidisciplinary manager with at least a general understanding of all facets of protected area management.

Tropical rain forests: a vanishing resource

Within the tropics, particular attention is being focussed on conserving rain forest ecosystems. This argument is forcibly presented in a paper by Roth and Merz (1980) from which much of the following discussion is drawn. For many years there has been alarm at the rate of rain forest clearance. Lanly (1982) estimates a global figure for the area being cleared every year of 157,000 sq km (about the area of England and Wales combined). The remaining areas of rain forest are shown in Table I.4. summarised from data compiled by FAO. Unless this destruction can be halted, the final demise of this irreplaceable sector of our planet will occur in only 72 years (Guppy, 1984).

The picture is just as gloomy on a regional basis. Tropical moist forests have been reduced by 45 per cent in Central Africa and by 72 per cent in West Africa, and the process of deforestation continues. In Ivory Coast alone, Roth and Merz (1980) estimate that by 1982 more than 90 per cent of the country's original rain forest will have been transformed into modified man-made landscapes. In the Indian sub-continent, 18 per cent of the land is still forested; but according to Mani (1974) the area remaining as undisturbed primary habitat is certainly less than 1 per cent. In Java only 2 per cent of the lowland forests survive.

These figures highlight the special urgency of conserving biotic communities representative of the different types of tropical humid forest, the most species-rich terrestrial habitats on earth. Unfortunately those rain forests which are most important from a conservation point of view due to their great diversity of plant and animal life – the lowland rain forests – usually also contain the most valuable timber. For example, the Taman Negara, a lowland forest park in West Malaysia, contains 60 per cent of the endemic mammal species of the entire Sunda Shelf region, 142 of the 198 species being dependent on rain forest for their existence (Medway, 1971). Of the 241 lowland bird species in Peninsular Malaysia, 172 have been recorded within this area (Wells, 1971). At the same time, this forest contains timber valued, in 1971, at about $US 3000 per hectare. Foregoing this revenue is part of the price of conserving the Taman Negara National Park.

Compared to rain forests, savanna areas, which particularly merit conservation because of their spectacular wildlife, are usually less threatened by economic exploitation. In savanna zones there may be pressure for grazing land or other agricultural lands but nowhere – except in the case of mineral exploitation – is there as strong an economic incentive for the ruthless exploitation of natural resources as in tropical forests with their valuable hardwoods. In fact many savanna conservation areas are economically marginal for agriculture due to unfavourable soil or water conditions or the presence of tsetse fly, which make it impracticable to keep livestock. Moreover, savanna areas lend themselves more easily to tourism development than do rain forests and can thereby contribute significantly to the local economy. As a result, some of the world's finest and best-managed protected areas are found in savanna zones, while protected areas in tropical rain forest are often under threat.

There are important ecological differences between primary rain forests and savanna which need to be taken into account when considering their conservation. Given appropriate protection and correct management, savanna areas, and the wildlife they contain, can recover in a relatively short space of time – even from levels of severe degradation – and reassume most of their original biotic features. Although rain forests are initially much more stable than savanna ecosystems, once forests have been destroyed they will never recover in the same form or structure as the original forest, nor contain the same plant and animal species.

The great diversity of plant and animal species in tropical lowland rain forest is associated with low density of species. This renders them particularly vulnerable to local extinction. To maintain the diversity of rain forest reserves, large areas must be protected and, as logging continues apace throughout the humid tropics, they must be protected soon.

Given the above facts, there is a strong case for preferential conservation efforts in the humid forest zones and a need for more and larger conservation areas in these habitats. However, if one examines the conservation situation on a worldwide scale it soon becomes obvious that tropical forests are still poorly protected. Of a total of approximately 935 million ha of moist forest, only about 39 million ha, i.e. 4.2 per cent, have been designated as national parks or equivalent reserves.

Given the rate at which tropical forests are vanishing, felled for timber or to open up agricultural lands, it is a matter of urgency to conserve as much as possible now. In general, savanna ecosystems are both less threatened and better represented within national systems.

The management of national parks and protected areas in rain forest zones is also quite different from that in savanna areas. From a physical point of view, protection and control, as well as routine observation of game populations, are more difficult in rain forests than open savannas, due to inaccessibility and limited visibility. Ecologically, as little human interference as possible is desirable in rain forests. This implies that utilisation of rain forest parks is more critical than for protected areas in savanna, and the two ecosystems sometimes require quite different management prescriptions.

3. Protecting blocks of tropical rain forest from the axe, saw and flame is the greatest challenge to
protected area managers in the humid tropics.
Photo: WWF/Claude Martin

Problems and challenges of establishing permanent reserves in tropical countries

'Right across the (African) continent there are still vivid examples of military coups, border disputes, civil confrontations and internal political tensions. All these have affected the atmosphere in which most conservationists work and changed national priorities to favour heavy investments into military expenditure. National budgets have consequently shown only small allocations to conservation ...

'Because of political uncertainty in some countries it has been difficult to make plans in the long term and as one director of wildlife conservation puts it, 'you just never know what will happen tomorrow'. Under the circumstances, it is quite possible – and this has happened on a few occasions – that assistance or support earmarked for conservation finds its way into other unrelated activities'

(Lusigi, 1984)

The above quotation illustrates some of the challenges involved in operating a secure system of protected areas in the tropics. These include severe limitations of funds, resources, public support and trained expertise.

High rates of illiteracy, low levels of institutional development, and complex land ownership systems are other obstacles. In addition, habitat modification due to economic forces and population growth in these countries is happening so fast that the reserve planner is usually working against severe time constraints. Often the manager must make bold decisions and recommendations on few facts and with little interest or support from a poorly-informed public. Together these limitations necessitate a different approach to protected area management to that accepted as the norm in temperate regions.

Political instability is another worrying factor in some tropical countries. Revolts, coups, guerrilla warfare and the presence of refugees can wreak havoc in protected areas. Political upheavals in Uganda and their well-documented and disastrous effects on wildlife populations and facilities in the parks are only too well-known (Kayanja and Douglas-Hamilton, 1984). Unfortunately, there is no foolproof management prescription to protect parks under such circumstances.

With a growing number of mouths to feed, it is only natural that politicians and government planners will be more orientated to agricultural and production development than to establishing natural reserves. Park managers must generate public support and persuade politicians of the long-term benefits of protected areas. It is a sad fact that protected areas are still generally undervalued, even when the economic return alone is comparable to, or better than, that from other patterns of land use. Too frequently there is a lack of understanding of environmental problems on the part of decision makers and priority is often given to short-term financial gain from logging or other forms of exploitation even where this conflicts with long-term environmental considerations.

This book is based on the theme of integrating conservation into the development process, stressing the multiple functions of protected areas. The linkage between protected areas and development is seen as the approach most likely to bring long term success in protected area management.

Example 1.2: Tropical countries of over 20,000 sq km with over 10% of the land area protected

Country	Size of country (sq km)	Population	No. of Areas	Area protected (ha)	ha/sq km (i.e. %)	ha protected per 1000 people
Botswana	574,978	726,000	9	10,439,300	18.16	14,379.20
Central African Rep.	622,996	2,610,000	12	7,499,800	12.04	2,873.49
Benin	115,763	3,377,000	5	1,377,550	11.90	407.92
Malaysia	330,669	12,600,000	20	3,839,084	11.61	304.69
Tanzania	939,762	16,553,000	15	10,830,700	11.52	654.30
Zimbabwe	389,361	6,930,000	25	4,394,400	11.29	634.11
Bhutan	46,620	1,250,000	11	950,000	20.38	760.00
Senegal	197,160	5,085,388	8	2,130,200	10.80	418.89
Rwanda	26,388	4,368,000	2	274,000	10.38	62.73

Source: IUCN, 1985b

Example 1.3: **Protected area coverage of biomes in tropical realms**

Biome and Realm	Number of areas	Total area (hectares)
Tropical humid forests		
Afrotropical	44	8,905,733
Indomalayan	122	5,092,774
Australian	53	7,776,347
Neotropical	61	17,277,197
	280	39,052,051
Tropical dry forests/woodlands		
Afrotropical	240	48,673,552
Indomalayan	238	10,420,406
Australian	10	934,272
Neotropical	93	5,501,447
	581	65,529,677
Evergreen sclerophyllous forests		
Afrotropical	41	1,620,967
Neotropical	5	38,795
	46	1,659,762
Warm deserts/semi-deserts		
Afrotropical	57	23,783,085
Indomalayan	35	1,628,854
Neotropical	7	1,446,751
	99	26,858,690
Tropical grasslands/savannas		
Australian	12	2,041,393
Neotropical	18	7,011,403
	30	9,052,796
Mixed mountain systems		
Afrotropical	38	5,104,626
Neotropical	86	11,037,282
	124	16,141,908
Mixed island systems		
Afrotropical	4	23,033
Indomalayan	177	10,426,372
Oceanian	51	4,108,584
Neotropical	26	1,190,599
	258	15,748,588
Lake systems		
Afrotropical	2	55,100
	2	55,100
TOTAL:	1,420	174,098,572

Source: IUCN, 1985b (IUCN Management Categories I-V)

Example 1.4: The world's principal tropical forest countries by area (in sq km)

Country	National Area	Undisturbed Forest	Logged/Managed Forest	Unproductive Forest	Total Forest Area	% World Total
Brazil	8,511,965	2,886,300	120,000	556,500	3,562,800	30.68
Indonesia	1,903,650	389,150	346,600	400,000	1,135,750	9.78
Zaire	2,345,409	797,400	3,800	255,300	1,056,500	9.09
Peru	1,285,215	373,200	60,000	259,900	693,100	5.97
Colombia	1,138,914	386,000	9,000	69,000	464,000	3.99
India	3,166,828	48,850	334,730	76,860	460,440	3.96
Bolivia	1,098,580	177,600	120,900	141,600	440,100	3.79
Papua New Guinea	475,300	138,150	2,200	196,750	337,100	2.90
Venezuela	912,050	76,000	116,100	126,600	318,700	2.74
Burma	678,030	141,070	90,090	80,770	311,930	2.68
Cumulative total		5,413,720	1,203,420	2,163,280	8,780,420	75.62
And 63 other countries		1,270,430	720,350	838,550	2,829,330	24.39
World total		6,684,150	1,923,770	3,001,830	11,609,750	100.00

N.B. Figures are for Broad-leaved Humid and Dry Forests with Closed Canopy
Source: Guppy, 1984

PART A

The Basis for Establishing Protected Areas

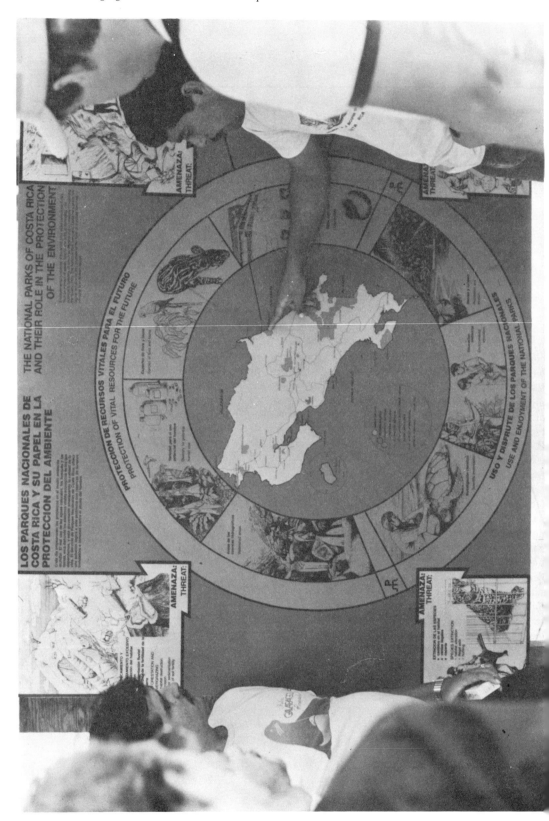

2

Categories of Protected Areas

Introduction

Most nations accept the desirability of protecting outstanding examples of their natural heritage and acknowledge that this is a contribution to the worldwide effort to protect living resources and conserve biological diversity. The national park has been the most common and popularly known form of protection, but national parks can be complemented by many other categories of protected area. The Commission on National Parks and Protected Areas (CNPPA) is the Commission of IUCN specifically responsible for promoting the establishment of a worldwide network of effectively managed terrestrial and marine protected areas and has distributed guidelines on this topic (IUCN, 1978a, 1984b).

One hundred and twenty-four countries have now proclaimed one or more national parks or similar reserves, although the level of legal protection and management objectives may vary even between areas with the same designation in the same country. Many countries recognise several different types of protected areas, each with different conservation and management objectives, including some which are heavily utilised, but all within one overall national system.

A protected area by definition should be secure from unrestricted use of its resources. Designating large tracts of land as national parks may be desirable from a conservation point of view, but it is simply not feasible for most countries. Any country limiting itself to protected areas suitable for national park status might find that it is doomed to have very small reserves or only areas of no alternative production value. Moreover, the protection agency would have no authority over extensive forestry and other wildlands, although such tracts would certainly contain most of the country's wild natural resources.

However, if in addition to 'total protection' areas, a country has alternative categories in which, for instance, limited selective forestry, hunting or controlled livestock grazing is permitted, the protection agency may be able to extend proper conservation practices over a much greater area. Thus land designated for productive forestry or hunting can be managed in such a way as to minimise loss of natural gene pools, and give prime attention to the goals of nature conservation.

In practice, most countries find it an advantage to have several categories of protected areas, each with different management objectives and each permitting different levels of manipulation. By applying sensible criteria to the designation of each area and applying strict controls on use, the protection authority regulates the management options possible and clarifies the manager's responsibilities. Having a range of protected area options can provide enhanced protection to the strictly protected categories by removing human pressures to those areas where heavier sustained use is permissible.

4. Iguazu Falls National Parks in Brazil and Argentina provide an example of the protection o
spectacular natural scenery as well as valuable biological resources
Photo: WWF/IUCN/Dolder

Criteria for classifying protected areas

The wise maintenance and development of the human habitat requires that some areas be retained in their wild state. The quality of water, protection of genetic resources, protection of scenic areas, the opportunity to enjoy and appreciate the natural environment and the continued availability of renewable natural resources on a sustained yield basis, all depend upon the conservation of natural areas.

Moreover, it should be possible to derive these benefits from natural areas or wildlands in perpetuity, if management is properly designed and implemented. However, there are types of benefits which compete with one another; for example, it is physically and biologically difficult to remove vegetation and study natural ecosystems in the same area. Controlled tourism and species conservation, however, can be compatible in both the terrestrial and marine environments. Management categories must be designed and implemented to accommodate compatible sets of benefits, without the pursuit of any one benefit excluding the possibility of others. Commonly known categories which encompass several management objectives include the national park and multiple use reserves. Even in areas with generally compatible objectives, however, conflicts may arise during certain seasons or at specific sites. For instance, it may be necessary to restrict visitor use during nesting or calving periods or within critical habitats. Such conflicts can be avoided by implementing a zoning system or in periodic restriction of activities in part or all of the reserve.

When setting up a national system of protected areas it is important to choose the right categories according to the objectives of management. The appropriate category of protected area depends upon the following considerations:

- Those features which the area is designed to protect, based on an evaluation of its biological and other features and the protection objectives thereby established.
- The degree of manipulative management needed for, or compatible with, the established protection objectives.
- The degree of ecological tolerance/fragility of the ecosystem or species concerned.
- The degree to which different types of utilisation of the area are compatible with the established objectives.
- The level of demand for different types of utilisation and the management practicality of accommodating these.

Features which the area is meant to protect

A protected area may be established to protect a wide variety of features, such as:

- Characteristic or unique ecosystems, e.g. lowland rain forest, endemic island faunas, tropical alpine systems.
- Special species of interest, value, rarity or under threat, e.g. rhinoceros, vicuna, quetzals.
- Sites of unusual species diversity.
- Landscape or geophysical features of aesthetic or scientific value, e.g. glaciers, hot water springs, waterfalls.
- Hydrological protective functions: soil, water, local climate.
- Facilities for nature recreation, tourism, e.g. lakes, beaches, mountain views, wildlife spectacles.
- Sites of special scientific interest, e.g. areas of long-standing research.
- Cultural sites, e.g., temples, shrines, archaeological excavations.

The relative value and importance of each feature will need to be considered, together with the compatibility of, or even need for, combining protection with different levels of manipulative management and utilisation.

Compatibility of protection objectives with management and utilisation options

In any protected area, the degree of disturbance from management or utilisation that can be accommodated will depend on the species or system that the area is supposed to protect. Some species populations, communities, and ecosystems are fragile and can tolerate almost no disturbance, while others are relatively adaptable or 'robust'.

Management actions for a given area could include a range of options:

- Maintaining trails, watchtowers, hides or cleared look-out points for management purposes or visitor use.
- Planting of food plants or creation of artificial waterholes, saltlicks, etc., to encourage selected wildlife species.
- Maintaining open feeding areas or clearing trailside vegetation to render wildlife more visible to visitors.
- Controlling predators, pests or competitors of species to be conserved.
- Culling or restricting the movements of wildlife considered to be too numerous, or for reasons of stock health, or to limit damage by wildlife.
- Cutting, burning or grazing of vegetation to maintain a certain vegetation stage, e.g. open savanna.
- Introductions, reintroductions or translocations (for genetic exchange) of wildlife.

According to the status of the protected area some of the following types of utilisation may be compatible with protection objectives. These activities are listed in approximate order of increasing disturbance to the ecosystem.

- No visitors permitted entry; only vital protective management allowed, e.g. catching poachers, putting out wildfires.
- Scientific research involving only measurements, counts and observations, e.g. behavioural studies of primates, census counts of migrating ungulates.
- Scientific research involving small-scale manipulative experiments and collection of specimens for identification.
- Controlled use by visitors on a simple trail system.
- Public access routes traverse protected area.
- Heavy use by visitors but a ban on all activities that threaten or disturb the natural setting.
- Collection of eggs, young or breeding stock for wildlife rearing industries, or restocking of denuded habitats.
- Collection by villagers of dead wood for firewood, also fruits, honey, and other minor forest products.

- Visitors fishing in waterways.
- Traditional hunting and fishing practices.
- Controlled seasonal hunting.
- Habitat management to increase the number of animals for hunting, fishing or wildlife viewing for visitors.
- Traditional human groups living inside reserve in close harmony with their ecosystem.
- Grazing of domestic animals within the reserve.
- Selective logging of timber.
- Small enclaves where mining or quarrying may proceed inside reserve.
- Limited agriculture within reserve.
- Agricultural mosaic landscape only preserved.
- Clear felling followed by reforestation.

Practicality of management

Some types of utilisation which may be compatible with the protection objectives of a given reserve are simply not practicable from a management point of view. For instance, it might be decided that small-scale harvesting of dead wood as firewood from the reserve would not threaten its biological integrity but this is not allowed because there is no way to control such collection and make sure it is 'small scale'; and the presence of firewood collectors in the reserve would threaten other objectives.

On the basis of management objectives as identified above and considering the selection of protected area categories available in that country, the protection agency should allocate the proposed protected area to the reserve category best suited for its protection and appropriate utilisation. Correct allocation is very important so that maximum benefits compatible with protective needs are achieved. In cases of doubt, areas should be allocated to the strictest or most protective option. It is comparatively easy to permit greater levels of use at a later date but not always possible to reduce levels of utilisation, nor repair the damage from overuse.

A review of the potential of all reserves in the country will reveal whether the national system of categories is flexible enough or whether other categories are needed. The actual allocation of protected status category to the individual reserve forms a basic part of reserve management and will be considered again in Chapter 9.

Developing a system of categories for protected areas

Each nation's system of protected natural areas should be designed to suit its own resources and its own requirements for conserving these resources in the interests of sustainable human development. A spectrum of areas with different management goals will usually emerge and there are advantages in classifying these areas, irrespective of the nomenclature applied to them, into a number of categories using well-defined criteria. For example, Miller (1978) provides a useful review of systems planning with examples from Latin America and the Caribbean.

System planning enables a nation to evaluate its own commitment to the protection of its finite resources and to assess its progress against internationally accepted norms. The classification of protected areas into a limited number of categories with differing management objectives helps facilitate many aspects of management, including:

- legislating for protected areas;
- planning management strategies;
- making appropriate management decisions;
- controlling both the type and intensity of utilisation;

- justifying the benefits claimed for the protected areas policy.

The exercise of evaluating the available national categories of protected areas and considering the desirability of creating new categories also forces a review of the status and category of existing reserves. This is useful as some areas will probably have been wrongly designated and in others the most current priority management objectives may be different from the reasons for which the reserve was originally established. For example, Indonesia (FAO, 1981-2) has just completed a review of all its reserves which proposed the 'dropping' of several small reserves, established during the Dutch colonial period, which have not been maintained and can now no longer fulfil their original purpose. Damaged strict nature reserves (Category I) have to be reclassified so that remedial management can be undertaken.

A range of protected area categories makes it easier to integrate reserve management into wider land-use planning and development. Where a conservation area becomes integrated into a regional development plan the budget for its management may also be picked up by outside funding. For instance, several protected areas in the Mahaweli area of Sri Lanka are being developed and funded under a USAID project in recognition of the vital role they play in the overall development of the area (de Alwis, 1984).

Having less strictly protective categories of protected areas enables the reserve planner to design layers or buffers of partially protected land or to evolve other management strategies. This makes the vital core area less of an ecologically isolated 'biological island', functionally larger and more acceptable to neighbouring communities (Lusigi, 1984).

Although it is generally more efficient for a country to have a single protected area management authority, this is not essential. Having several reserve categories permits more flexibility so that it may be possible to delegate the management of some areas to provincial rather than national government, or to different departments, or even to suitable non-government organisations or private trusts. Some mechanism for coordination is essential, however, if several agencies are involved.

When national categories can be related to internationally accepted classes this assists international agencies and other institutions to assess the worldwide distribution and status of protected areas and what they represent in the conservation of the human environment. This in turn brings recognition to particular protected areas and the national systems of which they are a part, particularly if relevant information about them is made available to IUCN's Protected Areas Data Unit (PADU). This documentation and conformity helps in the assignment of suitable technical assistance by international agencies, transfer of experience between comparable areas, even the establishment of 'sister' protected areas. It also provides IUCN with the information it needs to offer technical advice to international programmes like the Unesco Man and the Biosphere (MAB) Programme, the World Heritage Convention and UNEP's Global Environmental Monitoring System (GEMS).

International system of categories

The CNPPA recognises that while there is a confusing number of different names describing protected areas in different countries, in fact, there are really relatively few basic objectives for which areas are established and managed.

Accordingly, IUCN (1978a, 1984b) has proposed a system of ten management categories (see Table II.2), classified according to objectives for management.

Example 2.1: Categories and management objectives of protected areas

I. *Strict Nature Reserve/Scientific Reserve.* To protect nature and maintain natural processes in an undisturbed state in order to have ecologically representative examples of the natural environment available for scientific study, environmental monitoring, education, and for the maintenance of genetic resources in a dynamic and evolutionary state.

Examples include the Yala Strict Nature Reserve in Sri Lanka, the island of Barro Colorado in Panama, and the Gombe Stream National Park in Tanzania.

II. *National Park.* To protect outstanding natural and scenic areas of national or international significance for scientific, educational, and recreational use. These are relatively large natural areas not materially altered by human activity where extractive resource uses are not allowed.

Examples include the Royal Chitwan National Park in Nepal, the Etosha National Park in Namibia, and the Iguazu National Parks in Argentina and Brazil, and Volcan Poas National Park in Costa Rica.

III. *Natural Monument/Natural Landmark.* To protect and preserve nationally significant natural features because of their special interest or unique characteristics. These are relatively small areas focussed on protection of specific features.

Good examples include Angkor Wat National Park in Kampuchea, the Petrified Forests Nature Monument in Argentina and Gedi National Monument in Kenya.

IV. *Managed Nature Reserve/Wildlife Sanctuary.* To assure the natural conditions necessary to protect nationally significant species, groups of species, biotic communities, or physical features of the environment where these may require specific human manipulation for their perpetuation. Controlled harvesting of some resources can be permitted.

There are many good examples of this category of reserve in India including Manas Wildlife Sanctuary. Most of the national reserves in Kenya also fall in this category as do the biotope reserves in Guatemala.

V. *Protected Landscapes and Seascapes.* To maintain nationally significant natural landscapes which are characteristic of the harmonious interaction of man and land while providing opportunities for public enjoyment through recreation and tourism within the normal life style and economic activity of these areas. These are mixed cultural/natural landscapes of high scenic value where traditional land uses are maintained.

Examples include Pululahua Geobotanical Reserve in Ecuador and Machu Picchu Historic Sanctuary, Peru. The national parks of England are also classified under this category.

VI. *Resource Reserve.* To protect the natural resources of the area for future use and prevent or contain development activities that could affect the resource pending the establishment of objectives which are based upon appropriate knowledge and planning. This is a 'holding' category used until a permanent classification can be determined.

Few countries have yet applied this category but several resource reserves exist in Kenya including Kora and South Turkana National Reserves. Other examples include Brazil's Forest Reserves, and Tahuamanu Protected Forest, Bolivia.

VII. *Anthropological Reserve/Natural Biotic Area.* To allow the way of life of societies living in harmony with the environment to continue undisturbed by modern technology. This category is appropriate where resource extraction by indigenous people is conducted in a traditional manner.

The Gunung Lorentz Nature Reserve, Indonesia, Xingu Indigenous Park of Brazil and Central Kalahari Game Reserve of Botswana are all occupied by indigenous people and are classified as Category VII areas. Many protected areas in the South Pacific islands also fall in this category.

VIII. *Multiple Use Management Area/Managed Resource Area.* To provide for the sustained production of water, timber, wildlife, pasture and tourism, with the conservation of nature primarily oriented to the support of the economic activities (although specific zones may also be designated within these areas to achieve specific conservation objectives).

The most famous example is the Ngorongoro Conservation Area of Tanzania. Other examples are the Kutai National Park of Indonesia, Jamari and Tapajos National Forests, Brazil, Von Humboldt National Forest, Peru.

Two additional categories are international labels which overlay protected areas in the above eight categories.

IX. *Biosphere Reserve.* To conserve for present and future use the diversity and integrity of biotic communities of plants and animals within natural ecosystems, and to safeguard the genetic diversity of species on which their continuing evolution depends. These are internationally designated sites managed for research, education and training.

Good examples of this category include Sinharaja Forest Reserve of Sri Lanka, Mt. Kulal in Kenya and the Rio Platano Reserve of Honduras.

X. *World Heritage Site.* To protect the natural features for which the area is considered to be of outstanding universal significance. This is a select list of the world's unique natural and cultural sites nominated by countries that are Party to the World Heritage Convention.

As of 1985 there were 62 natural properties on the World Heritage List, including the Simien National Park of Ethiopia, the Darien Reserve in Panama, and the Great Barrier Reef in Australia. (For a map of the sites, see Ch. 12.)

Ed. note: This system of categories is currently under revision by CNPPA and will be published in mid-1986.

Example 2.2: *International categories of protected areas and corresponding conservation objectives*

Primary Conservation Objectives	Strict Reserve I	National Park II	Monument/ Landmark III	Managed Reserve IV	Protected Land-scape/Seascape V	Resources Reserve VI	Anthropological Reserve VII	Multiple Use Area VIII	Biosphere Reserve IX	World Heritage Site X
Maintain sample ecosystems in natural state	1	1	1	1	2	3	1	2	1	1
Maintain ecological diversity and environmental regulation	3	1	1	2	2	2	1	2	1	1
Conserve Genetic resources	1	1	1	1	2	3	1	3	1	1
Provide education, research, and environmental monitoring	1	2	1	1	2	3	2	2	1	1
Conserve watershed condition	2	1	2	2	2	2	2	2	2	2
Control erosion, sedimentation; protect downstream investments	3	3	3	3	3	3	3	3	3	3
Produce protein and animal products from wildlife; permit sport hunting and fishing				2	3	3	3	1	3	1
Provide recreation and tourism services		1	2	3	1		3	1	3	1
Produce timber, forage, or marine products on sustained yield basis				3	2		3	1	3	
Protect sites and objects of cultural, historical, and archaelogical heritage		1	3		1	3	1	3	2	1
Protect scenic beauty and open space	3	1	2	2	1			3	2	1
Maintain open options; manage flexibly; permit multiple use					3			3	2	1
Stimulate rational, sustainable use of marginal areas and rural development	2	1	2	2	1	3	2	1	2	2

Source: Adapted from IUCN, 1978a

Note: 1 — Primary objective for management of area and resources; 2 — not necessarily primary but always included as an important objective; 3 — included as an objective where applicable and whenever resources and other management objectives permit.

Example 2.3: Simplified scheme for assessing suitable protection category

			Recommended Status	IUCN Category
Protection of nature highest priority	Visitor use disturbing or of low priority	Primarily for preservation	Strict Nature Reserve	I
		Primarily for research	Scientific Reserve	I
	Zoned visitor use and/or some management desirable	Biologically valuable	Managed Nature Reserve	IV
		Geophysically or biologically spectacular	Natural Monument	III
	Visitor use high priority			
	Not for consumptive use	Global priority	World Heritage Site	X
		National priority	National Park	II
		Local priority	Provincial Park	II
	Consumptive uses for local people	Global interest	Biosphere Reserve	IX
		Regional interest	Anthropological Reserve	VII
Protection of nature secondary priority	Water catchment vital	High visitor potential	Protective Recreation Forest	VIII
		Low visitor potential	Hydrological Protection Forest	VIII
	Water catchment not vital			
	Hunting or harvesting value high	Hunting a priority	Hunting Reserve	VIII
		Traditional use a priority	Wildlife Management Zone	VIII
	Hunting or harvesting value low	Essentially natural	Agro-forestry Reserve	VIII
		Essentially agricultural	Protected Landscape	V

Example 2.4: Designing categories for protected areas: the example of the Indonesian system

---

General Criteria for Different Protected Areas

Taman Nasional (National Park)
Large relatively undisturbed areas of outstanding natural value with high conservation importance, high recreation potential, of easy access to visitors and clearly of benefit to the region.

Cagar Alam (Nature Reserve)
Generally small, undisturbed fragile habitats of high conservation importance, unique natural sites, homes of particular rare species, etc. Areas requiring strict protection.

Suaka Margasatwa (Game Reserve)
Generally medium or large areas of relatively undisturbed stable habitats of moderate to high conservation importance.

Taman Wisata (Recreation Park)
Small natural or landscaped area or site of attractive or interesting aspect of easy access for visitors where conservation value is low or not threatened by visitor activities and recreation orientated management.

Taman Buru (Hunting Reserve)
Medium or large-sized natural or semi-natural habitats with game hunting potential, i.e. large enough populations of permitted game species (pigs, deer, wild cattle, fish, etc.) where demand for hunting facilities exists and of easy access to would-be hunters. Such reserves should be of low conservation importance or have conservation values that are not threatened by the hunting/fishing activities.

Hutan Lindung (Protection Forest)
Medium to large areas of natural or planted forested land on steep, high, erodible, rainwashed lands where forest cover is essential to protect important catchment areas and prevent landslips and erosion but where conservation priorities are not so high as to justify reserve status.

Activities Prohibited (X) in Different Categories of Protected Area

	Taman Nasional (according to zones)	Cagar Alam	Suaka Marga-satwa	Taman Wisata	Taman Buru	Extra-limital Buffer Zones	Protection Forests
Growing food crops	X	X	X	X	X	X	X
Growing tree crops	X	X	X				
Human settlement	X	X	X	X	X	X	X
Commercial logging	X	X	X	X	X	X	X
Collecting herbs and firewood	X	X		X	X		
Hunting	X	X	X	X		X	
Fishing		X	X	X			
Camping		X					
Scientific collecting with permit		X					
Active habitat management		X					
Non-exotic introduction		X					
Collecting rattan + poles with permit	X	X	X	X			
Mineral exploration		X			X		
Wildlife control		X					
Visitor use		X					
Exotic introductions	X	X	X		X		

Source: Sumardja, *et al.*, 1984

Example 2.5: **Management categories of protected wild areas in Costa Rica** *(Example of a National System of Criteria)*

Legend:
- ● Primary objective
- ⊘ Not necessarily primary but always included as important objective
- ○ Included as objective where resources and other objectives permit
- | Not applicable

RESPONSIBLE INSTITUTIONS:
- National Parks Service (NPS): Biological Reserve, National Park, National Monument (Cultural), National Recreation Area
- General Forestry Directorate (GFD): Forest Reserve, Protection Zone (Water Production), Wildlife Refuge
- Indian Communities and CONAI*: Indian Reserve
- NPS, GFD, ADI* and Indian Communities: Biosphere Reserve

NATIONAL CONSERVATION OBJECTIVES

MANAGEMENT CATEGORY	Biological Reserve	National Park	National Monument (Cultural)	National Recreation Area	Forest Reserve	Protection Zone (Water Production)	Wildlife Refuge	Indian Reserve	Biosphere Reserve
Achieve conservation and integrate use of rural and marginal resources			⊘	⊘	●	●	⊘	⊘	●	●
Protect, administer and improve environmental quality			●	⊘	●	⊘	⊘	⊘				
Protect national cultural heritage			●	●	○	⊘					●	○
Provide opportunities for research, monitoring and education	●	●	●	●	●	●	○	●	⊘	●
Conserve genetic resources	●	●	⊘	⊘	●	●	⊘	●	○	●
Protect and administrate wildlife resources									●					●	⊘
Provide opportunities for recreation			●	⊘	●	●			○			⊘
Conserve representative samples of ecosystems	●	●	○	○	○	○	●	○	●
Conserve and improve timber and related forest resources									●	○					○
Prevent and control erosion and sedimentation	⊘	⊘	○	⊘	●	●	⊘	○	⊘
Conserve and improve hydrological systems	⊘	⊘	○	⊘	●	●	⊘	○	⊘

*The National Commission for Indian Affairs (CONAI) only advises on and coordinates the administration of the Indian Reserves.

*ADI: Agricultural Development Institute (lands and colonisation)

While Categories I (Strict Nature Reserves) and II (National and Provincial Parks) are well known and broadly applied, many of the other categories are not so well understood. Ideally, in all protected areas objectives and activities should be related to environmental protection and to economic and social development. All categories are of value, each with a different role, and only several together can adequately cover national and global resource management needs.

Example 2.1 provides a brief resume of the 10 categories of protected areas recognised by IUCN and gives examples of each category from protected areas situated in the tropics. There are eight functional categories and two additional international designations; the latter are usually chosen from, or overlap with, pre-existing protected areas which fulfil the extra criteria of Categories IX or X. The examples provided highlight the different nomenclatures used in different countries to describe protected areas with the same management objectives. It is worth emphasising that it does not matter so much what an area is called – what is important is the way in which it is managed.

Example 2.6: Native peoples and biosphere reserves in Central America

It is no coincidence that several of the largest remaining wildlands in Central America are also inhabited by indigenous peoples such as the Paya in Honduras, the Bribis in Costa Rica and the Chocoes in Panama. Their native technologies and forest knowledge have limited the imprint of their civilisation on fragile tropical ecosystems.

For the most part, wildlands planners in this region have sought to incorporate these populations into local conservation strategies and park development. The biosphere reserve concept has been embraced by conservationists as an administrative tool appropriate for integrating natural and cultural resource conservation. While results have been mixed, the ground work is being laid in several areas for wildland-based sustainable rural development, aimed primarily at native peoples.

In Honduras, the 500,000 ha Rio Platano Biosphere Reserve encompasses not only a variety of terrestrial and coastal habitats but also scattered Paya and Miskito Indian settlements. The management plan for the area addresses human need issues. Education programmes have focussed on interpreting the reserve concept and soliciting support and cooperation in management.

The Amistad Biosphere Reserve is not only Costa Rica's largest protected wildland but also the home of a large percentage of that country's native peoples. Between 11,000 and 19,000 Cabecares, Bribis, Tribes and Guaymies occupy the zone. Native land use and cultural characteristics are being studied in order to more effectively tailor reserve management and resource conservation to their needs and impact.

The Darien Reserve in Panama is also a large area – 575,000 ha. Initial management plans, developed before the area was declared a biosphere reserve, recommend relocating some native villages (Chocoes and Kunas occupy the area). Current management strategy, however, focusses upon working with these groups and facilitating their participation in management and protection programmes.

While all of these sites are still in the early stages of development and have suffered from inevitable 'growing pains', each is proving that nature and cultural resource conservation are compatible and that the biosphere reserve concept can facilitate this delicate merger.

Example 2.7: Biosphere reserves: an example from Mexico

The Man and the Biosphere Programme (MAB) was launched by the Unesco General Conference in November 1970. MAB is a long-term programme of research, training, and information exchange among States concerning environmental management.

Project 8 of the MAB Programme provides for the conservation of natural areas and of the genetic material they contain. Under this project a worldwide network of protected areas, called Biosphere Reserves, is being established for the purpose of conserving species and genetic diversity and for use in a programme of monitoring, research and training. In practice, most of these reserves overlap areas already established by national governments as protected areas.

Projects being conducted under the MAB Programme are expected to demonstrate the advantages of integration, inter-disciplinary involvement and participation by the local population.

A good example is the Mapimi Reserve in the State of Durango in Mexico. This reserve lies within a semi-desert basin which is the exclusive habitat of an endangered species of tortoise. Local people were involved in the selection of the site for the reserve. A strictly controlled core area was defined, surrounded by a buffer zone where wider uses are permitted.

The endangered tortoise used to be hunted by local residents for meat. After research and a public information campaign, local ranchers and farmers realised that over-hunting was not in their own interests and hunting of the tortoise virtually stopped. As part of the Mapimi programme and as a form of compensation, a series of studies is being developed to improve management and increase the production of livestock in the area.

Diverse social and political groups have been involved in the management of the reserve from the outset, including local and federal governments, the scientific community and the local population. A legally constituted association was formed to manage the reserve, including representatives of the local people. A measure of the success of the project is that there has been a notable absence of the clandestine exploitation of resources which is unfortunately characteristic of many legally protected areas throughout the world.

The Mapimi project demonstrates that an integrated approach with wide participation can achieve better results for both conservation managers and land owners, while eliminating the animosity and mistrust that might have occurred with a strict single-purpose reservation imposed without consultation.

Source: Halffter, 1981

3

Basis for Selection of Sites for Protected Areas

Assessment of global biogeographical coverage of reserves

The growing concern for the state of the environment during the early 1970s prompted international agencies and national governments to search for a more rational approach to the conservation of representative samples of the world's natural ecosystems. An international system of selecting protected areas based on well-founded biogeographical principles was prepared by IUCN to assess representative coverage of the earth's wild species and major ecosystems (Udvardy, 1975). Within the context of the *World Conservation Strategy* (IUCN, 1980), this basis was seen as a useful tool in evaluating the global conservation effort and for determining priorities for future action.

Biogeography – the study of the distribution of living organisms, and the natural processes that affect these distributions – can be used to classify the biosphere into distinct physical and biological entities which contain distinct biotic communities. As every living species is an integral component of some ecosystem or ecosystems, it generally follows that its conservation is dependent on the survival of those ecosystems or biotic communities.

The system for classifying terrestrial ecotypes proposed by Udvardy (1975), and periodically updated as better information is gathered, is generally accepted as a universal framework, based on biological reality, which is suitable for gauging the adequacy of protected area coverage at the global level. Udvardy recognises eight biogeographical realms overlapped by 14 biomes that occur in one or more of these realms (Fig. 3.1). While this is a gross over-simplification of the great diversity of the earth's natural ecosystems, it recognises types of vegetation cover that occur under characteristic geographical conditions within these realms. The 14 biomes are further divided into some 230 terrestrial biogeographical provinces. The Neotropical Realm, for example, is divided into 12 biomes comprising 47 provinces (Fig. 3.2).

A biome may be found in two or more provinces, with different faunal or floral characteristics, or be divided by a physical barrier. The savannas of South America, Africa, India and Australia reflect similar climatic conditions, but have different animal and plant associations and are provinces of the same biome separated by oceans. On the other hand, the Amazon rain forest stretches in a continuum from the Andes to the Atlantic Ocean and has been divided into several provinces on the basis of differences in the tree flora and other biogeographical criteria. To further complicate matters, a province classified according to its dominant biome type may include species or communities that are representative of other biomes.

The Udvardy system is useful for a global overview of protected area coverage, but it is of limited value for individual nations in the process of selecting reserves because of its gross scale. Many countries fall within a single biogeographical province and few include more than two or three.

It is, however, useful for each country to view its own resources in a global context and see how much international responsibility it has to protect examples of a given biogeographical province and with whom it may share that responsibility. It may

5. Example of a protected tropical rain forest system – Tai National Park, Ivory Coast – biologically the most important protected area remaining in West Africa. Tropical rain forests are biologically the richest terrestrial habitats on earth but also among the most fragile and threatened.
Photo: WWF/Wilhelm Barthlott

6. Example of a protected tropical desert system – Lauca National Park, a Biosphere Reserve in Chile.
Photo: WWF/H. Jungius

7. Example of a protected tropical savanna system – Ngorongoro Conservation Area, a World
Heritage Site in Tanzania.
Photo: J. Thorsell

Fig. 3.1: Biogeographical provinces of the world

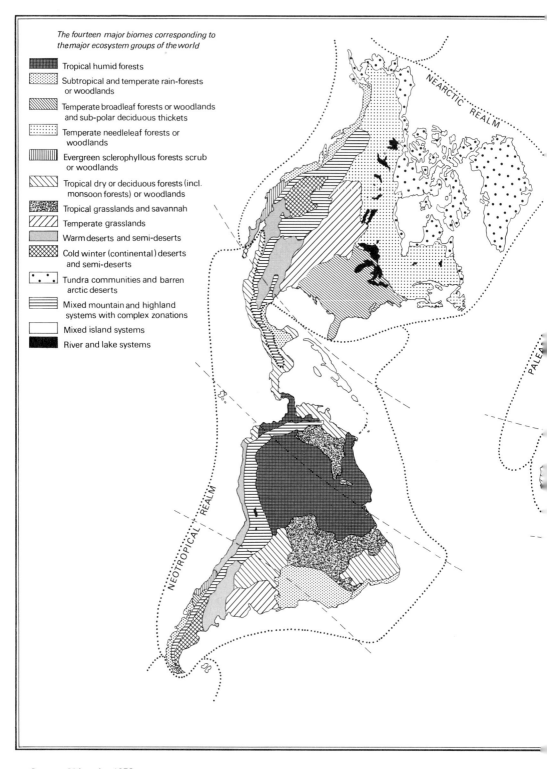

The fourteen major biomes corresponding to the major ecosystem groups of the world

- Tropical humid forests
- Subtropical and temperate rain-forests or woodlands
- Temperate broadleaf forests or woodlands and sub-polar deciduous thickets
- Temperate needleleaf forests or woodlands
- Evergreen sclerophyllous forests scrub or woodlands
- Tropical dry or deciduous forests (incl. monsoon forests) or woodlands
- Tropical grasslands and savannah
- Temperate grasslands
- Warm deserts and semi-deserts
- Cold winter (continental) deserts and semi-deserts
- Tundra communities and barren arctic deserts
- Mixed mountain and highland systems with complex zonations
- Mixed island systems
- River and lake systems

Source: Udvardy, 1975

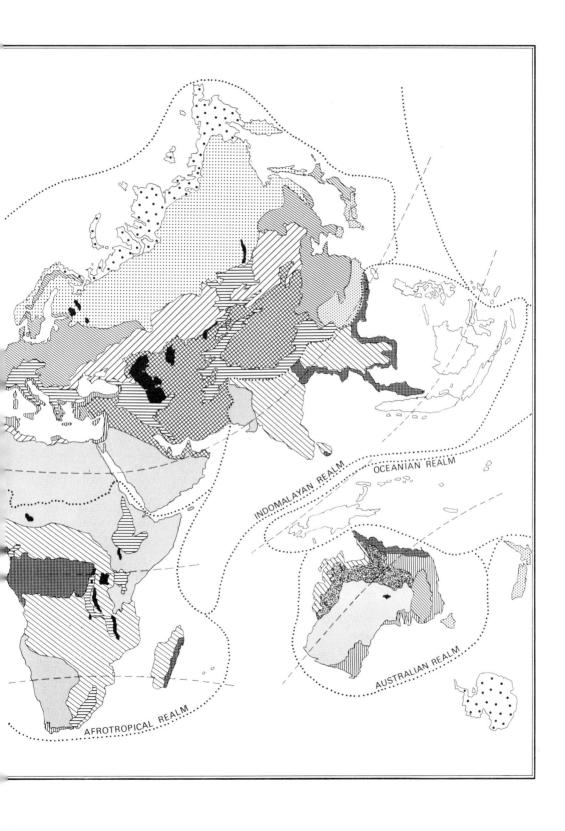

Fig. 3.2: *Biogeographical provinces of the neotropical realm*

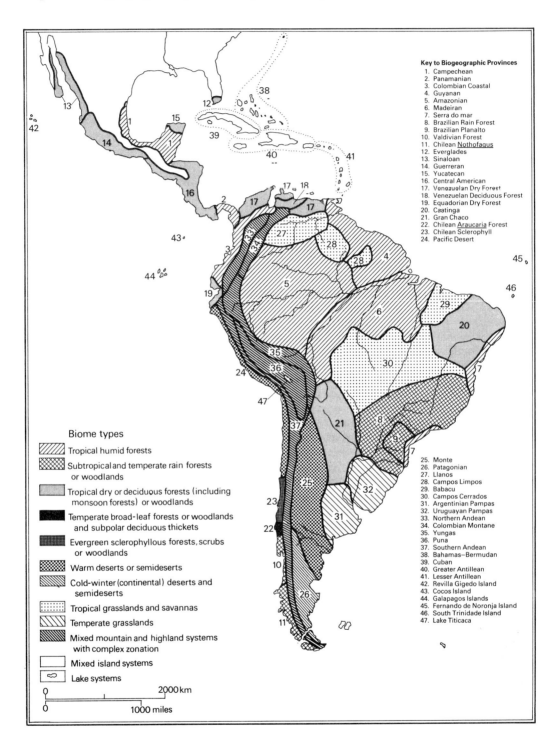

Key to Biogeographic Provinces
1. Campechean
2. Panamanian
3. Colombian Coastal
4. Guyanan
5. Amazonian
6. Madeiran
7. Serra do mar
8. Brazilian Rain Forest
9. Brazilian Planalto
10. Valdivian Forest
11. Chilean Nothofagus
12. Everglades
13. Sinaloan
14. Guerreran
15. Yucatecan
16. Central American
17. Venezuelan Dry Forest
18. Venezuelan Deciduous Forest
19. Equadorian Dry Forest
20. Caatinga
21. Gran Chaco
22. Chilean Araucaria Forest
23. Chilean Sclerophyll
24. Pacific Desert

25. Monte
26. Patagonian
27. Llanos
28. Campos Limpos
29. Babacu
30. Campos Cerrados
31. Argentinian Pampas
32. Uruguayan Pampas
33. Northern Andean
34. Colombian Montane
35. Yungas
36. Puna
37. Southern Andean
38. Bahamas–Bermudan
39. Cuban
40. Greater Antillean
41. Lesser Antillean
42. Revilla Gigedo Island
43. Cocos Island
44. Galapagos Islands
45. Fernando de Noronja Island
46. South Trinidade Island
47. Lake Titicaca

Biome types

Tropical humid forests

Subtropical and temperate rain forests or woodlands

Tropical dry or deciduous forests (including monsoon forests) or woodlands

Temperate broad-leaf forests or woodlands and subpolar deciduous thickets

Evergreen sclerophyllous forests, scrubs or woodlands

Warm deserts or semideserts

Cold-winter (continental) deserts and semideserts

Tropical grasslands and savannas

Temperate grasslands

Mixed mountain and highland systems with complex zonation

Mixed island systems

Lake systems

0 ———————————— 2000 km
0 ———————————— 1000 miles

Source: Udvardy, 1975

also become clear from such an exercise where new reserves should be established or that an existing or planned reserve is of greater international importance than previously realised. Moreover, a country that is making a significant global contribution can use this to seek international assistance and support for its conservation programme.

Sub-division of biogeographical provinces will differ with local needs but it is desirable to standardise the criteria and to have agreement on the sub-divisions to be used by States in the same region at least. These will then be divided into lesser units on more refined biogeographical criteria such as a biome mosaic for use at the regional or national level. Following this advice, countries in the Afrotropical Realm agreed to adopt the Unesco Vegetation Map of Africa (White, 1983) as the basic framework for recognising broad biogeographical units within the Realm. The Holdridge Life Zone System is often used in the Neotropical Realm.

There is no universally correct scale for mapping sub-divisions of biogeographical units, at the regional or national level. A small country like Singapore may prefer a larger scale than would be considered appropriate for a larger country such as Papua New Guinea. Nevertheless a map scale of 1:1,000,000 is often a convenient minimum scale and ties in with satellite imagery.

Example 3.1: Regional wildland protection strategies – WWF'S Andean Conservation Programme

---

The tropical Andes, which includes over 1.6 million sq. km of Bolivia, Colombia, Ecuador, Peru and Venezuela, have been identified by World Wildlife Fund (WWF) as one of the highest and most urgent conservation priorities in Latin America. The entire region – the montane and premontane forested belts in particular – is threatened by rapid deforestation and irreversible soil loss due to expanding populations and intensive human activities (e.g. logging, agriculture, ranching).

The region is considered an important centre of speciation in the Neotropics and the wet montane and premontane forests along the slopes of the tropical Andes compete with the luxuriant rain forests of the Amazon in species richness. The preservation of key areas in the region will not only help maintain ecological and evolutionary processes to support a wealth of species, but it will also ensure the conservation of natural genetic reservoirs of great economic value.

As a guide to designing an effective network of protected areas, a set of criteria and principles for selecting priority sites in the Andes was developed. The following are among the most important. First, an area ideally should encompass all altitudinal gradients from snow line to the adjacent lowlands. This will maximise diversity, and at the same time will ensure the integrity of entire watersheds, especially at mid-elevations (800-1800m) where forest conversion is occurring at alarming rates. The areas to be set aside should be large enough (at least between 200,000 and 500,000 ha), to support viable populations of as many species as possible. Emphasis should be given to wetter areas, which are likely to hold greater biological diversity than drier areas. Thus, the western slopes of Colombia and Ecuador, and the eastern slopes of Colombia, Ecuador, and Peru should be given preference.

Based primarily on these and other biological criteria, 16 top priority protected areas and 14 top priority unprotected areas (including the proposed enlargement of extant protected areas) have been proposed by WWF as priority sites for the long-term conservation of biological diversity in the region.

Source: Saavedra and Freese, 1985

Genetic and species conservation considerations in selecting sites for protected areas

To protect the widest range of global and national variations of biomes and species communities involves plotting the biogeographical divisions and making selections among the best available examples of each. Selection will favour large examples which are less isolated from other natural areas and which are expected to be richer in terms of species and more stable in terms of retaining the species they contain. Selection will also tend to favour areas of high endemism or distinctiveness.

Species do not live in isolation, they live within communities and in ecosystems. It has become widely accepted that habitat protection is fundamental to save species so reserves should be selected on the basis of representational coverage of habitat types. If this is done perfectly, most species' needs would be met, but in fact the degree of distinctions between habitat classifications is neither consistent nor always adequate. It is often more practical to select protected areas on the basis of which key species they harbour; in any case, this method is a useful independent check on the biogeographical approach.

Selection of reserves on the criteria of species presence is useful for several reasons:

- It identifies areas which require urgent protection.
  All ecotypes deserve protection but those whose conspicuous species are disappearing fast are obviously in need of more urgent action.
- Use of species criteria independently checks and complements the reserve coverage achieved by the biogeographical approach.
  From a biogeographical approach, we might conclude that we need to protect a sample, for instance, of Javan swampy lowland forests. From species considerations, we decide that we must have a reserve to save the last Javan rhinoceros. We combine the two approaches by protecting the last rhino locality as an example of swampy lowland forest, and this is a sensible choice for other reasons. Any examples of lowland swampy forest where rhinoceros are not present are lacking a major original ecological component and, irrespective of habitat condition, are less good examples of the original habitat type.
- Focussing on key species gives a good indication

of the effectiveness of management.
An area may be selected because of its basic habitat type, identified by its dominant vegetation, but it may be failing as a protected area because it is losing many other species unnoticed. Attention to the fate of the rarer species will give a good indication of management success. If the most conspicuous rare species cannot survive, then there is something wrong with the design or management of the reserve.

- Species provide a focal point or objective that people can readily understand.
  Local government officials and local people want to understand the point of a reserve. They cannot appreciate the need to preserve some minor biogeographic subdivision of what to them is just 'bush' or 'jungle'. Nor does it mean anything to them that 5 per cent of species in this habitat are quite distinct. What they can understand is that this is the only place in the whole world where you can still see a giant peccary or lion-tailed monkey, or in the case of the Mario Dary Biotope in Guatemala, one of the few places where one can see that country's national symbol, the Quetzal bird.
- Species have an appeal which wins sympathy, an important factor in raising public awareness and helping fund raising.
  Making the tiger – India's most well-known and evocative species – the focus of a special campaign helped raise more support and funds for conservation than a general campaign on Indian wildlife could ever have done. In the name of the tiger, a wide range of reserves was established in many different ecotypes, protecting examples of many of India's most beautiful wild areas and a vast range of plant and other animal species (Example 3.3). In Colombia, the La Planada Nature Reserve was initially established to protect the rare spectacled bear but also harbours numerous endemic plants and animals.
- Species lists for proposed protected areas provide hard data to back up the biogeographical approach.

What is so special about this particular area? What animals or plants does it harbour? Conservationists try to reduce loss of living resources with the claim that preserving biological diversity helps safeguard the sustained benefits we derive from wild species. Clearly not all species are equally valuable to man and selective bias must be given to those of known value or species which have been identified as having future potential. Such species would include:

- wild plant species related to man's domesticated food crops;
- wild relatives or forms of domestic animals;
- species with recognised potential for domestication;
- species harvested from nature for food; wild fruits, bush meat, or important for recreational hunting;
- species harvested by man for other forms of utilisation, e.g. for dyes, medicine;
- species whose value for food or other useful products is increasing due to increasing rarity;
- fodder plants for domestic animals;
- species vital for fulfilling functions on which other harvests depend, e.g. pollination by bees and bats, natural control of pests;
- species with capacity to improve soil structure, stability or fertility;
- animal species which are useful research models for studies of human behaviour and physiology such as our nearest relatives – apes and monkeys;

- species providing utilised or potentially useful drugs;
- species with a high capacity to modify their environment;
- species with specialised tolerance to extreme living conditions – to salinity, temperature extremes, deep shade, drought, fire and wind.

Clearly in many regions knowledge of individual species is insufficient to allow us to make such judgements about species values. Moreover, some species of no current recognised value to man may be found to be valuable in the future so it is important to preserve genetic distinctiveness *per se*. In theory, the smaller a family or genus the greater is the gap between it and the nearest family (or genus) and therefore the more distinct that group of species is from others. Other things being equal, priority should be given to species that are endangered throughout their range and to species that are the sole representatives of their family or genus - see Example 3.2. Species not known to be threatened but with highly restricted distributions should be closely monitored and protected within protected areas wherever possible.

Example 3.2: Formulation for determining priority threatened species

		imminence of loss →		
		Rare	Vulnerable	Endangered
size of loss ↑	Family	4	2	1
	Genus	7	5	3
	Species	9	8	6

- highest priority
- intermediate priority
- lower priority
- 1 — 9 suggested order of priority

A. Formulation for determining priority threatened species.

Example 3.3: *Integrating the species and ecosystem approaches to protected area selection in India*

By using the tiger as a symbol of national heritage, the Indian Government has been able to protect a wide range of tiger reserves selected to include all major ecosystems in the species range.

Tiger reserves established under Project Tiger

	Total area	Core area
	Sq. km	
Melghat (Maharashtra). Deciduous forests dominated by teak and bamboo	1571	311
Palamau (Bihar). Eastern peninsular forest with an interesting association of sal and bamboo	930	200
Simlipal (Orissa). Moist miscellaneous forests of the East (champ and sal)	2750	300
Kanha (Madhya Pradesh). Central highlands of Peninsular India (sal and miscellaneous forests)	1945	940
Bandipur (Karnataka). Miscellaneous forests of the Western Ghats	690	335
Corbett Park (Uttar Pradesh). Central foothills of the Himalayas with sal as the dominant species	520	320
Manas (Assam). Eastern foothills of heavy rainfall with *terai* riverain, reeds and swamps, semi-evergreen and evergreen forests	2840	391
Ranthambhore (Rajasthan). Dry deciduous open forests of the Aravalis and Vindhyas in the west	392	167
Sunderbans (West Bengal). Tropical estuarine mangrove grove forests and other littoral vegetation	2585	1330
Periyar (Kerala). Moist deciduous, tropical wet-evergreen and semi-evergreen forests	777	350
Sariska (Rajasthan). Dry deciduous forest in the heart of Aravalis Range, with sandy valleys carrying scrubthorn and grasslands.	800	498
Nagarjuna Sagar (Andhra Pradesh). Rugged hills in the middle reaches of Krishna with dry mixed deciduous forest	3560	1200
Namdapha (Arunachal Pradesh). Low level (200 m above MSL) riverain to alpine (6000 m above MSL) through moist deciduous and tropical wet evergreen forests	1808	695
Indravati (Madhya Pradesh). Tropical mixed moist deciduous forest with rich grasslands along Indravati River	2799	1258
Buxa (West Bengal). Riverain, *terai*-bhabhar, reed-swamps and semi-evergreen forest of the eastern foothills	745	313
Total:	24,712	8,608

Source: H.S. Panwar, 1984

By protecting useful species (and their relatives) and a wide range of genetic variation, we maintain the genetic diversity from which breeders and geneticists can select for improvements to produce future strains more specifically adapted to man's particular needs. To this end, the idea of gene pool reserves has been developed. (Example 3.4).

Example 3.4: In situ genebanks: a new category of protected area?

The conservation of genetic resources is a primary conservation objective of seven of the existing 10 categories of protected areas. *In situ* genebanks are sites where wild gene pools of value for plant and animal breeding, new domestications and biotechnology (including genetic engineering) are protected and maintained in their native habitats. Such sites can be protected within other categories of protected area or as protected areas in their own right. They are distinct from other protected areas in three main respects:

- *In situ* genebanks are established to protect gene pools rather than species, communities or ecosystems. The term 'gene pool' means the total number of different genes within a group of interbreeding plants or animals: that is, the pool of genes within a population. Obviously *in situ* maintenance of gene pools requires the protection of their habitats and hence of the communities and ecosystems of which they are part; but the object of conservation is the gene pool.
- The gene pools of concern are primarily of economic species. Some future use of the protected gene pools is envisaged: in crop and livestock improvement; in the selection of new species for domestication; and/or in the production of biochemicals. Accordingly, priority will usually be given to wild gene pools of actual or potential value for agriculture, horticulture, silviculture, aquaculture, or biotechnology.
- Provision is made for *use of the protected gene pools*. The purpose of an *in situ* genebank is the long term maintenance of the germplasm (genetic material) it protects; but the reason for maintaining the germplasm is so that it can be used. Provision should therefore be made for collection (at sustainable levels) of reproductive material (seed, budwood, etc.) by *bona fide* breeders and researchers and for supply of germplasm to *ex situ* genebanks.

Source: Prescott-Allen and Prescott-Allen, 1984

Example 3.5: Minimum critical size for reserves

According to the theory of island biogeography, creating a reserve, i.e. a 'biological island' will lead to a decrease in species diversity. The number of species that a reserve can hold at equilibrium will depend on its size, its distance from other areas of like habitat and the dispersal powers of the species concerned. The critical question is how large should the reserve be?

No matter how large an isolated fragment may be, it is likely to lose some species after isolation – this can be thought of as decay of the ecosystem. This problem of attrition of species from habitat fragments is being researched in the Amazon forests by a joint team from World Wildlife Fund and Brazil's National Institute for Research on Amazonia. In northern Brazil, where forested areas are being cleared for use as cattle ranches, patches of forest ranging from 1 ha up to 10,000 ha will be left standing. These patches, and replicates of different sizes, are being studied for data on species loss among various groups of plants and animals – mammals, birds, amphibians, reptiles and insects.

As well as the fate of individual species, the project will monitor the effects of fragmentation on the complex ecological interrelationships found in tropical forests. Especially important are the interactions of forest trees with animals species e.g. pollinators, herbivores, and dispersers or predators of fruits and seeds. These relationships are crucial in that they variously affect the tree's ability to reproduce and the ultimate success of that reproductive effort. Many of the relationships are obligatory for successful reproduction and recruitment of new individuals into the population, e.g. the Brazil nut tree *Bertholletia excelsa* has a single cross pollinator.

Preliminary studies of small forest fragments of 10 ha showed the following results after three years of isolation. Immediately after isolation both birds and primates showed unusually high densities, the result of an influx of animals into a remnant piece of forest. Very soon, however, species numbers in both groups declined and several birds and two of the three species of monkeys disappeared. Similarly, there have been local extinctions in the 10 ha reserve of large mammals such as margay cat, jaguar, mountain lion, paca and deer.

Within two years of isolation, there was evidence of ecological change in forest structure, reproductive behaviour of some individual trees and in plant-animal interactions. The most striking changes have been in the number and distribution of wind-thrown, broken and standing dead trees in the 10 ha reserve. As these trees fall, they provide colonisation sites for more light-loving species so gradually the tree species composition of the reserve will change. Some individual trees which flowered out of synchrony with others of their species (as a result of physiological stress) showed high loss of seeds to predators and low seedling establishment and survival. Similarly, seed predation increased as saki monkeys confined within the 10 ha reserve repeatedly returned to fruiting trees to eat less preferred green fruits, thereby destroying the seed crop.

The ecological changes observed in the 10 ha forest fragment – species loss, genetic drift, habitat changes – will all apply to larger isolated blocks of forest over a longer time span. The results are also applicable to ecosystems elsewhere in the world. Each ecosystem and each geographical region is likely to have its own particular minimum size to reduce shedding of species. Indeed, it may never be possible to know what is the minimum area necessary for a minimum population of a top predator in an ecosystem. In the last analysis, reintroduction programmes and other active management measures may be the only way to conserve such species.

Source: Lovejoy, *et al.*, 1983.

Implications of island biogeographic theory in selecting areas for protection at the national level

Island biogeographic theory is concerned with the distributions of plants and animals on oceanic islands and island-like areas on the mainland such as mountain tops, lakes and isolated forest patches (Diamond, 1984). It has been found that the number of species and, to a certain extent, the actual species inhabiting islands, is highly predictable and dependent on the size of the island and its relative remoteness from colonising sources. The number of species stabilises when the rate of local extinctions equals the rate of new immigration. The former is related to island size while the rate of immigration depends on the proximity and richness of the coloniser land mass.

According to the theory of island biogeography, small protected areas isolated by modified habitats behave like 'islands' and will lose some of their original species until a new equilibrium is reached, dependent on the size, richness and diversity of the area, and its degree of isolation from other similar habitats. Larger reserves lose fewer species at a slower rate, but *any* loss of natural habitat will lead to some loss of species (see Fig. 3.4). As a rough generalisation, a single

reserve containing 10 per cent of the original habitat will support just 50 per cent of the original species present (Diamond, 1975). Practical studies show that, by and large, this theory holds true.

An extensive literature exists on the theory of island biogeography and its relevance to protected area design, selection and management. Diamond (1984), Soulé and Wilcox (1980), Frankel and Soulé (1981), Simberloff and Abele (1976), and Wilcox (1984) provide useful synopses of the subject, with particular relevance to ecosystem conservation and the protected area manager. The main guidelines are summarised below, although it should be recognised that the field is a relatively new one and not all conservation biologists would concur:

• Protected areas should be as large as possible and preferably should include thousands of individuals of even the least abundant species. They should be of a compact shape with biogeographically meaningful boundaries. For example, watershed boundaries are preferable to rivers, which often bisect essential bottom-

Fig. 3.3: Key project areas in WWF/IUCN Plant Conservation Programme and centres of wild crop diversity

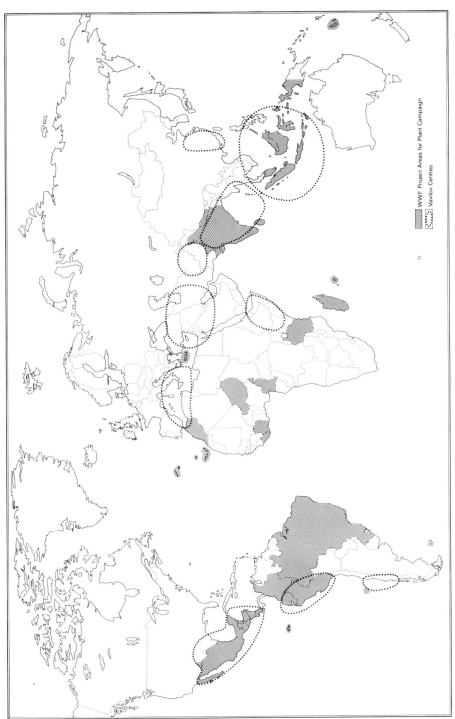

Key WWF Project Areas for Plant Campaign – selected as being of international importance due to extensive endemic flora under threat, support of national governments and opportunities for long-term conservation achievement

Vavilov centres – major centres of diversity of wild crop genetic resources (the inheritable characteristics of plants that are of use to people) identified by N.I. Vavilov, a Russian geneticist.

Credit: P. Virolle

land habitats of a range of species. Where a distinct vegetational type, such as a forest patch, is to be conserved it may be necessary to include the whole ecotone and a buffer of the neighbouring habitat type. So far as possible, a protected area should include the year-round habitat requirements of as many of the native animals as possible.

- Protected areas should encompass as wide a contiguous range of ecological communities as possible (e.g. altitude range) as few species are confined to a single community and few communities are independent from those adjacent to them.

- Precautions should be taken against protected areas becoming completely isolated from other natural areas. If possible, they should be located in clusters rather than dispersed, or they may be joined by corridors of semi-natural habitats.

However, these rules only relate to essentially similar blocks of habitat; for instance, two reserves close together in the same biogeographical sub-division will generally not preserve as many species in total as two reserves further apart and falling in different biogeographical sub-divisions.

While it may be true that no protected area is ever large enough to retain its full biological diversity once it becomes isolated from other similar habitats (and it is as well to realise this and expect some species losses), this does not mean that even small areas will not protect some of the component species, often with reduced niche competition (which can favour rare species). Further, overt manipulation of the ecosystems and their elements can reduce the loss of species, although this may become an on-going exercise which in the long run may be more expensive than acquiring more land at the outset. In any event, it is useful to set pragmatic goals which take into account the size of an area and the actions needed to conserve a realistic level of biological diversity they contain, bearing in mind that attempts to determine minimum or optimal-sized areas for protected areas and the genetic diversity they represent are still at the 'research and development' stage (Wilcox, 1984) and results may come too late to be applied.

It is worth noting that biological diversity is not uniformly distributed and 'hot spots' can often be recognised such as areas of high local richness or local endemism (Wilcox, 1984). The Amazonian Pleistocene refugia are such an example (see Example 3.6). Attempts should be made to include these 'hot spots' in the protected areas system to get better 'value' for number and uniqueness of species protected per area.

A useful general strategy is to include at least one large protected area in each biogeographical sub-division. This should usually include as many ecological communities as possible with omissions and variations being represented in smaller satellite areas.

In selecting areas for protection at the national level there is a need to select sufficient coverage to safeguard against the loss of the biogeographical features being protected due to some natural catastrophe, such as epidemics, flood, earthquake or changing lake levels. This insurance is enhanced if particular biogeographical entities are protected in more than one country as this reduces the risk of their loss through local political strife.

Example 3.6: Pleistocene refugia as sites for protected areas

In the mid-1970s, the Brazilian Institute of Forest Development established a new system of identifying conservation units based on highly relevant scientific criteria. The methods used to create seven new conservation units (covering 7 million ha) in the Amazon could be usefully applied elsewhere.

The Brazilian Amazon Conservation Plan utilised all pertinent scientific literature available, including data on biogeographic regions, vegetation formations, Pleistocene refugia for birds, lizards, plants and Lepidoptera and information on planned and existing conservation units, plans for development centres of the Brazilian Amazon and conservation areas proposed by the RADAMBRASIL project. All of this information was transferred to transparent maps drawn to the same scale so that when the maps were overlaid, it was possible to identify areas of apparent conservation potential. Field expeditions were made to evaluate areas with high potential.

Even though 90 per cent of the Amazon is tropical rain forest, other types of vegetation contribute to the area's biological diversity and should be protected in the conservation programme; these include liana forest, open forest, semi-deciduous forest, mangrove, Varzea forest and grassland and savanna. Every biogeographic region of the Amazon was assessed and national conservation priorities established according to three criteria. First priority was given to areas which two or more independent scientists identified as possible Pleistocene refugia, areas likely to support a high level of endemic plants and animals; second priority to areas likely to represent several vegetation formations and perhaps a refuge; and third priority to all other parks and reserves recommended by government and development projects.

Using this methodology, Brazil has already established 7 million ha of new national parks and biological reserves in the Amazon and plans to create 30 new protected areas, including a number of management categories not yet represented there.

Source: Jorge Padua and Tresinari, 1984

Fig. 3.4: Species numbers according to island size and distance from the mainland

---

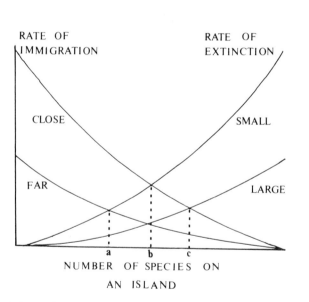

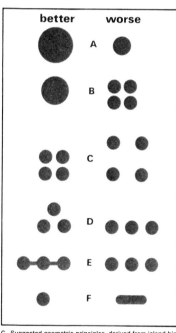

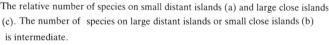

The relative number of species on small distant islands (a) and large close islands (c). The number of species on large distant islands or small close islands (b) is intermediate.

C. Suggested geometric principles, derived from island biogeographic studies, for the design of nature reserves. In each of the six cases labelled A to F, species extinction rates will be lower for the reserve design on the left than for the reserve design on the right. Source: 7.

N.B. These are theoretical patterns based on islands. The extent to which terrestrial systems actually behave like islands varies considerably and under some conditions these patterns prove incorrect.

Source: Diamond, 1975

Example 3.7: Selection of protected areas by biogeographic region in South America

The Amazon and Orinoco regions of South America, including tropical portions of nine countries, have been analysed from the standpoint of biogeographic coverage irrespective of political boundaries. This illustrates a multinational region-specific basis for selection of sites for protected areas. Utilising Terborgh's conclusions that Neotropical bird species in lowland rain forests require a minimum of 2500 sq. km to keep extinction rates at less than 1 per cent of the initial species complement per century, the Brazilian Forestry Department Institute has embarked on a programme to establish numerous parks and protected areas concentrating primarily on sites identified as Pleistocene refugia (Jorge Padua and Tresinari, 1984). Between 1971 and 1984, new parks and protected areas totalling more than 12,000,000 ha were formally established in the tropical forest areas of Bolivia, Brazil, Ecuador, Peru and Venezuela. This is a land area larger than Austria or Cuba. A summary of conservation units by Amazonian biogeographic region is shown below.

Existing Conservation Units by Biogeographic Region in 1981

Biogeographic Region	Per cent of Total Area	Proportional Allocation of Major Cons. Units		Proportional Allocation of Other Cons. Units	
		Recomm.	Existing	Recomm.	Existing
1. Atlantic Coastal	13.4%	3	Brazil: Cabo Orange NP Lago Piratuba BR (Gurupi FR)	3	Brazil: Piria-Gurupi ES Suriname: Coppename R. Mouth NER Wia Wia NER Brinckhuevel NER Galibi NER Hertenrits NER
2. Jari-Trombetas	8.3%	2		2	Brazil: Rio Trombetas BR Guyana: Kaieteur NP Suriname: Sipaliwini NER E. Gebergte NER Tafelberg NER Brownsberg NEP Raleighvallen-Voltzberg NER
3. Xingu-Madeira	19.2%	5	Brazil: Tapajos (Amazonia) NP, (Gorotire FR) (Mundurucania FR)	5	
4a. Roraima	2.6%	1	Brazil: (Parima FR)	1	Brazil: Maraca-Roraima ES
4b. Manaus	5.1%	1	Brazil: Jau NP	1	Brazil: Anavilhanas ES, (INPA has several small reserves near Manaus including Duke, Egler, and Campina)

5. Upper Rio Negro	7.9%	2	Brazil Pico da Neblina NP (Rio Negro FR) (Parima FR) Colombia: El Tuparro FT Venezuela: Serrania de la Neblina NP	2	Venezuela: Yapacana NP Duida Marahuaca NP Piedra del Cocuy NM Cerro Autana NM
6. Solimoes-Amazonas	9.4%	2	Ecuador: Yasuni NP Cuyabeno FPR	2	Colombia: Amacayacu NP
7. Southwest	34.1%	8	Bolivia: Isiboro-Secure NP Manuripi-Pando WR Huanchaca NP Brazil: Paacas-Novos NP Ique-Aripuana ES (Pedras Negras FR) (Jaru FR) (Juruena FR) Ecuador: Yasuni NP Peru: Manu NP Pacaya-Samiria NIR	8	Bolivia: Bella Vista NP, Ulla Ulla WR Brazil: Jaru BR Peru: Tingo Maria NP

Key: NP - National Park; WR - Wildlife Refuge/Reserve; RP - Regional Park; BR - Biological Reserve; FR - Forest Reserve; ES - Ecological Station; NIR - National Reserve; NER - Nature Reserve; NEP - Nature Park; FT - Faunistic Territory; NM - Natural/National Monument; FPR - Fauna Production Reserve; WH - World Heritage Site; MAB - Biosphere Reserve.

Source: Wetterberg, *et al.*, 1981

Tourism considerations in selection of protected areas

In many countries, tourism plays a major role in the establishment of protected areas and an area's 'tourist potential' is an important factor in the selection process. Some of the factors which make an area attractive to visitors are indicated in the checklist provided in Example 3.8. Growing numbers of vacationers seek recreation in a warm tropical country; they want to see something different, something new, something spectacular, something to photograph; they want to travel in comfort, with minimal effort; and they want to mix their 'adventure' with leisure activities such as sunbathing, swimming and shopping.

Consequently, the most successful tourist packages combine a number of different interests – sport, wildlife, local customs, historical sites, spectacular scenes, food and dancing and, most of all, water. The sea, lakes, rivers, swimming pools and waterfalls all have high recreation value.

Tourist potential in protected areas drops off fast, however, as the expense, time and discomfort of travel increases or when danger is involved in access to the tourist destination. Nairobi National Park receives more visitors than any other park in Kenya because it is the park closest to the capital and easiest for visitors to reach. The variety and close proximity of natural habitats protected by Costa Rica's Park System have made that country extremely popular for nature tourism groups. Wildlife tourism in Zimbabwe has declined since the well-publicised shooting of visitors by terrorists.

This latter incident highlights the fickleness of the tourist industry. A tourism boom may grow out of fashion and value for money but a switch in airline routes and prices, a change in exchange rates, the hint of political trouble or some other country making a better tourism offer can all reduce the tourist trade and leave the hotels empty.

Wildlife as a large-scale tourist attaction in Africa and parts of Asia is also a delicate matter. Certain animals such as lions, leopards, tigers, elephants, rhino and gorillas have big visitor appeal but other wildlife, just as fascinating to the scientist, seems to have lower 'star' quality. Reliability of sighting is also necessary. It is not enough to know you have a chance to see a tiger – visitors want to have a guarantee that they will see a tiger before they come in any substantial numbers.

Moreover, visitors may be 'spoiled' by the quality of wildlife television films and the quality of viewing in the really top parks and tend not to be satisfied with less spectacular reserves. One solution is, of course, to employ good knowledgeable guides to make wildlife viewing as interesting and rewarding as possible but even so certain habitats are easier of access and more open for viewing game. Tropical rain forests are particularly unappealing to most visitors, though they can be made more interesting with imaginative presentation: aerial walkways, board walks, indigenous people as guides, river-running (e.g. in Borneo), hides for wildlife viewing. Even so they cannot compete with African savannas in terms of interesting wildlife and are unlikely to attract such large numbers of overseas or domestic visitors.

Example 3.8: Checklist on tourist potential of protected areas

A Is the protected area
  - close to an international airport or major tourist centre?
  - moderately close?
  - remote?

B Is the journey to the area
  - easy and comfortable?
  - a bit of an effort?
  - arduous or dangerous?

C Does the area offer
  - 'star' species attractions?
  - other interesting wildlife?
  - representative wildlife? distinctive wildlife viewing, e.g. on foot, by boat, from hides?

D Is successful wildlife viewing
  - guaranteed?
  - usual?
  - with luck or highly seasonal?

E Does the area offer
  - several distinct features of interest?
  - more than one feature of interest?
  - one main feature of interest?

F Does the area have additional
  - high cultural interest?
  - some cultural attractions?
  - few cultural attractions?

G Is the area
  - unique in its appeals?
  - a little bit different?
  - similar to other visitor reserves?

H Does the area have
  - a beach or lakeside recreation facilities?
  - river, falls or swimming pools?
  - no other recreation?

I Is the area close enough to other sites of tourist interest to be part of a tourist circuit?
  - outstanding potential, other attractive sites
  - moderate potential
  - low or no such potential

J Is the surrounding area
  - of high scenic beauty or intrinsic interest?
  - quite attractive?
  - rather ordinary?

K Are standards of food and accommodation offered
   – high?
   – adequate?
   – rough?

3. Guatopo National Park in Venezuela is a good example of a superb forested area easily earning its protection status as a result of its valuable hydrological functions.
Photo: WWF

Hydrological criteria for selecting sites for protected areas

Natural vegetation cover plays a very important role in regulating the behaviour of water drainage systems. Particularly important is the 'sponge effect' by which rainfall is trapped and held by catchment forests and natural grasslands so that water drains out rather slowly and evenly into the river systems, reducing the tendency of floods in periods of heavy rainfall and continuing to release water during periods of dry weather. These functions are lost when the vegetation of upland catchments is destroyed.

In the tropics as a whole, 90 per cent of all farmers cultivate valley bottomlands, and thus are dependent on the activities of the 10 per cent of the population who live in watershed areas. The key example is the Ganges River system: 40 million people live in Nepal, Uttar Pradesh and other Himalayan foothills, while the floodplain supports 500 million people.

Water supplies are so vital to human life, to agriculture and industry, that protection of this water regulatory function of natural vegetation is of much greater value than alternative uses of such areas. Thus, specific areas must be set aside as hydrological reserves, as has been demonstrated in Malawi (Example 3.9).

Selection of areas in need of protection for the preservation of hydrological functions will depend on four main considerations;

- the susceptibility of the catchment to erosion
- the susceptibility of the river to flooding
- the seasonality of water availability
- the socio-economic importance of the particular watershed

Susceptibility to erosion

Various formulae have been developed to give an index of 'proneness to erosion' usually involving the combination of measures of: rain intensity, frequency of rain above critical intensity levels, soil fragility, land steepness and length of slopes. Despite some problems in measuring these features, crude estimates of climate, soil type and land steepness can be combined to give some indication of proneness to erosion. In some countries, (e.g. Thailand, Indonesia) such a formula has been used in classifying hydrological protection forests or reserves.

Susceptibility to flooding

The tendency of water systems to flood depends on the area of catchment, the ability of the catchment to absorb water and the details of land levels, bottlenecks, etc., in the drainage pattern. Anywhere which already has a history of periodic

Example 3.9: *The value of catchment conservation in Malawi*

It is not always easy to demonstrate directly the value of catchment conservation, usually because of lack of sufficiently long-term data for comparable controls. However, a good example is provided by comparing stream flow on the Bua and Dwangwa Rivers, which drain adjacent catchments in the Central Region of Malawi. The upper Bua catchment is largely open to cultivation and has experienced a massive expansion of agriculture over the last 10 years, particularly in the form of tobacco estates, at the expense of the indigenous vegetation, *Brachystegia* woodland. The upper Dwangwa catchment, by contrast, is largely protected by the Kasungu National Park.

It has recently been shown by the Department of Lands, Evaluation and Water that run-off from the upper Bua catchment, as measured by stream flow, was 50 per cent higher during 1970-1980 than during 1954-1964, a decade of rainfall comparable in quantity and pattern. The adjacent catchment of the upper Dwangwa, by contrast, showed no change in the amount of run-off between the two decades. The increased run-off from the Bua catchment can therefore be attributed to removal of the natural vegetation.

The problems associated with such an increase in run-off are of course well known, involving loss of topsoil, siltation of the lower catchment, and reduction of dry season flow. The stream flow data indicate that these problems may be anticipated in the Bua catchment, but not in the Dwangwa catchment, whose headwaters are protected.

Source: Kombe, 1984

destructive flooding with the water catchment under natural vegetation should certainly be regarded as a case for urgent protection, and no vegetation clearance should be allowed there.

Seasonality of water availability

In many areas streams which formerly flowed all year round now only flow in the rainy season as a result of denuding the upper catchment. In such cases, the need to protect remaining natural vegetation and reforest damaged areas becomes obvious. MacKinnon, 1983, reports a dramatic illustration of this in Sulawesi, Indonesia, where, during the dry season, adjacent river systems showed the effect of forest clearance, ranging from dry river beds in the cleared valleys to flowing waters in the river basins still clothed in natural forest.

Socio-economic importance of particular watersheds

The importance of any water system will depend on the number of people dependent on that water supply for drinking water and irrigation needs, the number of domestic stock similarly dependent together with their pastures, the area and value of agricultural land and the extent of industrial needs. Expensive investments such as hydro-electric or irrigation dams and irrigation canal systems add to the economic importance of the water course. In addition, boat transport systems depend on the continued navigability of the particular waterway.

The need to create a hydrological protection reserve will generally be more acutely felt and identified by the agency depending on the water supply or threatened by siltation damage than by the protection agency which is expected to manage these reserves. It is important that the selection of hydrological reserves is not left entirely to the authority managing these lands but that legal and institutional mechanisms exist for involvement of other agencies with interests in those lands. Braulio Carrillo National Park in Costa Rica was created primarily as a result of conservationist protest over the construction of a major new road through one of the country's most important watersheds. The road was built but a new national park will protect the watershed on either side of it.

Geographical aspects of selecting sites for protected areas

Locational considerations (in relation to selection of reserves) should rarely take precedence over the biogeographic, biological and hydrological considerations but are nevertheless crucial to the success of many protected area projects. A very remote and inaccessible location may be ideal for a reserve of Category I (Strict Nature Reserve) where the primary function is protection with minimal human disturbance. On the other hand, the reserve's remoteness will not be an asset if it means less effective protection, if guards refuse to be stationed there, inspectors never visit and local villagers are carrying out destructive activities unchecked.

Where a reserve's main function is as a site for recreation, nature-oriented tourism, or use by schools for education purposes, it must clearly be sited somewhere not too far from town and tourist centres and/or have easy access routes. Sometimes these factors will result in one area rather than an alternative being developed as a reserve.

As a general rule, groups with special interests such as hunters, fishermen, birdwatchers, and trekkers, are more willing to make difficult journeys to reach their desired objectives so that hunting reserves, for instance, can be located in more remote areas (e.g. Chirisa Safari Area, Zimbabwe, and Rungwa Game Reserve in Tanzania).

In addition to these practical, function-related aspects of the geographical location of reserves, there are several biological and management aspects to be considered. Geographical features such as steep ridges, broad rivers, and coastlines can be utilised as natural buffers both to human incursion and animal excursion from reserves. Irrespective of the actual biological content of the proposed reserves, serious consideration should be given to their geographical features before making a final selection. The use of meaningful geographic features may also be important when deciding upon their boundaries.

Political considerations in selecting sites for protected areas

The world is divided up into political units – countries, states, provinces, etc. Sometimes these divisions have meaningful geographical, even biogeographical, relationships, but more often political boundaries cut through biogeographical provinces and sub-provinces. These political factors must be given serious consideration in the selection of reserves and can sometimes be used to advantage in developing protected areas.

One of the reasons for the success of the national park concept is that it appeals to national pride. The name 'national park' inherently reflects an advertisement of national prestige. Countries simply do not want to be left behind, and all countries have some splendours of nature that should be protected as part of their national heritage. The same argument can be brought to bear at provincial, regional or district levels. When one provincial governor boasts of a national or provincial park in his province, the neighbouring governor will also want one. Strong local government support can be a justification for establishing a protected area where biological considerations alone might not have warranted it. Often local government can give considerable assistance in the form of free land, the loan of staff from other divisions, and even funds, provision of access roads, or vehicles.

Administrative aspects

There can be some strategic advantages in developing reserves on political boundaries. For instance, it has been noted (Chapter 3, pages 38-43) that it is important to establish very large reserves and that reserves should be linked where possible. Often, however, the head of a given region or province will only approve allocation of a certain proportion of his own region as a protected area. But by linking protected areas established along political boundaries, it is possible to get approval and local support for larger reserves. These amalgamated reserves also have management advantages in that only 'one side' of the reserve needs protection in each province or region. The responsibility can thus be shared. A good example is the Kerinci-Seblat National Park in Sumatra, Indonesia, which totals an area of 1.4 million ha, an impossibly large area to set aside for protection in any single province. In this case, however, the national park is rather evenly spread over four adjacent provinces. The positive aspects of administrative division of responsibility must be weighed against the possible negative aspects of poor communications or even bad cooperation between the respective agencies and duplication of functions.

Transfrontier protected areas

Biology does not respect political boundaries and it is sometimes useful for nations to set up their own parks and protected areas adjoining those of neighbouring countries. As well as the benefits of larger, contiguous protected areas and of shared responsibility, there are also additional advantages. First, such international reserves are not dependent on the political stability of any one nation. If law-enforcement and the political system in one country breaks down this does not invite the complete collapse of the reserve. For example the Ruwenzori-Virunga Volcanoes reserves system in Africa straddles three countries. Although the civil unrest in Uganda was disastrous for the Ugandan part of the reserve, the rest of the Virunga complex remained relatively unharmed. Now that better order has been restored, the Ugandan sector is slowly being restocked by animals emigrating from the adjacent reserves in Rwanda and Zaire.

The second consideration about transfrontier reserves is a military one. A country may wish to maintain, and like its neighbour to maintain, an uninhabited security zone along their frontier. A protected reserve where no human settlement is allowed makes an excellent security zone, so military planners will often support such protected areas, as was the case with the Boni National Reserve in Kenya on the Somalia border. Conversely, some 'demilitarised zones', such as the one between North and South Korea, can serve wildlife conservation objectives even without being a declared protected area.

Another example of international cooperation exists on the border between Malaysia and Indonesia in Borneo. The Game Department of Sarawak originally proposed creating the Lanjak Entimau Reserve along its border with Indonesia and asked the Conservation Department in Indonesia to consider making a comparable adjoining reserve on the Indonesian side. Quoting the Malaysian reserve as justification, the Indonesian authorities went ahead and authorised a large reserve, Gn. Bentuang dan Karimum, along the

9. The Volcanoes National Park of Rwanda is part of a transfrontier reserve, being contiguous with the Virunga National Park of Zaire which adjoins the Queen Elizabeth National Park of Uganda. Photo: WWF/H.D. Rijksen

border with Sarawak. The Malaysian Conservation authorities are now using the existence of this Indonesian reserve as justification for a considerable extension to Lanjak Entimau. As the whole area is a military security zone there has been no strong opposition to increasing the area of land allocated for reserves.

Practical considerations in selecting sites for protected areas

There is no point in establishing a protected area unless there is a good chance that its management objectives can in fact be achieved. If the potential reserve is simply not going to work, however justifiable or attractive the idea, then it must be replaced by a more realistic venture. Where this involves abandoning efforts for *in situ* protection of valuable resources an *ex situ* or translocation rescue operation may be considered instead.

The manager of protected areas must face realities. It is impossible to conserve a coastal swamp forest, if a development programme involving diverting the water sources or lowering the water table of the neighbouring area is clearly given higher government priority. The Klias National Park in Malaysia, for instance, was degazetted after only four years when the government decided to construct a pulp mill in the area.

Sometimes the levels of protective measures that would be needed to safeguard an area against local pressures of land hunger or general abuse may be impossible to achieve or justify. Some existing protected areas have failed or are failing to reach their objectives and should be abandoned unless the situation can be rectified; in such cases the land should be returned to the state govern-

Fig. 3.5: Major border parks of the tropics

Key
Neotropical (South America)

1. Iguazu (Argentina)/Iguaçu World Heritage Site (Brazil)
2. La Amistad (Costa Rica/Panama)
3. Serrania de la Neblina (Venezuela)/Pico da Neblina (Brazil)
4. Puyehue and Vicente Perez Rosales (Chile)/Lanin & Nahuel Huapi (Argentina)
5. Bernardo O'Higgins and Torres del Paine (Chile)/Los Glaciares (Argentina)
6. Cerro Sajama (Bolivia)/Lauca (Chile)
7. Los Katios (Colombia)/Darien (Panama)

Indomalayan (South and Southeast Asia)

8. Manas (India/Bhutan)
9. Wassur (Indonesia)/Tindu (Papua New Guinea)
10. Royal Chitwan (Nepal)/Udiapur and Valmikinagar (India)
11. Hutan Sambas (Indonesia)/Samunsam Tanjong Datu (Sarawak)
12. Lanjak Entimau (Sarawak)/Gn. Bentuang dan Karimum (Indonesia)
13. Yot Dom (Thailand)/Preah Vihea (Kampuchea)
14. Sunderbans (India/Bangladesh)

Afrotropical (Sub-Saharan Africa)

15. Serengeti (Tanzania)/Masai Mara (Kenya)
16. Tsavo (Kenya)/Mkomazi (Tanzania)
17. Boni (Kenya)/Lag Badana (Somalia)
18. Kalahari Gemsbok (South Africa)/Gemsbok (Botswana)
19. Volcanoes (Rwanda)/Virunga (Zaire)/Queen Elizabeth (Uganda)
20. 'W' (Benin/Burkina Faso/Niger)
21. Boucle de la Pendjari (Benin)/Arly (Burkina Faso)
22. Mount Nimba (Guinea/Ivory Coast)
23. Delta du Saloum (Senegal)/Gambia Saloum (Gambia)
24. Nyika (Malawi/Zambia)
25. Lower Zambezi (Zambia)/Mana Pools (Zimbabwe)
26. Mosi-Oa-Tunya (Zambia)/Victoria Falls and Zambezi (Zimbabwe)

Source: Thorsell, 1985b

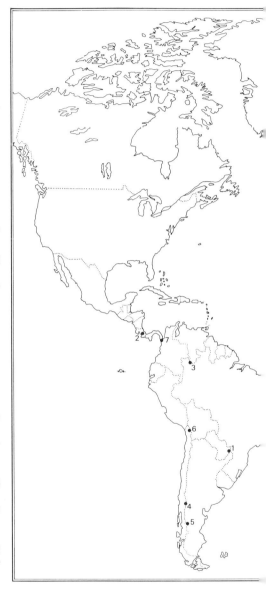

ment for reallocation for alternative use. This is particularly true of reserves which have always been too small to be viable or which, in periods of political instability or lawlessness, have been overrun, destroyed or hunted out, such as the Semliki Game Reserve in Uganda, the Mkomazi Game Reserve in Tanzania, and Queen Elizabeth National Park in the Solomon Islands.

Consideration of reserve practicability should rest on a number of ecological and human questions. Can the area's ecological integrity be maintained? On what internal and external factors does its survival depend and can those factors be controlled? Does management have the knowhow and resources to maintain these ecological factors? What levels of human pressure does the reserve face? Can these pressures be met practically by management with the resources and budgets likely to be available? Is there the potential to buffer the area against these threats?

These questions should be considered in turn for each of the several objectives or functions for which a given reserve may be selected in the first place. Some idea of the likelihood of success for each objective should be formulated and these probabilities weighed in the selection process.

Reserves for migratory species

The special needs of migratory species are often overlooked. Managers may feel that they are not responsible for migrants that visit their areas only in passage or for a few months, and that these migrants are the responsibility of the countries that harbour their breeding populations. However, because migrant species spend much of their lives outside the boundaries of protected areas, often make arduous and hazardous journeys and generally arrive in a weakened physical condition, they are particularly vulnerable. Resident human populations also view migrant animal

10. Wintering grounds of migratory species may need protection if these species are to be conserved. The entire tiny population of the western race of Siberian White Crane over-winters in the small Keoladeo National Park at Bharatpur in India.
Photo: WWF/P. Jackson

species as a bonus or free resource for exploitation and exhibit complete lack of constraint or responsibility in their harvesting methods. For example, villagers on the north Java coast harvest over one million migrating rails and waders each year for food.

The importance of migratory species and the responsibilities of those countries in which they settle during the non-breeding season, or on passage to and from wintering grounds, have been highlighted by the Migratory Species Convention concluded in Bonn in June 1979 (see Chapter 12, pages 255-260).

Each country should make a particular effort to make an inventory of migratory species using its territory, assess the status of these species and determine whether their particular requirements can be met.

Protective management for migratory species may in some cases involve the establishment of permanent reserves, as in the Djoudj Sanctuary on the Senegal delta and the Keoladeo National Park in India where tens of thousands of wintering wildfowl congregate on artificial reservoirs. Elsewhere it may be necessary to legally protect migrants, to prohibit hunting of wintering populations or to apply seasonal protective measures to important feeding areas and roosts, which can be used for other purposes during the rest of the year. It can also be helpful to provide grain at migration 'stations' or to compensate local landowners for loss of grain to migrating birds, as is done along the geese migration routes on the eastern seaboard of North America.

Long migration routes are often dependent on key transient points where animals stop to rest, water, and feed before continuing their journey. Inadvertent destruction of such key sites – for instance, pollution of a muddy estuary important to migrating waders – can prove disastrous to some species.

Example 3.10: Criteria for consideration when selecting protected areas

The following criteria for judging the conservation value of an area are adapted from Ratcliffe (1977). In applying these selection-criteria, the following should be taken into account:

- some of the criteria may overlap, be equally important or cumulative
- some are mutually incompatible (e.g. 'rarity' versus 'typicalness').

1. *Size*: The conservation value of an area is a function of its size. In principle, the area must be of a size and form sufficient to support entire ecological units or viable populations of flora and fauna. As a general rule, the area's conservation importance increases with size.
2. *Richness and diversity*: Richness and diversity of species is usually linked with diversity of habitat. Ecological gradients (catenas, ecotones, altitudinal transition zones) should be represented because of the important transitional communities they support.
3. *Naturalness*: There are few places on earth that have not been modified through the influence of man. Areas where this influence is minimal or which have potential for restoration are particularly valuable.
4. *Rarity*: One of the most important purposes of many national parks and conservation areas is to protect rare or endangered species and communities. Rarity of a species may be related to extremely specialised habitat requirements or to direct human pressure (trapping, collecting, hunting, poaching) or indirect human influences (destruction of habitats).
5. *Uniqueness*: For the purposes of selection, an area may be unique because the biome it represents is not adequately represented in the national system or because it exhibits particular natural processes. Thus Lake Malawi is unique because of its many endemic forms of cichlid fish, the result of rapid speciation.
6. *Typicalness*: In addition to unusual features, it is important to represent typical areas of common habitats and communities of the biogeographic unit.
7. *Fragility*: Fragile habitats, species and communities have a high sensitivity to environmental changes. Climax vegetations, such as the humid tropical forest, are inherently stable, but other vegetation types may be very fragile and easily affected by minor climatic or hydrological changes. Fragility is often linked with rarity.

8. *Genetic conservation*: Richness and diversity usually reflect genetic diversity but there may be other genetic considerations that justify protection, e.g. the occurrence of wild forms of domesticated plants and animals.

9. *Historical records*: If an area has been studied and monitored for a long period of time, its value for research objectives is greater than a comparable unmonitored area and this value would be reduced if studies did not continue.

10. *Position in an ecological/geographical unit*: Include within a single large area as many as possible of the important and characteristic formations, communities and species. Such areas will be more valuable than those representing a single formation or community.

11. *Indispensability*: An area may deserve protection because it protects a vital watershed catchment or because it is indispensable at a higher level of biogeographic subdivision, e.g. bottom lands in a major river valley, or represents a seasonal habitat component of a migratory species.

12. *Potential value*: Areas once known to be of exceptional quality but which have been recently damaged could, with appropriate management and protection, regain the former quality. Of course, there is no reason to select such areas if unimpaired examples are available elsewhere.

13. *Intrinsic appeal*: The area should provide opportunities for recreation. However some features have more appeal to humans than others. Birds and larger mammals are more interesting to most of the public than invertebrates. Similarly, orchids arouse more enthusiasm than sedges and grasses. While science may view all creatures as equal, in nature conservation it is more realistic to give more weight to some groups than others.

14. *Modified landscapes augmenting biological values*: National or cultural sites or particular forms of land use which have a significant influence on the region's biogeography may require protection.

15. *Opportunities for conservation*: The socio-political climate is highly relevant in determining conservation priorities. Often a lack of support, and perhaps even overt resentment toward park development by local peoples results in limited conservation success and even complete failure, despite the richness or value of the wildland. Conversely, some second choice areas have been so enthusiastically supported that, despite the less than optimal resources, they have been rousing successes as parks.

4

Policy, Law and Administration for Managing Protected Areas

Introduction

Protected areas policy, law and administration are important inter-connected aspects affecting the successful long-term management of protected areas. Policy, law and administration involve many interdisciplinary facets merging to achieve clear objectives, effective planning, competent execution and, above all, public support and participation.

This chapter is divided under four principal headings: overall policy; legislation; administration; and broadening participation in protected area management. Sound policy based on ecological evaluation in combination with economic, social, and political factors should set a protected area's goals as an integral part of development planning. Legislative mechanisms must be consistent with protected areas policy and specially-tuned to the specific programme needs in administration, management, and enforcement. Strong and competent institutions to administer protected areas laws and programmes provide the third key element for effective management. Finally, increased efforts to broaden participation of all interested and concerned individuals and groups in protected areas management may provide the best opportunity for improving long-term success of protected areas programmes. For a more detailed discussion of each of these elements, see Lausche (1980).

Policy matters relating to protected areas

National Conservation Policy

The basis for responsive legislation and administrative authority for protected areas should lie in national policy on resource conservation and development. Such policy may be written into the national constitution, enshrined in legislation or declared in government programmes and manifestos. National conservation policy should include a statement of the nation's commitment to the sustainable use of the nation's living resources, including the protection of representative ecosystems and species by means of a programme of protected area management.

The World Conservation Strategy (WCS) gives broad general guidelines on the contents and objectives to be formulated in each country's conservation policy, stressing the need to underline the importance of conservation and protected area management in furthering sustainable development. The WCS also urges each country to clarify its conservation needs and define its conservation policy through the preparation of its own national conservation strategy (NCS).

The NCS provides the framework for the execution of policy. It identifies the country's conservation needs and objectives, as well as areas and resources of particular significance which are in need of protection. It describes the programmes needed to achieve these conservation objectives, identifies the institutions responsible and suggests or reviews the appropriate legislative and administrative framework necessary for implementation.

Where an NCS does not exist, other tools influencing government operations may provide important guidance on conservation policy. Economic development plans and national planning legislation frequently contain sections related to development and use of natural resources. Such sections should incorporate conservation goals and considerations with land-use planning and other resource development considerations.

Further policy guidance for conservation purposes may be derived from any relevant multilateral obligations or responsibilities which the country may have assumed related to resource conservation. Some international programmes or obligations such as the World Heritage Convention contain conservation principles which should be recognised in national policy and, in some cases, are automatically incorporated in national policy upon acceptance of the obligation.

Protected Areas Policy

In each country, a policy on protected areas should be developed for the national programme as a whole. In addition, each protected area may be guided by its own specific policy considerations. These considerations may be the basis for particular objectives or goals. For example, some areas may be established primarily for scientific research or for preservation of an ecosystem or species threatened with extinction. Other areas may serve a combination of purposes including recreation or protection of cultural values. Policy guidelines for individual areas may also relate to the buildings, roads, and other development activities associated with the area. Each area will have its particular role and policy basis within the comprehensive policy of any national or subnational programme. Definition of each area's policy is important to guide legal and administrative elements associated with the area. Moreover, specific objectives and purposes for each area may be defined largely by the kind of policy statement developed for the area. Thus, it is important to develop a clear policy basis for each protected area wherever possible (for a sample outline see Moore, 1984).

Legal aspects of protected areas management

(a) Preliminary considerations

A sound and lasting protected areas programme requires careful, realistic deliberation to ensure the existence of adequate legal strategies and institutional arrangements. These strategies may take a variety of forms, from government agency decision-making, laws and regulations, to other means of formally or informally influencing human behaviour to effect change and achieve the desired conservation objectives and goals. Thus, legislation for protected areas must be seen within a broad context, if it is to be properly used and understood. A number of preliminary considerations are relevant to the appropriate form and scope of protected areas legislation in any particular country.

The nature of law

Understanding the country's formal and informal legal system is a prerequisite to using law effectively for protected areas management. Societies differ fundamentally in their attitudes towards law and the extent of their use of an active court system. In some countries, more informal negotiation may be the preferred method for accomplishing protection goals, usually through the strong persuasive role of key individuals or an agency which exercises ultimate authority. In this latter instance, the courts may play a less active role. Many different legal systems (for example, statutory or codified law, traditional or customary law, and religious law) may operate simultaneously or at various levels. They may have their own authority structures that include decision-making bodies parallel to formal courts.

Traditional laws and customs

In many tropical countries strong traditions and customs relate to natural resource use, involving, for example, sacred sites, or respect for environmentally important features like waterholes, caves, reefs, forests protecting water sources, or forests protecting villages from landslides. Many such traditional laws concern the individual use of communal lands or resources and sometimes have extra-legal punishments incorporated for rule-breakers.

In many cases, these traditional rules may now be incompatible with modern religion or national legislation. Some, however, do not conflict with modern government and can be highly relevant to the protection of natural areas, especially in remote inhabited regions where villagers show greater respect for their ancient traditions than they do for modern and often poorly understood statutory laws. Under such circumstances it may be most effective for the manager to persuade the villagers of the local benefits or religious traditions of a neighbouring protected area and let them assume a significant role in protecting the area. For example, the Gunung Palung Reserve in Kalimantan, Indonesia, is avoided and respected by newly-arrived settlers who quickly adopt the local belief that it is haunted by spirits. As a result, the reserve survives with virtually no protective guard force at all. The manager's role in such a case can be focussed on monitoring the area and educating the people on local benefits to ensure that the area is maintained over the long term even though traditional beliefs may eventually change.

Evoking religious traditions can also be a useful tool for the protected area manager. Villagers in remote areas are often devoutly religious, giving special meaning to such natural events as volcanic eruptions, floods and droughts and even relating them to forest disturbance. Similarly, many tribal peoples have food taboos; the Masai, for example, rarely consume the meat of wild animals. It may be possible to get the backing of teachers in certain regions with protected areas to reinforce those religious ideas that emphasise respect for nature. Individual teachers can highlight special conservation problems – for example, the harm in eating turtle eggs or other species that need local protection. Similar messages can be emphasised throughout the educational system.

Conversely, the protected area manager who fails to win the support of local people will find them invoking traditional laws and beliefs to justify continued exploitation of the reserve. This often means that more extension work is needed, or perhaps that a new compromise must be reached between utilisation and protection to compensate for the loss of legitimate pre-existing rights. If alternative supplies of resources are available, villagers are more likely to accept an arrangement involving loss of some use rights within a protected area.

An understanding of traditional rules is also important in determining exploitation rights of buffer zones around reserves. In such cases some fair and workable system of exploitation must be found for what is usually a community resource. This aspect will be covered more fully in Chapter 6.

Status of land for protected areas

The legal status of land designated as a protected area is a critical preliminary consideration which may require different approaches in different countries. In some countries, such as China, much of the land is State-owned, while in others, such as Papua New Guinea, most land is held communally. In contrast, European countries have little remaining public land and must use private land where it is in the overriding public interest to create protected areas.

In some cases, it may be necessary to acquire privately-owned land or land held by other public interests. Where this is a possibility, the protected area legislation should provide clear procedures for acquisition, compensation and, as appropriate, expropriation.

Communal or customary land-use rights and practices should be recognised in protected area legislation and management directives for individual areas as it is essential that land arrangements for protected areas are acceded to by local community authorities.

In some cases, it may be necessary to make special arrangements with community officials for the use of customary land, for instance, a lease with perpetual use and control by the protected area authority in return for some compensation to traditional users relinquishing their use rights. Elsewhere, protected areas may be established to safeguard the land use rights of indigenous peoples by providing special protection for certain traditional practices. This has occurred, for example, with the land of the Kuna Indians of Panama and in the 'Traditional Use Zones' of Siberut Island, Indonesia.

(b) The need for protected areas legislation

Various categories of protected areas call for different levels of protection and utilisation. No matter what the type or purpose may be, protected areas can be effectively established and safeguarded only if there are responsive legislative and administrative arrangements for their protection and management.

Example 4.1: *Owner involvement in protected areas in Fiji*

A unique iguana species on the small island of Yadua Taba in Fiji was threatened with habitat destruction through goat grazing and slash and burn agriculture. The land was under customary ownership of the Matagali people who have signed a lease agreement with the National Trust for Fiji to return the island to a natural state.

The land owners now receive an annual payment of $US 1500 to act as honorary wardens and to control unauthorised landings on the island. Compensation was paid for removal of the goat population; burning of vegetation is no longer allowed. The crested iguana itself has traditional significance to the local people as a totem, and its preservation has been an event of some pride to the elders. The rarity of the iguana and the scientific interest it created also facilitated the raising of funds for establishment of the sanctuary.

Source: Eaton, 1985

The existence of adequate legal machinery is fundamental to the long-term success of any protected area programme. Such machinery provides the manager with essential support in meeting his or her responsibilities. It is to the manager's advantage to work closely with the legislative process so as to ensure that this legal base provides the necessary authority for action.

As a primary consideration, the manager's input is important to help ensure that protected areas legislation is realistic and enforceable. Legislative and institutional mechanisms which are not technically, socially or economically feasible are unlikely to be effective. Too much law or authority can be as harmful as too little and can lead to confusion and dissipation of effort. Moreover, if laws are ignored or become redundant, the manager's authority and credibility are likely to be undermined.

The lack of legislation specifically responsive to the needs of protected areas is a weakness in the conservation effort of many countries. Moreover, much existing protected areas legislation was enacted decades ago and has little regard for internationally evolving norms in protected areas management. Revising legislation to adapt internationally accepted standards to local circumstances may be one means of generating support for viable national systems of protected areas. It may also provide a basis for public awareness programmes on the importance of such protected areas for human well-being at the local, national and international levels.

The following points are important considerations when reviewing the adequacy of national legislative frameworks for protected areas:

- Legislation should authorise a competent body to protect the area by force of law.

- Such an authorised body should be responsible only to the highest governing authority and should not be subordinate to any government agency which has conflicting policies or objectives.
- Legislation should be based on a thorough understanding of international conservation agreements but should also be in harmony with local traditions, institutions and ecological conditions.
- When protected areas are first planned, all inhabitants in and around the areas should be well informed about the protected area, and how it will affect their livelihood and lifestyle.
- Protection of the natural environment which includes the protection of areas occupied by indigenous people may need to specifically recognise their traditional land-rights.
- Any legislation to establish, de-list or reduce the size of protected areas should be enacted only by the highest authority in the country; de-listing should be permitted only in the most extraordinary circumstances.

Finally, there is a tendency for statutes and organisations to evolve in a somewhat *ad hoc* manner over time. In any protected areas programme, it is desirable to undertake periodic reviews and re-appraisal of the legislation and, as appropriate, streamline and restructure the legal and administrative arrangements, drawing on experience from other disciplines and situations and adapting these to local circumstances.

(c) Key aspects of protected areas legislation

In drafting or strengthening legislation for protected areas management, attention should be paid to three general principles:

i) Conservation and management objectives must be ecologically sound and achievable with the technical and financial resources available or likely to become available. Here it should be noted that national treasuries are usually more sympathetic in allocating funds for activities that are required by law or International Convention than for less formal programmes.
ii) Existing institutions should be used as much as possible in order to minimise the need for a new and expensive infrastructure.
iii) A high level of national and local public participation should be encouraged to ensure broad social and political support.

Protected areas policies and objectives

Legislation for protected areas should provide a general framework as to how an area, or different classes of areas, should be protected. This guidance provides the foundation for the policy framework within which more detailed programmes and area plans can be elabaorated.

A solid policy framework for protected areas should be developed at the national level, and at any appropriate regional level. The policy should be based upon fundamental ecological principles, in combination with economic, social and political factors. As part of a national development policy, it should be implemented hand-in-hand with land-use planning and other development goals.

While policies and objectives may be communicated legislatively in a number of ways, the most direct method is to include them in the principal law. An alternative is to use subsidiary documents flowing from the legislative process, such as ministerial or departmental regulations. The latter approach may be useful where there is a need to make reference to management concepts that deny precise definition in law, or where changes in details are envisaged but the process of revising the principal law is slow and difficult. Under such circumstances, the principal legislation may provide for the preparation of more specific subsidiary documents framed within the spirit of general legislative policy guidelines.

Protected areas authority

In countries with a constitutional framework, constitutional provisions may exist which allocate jurisdiction for matters related to protected areas. In addition, legal provisions on public health and welfare, social good, or interstate matters may contain some constitutional delegation of authority over conservation-related matters. Where appropriate, protected area legislation should make reference to relevant constitutional provisions to establish a suitable protected area authority to which the country's highest law-making body can delegate powers. Where more than one level of government has constitutional powers for protected areas matters, cooperation is particularly critical.

With respect to specific provisions concerning protected areas institutional authority, legislation should include the following items to the extent possible:

- Designation of Protected Areas authority, or authorities
- Statement of functions, jurisdiction, powers, and duties over protected areas management
- Method to appoint top management
- Degree of authority to initiate and regulate
- Activities envisaged
- Powers to raise and expend funds, and government obligation to ensure adequate and continual funding
- Personnel
- Accountability to legislature and/or judiciary relation to other legislation
- Ministerial discretion to override agency
- Method of reporting
- Liaison with external organisations
- Method of appeal against agency decisions

Management needs

Each protected area will have its own management needs, including the associated monitoring, research and support services required. The Manager should provide input to ensure that the legislation contains authority and resources for appropriate management. Here the language should be sufficiently specific to guide the design of any regulations that may be promulgated under the parent legislation.

One of the most important provisions in protected areas legislation is the requirement of a management plan for each protected area established on the basis of the legislation. To encourage prompt development of the first plan once an area has been established, some countries specify in the legislation a reasonable amount of time after establishment within which a plan must be operational. In other countries this may be an unrealistic ideal. Indonesia, for instance, has over three hundred protected areas which do not yet have management plans but still needs to acquire more land for protection. It will certainly take a number of years to complete plans for all these areas. To ensure effectiveness of the management plan as a conservation tool, legislation should cover procedures for adoption, approval, and review of the plan, along with identification of key institutions or individuals responsible for each activity.

Legislative provisions designed to orient management needs also can provide for:

- Clear statement of purpose of protected area
- Identification of management authority
- Buffer zones with compatible land use
- Secure tenure, permitting modifications only with due notice and review
- Requirement for management planning
- Appropriate public participation
- Close on-going relationship with indigenous and other affected people
- Accountability of any concessions
- Enforcement needs, both concerning powers and equipment

Finally, the legislative sections related to management should require a clear description of protected areas boundaries. Protected areas boundaries should meet the conservation needs of the area to the extent feasible and should be defined in subsidiary legislation (usually a Ministerial Order or Decree issued under the provisions of the relevant basic legislation) as precisely as possible so as to avoid later disputes. Tables, appendices or schedules to the legislation are often a convenient way of describing such boundaries and any sub-divisions of the area which may need to be recognised in law. The Manager should also provide a simple but clear map showing the boundaries of the area. Where maps of remote parts are thought to be unreliable or inaccurate, for example with incorrectly marked watercourses, they should not be used as legal documents but only as secondary information to clarify the legal description of boundaries. Private in-holdings within a park or buffer zones screening the area from conflicting forms of land use should also be well defined.

Regulation of use

Regulations of activities concerning protected areas are of three types: regulations applied inside the protected area; interim regulations to maintain the *status quo* where an area has been identified for protection but the designation takes some time to finalise; and regulations applied outside the protected area to prevent or minimise adverse impacts due to potentially detrimental external activities (e.g. buffer zones, pollution control). The extent of these measures will be determined by the area in question and in each case the protected area manager must communicate his needs to the legal drafter.

The very concept of protected areas, their legal definition and whatever formal or informal legislation or regulations are developed will all require the establishment of firm controls. There must be regulations to control people living in protected areas, visitor activities, concessions to sell food or other items in protected areas, levels and types of utilisation in reserves, etc. The types of controls needed and their appropriate implementation will vary from country to country and area to area. Effecting these controls will be much easier if the proper machinery for control is instituted at the time of establishing the protected area.

Some controls will actually be written into the legislation or regulations of the protected area concerned. Others may be implicit by general powers contained in legislation. It is important to plan how these controls will be implemented. Will issue of permits and setting of quotas be done at central headquarters or by local staff? If by local staff, appropriate authority and guidelines will be needed on how to proceed. Strong supervision and counter-checking will be needed to prevent abuses of any regulatory controls. The individual manager will be responsible for controlling many of the activities in his area by such methods as:

- issue of tickets, permits, or passes for entry;
- issue of special letters for entry to utilise resources;
- setting quotas, checking quotas and harvested materials;
- demarcation of special areas or zones;
- delegation of control authority to other agencies, e.g., police, local government, forestry (for forest products), tourism, etc.

In some cases, it may be necessary to restrict activities (e.g. banning of burning and hunting) on land outside the protected area itself. To effect such control it will be necessary to invoke other related legislation such as laws pertaining to agriculture, forestry or the environment. The full range of legal tools should be used to protect areas against ever increasing external threats. Other laws with potential for use in support of conservation and protected areas may include:

- Land use planning laws
- Environmental laws
- Natural resources conservation laws
- Nature conservation, game, forest or wildlife conservation laws
- Public health and safety laws
- Pollution control laws and guidelines for solid waste disposal
- Mining laws
- Building laws, zoning laws, and those relating to the acquisition of land for national development programmes.

Enforcement

Implicit behind the creation and use of law to protect national parks and other protected areas is the need for its enforcement. Protected areas legislation should specify the enforcement agency and detail the extent of that agency's powers. Countries may differ significantly on how much law enforcement power they care to delegate to the protected area management authority itself. In some countries protected area staff are armed and authorised to use firearms if necessary in carrying out their duties. In other countries protected area staff may have no powers of arrest, con- fiscation of prohibited articles, or fining of trespassers.

Increasingly, countries are giving protected area management staff the authority to act as law enforcement officers in protected areas matters. It is essential that staff do have such authority as without it effective management is virtually impossible, especially in remote areas where the nearest policeman may be 100 km away. This authority should include powers of search, arrest and seizure. In cases where it is not possible to give protected areas staff policing powers, the management authority must develop particularly close working relationships with other law enforcement agencies. In addition, increasing attention should be given to incentives that encourage self-enforcement and local participation with enforcement programmes, a point discussed further below.

Where protected area staff are given law enforcement powers this necessitates special training. Such officers must be very familiar with the laws they are meant to enforce and their own powers to do so. They must know the correct procedures for making arrests and collecting evidence for prosecution, and may need special training in the use and handling of firearms.

11. Kenyan guards catch a party of poachers red-handed but too late to save the elephant. In many African reserves the 'war' against poachers is the primary management activity.
   Photo: WWF/IUCN/Kenya Information Service

Subsidiary legislation and regulations

As the name implies, subsidiary legislation usually flows from a parent law in which the legislature delegates authority to a Minister or an official – e.g. the director of the Parks Service, to promulgate regulations for implementing the law. For example the law may provide for the control of visitor access to a protected area and for regulations which stipulate how this access is to be controlled. Regulations may also specify what may or may not be done in the Park or in different parts thereof, where entry shall take place and whether or not fees should be levied and the amount of such fees. They may control hunting, fishing, the cutting of plants, the lighting of fires, the digging of soil, the use of motor vehicles, boats or aircraft, and many other activities. This list is almost endless and must be tailored to an individual protected area, a class of protected areas and the national system of protected areas.

Properly constituted regulations have the force of law and carry the penalties prescribed by the parent Act. As with the parent Act, any regulations should be reasonable and realistic for the situation. If they are too stringent they may result in retaliatory behaviour, but if they are too weak they may be ignored.

One of the principal advantages of reserving detailed regulations for subsidiary legislation is the flexibility for adjustment and revision when needed. In many countries, changes in the parent law may be very difficult and require much time to effect. Conversely, one of the disadvantages of leaving too much substance to subsidiary legislation is that a change in government may be able to quickly abolish fundamental aspects of the programme. Thus, fundamental elements of the programme always should be grounded in the parent Act, with only details on implementation left to subsidiary legislation.

Example 4.2: How India protects her wildlife and protected areas (an example of a National Wildlife Act)

The Wild Life (Protection) Act, 1972

An Act to provide for the protection of wild animals and birds and for matters connected therewith or ancillary or incidental thereto.

WHEREAS it is expedient to provide for the protection of wild animals and birds and for matters connected therewith or ancillary or incidental thereto.

Definitions:

(1)   'animal' includes amphibians, birds, mammals and reptiles and their young, and also includes, in the cases of birds and reptiles, their eggs.
(15)   'habitat' includes land, water or vegetation which is the natural home of any wild animal.
(21)   'national park' means an area declared, whether under section 35 or section 38, or deemed, under sub-section (3) of section 66, to be declared as a national park.
(26)   'sanctuary' means an area declared, whether under section 18 or section 38, or deemed, under sub-section 66, to be declared as a wild life sanctuary.
(36)   'wild animal' means any animal found wild in nature and includes any animals specified in Schedule I, Schedule II, Schedule III, Schedule IV or Schedule V, wherever found.

Sanctuaries:

18.(1)   The State Government may, by notification, declare any area to be a sanctuary if it considers that such area is of adequate ecological, faunal, floral, geomorphological, natural or zoological significance, for the purpose of protecting, propagating or developing wildlife or its environment.

(2)   The notification referred to in sub-section (1) shall specify, as nearly as possible, the situation and limits of such area.
   Explanation: For the purpose of this section, it shall be sufficient to describe the area by roads, river, ridges or other well-known or readily intelligible boundaries.

National Parks:

35.(1)   Whenever it appears to the State Government that an area, whether within a sanctuary or not, is, by reason of its ecological, faunal, floral, geomorphological or zoological association or importance, needed to be constituted as a national park for the purpose of protecting, propagating or developing wildlife therein or its environment, it may, by notification, declare its intention to constitute such area as a national park.

(2)   The notification referred to in sub-section (1) shall define the limits of the area which is intended to be declared as national park.

(3)   Where any area is intended to be declared as a national park, the provisions of sections 19 to 26 (both inclusive) shall, as far as may be, apply to the investigation and determination of claims, and extinguishment of rights, in relation to any land in such area as they apply to the said matters in relation to any land in a sanctuary.

(4)   When the following events have occurred, namely:

a)   the period for preferring claims has elapsed, and all claims, if any, made in relation to any land in an area intended to be declared as a national park, have been disposed of by the State Government, and

b)   all rights in respect of lands proposed to be included in the national park have become vested in the State Government, the State Government shall publish a notification specifying the limits of the area which shall be comprised within the national park and declare that the said area shall be a national park on and from such date as may be specified in the notification.

(5)   No alteration of the boundaries of a national park shall be made except on a resolution issued by the Legislature of the State.

(6)   No personnel shall destroy, exploit or remove any wildlife from a national park or damage the habitat of any wild animal or deprive any wild animal of its habitat within such national park except under and in accordance with a permit granted by the Chief Wild Life Warden and no such permit shall be granted unless the State Government, being satisfied that such destruction, exploitation or removal of wildlife from the national park is necessary for the improvement and better management of wildlife therein, authorises the issue of such permit.

(7)   No grazing of any cattle shall be permitted in a national park and no cattle shall be allowed to enter therein except where such cattle is used as a vehicle by a person authorised to enter such national park.

(8)   The provisions of sections 27 and 28, sections 30 and 32 (both inclusive), and clause (a), (b) and (c) of section 33 and section 34 shall, as far as may be, apply in relation to a national park as they apply in relation to a sanctuary.

Game Reserve:

36.(1)   The State Government may, by notificaton, declare any area to be a game reserve.

(2)   No hunting of any wild animal shall be permitted in such reserve except under and in accordance with a licence issued under this section by the Chief Wild Life Warden or the authorised officer.

Closed Area:

37.(1)   The State Government may, by notification, declare any area closed to hunting for such period as may be specified in the notification.

(2)   No hunting of any wild animal shall be permitted in a closed area during the period specified in the notification referred to in sub-section (1).

Sanctuaries or National Parks Declared by Central Government:

38.(1)   Where the State Government leases or otherwise transfers any area under its control, not being an area within a sanctuary, to the Central Government, the Central Government may, if it is satisfied that the conditions specified in section 18 are fulfilled in relation to the area so transferred to it, declare such area, by notification, to be a sanctuary and the provisions of section 19 to 35 (both inclusive), 54 and 55 shall apply in relation to such sanctuary declared by the State Government.

(2)   The Central Government may, if it is satisfied that the conditions specified in section 35 are fulfilled in relation to any area referred to in sub-section (1), whether or not such area has been declared to be a sanctuary by the Central Government or the State Government, declare such area, by notification, to be a national park and the provisions of sections 35, 54, and 55 shall apply in relation to such national park as they apply in relation to a national park declared by the State Government.

(3)   In relation to a sanctuary or national park declared by the Central Government, the powers and duties of the Chief Wild Life Warden under the sections referred to in sub-sections (1) and (2), shall be exercised and discharged by the Director or by such other officer as may be authorised by the Director in this behalf and references, in the sections aforesaid, to the State Government shall be construed as references to the Central Government and reference therein to the Legislature of the State shall be construed as a reference to Parliament.

Sources: Government of India, 1972; Rao, 1985

Administrative matters relating to protected areas

Administrative organisation

The type of administrative organisation best suited for protected area management will vary according to the country's size, needs and conservation objectives. Present conditions may well reflect the political evolution of the department in question more than its current functional purpose. As scientific information has improved about the management needs of protected areas, many administrative structures may be insufficiently flexible or equipped for the technical demands of agencies entrusted with management of protected areas. Also, conservation departments commonly have grown up within other government agencies (e.g. forestry, game or agriculture departments) and have inherited their administrative infrastructure without regard to their suitability for present protected area needs. A review and revision of the administrative arrangements of conservation departments may help ensure effective decision-making.

Position of the protected area management authority within government

When the protected area management authority is first established, government notices should clearly state how it will relate to other ministries or departments. It is important that the agency carry out fundamental government policy in a position of authority appropriate to its responsibilities. In practice this may mean placing the authority under a ministry with no responsibility for revenue-production. In some countries this may mean, for example, the Ministry of the Environment, rather than the Ministry of Agriculture or Forestry where the latter ministries are obliged to maximise revenues from their respective resource programmes. Where a primary justification for protected areas is wildlife-based tourism, recreation and hunting (as in Kenya and Sri Lanka) placing the authority for protected areas within a Ministry of Tourism or Home Affairs may be considered.

There are obvious advantages for the protected area management authority being placed under a powerful ministry. Provided the authority can get its plans approved within its own ministry, it could have considerable influence with other government ministries in carrying through programmes. In some countries (e.g. Uganda and Tanzania) parks, are operating outside the government structure under parastatal arrangements, an approach which can provide a certain amount of independence with the right ministerial support.

It is sometimes convenient if the same authority is responsible for management of all categories of protected areas to minimise duplication of effort and skills, competition for staff, land, projects and budgets, and inter-department jealousies. If more than one agency is involved, very close coordination should be established.

It is useful to clarify in an organisational chart the exact position of the protected area management authority within government, indicating all formal linkages. This chart should be familiar to management staff so that the administrative hierarchy can utilise appropriate channels of communication with all other agencies.

Administrative structure of the protected areas management authority

Protected area management authorities are often composed of a number of specialised sub-units, according to the needs of the protected areas programme. These sub-units may include all or most of the following:

- a directorate supported by a central policy and planning unit;
- monitoring and data compilation services;
- research units;
- operational management including:
  - field operations (e.g. law enforcement and ecological management);
  - visitor services;
  - interpretive services; education and extension;
  - engineering, construction and maintenance.

Other duties must be performed, such as public relations and liaison with tourist authorities, concessionaires, local and central government agencies, and the public at large. There are also internal administrative functions including personnel management, financial control, account-ability, legal matters (including the preparation and administration of agreements), and stores functions (e.g. the purchase of stores, and the control and allocation of movable assets).

The degree of centralisation or decentralisation of park management and control is a key issue. Central control simplifies planning and coordination and enables development of a more uniform and integrated protected area system. At the same time, regional disparities, different ecosystems and the need for local knowledge are sound grounds for some delegation of decision-making to regional park managers.

Countries will vary as to how much authority is delegated to field operations, i.e. to the warden or supervisor of a protected area, and how much authority is retained at regional or central headquarters. Whatever the approach, the essential consideration is that different levels and types of decision making be clearly specified and that channels of authority and responsibility be clearly identified. It is useful to show these relationships in chart form (see Figs. 4.1 and 4.2) so that individual staff members know their powers and channels of access to higher authorisation. Since management decisions often have to be taken quickly the more regional delegation of responsibility the better, provided that trained and competent personnel are available.

A final consideration in administrative structure should be to avoid too much bureaucracy and too many administrative levels. The director must not lose touch with ground operations. It is good for morale if the field guards and rangers know and have access to the director.

Organisational procedures

Organisational procedures may be determined by the government protocol or be developed within each programme to formalise certain administrative functions within the agency itself. Organisational procedures may cover such items as specific implementation of policy, accounting or personnel management, rules and regulations affecting staff and their conduct, communicating management recommendations and decisions, linkages to political leaders, and the form of formal liaison or coordination to be taken with other Government agencies or external institutions.

Fig. 4.1: A hypothetical flow chart for decision making within a nature conservation agency

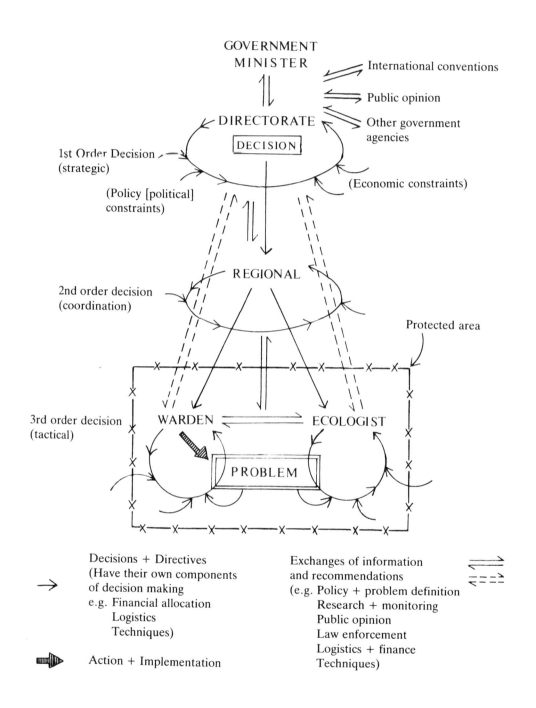

Source: Bell, 1983

Fig. 4.2: *Interaction of law and the protected areas programme*

Law and legal processes		
Input from legal authority:		*Important input of the manager involves:*
Legal style and practice		Identifying objectives and benefits
Legislative format and interpretation		Identifying boundaries and any outer
Legal proceedings		or internal zones needing special protection
Enforcement and penalty	FLOW	Identifying operational needs for:
Standards	OF	research; management; administration
Institutional mechanics,	INFORMATION	Identifying regulatory needs to
e.g. formation, inter-		ensure adequate protection
governmental coordination,		
infrastructure		
Other laws and institutions		

Source: Lausche, 1980

Broadening participation and cooperation in the management of protected areas

(a) Inter-agency cooperation

The management of protected areas covers such a wide range of activities that it is impossible for the management authority to carry out all conservation related functions by itself. It must delegate some duties and coordinate closely with other agencies.

- Law enforcement requires coordination with the police and perhaps the military authorities as well as local government at all levels. Close coordination with the judiciary prosecutors is also needed. These links may be formalised as well as on a personal basis between the officers responsible. In some countries protected area managers may have no law enforcement capacity, but must depend upon the legal department to process prosecutions. Under such circumstances, law enforcement in protected areas is totally dependent on good relations with other agencies.
- The development of recreation facilities should be planned hand-in-hand with other forms of tourist development in the region and should be coordinated through the local tourist board.
- The use of buffer zones peripheral to reserves will inevitably involve working closely with forestry and agriculture departments, local farmers and smallholders, industrial plantations, and other concerned or affected interests.
- Where reserves contain tribal peoples still living in traditional patterns, coordination is important with departments of tribal affairs, and the elders and village councils of local tribes.
- Where reserves are established to protect vital watersheds, the protection authority should liaise with concerned departments involved with public works, irrigation, agriculture and others.
- Where departments of public works or transport, communications, mining and others have installations within, or need access across, protected areas, there should be some forum to negotiate such access with the minimum disruption of the management objectives of the protected area.
- The military authorities may need to use large open areas for military exercises. It is better to have proper channels of communication than to have no cooperation and find out too late that the reserve is full of tanks. At the same time, it is worth noting that some closed military exercise areas succeed in protecting a great deal of wildlife, e.g. Stanford Battle Area in the United Kingdom, the demilitarised zone in Korea, areas adjacent to De Hoop Nature Reserve in South Africa and the Suffield Military Range in Canada.
- The protected area manager may need to liaise with biologists or other scientists outside his agency. This may require special relationships with universities or a national biological institute, sometimes designated as the scientific authority for certain conservation matters.

Finally, while official relationships always exist between departments, the best results will be obtained through regular personal contact. Thus, it is always advisable that the manager maintain some level of personal contact with the other agencies involved with the protected area.

(b) Broadening participation of outside groups

Protected area management authorities commonly suffer from shortages of money and trained manpower. Encouraging others to participate in aspects of protected area management can strengthen substantially the manager's position and augment his performance. Involvement of outside groups in protected area management may range from giving advice or donating funds or equipment, to assistance in monitoring and law enforcement, to total adoption of management responsibilites for a whole protected area.

(c) Cooperation with local authorities

State or provincial governments may have resources and authority to manage their own reserves or may provide valuable assistance to central or national management authorities. Where local pride is reinforced or the local region derives clear benefits from the existence of a protected area (see Chapters 5 and 6), local authorities may well give strong backing to protected areas programmes where central government is unable to meet its full responsibilities. In cases where benefits are more local (e.g. recreational) than national, this regional or local delegation of management functions may be a sensible way to ease the responsibility of central authorities. Generally, the manager of a protected area will have to rely on local police, customs officers, forestry inspectors, magistrates, district officers and others to assist with control of

12. Enlisting public participation in management activities gets the job done and helps promote wider interest in the park. Students from the local university assist in a reafforestation programme in the buffer zone of the Dumoga Bone National Park, Sulawesi, Indonesia.
Photo: WWF/Berend Wegman

public activities and protection of the reserve, and to enforce the relevant laws and regulations.

(d) Strengthening relationships with non-government organisations (NGOs)

Non-government special interest groups – clubs, youth groups, conservation- orientated societies and foundations, can play a useful role in assisting protected area management and in some cases can also be entrusted to exercise management responsibilities for some protected areas. A hunting club, for instance, may manage its own hunting reserve or a bird preservation society may undertake the protection of an important nesting area. This is particularly attractive if protected areas are located on private lands. In government-run reserves, certain NGOs may be given responsibility for limited aspects of management such as operating an educational unit, producing information materials, anti-litter campaigns, or assisting in biological monitoring or other surveys. They may provide valuable volunteers to assist protected area staff in a wide range of ongoing activities. The Bombay Natural History Society is an excellent example of an NGO reinforcing the efforts of the protected area agencies in India.

(e) Involving local communities

Protected area authorities vary in their willingness to involve local communities in the daily management of protected areas. In some countries, public participation is avoided, in others it is encouraged. Generally, however, where public participation is allowed, public support for protected areas is increased.

At a minimum, local communities commonly should be involved in the management of buffer zones. Where the situation allows, local communities should also be involved in controlling the harvest of resources from reserves (where harvesting such as hunting and firewood collection, is in line with management objectives), running of concessions within reserves, serving on advisory committees, and other aspects affecting local management (see Chapters 6 and 7 for a more detailed discussion of local community involvement).

Example 4.3: *Private foundations supporting public parks – the case of Costa Rica's 'Fundacion para Parques Nacionales'*

While the Government of Costa Rica has done an outstanding job of establishing a wide array of parks and reserves, its ability to provide adequate funding for system maintenance and protection appears uncertain at this time. In response to this urgent need for assistance, a group of dedicated Costa Rican conservationists have established the "Costa Rican Foundation for National Parks ".

The primary objective of the Foundation is "to assist in the protection and development of the National Park System and the promotion of enviromental education". These efforts are supported entirely by private donations which the FPN has raised itself. Fund raising efforts have been very successful both in Costa Rica and in several other countries (the FPN maintains both a San Jose office and an office in Washington, D.C.). A variety of fund raising techniques have been employed. These have ranged from direct appeals to individuals and institutions interested in tropical conservation to sponsoring the premiere of a major motion picture which was filmed in a tropical rain forest. As a non-governmental entity the FPN is able to react quickly to Park Service needs and has provided funds and technical assistance for emergency land purchases and management actions. Also, more long-term efforts such as environmental education programmes have been supported by Foundation grants.

Example 4.4: *NGOs and wildland protection in Latin America*

Several non-governmental entities in Latin America have gone beyond merely advising or criticising wildland management agencies and are actually trying their hand at establishing and operating nature reserves. In many cases they have been successful in their endeavours and by example have served as a catalyst for increased governmental support for national conservation programmes. There are both advantages and disadvantages of NGO wildland management but in most cases private conservation groups have proved themselves to be technically and financially efficient in the operation of small parks and refuges.

In Guatemala, the University of San Carlos has established an entire system of biological reserves called 'biotopes'. Each one protects an outstanding example of an important Guatemalan ecosystem and several harbour endangered species such as the quetzal and the manatee. The Tropical Science Center in Costa Rica has, for several years, managed one of the first protected wildlands in that country, the Monteverde Cloud Forest. Revenue is generated by charging admission to forest visitors and by leasing reserve mountain top to a telecommunications firm. This income helps to pay for reserve management. The Fundacion Natura in Ecuador is developing a nature centre at Pasachoa Reserve near the capital city of Quito. The centre will be utilised for both educational and tourism activities by national and foreign visitors. In Colombia, the Fundacion para la Educacion Superior (FES) is developing the La Planada Nature Reserve which is fast becoming a prototype for wildland managers who are seeking to integrate their reserves with surrounding rural development.

Another innovative example of NGO participation in governmental park development is provided by Belize. In 1984, the Government of Belize formally delegated a major share of the responsibility for managing and developing a national system of protected wildlands to the Belize Audubon Society (BAS). The Audubon Society already manages several small nature reserves and is beginning to formulate wildland tourism plans which will help pay for their establishment and maintenance.

13. Protected areas managers must encourage NGOs to carry the conservation message to a wider audience. Here the Conservation Clubs of Zambia stage a display of educational materials.
    Photo: WWF/R. Jeffrey/WLCS Zambia

PART B

Winning Support for Protected Areas

Key elements in the work of today's protected area manager are public relations and communications. The General Manager of Ethiopia's Wildlife Conservation Organisation discusses plans for resettlement of local people in the Simien Mountains National Park.

5

Integrating Protected Areas in Regional Land-use Programmes

Introduction

Although protected areas are often viewed as islands in isolation from their surroundings, they are subject to many outside influences and in turn affect neighbouring lands. These relationships may be primarily ecological or physical, but also include cultural, social and economic considerations. Protected areas are not established to remove them from the mainstream of development but rather constitute a form of land use that must be complementary to their hinterlands if they are to survive. This Chapter suggests principles for integrating the development and management of protected areas with other forms of rural land use.

The *World Conservation Strategy* stresses the need to integrate conservation with regional development. In addition, Objective 5 of the *Bali Action Plan* aims: 'to promote actively the linkage between protected areas and appropriate sustainable development' (IUCN, 1984a). If protected areas are to be part of the pattern of land use covering a much larger area than the park or reserve itself, they must be managed as such.

This Chapter touches on some of the positive and negative relationships that may exist between a protected area and adjacent lands and suggests how the conflicts can be reduced and their benefits to local communities enhanced. It also demonstrates how the security, support for and appreciation of protected areas can be strengthened by underlining and further developing their contributions to the regional development process and forging links of mutual interdependency with other departments and agencies.

Integrating protected areas into regional development plans calls for continuous liaison between the various planning and management authorities and local communities so the protected area management authority must evolve a good working relationship with the other agencies concerned. Clear formulation of local conservation needs and objectives can provide a useful input into the development of a regional plan and its implementation. Such strategies and plans should try to set goals and standards for development and conservation of natural resources with an aim to obtaining optimal sustainable production from a multiple land-use system without foreclosing options for future use.

How protected areas contribute to regional development

As demands for efficient and immediate utilisation of natural resources increase worldwide, particularly in tropical countries with fast-growing populations, the need for protected areas must be clarified. To survive these pressures protected areas must be justifiable in both biological and socio-economic terms. Since government officials and the public generally undervalue the role of protected areas in environmentally-sound development, protected areas should be designed and managed in ways that bring real benefits to local and national human communities. Conservationists must arm themselves with all the facts to defend the area's protected status in the first place; they must be able to counter in a convincing, cogent and eloquent manner such challenging questions as:

'Why do you need a reserve here?'
'Why must it be so large?'
'Couldn't you manage just as well with half the area?'
'Why can't we collect wood in the reserve?'
'Why should I tolerate my cows being eaten and my wife being terrified by your tigers?'
'Why bother to save jaguars at all?'
'What's in it for us?'
'We need this land for agriculture to survive; why is it more important to save elephants than to let us live?'
'These turtle eggs provide an important source of income for my family. Why can't I sell them?'

Vague, ignorant, incorrect or evasive replies to such questions can be highly counter-productive and may strengthen the hand of those who want to use the protected area for more exploitative purposes.

There are at least 16 main ways in which protected areas can bring valuable benefits to communities in the region:

1) *Stabilisation of hydrological functions*
Natural vegetation cover on water catchments in the tropics plays a valuable role, acting like a 'sponge' to regulate and stabilise water run-off. Deep penetration by tree roots or other vegetation makes the soil more permeable to rainwater so that run-off is slower and more uniform than on cleared land. As a consequence, in forested regions streams continue to flow in dry weather and floods are minimised in rainy weather. In some cases these hydrological functions can be of enormous value, worth many millions of dollars a year per catchment.

2) *Protection of soils*
Exposed tropical soils degrade quickly due to leaching of nutrients, burning of humus, laterisation of minerals and accelerated erosion of topsoil. Good soil protection by natural vegetation cover and litter (especially significant in grassland ecosystems) can preserve the productive capacity of the reserve itself, prevent dangerous landslides, prevent costly and damaging siltation of fields, irrigation canals and hydroelectric dams, safeguard

coastlines and riverbanks, and prevent the destruction of coral reefs and coastal fisheries by siltation.

3) *Stability of climate*
There is growing evidence that undisturbed forest actually helps to maintain the rainfall in its immediate vicinity by recycling water vapour at a steady rate back into the atmosphere and by the canopy's effect in promoting atmospheric turbulence. This may be particularly important in the production of dry season showers which are often more critical for settled agriculture than the heavier monsoon rains (Dickinson, 1981; Henderson-Sellers, 1981). Forest cover also helps to keep down local ambient temperatures, benefiting surrounding areas both for agriculture (lowered transpiration levels and water stress) and for human comfort.

4) *Conservation of renewable harvestable resources*
Biological productivity under natural conditions is 'cost free' and generally higher than for any form of artificially planted alternative (Odum, 1971). The quantity and value of natural materials that can be harvested on a sustained basis will vary considerably, depending upon the protection category of the reserve, and may be of as much value to the local community as any alternative land-use.

5) *Protection of genetic resources*
Man makes use of several thousand species of tropical wild plants and animals for foods, medicines and utilities, many to a commercially important degree. Many thousands more species may be of potential use. All domestic plants and animals were originally derived from the wild and many can only be maintained and improved by regular recrossing with wild forms and relatives. The short- and long-term values of these genetic resources are enormous and most improvements in tropical agriculture and silviculture depend on their preservation. Protected areas are of great value as *in situ* genebanks but only for as long as they are protected. Moreover, the gene pool value of reserves will increase as remaining natural habitats become scarce.

6) *Preservation of breeding stocks, population reservoirs and biological diversity*
Reserves may protect crucial life stages or

elements of populations that are widely and profitably harvested outside reserves. They are sources of seed dispersal, wildlife, and fish spawning areas. They act as 'refugia' wherein biological diversity can be maintained.

7) *Promotion of tourism*

Where protected areas are developed for tourism, local economies can benefit considerably. At the national level, tourism brings valuable foreign exchange into the country and at the local level it stimulates profitable domestic industries – hotels, restaurants, transport systems, souvenirs and handicrafts and guide services.

8) *Provision of recreational facilities*

Local communities as well as other domestic and foreign visitors benefit from the recreational facilities provided by most categories of protected areas. These benefits will become ever more valuable as the availability of other wild recreation areas is further reduced.

9) *Creation of employment opportunities*

Apart from the employment created within the protected area itself, additional employment is generated by auxiliary services, tourist development, road improvements and professional services. Such benefits are particularly relevant where the land set aside for the protected area has little or no value for agriculture.

10) *Provision of research and monitoring facilities*

Man has much to learn on the subject of how to get better use from tropical environments. His agriculture and plantations are disease and pest-prone, delicate, require fertilisers and result in soil degradation. Much applied research still needs to be done in natural tropical ecosystems to find the secrets of high, stable productivity on poor soils. Protected areas provide excellent living laboratories for such studies, for comparison with other areas under different systems of land use and for valuable research into ecology and evolution.

11) *Provision of education facilities*

Protected areas provide valuable sites for school classes and university students to gain practical education in the fields of biology, ecology, geology, geography and socio-economics. Such uses can extend to, and

ultimately benefit, a large proportion of the local population.

12) *Maintenance of a quality living environment*

Inhabitants close to a protected area are often privileged to enjoy a quality living environment – cleaner, more beautiful and more peaceful than elsewhere. The values of property adjoining protected areas may become enhanced as outsiders choose to have holiday homes in the area, such as occurred at Cibodas adjacent to Gn. Gede-Pangrango National Park in West Java.

13) *Advantages of special treatment*

Because of their proximity to environmentally critical areas and places of showcase status, local residents near parks and reserves may be eligible for special treatment – improved social services, communications, loans, irrigation and housing projects. For example, the Indian Board for Wildlife in 1983 recommended that areas surrounding wildlife reserves should be recognised as Special Areas for Ecodevelopment (see Example 6.11).

14) *Preservation of traditional and cultural values*

Protection of natural reserves can result in the preservation of locally important cultural sites and traditional practices which would otherwise be destroyed. Whilst such benefits as continued access to shrines (as in Ranthambhore National Park, India) may have little or no economic value they will be highly appreciated by local people.

15) *Natural balance of environment*

The existence of a protected area may help maintain a more natural balance of the ecosystem over a much wider area. Protected areas afford sanctuary to breeding populations of birds which control insect and mammal pests in agricultural areas. Bats, birds and bees which roost and breed in reserves may range far outside their boundaries pollinating fruit trees in the surrounding areas.

16) *Regional pride and heritage value*

The development of sources of regional and national pride have benefits which are not easy to evaluate but are nevertheless real credits. The fact that individuals and organisations will donate money for the preservation of their local heritage, is a clear indication that they appreciate the value of the protected areas in their region.

The benefits described above are of different scales of magnitude, accrue over different time-spans and fall to different groups in the local community, but they are cumulative and the total value to the region as a whole can be considerable. Not all benefits will necessarily derive from all reserves. Some of the benefits will occur automatically with the establishment of the reserve, while others will require management to reach their full potential. Whether establishing a reserve is the best land use for a particular area will depend on the sum of these benefits compared with the potential values or benefits attainable if the area was designated for alternative use. It is easy to find socio-economic justification for establishing reserves in inhospitable marginal lands but much harder to justify reserves in areas of high agricultural or urban potential. Unfortunately, though not surprisingly, areas of high agricultural potential are often biologically the richest and the

most valuable for conservation.

IUCN and other conservation agencies are concerned to promote the quantification of values which relate conservation to development, including such benefits as watershed protection, genetic resources, pollution control, soil formation, amelioration of climate, provision of recreation and tourism. As human pressure on land increases, it becomes more important for the protected area management authority to put an economic value on both the tangible and intangible benefits provided by the national system of reserves and to predict the likely immediate and future costs to the community if the land is designated for alternative uses instead.

Example 5.1 is based on a simplified scheme used in the preparation of the National Conservation Plan for Indonesia to assess the socio-economic justification of reserves by scoring the benefits of their protective functions against alternative land use values.

A few of the key benefits will be discussed in more detail in the following section.

Example 5.1: Guidelines for measuring socio-economic justification for protected areas in Indonesia

Areas are scored for their economic importance for seven different criteria, each of which is weighted according to its priority in government planning. Potential reserves can score a maximum of 20 points and only those scoring 10 (50%) or more qualify for selection or retention as reserves.

The largest contributor to the score is the 'environmental protection function' with a maximum of 4 points. Thus areas which are essential for maintaining the human living environment, such as important water catchment areas, require little further justification. Areas which have high alternative land-use value and no environmental protection function have to score almost full marks in all other categories to justify establishment as reserves.

The seven contributing criteria are scored as follows:

1. *Environmental Benefits of Protection* (0-4 points)
    This score gives high points to areas which protect important water catchments, particularly in areas prone to erosion, areas of seasonal rain and water shortages and areas providing water for large populations or extensive agricultural areas, industrial plants, hydroelectric schemes, etc.

2. *Low Land-use Conflict* (0-3 points)
    This score gives high points to areas where protection does not compete with valuable alternative land uses.

3. *Conservation Priority* (0-3 points)
    This score is based on the need to preserve examples of all ecotypes. Thus an area not represented elsewhere in the national system will score highly.

4. *Special Value of Contents* (0-3 points)
    This score is based on the value, interest or usefulness of the species being protected. Such species include wild relatives of domesticated animals and plants, wild species that are already economically exploited, species with high trade value or rare endangered species of special interest

5. *Tourism, Recreation, Research and Education Potential* (0-3 points)
   This score assesses the value of additional uses and benefits that can be derived through protection. Tourist and recreational potential is only scored as high if the area is easily accessible from a major town or tourist centre as well as being interesting and beautiful. Research and education potential is also based on accessibility and proximity to universities as well as on the biological suitability of the area for such activities

6. *Geological and Ethnic or Cultural Benefits* (0-2 points)
   Under this criterion areas score additional points where protection of the natural habitat will also bring benefit by protecting rare or interesting geological, anthropological, historical or cultural features such as indigenous peoples following traditional life-styles, shrines and megaliths

7. *Research Investment* (0-2 points)
   Areas which include sites of past or ongoing scientific research should be protected whenever possible since they provide a data base against which to measure patterns of change. This is very important in monitoring the rate of environmental change both in these areas themselves and in similar areas where different management is applied.

Source: MacKinnon/FAO, 1981

Protected areas and hydrological relationships

Water resources are so vital to human life, agriculture and industry that their proper management is of fundamental concern to society. In the tropics, where almost the only way to cope with the fast growth of population is to expand the area under agriculture and increase the productivity of existing croplands, many of the day-to-day problems arise from the fact that at any one time there is usually too much or too little water on the land. The most common means employed to achieve better control of water flow are the development of irrigation schemes and improved drainage. Colossal sums of money are invested in water canals and dams to enhance water supplies but these investments can be jeopardised easily by poor protection of the water catchments on which they depend.

Watershed protection has, therefore, been used to justify many valuable reserves which otherwise might not have been established, and irrigation agencies can make powerful potential allies for protected areas which protect watersheds. For instance, the magnificent Guatopo National Park in Venezuela (Example 5.2), is justified by its contribution to the welfare of the nation in providing the water for Caracas, the capital. The Canaima National Park, also in Venezuela, safeguards a catchment feeding hydroelectric developments which Garcia (1984) estimates will save the nation $US 4.3 billion per annum in fossil fuel oils (Example 5.3). The watershed protection function of Canaima is so important that the Venezuelan Government recently tripled the size of the park to 3 million ha to enhance its effectiveness.

In many parts of the world, the total costs of establishing and managing reserves which protect catchment areas can be met and justified as part of the hydrological investment. MacKinnon (1983) examined the condition of the water catchments of 11 irrigation projects in Indonesia for which development loans were being requested from the World Bank. The condition of the catchments varied from an almost pristine state to areas of heavy disturbance, due to deforestation, logging or casual settlements. Even where hydrological protection forests existed, these were porly protected by the Forestry Department as the areas were considered of low priority and provided with inadequate budgets. By using standard costings for the development of proper boundaries, establishment of guardposts, recruitment of guards and purchase of basic equipment, plus the costs of reforestation where necessary, and even resettlement of families in some cases, the costs of providing adequate protection for the catchments were estimated. These ranged from less than 1 per cent of the development costs of the individual irrigation project in cases where the catchment was more or less intact to 5 per cent where extensive reforestation was needed and a maximum of about 10 per cent of development costs in cases where resettlement and reforestation were required. Overall these costs were trivial compared to the estimated 30 per cent to 40 per cent drop in efficiency of the irrigation systems expected if catchments were not properly safeguarded.

It is evident that the costs for protecting watersheds should be an automatic component of irrigation loan requests and that the protected area management authority should provide the necessary management paid for out of the irrigation budgets. In one case in Indonesia, the Dumoga-Bone National Park (see Example 12.4), this has already been done in collaboration with the World Bank, helping to establish one of the country's model protected areas (Sumardja, *ct al.*, 1984). Protected areas can also be threatened by development projects outside their boundaires which cause changes in hydrological regimes. Upstream catchments may need to be protected to prevent flooding, siltation or pollution of a protected area. Abnormal depositions of sediments may influence key ecosystems or communities in reserves. Such pollution can be a particular threat

to coastal systems such as coral reefs, which are sensitive to the quality of effluent streams.

Hydrological projects may also cause changes in the water table which may threaten the integrity of natural ecosystems in protected areas. For instance, a planned dam and hydroelectric plant in Silent Valley, India, would have flooded a large area of unique habitat in that reserve. The Manu National Park in Peru is threatened by the planned construction of a canal which will cause major changes in the water regime of the area. Modification of river flow in the Zambesi River below the Kariba Dam has resulted in accelerated bank erosion and the river has become wider and shallower in the Mana Pools National Park of Zimbabwe.

Clearly it is vital that the protected area management authority has close working relations with the water resources agencies to avert such threats where possible and to ensure that safeguards are included in major projects to protect the hydrological regimes of the affected protected area.

14. Slash and burn agriculture is one of the greatest conservation problems in the humid tropics. Thi hillside in Nepal is typical of many scenes in tropical countries. To a hill farmer this photo bring images of a rich crop to come, but to the conservationist a gloomy prospect of irreversible natura loss, soil erosion, floods and future wasteland.
     Photo: WWF/T. Cronin/H. Emery

Example 5.2 The Guatopo National Park, Venezuela, as an example of a protected catchment serving urban water needs

Caracas, the capital of Venezuela, is a modern city of over 7,000,000 people. A substantial proportion of its water emanates from the Guatopo National Park, one of 10 national parks in Venezuela which serve the country through the conservation of important river catchment areas.

The park, which covers 100,000 ha of magnificent rain forest, is situated in attractive mountainous country less than two hours drive from the city. It was established and depopulated at considerable expense in compensation ($US 16.4 million) in 1958 in order to protect the catchment areas serving four dam sites. In 1982 the park supplied the metropolitan area with 3500 litres of very high quality water per second and this is expected to rise to 20,000 litres per second by 1985.

This example provides an especially useful illustration of a very tangible and quantifiable value of a national park. This is in addition to its very considerable natural values and its use as a site for visitor recreation close to a large urban complex.

Source: Garcia, 1984

Example 5.3. The Canaima National Park, Venezuela, as an outstanding example of conservation for development

The Canaima National Park in the Guayanan region of southern Venezuela is an area of outstanding natural values. Although probably best known for its spectacular waterfalls, (including the world famous Angel Falls which with a free fall of 670 m are believed to be the highest waterfalls in the world), the area has rich forest and savanna ecosystems and spectacular tepuys (table-like mountains) and exhibits a high level of plant endemism.

The Government of Venezuela increased the area of the park from 1,000,000 to 3,000,000 ha in 1975 in recognition of its value as a source of water for the Caroni River system, which is scheduled for intensive hydro-electrical development to serve a large industrial complex to the south of the Orinoco River. By 1985, the Guri Dam Hydro-Electrical project is due to produce 9,000,000 kw and in time the whole system will yield 20,000,000 kw. Generation of this electricity using oil would consume some 144 million barrels per year, worth about $US 4,300,000,000 per annum at 1982 oil prices.

The habitats in this region are especially fragile and susceptible to modification by man or fire. They also have a very low agricultural potential. Destruction of the natural vegetation would affect both the water-generating capacity of the catchment and the quality of the water reaching the hydro-electric projects, thereby threatening the efficiency of these projects and the massive investments they represent, as well as the growing industrial complex they serve.

Allocating such a large area as a protected catchment is clearly a sensible precaution in the interests of the many people who will benefit from this industrialisation in the long term. Giving the area national park status and managing it with these objectives in mind represents a rational form of land use in keeping with the area's outstanding natural qualities. Together these values far outweigh any potential value the area might have had for agricultural development.

Source: Garica, 1984

Protected areas and forestry

Forestry here is taken to be the production and harvesting of forest products generally and not just the exploitation of timber. Certain forms of forestry can take place in protected areas of Categories V and VIII and forestry lands often lie adjacent to protected areas of all Categories. Forestry practices can have serious effects on wildlife species varying from almost total elimination of wildlife when natural forests are clearfelled and replaced by exotic monocultures to slight reductions of arboreal species, and even increases in some terrestrial species when forests are thinned by more selective logging systems (Wilson and Wilson, 1975, Johns, 1981). In areas where selective logging is combined with the practice of leaving untouched patches of natural forest as reseeding stock (as in the Malaysian virgin forest system), forestry can be performed in a profitable sustained manner and serve an important nature conservation function. On the other hand, modern methods involving heavy tractors, wide unmetalled roads and chain saws, can be very destructive to wildlife and any subsequent timber crop, yielding only short-term benefits. But with more attention to the effects of logging techniques it is often possible to improve forestry yield and reduce damage to the environment and wildlife. Modification of patterns of cutting, such as strip logging, can increase the chances of local wildlife surviving logging operations and allow recolonisation of areas of logged forest.

In many countries, forestry resources are wasted by having too sharp a classification between production forests, where very destructive mechanised logging is permitted, and protection forest where no logging is permitted. There is certainly more room to explore the possibilities of having intermediate categories of production. Not only is the present system of logging wasteful and environmentally destructive but the profits are drawn out of the region (and often out of the

country) by large timber companies and little benefit accrues to the local people, whose living environment – former source of wood, fruits, meat, etc., is effectively destroyed, and who, predictably, become alienated. The need to direct forestry more towards the welfare of local people – 'Forests for the People' – was the central theme of the 1978 World Forestry Congress in Jakarta. Forestry aimed more at providing forest products for local people rather than for international or domestic timber markets will also benefit adjacent protected areas by reducing the need for local villagers to seek forest products inside protected areas.

For these and other reasons, the protected area management authority should work closely with the forestry department in both formal and informal ways. The clear-cut separation of function between the two departments is not in accordance with current thought, since significant protection and conservation can be achieved on forestry lands and some forestry can be performed in some protected areas. The 'minor' forest products – wildlife, medicinal plants, fibres, animal fodder thatch, edible mushrooms, fruits, honey, even the production of clean water, harvested in a sustainable way can often exceed the value of timber. Tropical forestry would benefit by expanding its purview to include all types of valued production on forest lands, thereby strengthening the linkage between conservation and development.

Protected areas and harvesting of wildlife and other natural resources

In some categories of protected areas hunting and other forms of direct harvesting of wildlife are appropriate and economically important. In Zimbabwe, for example, controlled culling of excess elephant populations and recreational hunting in the Chirisa Safari Area brought $US 556,230 in income to the local District Council at a critical stage in the history of the area (Child, 1984). Where wildlife harvesting is conducted with proper controls and the application of sensible quotas, it can be regarded as sound conservation and can help justify the maintenance of wild populations in protected areas.

Local communities may also benefit by being allowed into protected areas at certain times to harvest some natural resources. In Nepal's Royal Chitwan National Park, for instance, the local

people are allowed into the park during a specific two-week period each year to harvest thatch grass, worth some $US 600,000 per year to the local community. Since almost the entire area around Chitwan has been denuded of natural vegetation, the park now provides virtually the only source of thatch, the most important traditional roofing material in the region (Mishra, 1984).

Protected areas may also serve a vital function by protecting a vulnerable life stage of an animal population harvested by local villagers, e.g. by protecting fish spawning areas or bird nesting colonies. This function may be of high economic importance. In India, for example, the prawn production from partially protected mangrove swamp was estimated at 110 kg/ha/year, while in a nearby estuary where the mangroves were damaged or

15. A herd of wild elephants being rounded up for capture in Mysore, India. Elephants are domesticated in many Asian countries but do not breed well in captivity. Unless wild populations are maintained these valuable domestic animals will be a sight of the past.
Photo: WWF/P. Jackson

removed, prawn production was just 20 kg/ha/year (Krishnamurthy and Jeyaseelan, 1980).

Since many wildlife-based industries depend on wild stocks – either for initial breeding stock or for eggs or young animals to rear in captivity – protected areas serve a valuable economic function by protecting the wild populations on which such enterprises depend. Species regularly bred for wildlife products include deer for velvet and venison, and snakes for their skins and venom. Animals reared from wild-gathered stocks include crocodiles (sometimes also bred), ornamental fish and butterflies (see Example 5.4). Such enterprises can be highly profitable, contribute to a country's export trade and bring much-needed revenue to communities in remote areas which can produce little else beyond substenance food.

Dependence on wildlife for food and other products is likely to increase in coming years and it is important that these wild resources be used wisely, and that harvesting be on a sustained yield basis. Game farms could be established in Category VIII protected areas, such as Cuyabeno Fauna Production Reserve in Ecuador and the El Angolo Hunting Reserve in Peru. Although the potential of wildlife for food has not yet been fully exploited, considerable progress has been made recently in South America. Capybara farms exist in Venezuela and Brazil has established an experimental game farm to develop the technology for semi-domestication of Amazonian wildlife preferred as food for human consumption.

16. With proper farming procedures crocodiles can become a valuable renewable resource. Such utilisation of wildlife is an important justification for the protection of the wild populations upon wich the industry is ultimately dependent.
Photo: WWF/F. Vollmar

Example 5.4. Butterfly industry in Papua New Guinea

New Guinea is the centre of the distribution of the beautiful birdwing butterflies (Ornithoptera), many of which are highly priced and prized by collectors. These butterflies live on *Aristolochia* vines. Villagers are encouraged to grow these vines in their abandoned gardens and this attracts wild females from nearby forests to lay their eggs in the gardens. Villagers care for the resulting caterpillars, protect them from predation and collect the pupae. Hatching adults are killed and marketed through the Insect Farming and Trading Agency (IFTA), a non-profit government organisation, which uses mission planes to collect packages from remote villages. Because the packages are light in relation to their value they can be transported profitably by air and guaranteed prices are maintained per species for undamaged adults. This system ensures a quality product which makes wild-caught adults almost valueless. Damaged captive specimens and all the caterpillars that are overlooked during collection return to the wild population. Encouragement of the food plant and greater appreciation of the natural forest patches as the source of stock also leads to better conservation of the wild populations. The trade brings appreciated revenue into poor areas with little else to sell and is much less destructive than harvesting some other forms of forest produce.

By providing employment in rural areas where other income-producing activities are difficult to establish or are harmful to traditional lifestyles and fragile environments, the butterfly farming programme is also conserving butterflies and their habitats. The bulk of the land around the villages is left intact, which means that villagers can also retain their traditional hunting grounds. The project has focussed attention on the status of all butterfly species in the country. The Government has already established wildlife management areas to save Queen Alexandra's birdwing *Ornithoptera alexandrae*, the largest and most threatened butterfly in the country, and is also setting up refuges administered by village councils to preserve and protect other birdwings.

Now after 10 years of operation, there are more than 500 butterfly farmers in all 10 provinces of Papua New Guinea. They rear butterflies, beetles, stick and leaf insects, moths and other insects for export all over the world. Papua New Guinea is also applying the same concept of combining the conservation of species endangered by trade with economic gain at the village level to other animals. The Division of Wildlife is farming crocodiles, rusa deer, wallabies and two native bird species, the megapode and the cassowary.

Source: Hutton, 1985

17. The saving of the Vicuna from the brink of extinction has depended largely on protection for utilisation. There may be controversy about whether this is humane but it has certainly proved to be effective conservation.
Photo: WWF/Dr.J.Esser

Example 5.5: Revenue from hunting in Botswana

The revenue derived from hunting can be very important for a country's economy. In Botswana (area 577,000 sq km, 691,000 inhabitants in 1975), the total government revenue derived from hunting amounted to almost $US 8.5 million in 1974:

A. Direct Revenue paid to Central Government	$US
Hunting licences	366,241
Entrance fees to national park	28,631
Sale of ivory and trophies	544
Export tax of trophies	24,468
Traditional hunting licences	33,989
Rent of hunting zone concessions	49,194
Total direct revenue	503,067

B. Indirect Revenue	
Value of meat of hunted animals	1,019,543
Value of sale of trophies	454,182
Value of locally utilised hides, skins	353,323
Expenses of hunters	4,526,068
Expenses of non-hunter visitors	543,690
Expenses of caretakers of lodges, camps, etc. and trophy dealers	1,059,709
Total indirect revenue	7,956,515
Grand Total	8,459,582

Source: Von Richter, 1976

Protected areas and tourism

Protected areas can make a substantial contribution to regional development by attracting tourists to rural regions. Protected areas are major tourist attractions in many tropical countries, bringing significant economic benefits to the country and, with proper planning, to local communities. In Kenya, for instance, where the tourist industry is the largest earner of foreign exchange, 1977 foreign earnings from tourism totalled $US 125 million of which a third was provided by seven national parks. Much of the other revenues expended outside reserves from international travel, hotels, souvenir sales, were also largely dependent on the attractions of the protected areas.

Tourism is an industry which, with proper planning and investment, can show spectacular growth and protected areas can contribute to this growth.

Example 5.6 shows how the Virgin Islands National Park earned an estimated tenfold annual return in benefits over investments.

Tourism development in and around protected areas can also be one of the best ways of bringing economic benefits to remote areas by providing local employment, stimulation of local markets, improvement of transportation and communications infrastructures. But careful planning is necessary to avoid some of the negative side-effects of tourism, particularly the tendency for local people to view protected areas as being established for the benefit of foreigners rather than for themselves.

There are other dangers inherent in promoting the idea of protected areas as tourist attractions. First, many areas of important conservation value have very little appeal to tourists (e.g. extensive tracts of tropical forest and most mangrove swamps). Second, if decision-makers are led to believe that parks exist primarily for economic gain, and their expectations in this direction are not fulfilled, they may begin to look for more profitable alternative uses for the land. There is also the danger that governments will seek to maximise economic returns from parks through inappropriate developments. Large hotels, highways or golf courses designed to attract more visitors can diminish a park's natural values and eventually turn it into an area for which the main objective is mass tourism rather than conservation.

The role of protected area management in providing tourist objectives and facilities must be developed in close coordination with the regional and national tourist authority. The tourist board may sometimes even provide financial assistance for developing tourist facilities in reserves. Managers of protected areas must also explain to the tourist authorities what limits the respective protected areas must place on visitor use so that carrying capacities are not exceeded. Unless carefully controlled, the volume of visitors may have a deleterious impact on parks and eventually destroy the very resource on which tourism depends (see Example 5.7). In Amboseli, for instance, heavy visitor traffic concentrated in a small area and numerous vehicles located round a single predator have resulted in severe stress on sensitive species such as cheetah, unnecessary habitat destruction and deteriorating visitor satisfaction (Western, 1984).

18. Visitors, driving off-road, surround a pride of lions in Amboseli National Park, Kenya. Such intensive use is not only damaging to the park resource, but reduces the level of visitor satisfaction as well.
Photo: J. Thorsell

Example 5.6: *Comparisons of annual costs and benefits: economic impact of Virgin Island National Park (VINP) on St Thomas/St John economy*

Direct	Indirect (thousands) $US	Total (thousands) $US	(thousands) $US
Costs			
Operation and Maintenance of VINP	1,250		
Interest on Federal Investment in VINP Properties		670	
Taxes Lost on Property Removed from Local Government Rolls		176	
TOTAL	1,250	846	2,096
Benefits			
Outlays of VINP in Local Economy	830		
Outlays of VINP Concessionnaires in Local Economy	2,500		
Imputed Benefits from VINP Impact on Tourism		12,061	
Imputed Benefits from VINP Impact on Boat Industry		3,000	
Imputed Benefits from VINP Impact on Increased Land Values on St John, as an Indicator of Increased Economic Growth on St John		5,000	
TOTAL	3,330	20,061	23,391

Reduced to ratios, the above tabulation indicates:

The Benefit/Cost Ratio of the existence of the VINP on the local economy, based on direct costs and benefits only is   2.7 to 1

The Benefit/Cost Ratio of the existence of the VINP on the local economy, based on indirect (imputed) costs and benefits only is   23.7 to 1

Total Benefit/Cost Ratio of the existence of the VINP on the local economy, based on all costs (direct and indirect) is   11.1 to 1

These ratios are, of course, approximations. It would take very little change in assumptions to alter them substantially – in either direction. In sum, however, they support the proposition that the VINP even if measured on only a dollar and cents basis, plays a very significant role in the economy of the islands of St Thomas and St John – well beyond the costs incurred in its operation and maintenance.

Source: Island Resources Foundation, 1981
Credit: U.S. Department of the interior, National Park Service, Virgin Islands National Park.

Example 5.7: *Potential environmental effects of tourism in protected areas (E. Africa): the types of negative visitor impact that must be controlled*

Factor Involved	Impact on Natural Quality	Comment	Examples
Overcrowding	Environmental stress, animals show changes in behaviour	Irritation, reduction in quality, need for carrying-capacity limits or better regulation	Amboseli
Overdevelopment	Development of rural slums, excessive man-made structures	Unsightly urban-like development	Mweya, Seronera, Keekorok, 01 Tukai
Recreation			
Powerboats	Disturbance of wildlife and quiet	Vulnerability during nesting seasons, noise pollution	Murchison Falls
Fishing	None	Competition with natural predators	Ruaha, Nile
Foot safaris	Disturbance of wildlife	Overuse and trail erosion	Mt Kenya, Kilimanjaro
Pollution			
Noise (radios, etc.)	Disturbance of natural sounds	Irritation to wildlife and other visitors	Many areas
Litter	Impairment of natural scene	Aesthetic and health hazard	Many areas
Vandalism	Mutiliation and facility destruction	Removal of natural features, facility damage	Sibiloi
Feeding of animals	Behavioural changes of animals	Removal of habituated animals - danger to tourists	Masai Mara, Ruaha
Vehicles			
Speeding	Wildlife mortality	Ecological changes, dust	Amboseli, Mikumi
Off-road driving, night driving	Soil and vegetation damage	Disturbance to wildlife	Ngorongoro, Amboseli

Miscellaneous

Souvenir collection	Removal of natural attractions	Shells, coral, horns, trophies, rare plants	All areas
Firewood collection	Small wildlife mortality and habitat destruction	Interference with natural energy flow	All areas
Roads and murram pits	Habitat loss, drainage changes, natural scars if not well-sited and constructed	Aesthetic scars Ecotones damaged	All areas
Power lines	Destruction of vegetation	Aesthetic impacts	Tsavo, Bale Mts
Artificial water holes and salt provision	Unnatural wildlife concentrations, vegetation damage	Replacement of soil required	Aberdares
Introduction of exotic plants and animals	Competition with wild species	Public confusion	Many areas, Mt Kilimanjaro, airstrips

Source: Thorsell, 1984a

Protected areas and agriculture

Protected areas often perform a useful service for neighbouring agricultural areas in safeguarding against floods, by providing water through dry periods and fertile silt in the rainy season (as in the Mekong and Red River areas of Vietnam). Moreover, many of the wild species resident in the protected areas are vital to the well-being of the surrounding agricultural lands. Birds help control levels of insect and rodent pests, bees perform vital fertilisation functions, and bats control insects and pollinate many tropical fruits.

A good illustration of the importance of bats is the case of durians *Durio zibethinus*, a highly-prized fruit in S.E. Asia, which is very seasonal in its fruiting and depends on wild nectar-feeding bats for its pollination. When the durians are not in flower, the bats (especially *Eonycteris spelaea* and *Macroglossus minimus*) depend on other wild tree species for nectar so loss of protected areas can lead to loss of the bats and failure of the valuable durian crop (Start and Marshall, 1976).

Where such benefits are clear, the agricultural authorities and neighbouring agricultural communities can become good allies for the protected area, but there are also many less beneficial relationships. Many species of wildlife move out of reserves into agricultural lands where they are a

serious nuisance and can cause considerable damage – parrots, monkeys, deer, rodents, antelope, pigs, elephants and large carnivores are among the main culprits. Some measure of control is often needed and it is important that the protected area management authority is involved. Inappropriate control measures can pose a serious threat to protected wild populations. In particular, any use of poisons must be carefully monitored to prevent their spread through waterways and food chains into the ecosystem. Specific guidelines on the control and restraint of wildlife are given in Chapter 8.

Reserves may also harbour reservoirs of certain diseases which are a danger to man and/or his domestic species (e.g. malaria, malignant catarrah, and trypanosomiasis). These, too, may need control measures to reduce health risks but they can also threaten the integrity of the reserves if applied inappropriately.

Accidental spraying of selective weed killers, fungicides or insecticides onto protected areas could be disastrous to the natural ecosystem and such chemicals introduced into upstream water sources may have serious ecological impacts. Chemical pollution of waterways from urban or industrial waste poses a similar threat.

19. The wildlife souvenir trade can be an important source of foreign exchange in some countries and helps to justify the establishment of wildlife management areas. However, such trade must be developed very carefully, with effective controls, if it is not to place an unacceptable pressure on wildlife.
Photo: WWF/Mark Boulton

Spread of fire into protected areas from deliberately burned fields, wind erosion of protected areas resulting from clearing of neighbouring agricultural lands, and the invasion of protected areas by agricultural weeds, exotic species, domestic animals and man himself, are other threats to reserves. These further underline the need for the protected area management authority to develop close links with neighbouring agricultural communities to avoid such negative interactions and to settle any problems that may arise.

As a general principle, intensive agriculture and protected areas do not make good neighbours and the development of buffer zones or some areas of intermediate land use is needed between the two. Sometimes there is an adequate natural barrier such as a river, estuary, ridge crest or swamp that forms a deterrent to human incursion and wildlife excursion and no further buffering is needed. In other cases, the same function can be served by a less strictly controlled category of protected area, production forest, plantations that are unattractive to wildlife, an airport, golfcourse, or reservoir. In many cases, however, it is necessary to plan and develop a specific buffer zone to reduce direct interference between protected areas and areas of conflicting land use.

Development of protected area buffer zones

Definition

Buffer zones can be defined as areas adjacent to protected areas, on which land use is partially restricted to give an added layer of protection to the protected area itself while providing valued benefits to neighbouring rural communities. Buffer zones may serve two main functions:

Extension buffering, which in effect extends the area of those habitats contained within the protected area into the buffer zone, thus allowing larger total breeding populations of plant and animal species than could survive within the reserve alone. Examples of such buffering can include selectively logged production forests, hunting areas, natural forests used by villagers for firewood collection, unused wilderness and grazing pastures.

Socio-buffering, where wildlife use of the buffer zone is of secondary importance and management is aimed primarily at providing products of use or value (cash crops) to local people; but such land use should not conflict with the objective of the protected area itself. This generally involves planting species that are unattractive as habitat for local wildlife or allowing a controlled harvest of wildlife.

Buffer zone requirements and restrictions

In determining the type and extent of buffer zones needed, the following factors should be considered:

- Needs of threatened wildlife species for use of additional habitat outside the reserve boundaries. Knowledge of the size and habits of the species will give some indication of the extent of an adequate buffer zone.
- The need for the buffer zone to serve other protective functions, such as soil and water conservation or fire-break protection.
- The need to contain wildlife species likely to move out of the reserve.
- The reasonable needs of local people for land, forest products, grazing areas or meat.
- The amount of land available for buffer use, whether it is currently under natural or other vegetation, and whether it is vacant or being used.
- The suitability of possible buffer crops for the particular land type and climatic conditions and the interests of local wildlife. For instance,

bananas or oil palms should not be planted if the buffer zone is next to an elephant reserve, and maize would be unsuitable near macaques or baboons.

As a general rule, first priority should go to protection needs, second to villagers' requirements for harvestable products, and third to cash crops. All planned buffer zones should adopt the following restrictions:

- Prohibit permanent settlements in buffer zones.
- Generally prohibit burning of vegetation in buffer zones. Highly inflammable standing crops (e.g. long grass or pine plantations) should be avoided. Exceptions may be permitted in natural tropical grasslands where species communities are adapted to regular fire.
- Prohibit introductions into the buffer zone of animal or plant species likely to invade or threaten the protected area.
- Prohibit any activities (e.g. poisoning or hunting) within the buffer zone which are likely to endanger threatened species in the reserve.
- Avoid planting crops likely to encourage wildlife to forage outside the reserve
  (see Example 5.9).

A major function of socio-buffers is to ensure that rural people do not need to seek forest or other products inside reserves. Villages, for instance, have predictable needs for firewood and building timber, so the buffer zone should be large enough to meet these requirements or provide a cash equivalent. Location of buffers should also take into account access by villagers. The buffer zone does not necessarily need to be a thin linear strip following the reserve boundary. A more compact plantation sited close to the village will fulfil the same function of meeting village needs for firewood and timber and remove the need for villagers to seek such resources n the reserve.

Types of Buffer Zone

The main types of buffer zone for protected areas include.

1) *Traditional Use Zones inside protected areas.* There are situations when no suitable land exists outside reserves for buffer zone establishment and it is preferable to permit collection of certain natu-

Fig. 5.1: Examples of buffer zones for parks and reserves

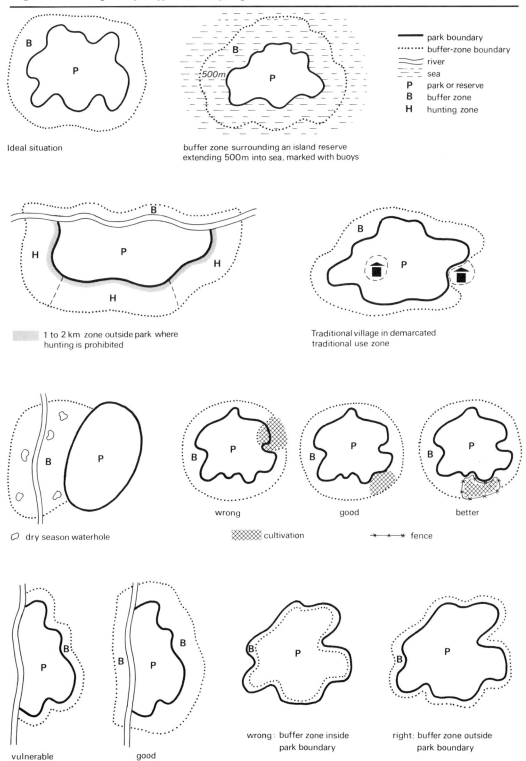

Source: Van Lavieren, 1983

ral products from some parts of the reserve or at certain times rather than have to excise valuable lands as buffers. Examples occur where indigenous people still live within large protected areas or where a good natural boundary for the reserve includes damaged or previously destroyed habitats of reduced conservation importance. Such conclaves could be used to satisfy some of the needs of local people for forest products. Activities permissible inside traditional use zones might include:

- Fishing without poisons or explosives
- Traditional hunting of non-protected species without traps, modern weapons or use of fire
- Collection of gums and resins (provided trees are not killed in the process)
- Gathering of wild fruits and honey (provided trees are not cut or burned)
- Collection for own use of naturally fallen wood for lumber or fires
- Cutting of bamboo, reeds, thatch or rattan
- Seasonal grazing of domestic animals, where native grazing species are not an important component of the park's resources

Activities that should be strictly banned in traditional use zones within protected areas include:

- Grazing of exotic or domestic animals liable to go feral
- Plantations of any kind
- Cutting of live trees
- Burning of vegetation
- Settlements inside the protected area (if these are inevitable, they should be zoned into enclaves)

2) *Forest buffers.* These include fuelwood or timber forests outside protected area boundaries but on public land. These may be natural forests, enriched secondary forest or even plantations where the emphasis is on maximising sustained yield for local village use, while maintaining good soil and water protection. The encouragement of plantation forests in buffer zones is probably the single most effective resource management strategy for ensuring long-term integrity of protected areas themselves.

3) *Economic buffers.* Sometimes economic buffering is needed to reduce the needs of villagers to take resources from protected areas. This could take the form of special agricultural, social or communication assistance in lieu of, or as well as, provision of productive buffer lands. Other examples include cash tree plantations, and wildlife cropping outside protected area boundaries, but on state land, where the emphasis is on maximising cash returns to benefit villagers. Such buffer lands could be provided on public or other land around protected areas if the necessary legislation exists. Alternatively, villages may receive some cash from park revenues, a system applied in some African reserves.

In some cases, hunting may be permitted or even beneficial in buffer areas adjacent to reserves provided that such hunting activities do not constitute a threat to the reserve's objectives. Controlled hunting of excess animals or agricultural pests can be an important source of protein and recreation for local people but the management authority must regulate which and how many animals are killed. These topics will be covered in more detail in Chapter 8.

4) *Physical buffers.* Where no land is available for buffer zone development the boundary itself must serve as a buffer and there is sometimes a need for physical barriers such as fences, ditches, canals, walls or spiny hedges. These help discourage wildlife from leaving the reserve and deter people and domestic stock from entering. In some cases all that may be required is a clearly visible boundary such as a cut trace line or single row or thin belt of distinctive tree (bright leaves or flowers) as a living boundary.

Administrative responsibility for the management of Buffer Zones on state land may rest with the management authority of the protected area. This has management advantages but may lead to conflicts of interest to *produce* in what is essentially an agency to conserve. More often management authority over buffer zones would be vested in the most competent or suitable agency e.g. reforestation schemes under the control of the Forestry Department, cash crop plantations under the department responsible for Industrial Plantations. In such cases, however, it is important that there is adequate coordination between the selected agency and the adjacent conservation agency to ensure that the protective functions of the buffer zone are not lost to other interests.

Example 5.8. Controlled buffer zones

A buffer zone adjoining or surrounding a protected area can allow limited levels of use intermediate between the strict limitations of the protected area and the more liberal land uses of the general region. An example of this approach as applied to Kenya was provided by Lusigi (1981). He suggested that the ecosystem affecting national parks be designated a wildlife conservation unit with three land-use categories – the national park, the protected area and the multiple use area.

The national park area containing the wildlife populations and unique scenic areas would be strictly protected. It would be retained in a wilderness state with minimal development and roading. The protected area would surround the national park and contain the more intensive touristic facilities and maintenance and staff facilities. Restricted local grazing would be by permit only. Some managed harvesting of wildlife on a sustained yield basis would occur in this area.

In the multiple use areas, tourism facilities would be permitted, but the major purpose of the area would be wildlife management coordinated with resident livestock operations. Resident pastoral tribes would be permitted to establish or continue their traditional ways of life.

This particular system will not suit every situation, but the general concept of buffering the strictly protected area with partly controlled areas is important. The specific means of implementing such a system will also vary in different countries according to their customs and laws. Implementation is easiest when all the land involved is in public ownership, and the various uses can be established as leases or concessions, or undertaken by a government agency.

Fig. 5.2. Diagrammatic model of a Wildlife Conservation Unit (WCU).
The entire unit would be managed as a single entity with distinctive land uses for the national parks, the protected areas and the multiple use areas.

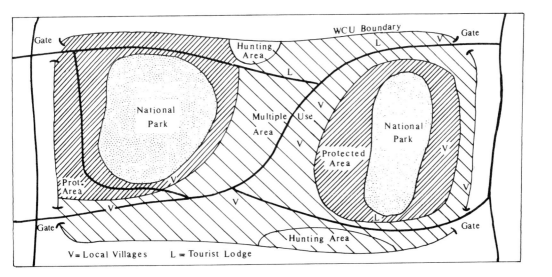

V = Local Villages   L = Tourist Lodge

Source: Lusigi, 1981 (taken from Ambio, Vol. X, No. 2-3, 1981)

Example 5.9. Selection of crop for buffer zones

The merits of various plantation types as buffer zones and their attractions for wildlife have been identified below. Although the list was prepared for Indonesia many of the principles are applicable elsewhere, especially in the tropics.

1. Natural forest, disturbed forest and secondary forest provide additional habitat for wildlife species and excellent protection of the soil.
2. Fast-growing firewood plantations (various species) are of some use to wildlife species and provide good soil protection. This solution is most suitable in areas where land is limited and where the demand for firewood is pressing. Coppiceable species should be selected.
3. Timber plantations (various species) give good to excellent soil protection i.e. reforesting steep slopes.
4. Mixed plantations providing firewood, poles and timber are of some use to wildlife and give good soil protection.
5. Fruit plantations protect the soil and provide cash and food, but problems may arise with certain wild species, e.g. monkeys or bats raiding the crops.
6. Cinnamon provides cash and firewood but is of no use to wildlife; soil protection is good although the trees have to be cut every few years. Cinnamon plantations are suitable on less steep, lower mountain slopes.
7. Cloves provide cash but require suitable climate and soil. Clove plantations are of no use to wildlife and provide only moderate soil protection. They can be undercropped for fodder or grazing.
8. Coconuts provide some cash, some food, some wood, but are of little use to wildlife and provide poor soil protection. Undercropping is possible. Raiding sunbears can be a serious problem.
9. Rubber and oilpalm provide cash crops and some firewood but are of little use to wildlife. Both species need moderately level ground and give good protection to the soil. Oil palm is unsuitable when the conservation area contains elephants.
10. *Eucalyptus* and *Melaleuca* provide valuable resins, are of no use to wildlife, but give a good soil protection. Both species grow in seasonal rainfall areas and are rather susceptible to accidental fires.
11. Tea is a profitable cash crop in wet climates at higher altitudes, but is of no use to wildlife and soil protection is poor. Tea may be acceptable if erosion susceptibility of the soil is low.
12. Coffee requires good soils, is of little use to wildlife and gives poor to moderate soil protection. It can be mixed with other crops but is not suitable on steep slopes.
13. *Leucaena* provides fodder (edible leaves and pods) as well as fuelwood, but gives poor soil protection. *Leucaena* is a fast growing coppiceable tree, which fixes nitrogen in soil. It can be seeded by air and is a good species to cover grassland quickly. Horses lose hair if they eat too much of it.
14. Bamboos (various species) provide cash, building material and some fuel. Bamboos are fast growing and coppiceable and give moderate soil protection.
15. Rattans (various species) provide cash and are useful to wildlife; the degree of soil protection varies with conditions. Rattans can be mixed with other tree crops and can be a valuable investment as prices still soar as wild stocks dwindle. Good silvicultural techniques have been developed in the Philippines.
16. Sago provides food and fodder and gives an excellent cover in damp, or swampy areas.
17. Mangrove plantations provide tannin, timber, seafood and firewood. They are good for wildlife and soil protection and are an excellent use of saline swamp areas. Plantations can also be combined with fishponds.
18. Herbs and grasses (undercropping) provide fodder, cash and medicine. Numerous herbs and grasses are suitable for planting under tree cover.

Source: Mackinnon, 1981a

Public works installations in protected areas

To maintain a variety of services to surrounding human settlements, public works and other departments may require access through, or installations within, protected areas. Examples include:

- Roads, canals, railways, paths crossing reserves
- Water pipes, oil and gas pipes, power lines, telephone cables
- Water stations, sewage works
- Hydroelectric dams, geothermal plants
- Telecommunication stations
- Meteorological stations, astronomical observatories
- Quarries or gravel pits

Whenever possible, the protected area management authority should persuade the departments concerned to consider alternative sites outside protected areas. If installations must be accommodated within a protected area, the management authority must press for prior consultations on siting and dictate the terms under which such installations are to be accepted. However, sometimes public works projects can generate funds for park management. At the Monte Verde Cloud Forest Reserve in Costa Rica, a yearly rental fee is paid to the park for the use of one of its mountain tops for telecommunication structures. This provides a supplemental source of income which is used for park management programmes.

For example, the management authority might agree to the construction of a telecommunications station provided:

- it is discreet in location and design;
- it is not permanently manned;
- controls during the construction phase are agreed to;
- staff attending it are obliged to adhere to normal visitor regulations pertaining to behaviour in the reserve;
- the telecommunications department constructs and maintains a service road to the station, along a route approved by the management authority (who will suggest the route most useful for other aspects of management or making least impact on the natural environment);
- compensations are made by way of adding extra land elsewhere to the protected area;
- data collected by the station are routinely provided to the management authority.

Such installations should either be officially excluded from the reserve land or built in special use zones.

By accommodating the needs of other departments in this way, the protected area management wins support and, perhaps, extra help. While engineers and machinery are on site for other purposes the manager may get a few jobs done on the side – levelling a site for building, clearing a ditch, grading a road, or digging a well.

Integrating protected areas into regional development programmes

The previous sections have stressed the importance of protected area managers consulting and cooperating with other agencies and programmes involved in regional development. Such links are important for several reasons:

- *Settling inter-agency land-use conflicts and overlaps in planning.*
  Protected area managers often find themselves involved in disputes regarding the use of land or resources. The use of an integrated planning approach can often reduce or avoid such conservation versus development conflicts, but this depends on good working relationships and a forum for discussion between the agencies involved.

- *Achieving modifications in other agencies' plans to reduce threats to protected areas or to strengthen their integrity.*
  In planning a road, siting a dam or planning a resettlement programme or agricultural development project, the planning agency may not be aware of the impact, direct or indirect, that its project may have on a nearby protected area. It is up to the protected area management agency to protect its own interests by identifying potential conflicts and trying to avoid or mitigate them by influencing other agency's plans at the earliest stages. For example, intervention by the conservation authorities during the planning stages of Sudan's Rahad irrigation

scheme (a World Bank project) led to the design of a canal being altered to avoid an important wildlife migratory route (Goodland, 1984).

- *Developing mutually beneficial inter-agency cooperation and dependencies.*

Where the interests of two or more agencies are in line these agencies can benefit from an alliance to promote their joint case. Moreover, where the management authority for protected areas can form strong alliances with other departments who are dependent on the benefits deriving from the protection of reserves, these departments may also support other activities of the protected area authority even when they are not directly involved. An example is the linkage between the Park Service, Tourism Department, and Education Department in Dominica (Thorsell, 1984b).

- *Achieving wider acceptance for the role of protected areas in the regional context.*

The more firmly integrated the establishment and management of protected areas are in the functions of other departments, the wider will be the general support for the whole protected area programme.

- *Obtaining approval for protected area development in wider multiple land-use packages.*

Major developments generally involve several departments and this results in the need to develop rather broad cross-sectoral plans, regional development plans and the like. If the protected area management authority can underline its contribution to such plans, even if its inputs are small, it can often get its own projects included and approved as part of a larger total packsage.

- *Funding for vital protective functions from those projects and programmes which derive the most benefit.*

By having plans for the development of protected areas included in larger projects it is sometimes possible to have their development funded by other agencies. For instance where the protection of a water catchment is vital to the success of a large irrigation or hydrological project the development and protection of the catchment area can be included as a relatively minor component of the development project, e.g. Dumoga National Park, Indonesia (Sumardja *et al.*, 1984).

Example 5.10 La Planada – looking beyond park borders

La Planada is an isolated nature reserve (1667 ha) located in the forested mountains of southern Colombia. The area is notable for its high number of endemic plants and animal species as well as a resident population of spectacled bear.

Initial management planning for the reserve was carried out in 1982. Resource inventories made it glaringly obvious that because of it small size, long-term conservation of flora and fauna could only be assured if the natural habitats outside reserve borders were also protected. Though largely undeveloped, this surrounding area is undergoing rapid colonisation by both indigenous and Latino cultures. Consequently, the management plan focusses more attention on activities adjacent to the unit as it does to development within the reserve itself.

By design, La Planada is becoming the catalyst and coordinator of sustainable regional development in the area. This includes organising not only conservation programmes but also health, education and other human service activities. Such attention to basic human needs has paid off in strong community support for the project and its goal of sound natural resource management both within and outside the reserve.

Personnel at La Planada and the residents of the adjacent communities are realising that land-use practices that are good for long-term rural development can also be good for conservation. While public health and education, agricultural extension and even road and trail construction seem to be outside the realm of a park managers duties, at La Planada they are proving to be the keys to assuring the long-term survival of the area's impressive biological diversity.

20. Where national parks can be integrated with larger regional developments, they will gain more support. This weir being constructed at Toraut, Sulawesi, Indonesia, is part of a large irrigation system financed by the World Bank. To safeguard their investment, the Bank provided extra funds to help establish and maintain the Dumoga National Park which protects the water catchment on which the scheme depends.
Photo: WWF/Michéle Dépraz

Example 5.11 Development without destruction – the Mahaweli River Development Scheme in Sri Lanka

The Mahaweli River Development Scheme involves the harnessing of Sri Lanka's largest river to irrigate its lower basin as well as the valleys of several other rivers. This is a rich biogeographical region with 90 known endemic plants and animals and many large mammals, including some 800 elephants. The development of the basin for agriculture threatened to reduce these prime wildlife habitats. Besides causing the displacement of animals and their being crowded into surviving natural areas with all consequent problems, there was every likelihood of increased human/animal conflicts.

In response to these and similar problems elsewhere in Sri Lanka, the Government has placed a high priority on the upgrading and establishment of protected areas in prime wildlife habitats and the protection of the catchments of reservoirs. This applies in the lower Mahaweli basin where the existing Somawathiya Sanctuary is to be expanded by 52,000 ha and elevated to national park status. The Wasgomuwa Strict Nature Reserve of 27,500 ha will be made into a national park to afford it greater public appeal, and two new areas, representing prime wildlife habitats and totalling 55,000 ha, will be established. This system of parks will be interlinked by forest reserves and jungle corridors to promote maximum ecological and genetic resilience in the system and so as to protect elephant migration routes. In addition each park will be surrounded by a 1.6 km buffer zone in order to reduce conflicts between it and neighbouring communities.

This progressive programme of integrated land use involving a range of different types of protected areas in support of sustainable development is in line with the ideals of the *World Conservation Strategy* and is based on the realisation of benefits that nature conservation in some 135,000 ha can bring to people on the 107,000 ha of land being improved for agriculture. Benefits from the conservation of these natural areas include flood control and reduced downstream sedimentation, bank stabilisation, reduced conflict between wild animals and crops, conservation of fisheries, the creation of tourist and recreational opportunities, local employment opportunities, the conservation of genetic resources and opportunities for research and education.

Source: de Alwis, 1984.

Conclusion

Protected areas can make significant contributions to regional land use in the fields discussed in this Chapter. Because of their proximity to environmentally critical areas and places of show-case status, well-managed protected areas can serve as the focus for regional development, helping to maintain a more natural balance of the ecosystem over a much wider area.

6

Local People and Protected Areas

Introduction

The previous Chapter discussed the problems of integrating protected areas of various categories into the regional land use fabric. This Chapter considers more specific questions of how to derive sustainable benefits for rural populations around and within protected areas.

The success of management depends very much on the degree of support and respect awarded to the protected area by neighbouring communities. Where protected areas are seen as a burden, local people can make protection impossible. When the protected area is seen as a positive benefit, the local people will themselves become allied with the manager in protecting the area from threatening developments.

There are many ways in which local people can benefit from protected areas, including utilisation of some resources from certain protected areas and buffer zones, the preservation of traditional rights and cultural practices, and special preference for local residents in employment or social services. Nevertheless, there are limits that must be placed on exploitative uses if reserve areas are to fulfil their primary protective functions. Managers must know where to draw the line.

Protected areas and indigenous people

Some protected areas, particularly Protected Landscapes (Category V), Anthropological Reserves (Category VII) and Biosphere Reserves (Category IX), may be inhabited by indigenous people. In other categories of protected areas, the presence of indigenous peoples may sometimes be acceptable where these people are living in close and balanced harmony with their environment and can be said to have become a part of the natural ecosystem. In other cases, where no people live in a reserve, traditional harvesting of various resources may be permitted on a seasonal basis and the use of traditional cultural sites for religious or spiritual purposes may continue.

The whole question of protection of indigenous cultures is highly sensitive. Where planners have forbidden the continued practice of traditional rights in national parks or other protected areas, they have been strongly criticised. On the other hand, those who seek to preserve 'primitive' cultures are often accused of preventing indigenous people from pursuing the advantages of modern development and of trying to establish 'human zoos as scientific curios or tourist objects'.

There are many areas in which native populations, following their traditional cultures on their own land, protect large areas of essentially natural ecosystems and harvest the renewable resources of their environment on a sustained yield basis (see McNeely and Pitt, 1985 for case studies). These people and protected area managers can be appropriate allies and the need to reach a mutual understanding is urgent. Managers can learn much about resource conservation and use, while

21. To win the support of local people, park managers attempt to integrate as much traditional use of the protected area as possible without compromising its management objectives. How far to go in this direction is a matter of delicate balance. Traditional hunting of lions by the Masai might be countenanced in some protected areas but would be unacceptable in others.
Photo: WWF/Kenya Information Services

the conservation of natural areas can provide the opportunity for traditional cultures to survive. The social and behavioural patterns of these allegedly 'primitive' peoples have become so integrated with their natural environment that they often achieve ecologically sound long-term use of an area. Both are easily disturbed by insensitive forces from outside.

The launching in March 1981 of the *World Conservation Strategy* brought the convergence of indigene and conservation interests into sharp focus. Deforestation, desertification, depletion of fisheries, soil erosion and misuse of crop lands are all matters of direct concern to aboriginal populations. The logic behind this compatibility of interests has already been recognised by the World Council of Indigenous Peoples (WCIP) which was invited by the United Nations Environment Pro-

gramme in 1980 to prepare a study on 'environmental degradation in indigenous areas'. The WCIP is following closely the operation of the international agreements such as the World Heritage Convention and the Man and the Biosphere Programme. Many 'biosphere reserves' have a direct effect on the indigenous peoples *in situ*; The Rio Platano Biosphere Reserve in Honduras, for example, is designed, among other things, to protect two indigenous tribes.

Outright conflict between conservationist and indigenous objectives has occurred in the past. Tribes have been expelled from national parks or denied the use of resources within the park: for example, the Rendille were excluded from the Sibiloi National Park in Kenya and the Ik expelled from Kidepo National Park in Uganda with disastrous results for the tribes concerned (Turnbull,

1973). Understanding of modern conservation objectives by aboriginal peoples remains low (battles erupt in Ethiopa's Simien Park over woodcutting rights, for example). Some conflicts even have an international dimension; enforcing the Migratory Birds Convention and accommodating native Indian demands have caused problems for governments in Canada and the USA. As another example, the International Whaling Commission attempts to compromise with those who oppose bowhead whale-hunting prohibitions, and argument revolves around Inuit rights to use modern whaling technology.

Several commentators have advanced suggestions for successful involvement of indigenous groups with an interest in territories in which restrictive land use policies are tied to conservation objectives. Brownrigg (1985) offers four land-use options for consideration:

- *reserves*, where a protected natural area corresponds with the territory of a particular native population;
- *native-owned lands*, where the protection of the area is by native peoples;
- *buffer zones*, where a protected area serves as a physical or ecological barrier between native lands and the lands of others;
- *research stations*, where certain areas under native management are organised as agricultural or ecological research stations.

The option which is most appropriate will depend on the cultures of the native peoples and the specific objectives of the protected area. In general the best indigene/conservationist relations occur when indigenous peoples see the protected area as helping to maintain their culture (and to provide tangible benefits such as employment);

- indigenous organisations have strong bargaining positions (related to unambiguous title to their lands);
- permitted land-use in the protected area is well-defined.

Tribal lands include not only those areas inhabited at all times, but other sites which are used only intermittently. There are two possibilities here. First, many countries permit acquisition of rights to land by prescription, i.e. continuous and uncontested use of the land for a determined number of years. A wider definition of particular aboriginal land 'uses' can lead to successful tribal land claims (and therefore to more lands put outside the reach of 'development'). The second pos-

sibility concerns the systematic, non-damaging land use practised by intermittent users such as hunter-gatherers following traditional practices (the Kalahari Bushmen or Australian Aboriginals) or pastoralists (Fulani or Masai of Africa, the Gujjars of India or the Bedouins of Arabia). The advantages of these practices need to be demonstrated quantitatively to national authorities.

It is imperative to undertake a socio-economic survey of the communities affected by park management decisions when considering any of the above options. Such a survey should delineate the ethnic diversity of the communities and their social structure, including the traditional location and proximity of householder and kin groups for ritual, labour exchange and other important community activities. This approach provides park management with an in-depth perception of local people and can avoid misunderstandings and disruptions when implementing policy. After studying the options suggested from such a study, the Nepalese Parks and Conservation Department were able to effectively implement a resettlement programme for the community of Padompur Panchayat, Chitwan, which met the needs of the people involved (Milton and Binney, 1980).

Indigenous peoples can and should benefit from the establishment of protected areas. In one outstanding case, that of Panama's Kunas, the encroachment of slash-and-burn cultivation from outsiders was countered by the Kuna themselves turning part of their traditional territory into a protected area that includes research facilities for foreign scientists and tourist facilities for visitors. By establishing a protected area the Kuna have maintained control of their traditional land and culture, served conservation objectives, brought in foreign exchange and fostered economic development (Breslin and Chapin, 1984).

This section has dealt with the compatibility of preserving indigenous traditional life styles and protecting semi-natural ecosystems with which these life styles are in harmony. Where this harmony breaks down, difficulties relating to accommodating legitimate traditional rights within protected area management objectives assume the dimensions of a rural land-use problem and become an issue of properly integrated regional planning (Chapter 5). In either event, attempts to transplant applications of the concepts that are relevant in one part of the world to another should proceed cautiously, as each situation is unique and demands an individual solution.

22. Permitting local people to continue traditional practices in or around protected areas can win allies
for conservation as well as preserve valuable traditional knowledge. On Siberut Island, off
Sumatra, where this medicine man or Sikerei still practises his art, wide 'traditional use zones' have
been proposed as buffers around smaller sanctuary areas to protect the endemic fauna.
Photo: WWF/Tony Whitten

Example 6.1: Anthropological reserves: some useful guidelines

Where a protected area is designated to correspond with the territory of a particular native ethnic group, the traditional residents should be given the authority to oversee the activities of their own group and to expel any unauthorised invaders. The national conservation agency may remain the official administrator of the area, but managers should work closely with the resident native population.

- When establishing protected areas, resettlement of native peoples should be avoided whenever possible. A native culture will remain intact only in its home territory, where the productive capacity of the environment is intimately understood.
- The protected area should be sufficiently large to accommodate its dual functions, a reserve for nature with a reserve for native populations. The creation of reduced reserves serves only a symbolic end and begins a process of cultural devolution and ecological degradation if the native population does not have access to the resources they require.
- Protected areas planning must also anticipate population increases and culture change. It is unrealistic to expect a group to atrophy, or worse, to 'return' to some traditional technology long ago discarded in favour of a more modern alternative.
- Official park guards should be drawn from the traditional residents. The threat to the integrity of a protected area originates largely from the outside. If reserve administrators expend their expectably meagre resources controlling the native residents, they will have neither sufficient force nor the peoples' good will to expel outsiders.

These rules all require the participation of the native population in the planning and implementation of the reserve. This requires good communications between reserve planners and the native peoples. There are examples from Latin America of planning anthropological reserves without any basic facts about the resident groups – where they were located or what language they spoke, let alone how their settlement patterns fit into their total ecological adaptation to the environment.

    This model is attractive for those native populations which do not have formal rights to their land, nor an avenue to pursue land titles within the juridical structure of their country. It also has particular merit for some smaller, rarely contacted groups, which are not capable of pursuing the involved legal struggles to obtain rights to their own land.

Source: Brownrigg, 1985

Example 6.2: Involvement of indigenous people in park management in Nepal

Some 2500 of Nepal's estimated 20,000 Sherpa people live in the 124,000 ha of the Sagarmatha National Park (which also includes the Khumbu area, famous for Mount Everest). Prior to the influx of tourism and mountaineering, the Sherpas were managing a partly modified landscape under a system of social and community controls which ensured wisest use of forest resources and minimised long-term forest degradation.

    The trekking and mountaineering which followed the opening of the area to outsiders in 1950 has led to worrying changes in traditional Sherpa life, associated with the depletion of manpower (for porters) and firewood (it is estimated that each mountaineering expedition needs 30,000 kg of wood for fuel).

    In association with New Zealand rangers, the park's managers have determined upon the following objectives to include the indigenous Sherpas in the park's activities:

- *constant liaison* with monastery lamas;
- *restoration* of religious structures within the park;
- *retention and protection* of all monastery buildings;
- *maintenance* of traditional village water supply schemes;
- *active encouragement* of the traditional character and architectural styles of villages within the park;

- *prohibition* of all trekking within sacred areas (including whole mountains) where guardian spirits reside;
- *employment* of Sherpas as rangers on a preferential basis;
- *retention* as far as possible of firewood as the Sherpas' fuel (rather than displacement by kerosene or other new – and imported – fuel technology);
- *internal modification* where possible of traditional Sherpa houses to minimise heat losses and consequently reduce firewood consumption;
- *revival* of Sherpas' traditional forest-use control system, i.e. the *Shing-i Nawas* ('protectors of the forests') who were empowered to allocate wood for families.

These objectives demonstrate an active involvement of a partially-acculturated indigenous people in a park which is part of the indigene territory. Briefly, the conservation objectives of Sagarmatha are to correct a situation where over half of the forest cover within the park territory has disappeared and to revive, within a system catering also to outsiders' mountaineering expeditions, a pattern of traditional use.

Source: Clad, 1982

Example 6.3: Involvement of local people in Siwi-Utame Wildlife Management Area, Papua New Guinea

Siwi-Utame, a 12,450 ha wildlife management area in the Southern Highlands of Papua New Guinea, is a favoured habitat for wildlife since it contains one of the largest continuous areas of forest in a densely populated region. The area is rich in bird life, including seven birds of paradise, cassowaries, bower birds, and the New Guinea Eagle. Mammals include tree kangaroos, bush wallabies, bandicoots, cuscus and different types of phalangers. In the past, all these species have been hunted, with the exception of the bower bird which was protected in its nesting area because of traditional beliefs concerning its magic powers, especially with regard to its assistance in finding wives for young men.

There are 19 villages in the area which hold traditional tribal rights to the land. The main occupation of the population of about 6000 persons is subsistence farming with sweet potatoes and taro being the main crops. There has been little social or economic development and there are very few sources of cash income.

The wildlife management area was officially gazetted in 1977. The rules restrict hunting in the area and forbid the use of bows and arrows, shotguns, slings, metal traps and dogs. The taking of eggs is also prohibited and rules were made later forbidding the damage and removal of trees without the permission of the land-owners. There are also general rules restricting the felling of trees that provide fruit or shelter for wildlife; bird of paradise display trees in particular are protected.

Siwi-Utame has a wildlife management committee which consists of 14 members representing different villages who meet about twice a year. Members of the committee each have a badge, but do not receive any cash payment. Siwi-Utame is one of the few wildlife management areas where relatively large numbers of people (35) have been prosecuted for breaking the rules. Some offenders have been fined by the committee or by village courts; others have been brought before local courts and serious cases (e.g. killing birds of paradise with a shotgun) are heard by district courts.

A wildlife centre has been established at Kume in a 4 ha area adjacent to the highway, where cassowaries are reared in several pens. Most of these have been bought as young from other parts of the Southern Highlands. They are fed on sweet potatoes and concentrated foodstuffs and then sold when mature. They are in considerable demand for ceremonies and bride prices and are sold at a price averaging more than $US 8 per kilo.

In addition to the cassowaries, Kume has a small information centre, a picnic place and a small hut where visitors can spend the night. A recent development has been the start of an orchid farm. The centre has attracted a small number of visitors, scientists and educational parties; an entry fee is charged for visitors. Some of the costs for constructing facilities at the centre came from provincial rural development funds. The land was purchased from the traditional land-owners by the national government, which may also purchase a further 2,400 ha of primary forest as a bird of paradise conservation area.

There have generally been few problems caused by competing land use in the area. In 1982 a proposal to start a logging project was refused with the agreement of the land-owners. Population pressure has led to some areas of forest near the village of Kirune being cleared for subsistence cultivation. The people of the area seem to have kept to the rules restricting hunting and there have been few incursions by outsiders.

In comparison to some other protected areas in Papua New Guinea the Siwi-Utame wildlife management area seems to have been a success. The people of the area are aware of the need for conservation and are involved in the management and protection of their wildlife resources. Their rules not only protect the fauna of the area, but also the habitat. All seem agreed that since the establishment of the area, the numbers of wildlife have increased and many of the threatened species are becoming more common.

Source: Eaton, 1985

Example 6.4: Conmarca de la Biosfera Kuna Yala – an indigenous group establishes its own park

---

Spontaneous colonisation by non-indians and the construction of a new road through the previously isolated Kuna Yala Reserve in Panama prompted indigenous residents to devise a land management plan that would protect their outstanding natural and cultural resources. With the assistance of several international agencies, the Kuna began exploring the possibility of establishing a protected conservation unit on tribal lands in the late 1970s and by 1980 they had established their PEMASKY effort (Project for the Study of the Management of Kuna Yala Wildlands).

A team of 20 Kuna Yala (several of which have attended wildland management training courses) have identified and marked the reserve boundaries and are completing and implementing a management plan. The area will be administered much like a biosphere reserve with both protection and sustainable development integrated into one umbrella management scheme. While the Kuna are still receiving some outside assistance in the planning and operation of the project, ongoing training will assure technical self-sufficiency in the near future. A scientific tourism component will also help to finance the operation of the unit.

The project is unique in its utilisation of both modern wildland conservation techniques and indigenous natural resource knowledge. In addition, the Kuna have demonstrated that cultural and natural resource conservation can be achieved through appropriate park and reserve protection programmes.

Source: Wright, *et al*, 1985

Human enclaves within protected areas

Wherever possible, reserve boundaries should be selected or adjusted so as to exclude human settlements. Resettlement of small numbers of people is sometimes desirable if alternative and acceptable sites can be found for their villages. Where this is impossible, it may be necessary to declare an enclave inside a reserve. The fishing villages inside Queen Elizabeth National Park in Uganda are one example where unfortunate consequences have resulted. When the villages grew unchecked, the lake became overfished and villagers turned to poaching in the park instead, leading to antagonism between villagers and park authorities.

The danger of enclave settlements is that they tend to expand at the expense of the reserve and that they invariably have access routes that cut through the reserve. Ultimately these will split the reserve unless firm controls are applied. The following regulations are suggested:

• As a check on growth, immigration of outsiders into the enclaves is prohibited, i.e. no land may be purchased or cleared, or houses erected, by non-residents or new immigrants to the enclave.

- The limit of agricultural spread that is tolerable must be clearly defined in the field and an appropriate buffer zone established. No expansion beyond these limits will be permitted.
- Road access to and from the enclave must be limited to traditional routes (i.e. no new trails or roads) and no clearing allowed along the sides of the roads.

With restrictions on the spread of agriculture and prohibition of further immigration, population growth within the enclave should be minimal or even drop as young people move away to find employment. In an expanding population there will be economic pressure for emigration both as a result of the lack of growth potential within the enclave and the settlement's general remoteness. As enclaves are abandoned the land can be absorbed into the reserves.

Protection of cultural sites

Many cultural sites are located within natural protected areas and nature conservation often benefits from the protection of important cultural features. Examples include the Tikal National Park of Guatemala, Tassili N'Ajjer National Park in Algeria and Angkor Wat National Monument in Kampuchea. Some such sites may be spectacular and well publicised while others may be less conspicuous and kept secret by the people for whom they have a special significance. The former often attract visitors and it is usually a relatively simple matter for the park manager to provide for their appropriate use. This is more difficult in the case of the more secret sites as the manager may not know of their existence or of their importance and may unwittingly prevent their use or permit their desecration. A sensitive manager will try to establish the location of these sites (or other cultural features such as traditional pilgrimage routes) and provide adequate protection without becoming too intrusive in his enquiries about their cultural significance.

In any case, the proper use of cultural sites calls for close liaison with a range of interested parties from professional scientists to informed and influential members of local communities.

Direct harvesting from protected areas and buffer zones

Development of buffer zones can be a useful way of providing some compensation to rural communities in cases where they have lost traditional harvesting rights or privileges through the establishment of the reserve. These zones can provide essential products (e.g. firewood, timber, building poles, thatch, meat, fish) which could otherwise be obtained only by illegal collection from the protected area itself.

The buffer zones should benefit the whole community and not just a few privileged individuals; otherwise the 'have-nots' will still exploit the protected area. It is, therefore, recommended that buffer zones should be established for use only by specified villages and that exploitation is controlled by a village cooperative in which every household has a share. The cooperatives must ensure fair harvesting rights and organise profit-sharing from cash crops. In areas where there already exist traditional laws concerning community

rights, these would form an excellent basis for determining sharing of buffer zone produce. Elsewhere, the park management authority could help in drawing up regulations for use and distribution of benefits (see Chapter 10, pages 227-230).

Some Categories of protected areas (V, VIII) may contain products that are useful to local communities and which may be harvested without detriment to the area itself. Naturally this will depend on the nature of the product, how it is to be harvested, and the particular protective status and management objectives of the area. Clearly, situations vary and there is a need to lay down very clear policy guidelines so that the protected area manager can act with consistency within a framework that is understood, if not always warmly accepted, by neighbouring communities.

Examples of useful products that may sometimes be harvested from a protected area by peo-

23. Traditional hunting methods used here to kill hartebeest in Uganda are far less likely to threaten game populations than uncontrolled use of modern firearms. Care must be taken to restrict the use of fire as a traditional hunting method and the use of snares and nets which can be very destructive. Photo: WWF/J. Allan Cash

ple from surrounding areas include firewood, thatching grass, surplus animals, traditional medicinal herbs, honey, fruits and seeds, and clay for traditional pottery. Where such harvesting is permitted, it should be viewed by those who benefit as a privilege rather than a right and in this regard some form of payment in cash or kind may have advantages. For instance, grass cutters harvesting thatching grass in the Matobo National Park in Zimbabwe, pay in kind by donating one bundle of thatch from every ten collected to the park (Example 6.5).

Harvesting must be strictly controlled and integrated into the programme for managing the natural resources of the protected area. Conversely, where resources have to be managed for sound ecological reasons and this results in a harvest of useful products, these should be disposed of to the best advantage of the protected area. Earning good will for the area among its neighbours may outweigh any revenue foregone. In Zimbabwe, trophy hunters and sportsmen pay to shoot large

mammals in some reserves under warden supervision; this brings revenue to the parks and the meat is distributed to local communities.

Mishra (1984) describes a system in the Royal Chitwan National Park in Nepal where the controlled harvesting of grass and reeds for the thatch helps to compensate the local people for the loss of potentially rich agricultural land and for the inconveniences they suffer due to the proximity of the park. Similarly, native Indians are permitted to harvest wild nuts in the Grand Canyon National Park in the USA.

These examples represent the way in which products from a national park can be harvested by local people under appropriate controls, to the benefit of both the park and its neighbours, without affecting natural values to any significant extent. Such interchanges build up good public relations at little or no cost and remove the need for local populations to engage in activities which may be more damaging to the protected area.

Example 6.5: Thatching grass as a means of promoting local public awareness of park values in Zimbabwe

The Matobo National Park in Zimbabwe is an area of superlative natural and cultural values, but it is threatened along most of its boundaries by dense peasant settlement in degraded habitats. Neighbouring villagers belong to a cattle-raising culture and are tempted by the lush grazing in the park; their own lands are over-grazed and denuded, and until the mid-1950s some of the villagers resided within the present park boundaries.

Thatch is the main roofing material in this part of Zimbabwe but is now in extremely short supply due to overgrazing. It occurs in fair quantities within the park where manipulative management for large indigenous mammals requires it to be burned periodically in order to prevent a build-up of moribund tissue.

In 1962, the park authorities, in liaison with the local communities, decided to permit the strictly controlled harvesting of this grass on the understanding that the local people would not poach, trespass with their cattle or cause fires within the park. Village elders nominate villagers, mostly women, who are licensed to cut a given number of bundles of thatch according to a pre-determined annual quota and 'pay' the park authorities one bundle for every ten cut. The park's share of the grass is used to roof visitor facilities and service buildings in the park.

Annual quotas have ranged from around 40,000 to 115,000 bundles, worth at least 50 cents each at present values. This income of $US 20,000 to $US 60,000 has been a welcome annual addition to the livelihood of the community, representing an income of $US 200 to $US 600 for each villager involved for six to eight weeks' work each year. Poaching and wild fires have been minimised and cattle trespass is much less serious than might otherwise be the case in a politically sensitive region. Other benefits include reduced pasture management costs, and the protection and rehabilitation of important water-generating catchments, the availability of a steady supply of attractive cheap roofing material to the park, and improved relations with neighbouring villages.

Source: Child, *in litt.*, 1984

Example 6.6: The economic values of wildlife

Apart from the genetic and aesthetic value of plants and animals or their value as tourist attractions, certain species of wildlife are of considerable importance in local and national economies.

- Preliminary information from a study on hunted wildlife in Sarawak shows that Sarawak villagers eat considerable quantities of wild meat (mostly bearded pig) conservatively estimated to be worth $US 50 million every year, at current prices. The loss of this cheap source of protein would have a crippling effect on many village economies. If the wild meat were to be replaced with imported tinned food there would be an adverse effect on Sarawak's balance of payments.
- It has been estimated that more than 80 per cent of the fresh meat consumed in Ghana is bushmeat. This indicates that if bushmeat could be rationally exploited on a sustained yield basis in Africa, it would lead to an economic justification for wildlife conservation. It also would give stiff competition to poachers and possibly make poaching uneconomical to the tribal villager, as well as to the big businessmen and executives who are behind the scenes of illegal hunting in some countries.
- The worth of products from a single female estuarine crocodile, *Crocodylus porosus* and her lifetime's offspring has been estimated at $US 280,000 (Whitaker, 1984).
- In the USA alone, as many as half of all prescriptions written every year contain a drug of natural origin; these have been valued at well over $US 3 billion. The two richest areas in the world for natural production of the complex chemicals that may be used in pharmaceuticals are tropical rain forests and coral communities.
- Brazil imports two-thirds of its rubber yet could be self-sufficient from wild trees being felled and burned in land-clearance schemes in the Amazon Basin (rubber tappers earn as much as the best-paid factory workers).

- Fish which breed in the Amazon rivers when they flood the rain forests produce more protein per hectare than cattle.
- In Sabah, recent studies suggest that high densities of wild birds in commercial *Albizia* plantations limit the abundance of caterpillars that would otherwise defoliate the trees. The birds require natural forest for nesting.
- Rhesus macaques and long-tailed macaques are used for testing live vaccines, an essential part of immunisation programmes which have been instrumental in saving the lives of hundreds of thousands of children worldwide every year. This gives these monkeys, often regarded as pest species, a considerable economic value.

All of these benefits accrue from wild populations of species which can best be conserved in their natural habitats by establishment of national parks and other protected areas.

Sources: Kavanagh, 1984; Guppy, 1984

Example 6.7: Economics and conservation in Kenya's Amboseli National Park

Kenya is one of the few countries to have an explicit policy of making wildlife pay. The table below calculates the economic potential of various options for land use in the Amboseli ecosystem. This arid region will support little apart from ranching and wildlife exploitation, and from the national point of view the latter use is more economically profitable. In 1972, wildlife exploitation grossed 166 times the cash income of livestock, or more realistically, over twice the subsistence value of livestock to the pastoralists. Projecting tourism to full development, it was shown that wildlife could earn 18 times the annual income of a fully developed and commercialised beef economy.

Gross revenues from existing and potential uses of Amboseli as calculated in 1973

	$US Gross Return	
	Park	*Ecosystem*
Total wildlife 1972	1,200,000	+1,202,710
Total livestock 1972		
(Cash returns only)	3,000	4,200
Subsistence value livestock 1972	199,188	597,562
Wildlife potential (no livestock)	6,560,000	+8,030,000
Commercial livestock potential		
(no wildlife)	69,300	445,930
Combined wildlife and commercial		
livestock potential	6,560,000	8,285,580

The economic exploitation of national parks, when rationally planned, need not be at odds with the other goals of conservation. In fact putting an economic value on wildlife species can help to protect them. An analysis of the value of lions in Amboseli shows their gross worth (in visitor attraction) to be $US 27,000 each per year. The elephant herd is estimated as worth $US 610,000 per year. Such animals are worth far more alive as a tourist attraction than dead; the comparable gross yield from hunting would be appreciably less than 10 per cent of this value. Moreover, the total park net returns (due mainly to tourism) amount to $US 40 per ha a year compared to 80 cents per hectare under the most optimistic agricultural returns.

The principles applied in Kenya could be usefully applied in other tropical countries. An economic justification of national parks should be clearly and objectively stated in national park policies. This is a prime conservation aid. More important, it argues for comprehensive planning and management to ensure the sustained profitability of the resource, which depends ultimately on reconciling the dilemma of use and preservation – a universal challenge that applies to all parks whatever their objectives.

Sources: Western and Henry, 1979; Western 1984

Example 6.8: Terrestrial wildlife as a source of food in selected countries of Africa

Country	Food consumption and Species Concerned
Botswana	Over 50 species of wild animals, ranging from elephant through ungulates to rodents, bats and small birds provide animal protein exceeding 90.7 kg per person per annum in some areas and contribute some 40% of their diet.
	3.3 million kg of meat from springhare are obtained yearly by Botswana hunters.
Ghana	About 75% of the population depends largely on traditional sources of protein supply, mainly wildlife, including fish, insects, caterpillars, maggots and snails.
	During the period December 1968-June 1970 (17 months) a total of 157,809 kg of bushmeat from 13 species of animals was sold in Accra in one market only.
Ivory Coast	In the northern part of the country 27g of bushmeat were consumed per person per day.
Nigeria	The Isoko tribe (Niger delta) obtain 20 g/day of animal protein, mainly game.
	Game constitutes about 20% of the mean annual consumption of animal protein by people in rural areas.
Senegal	A minimum consumption rate of 373,631 metric tons of wild mammals and birds per annum for the country's human population of 5,000,000.
Togo	Various species of wildlife, including rodents, are eaten. The per capita per day intake of rodents varies from 0.5-12g.
Zaire	75% of animal protein comes from wild sources, including mainly three species of *Cephalophys* and three species of *Cercopithecus*. Rats and other rodents are also eaten.
Zambia	22% of those interviewed in the Serenji district reported having eaten small animals, including rats, mice and mole rats.
Zimbabwe	Game yielded 5-10% more than the beef industry at a conservative estimated production of 2.5 million kg.

Source: Sale, 1981

Example 6.9: Multiple use in a wetland environment – Pacaya Samiria National Reserve, Peru

The giant Pacaya Samiria Reserve (2,080,000 ha) was initially established as a fishery reserve in 1940. As a result of studies demonstrating the need to protect Amazonian flora and fauna, it was later upgraded to a National Reserve although its primary management goal is still natural resource conservation for sustainable utilisation.

In 1982, an Inter-agency Working Committee for the reserve was formed to coordinate the many diverse government institutions involved in the development of the site. The Committee has elaborated an operational plan which details short-term management objectives many of which relate directly to multiple use programmes for flora and fauna of economic value.

In addition to illegal poaching of plants and animals, a major threat to the integrity of the reserve is the recent influx of oil extraction operations. However, a new tax levied on oil produced in the Amazonian region has been utilised to create the Research Institute of Peruvian Amazonia. This institue has been actively carrying out studies on the environmental impact of contamination caused by petroleum related activites in the reserve.

Preliminary investigations have revealed that, if properly managed and harvested, the area's fauna alone has the potential to generate at least 6 million dollars (1985) per 500 sq. km per year on a sustainable basis. Added to this amount could be an additional income produced from the harvest of the tree and plant species as well as from nature tourism which has yet to be developed in the region. However, before such programmes can be established, resources must be well studied and even more important, well protected. For this reason major emphasis is being placed on baseline ecological investigations and reserve vigilance. Despite the many problems associated with conservation projects of this magnitude, Pacaya-Samiria is well on its way to becoming the world's largest tropical multiple use project.

Grazing in protected areas

Grazing by domestic animals within some protected areas (for example Category VIII) may be allowed where it does not conflict with management objectives for the area. Any grazing must be strictly controlled as domestic animals can have a profound influence on the local environment. In many situations, however, the goat and the cow, like the plough or the axe, are incompatible with the aims of protection. This is particularly true in areas devoted to the protection of natural ecosystems or where the management of wild browsing and grazing animals is an important objective of the area. It is especially significant where such wild animals are a dominant ecological consideration, or where local people may come to view the protected area as an emergency grazing area for their stock in poor seasons. In this kind of situation, the acquiescence of the protected area manager in permitting livestock into his area can be a disservice both to the park and the areas surrounding it. The practice allows local herdsmen to overstock, thus promoting over-grazing and habitat degradation outside the park, and can result in habitat modification and a loss of species within the reserve itself.

Role of protected areas in improving tropical land-use practices

The poverty of many tropical countries is aggravated by poor land use. There has been a long history of population growth at the expense of land fertility. Original tropical ecosystems were highly productive but produced little human food per hectare so many have been converted to agriculture. While this has been very productive on the best lands, especially those which have been converted to irrigated rice, the cutting of trees and opening of the land to the effects of rain, sun, and wind and the added loss of organic material due to regular burning, have resulted in speedy deterioration of agricultural potential in many of the hilly or less fertile areas. Only where man is able to apply expensive irrigation, terracing, fertilisers and insecticides does tropical agriculture approach the productivity of temperate farmlands.

Some peoples in the humid tropics have developed quite complicated integrated multicrop systems with intensive cropping under trees. Cardomum in India, for example, has traditionally been grown under a wild tree canopy. Many indigenous peoples also have well-developed harvesting and management practices from which a great deal of valuable scientific knowledge could be gleaned. Such systems could be improved with more research and experimentation.

In more open areas, the use of wild or modified wild savannas and rangeland can also be greatly improved. In Zimbabwe the ranching of wild ungulates has been shown to have considerable commercial potential and many advantages over the use of cattle or other domestic stocks.

The research needed to improve tropical land-

24. Permitting limited grazing in a wildlife sanctuary in Nepal maintains good relations with local communities at the cost of some disturbance to the natural system. Balancing trade-offs in this way is a delicate matter. As a general rule, it is wiser not to allow grazing of domestic livestock in reserves.
Photo: WWF/J. Juan Spillett

use practices involves preservation of a wide range of natural species for selection and the provision of opportunities to study such species in the wild to determine their properties and the best ways of harvesting and marketing the benefits. National scientific institutes in tropical countries should give high priority to research programmes aimed at determining the potential uses of wild species, improving the qualities of wild genetic resources and making better use of tropical soils and ecosystems.

Protected area management authorities must recognise the importance of such research and encourage and accommodate as much research as is compatible with the objectives of a particular protected area. To do this they must foster good relationships with the scientific authorities in their respective countries.

As well as being excellent living laboratories for the pursuit of research objectives, and providing benchmarks against which to measure the environmental effects of alternative forms of land use, protected areas offer valuable facilities for the practical elements of education in many fields such as biology, botany, zoology, entomology, evolution, ecology, socio-biology, ethology, forestry, and agriculture. These sciences cannot be taught solely in a classroom. Practical learning from the examination of wild living creatures is necessary, and such educational benefits help justify the existence of the protected areas.

Local preference in employment

Directly and indirectly, a protected area can enhance employment opportunities in the region. A certain number of local people may be employed directly by the management authority, or in catering for visitors to the area or providing ancillary services. In some cases a park or reserve can stimulate the whole local economy, especially if the monies deriving from the reserve and its visitors are used and circulated within the region. Paid employment may be less easily recognised as a benefit by the local communities, however, because payment for labour is not always clearly related to the protected status of the area. It is valuable to underline the relationship between regional employment and other benefits through the protected area extension and information programme. Whenever possible, local people should be employed as reserve staff or as concessionaires in preference to outsiders from more distant towns. This keeps locally generated wealth within the communities immediately adjacent to the protected area (see Chapter 10, pages 209-215).

Provision of social service – roads, health, assistance grants

Expanded social services should be provided to local people as a benefit of their proximity to a protected area and to reduce their dependence on the adjacent protected area for harvestable products.

Many of the threats and abuses to reserves result because people simply have no alternative but to steal wood or poach. Since these activities are often hard work, uncomfortable, risky or even dangerous, and are often only marginally profitable, many offenders can be persuaded to halt their illegal activities if they are provided with other ways of earning a living. The management authority of a reserve may solve the problem more effectively by investing in development of social services and alternative employment than by increasing law enforcement.

Government can provide many forms of special assistance to rural people including:

- Agricultural and grazing improvement schemes
- Road improvement schemes
- Water, sewage and electricity services
- Schools, clinics and dispensaries
- Direct grants for land impovement
- Loans or credit facilities for individual farmers
- Alternative land rights
- Establishing plantations on village lands or in buffer zones
- Creating local employment by stimulating local industry.

As a guide to understanding what the needs of local villagers are, Example 6.10 provides an outline of a survey conducted in Liberia on this topic.

Since protected areas which are developed for tourism become showpiece areas of a country, local government may be willing to promote development in surrounding areas. It pays to make clear to the local people the fact that they are getting preferential treatment, and that this is due to their privileged location close to the protected area. These benefits should be emphasised by the extension and information programme of the reserve. The examples of Amboseli National Park in Kenya and India's rural community policy show how successful this approach can be (see Examples 6.7 and 6.11).

Example 6.10: Understanding village needs through use of village data sheets

(The following data sheet was developed for use in a survey of villages surrounding protected areas in West Africa)

Date _Jan. 18, 1982_

Village/Town name _Jalays Town_   Town chief _Sobah, Sammy_   Age _56 yrs_

Location _3 mi. E. of Sinoe Road – 3 mi. N. of Juarzon_

No. Houses _20_   District _Pynelown District_

Chiefdom data _Paramount Chief – Harry Wallace (living in Pynetown)._

Languages (1) _Sarpo_   (2) _____   (3) _____

Population: Total _140_   Men _____   Women _____   Children _____

Historical data _Town is 50+ years old._

Electricity: yes (no)   Water system: yes (no)   Telephone: yes (no)

Occupational data _1. Subsistence farmers_

2. Public workers – three

3. Teacher – one

Health care _at Juarzon – 1 hr. 30 min. walk to clinic_

Transportation _no vehicles owned in village – passenger bus comes twice weekly to village_

Road access _good Laterite road – completed 1967._

Food supply/Food crops grown _rice, cassava, plantain, bananas, sweet potato, corn, country beans, egg plant, palm nuts_

Cash crops _rice, plantain, sweet potato, some corn_

Livestock raised _sheep, goats, chickens, cattle_

Primary meat sources: beef _5_   fish _3_   poultry _2_   pigs _no_   goats _4_   bushmeat _1_

Secondary meat sources _(especially "deer" and monkeys)_

Closest market _Juarzon_

Education/Schools _temporary primary school – need permanent structure_

Closest 1 _Jalays Town – Grades 1-6 – 125 students (40 from Jalays Town)_

Closest 2 _Greenville_

Teachers: _two_

Names: _J. Isaiah Sanwon, Harry Suo_

Resident with most education _Isaiah Sanwon_   Age _40 yrs_

Famous residents (or past residents) _Commissioner Worjest (Pynetown)_

Primary needs: Plans for primary needs
1 _Health care_   _no plan_
2 _Drinking water supply_   _possibility of self-help program_
3 _Permanent school structure_   _promised by govt. but never built_
4 _Transportation for marketing_   _/_

Enter data: (Best): __Peter Triesh – interviewed him__
__Phillip Whie__
__John Sunday__

Wildlife:
Proximate wildlife _(W. side of Sinoe River) – Maxwell's duiker, Black duiker,_
cane rat, chimpanzee, bush cow, Jentinck's duiker, pigmy hipp.
Zebra duiker, crocodile
Secondary wildlife _Red colobus, Black colobus, bongo, Leopard, forest hog,_
otter

Tertiary wildlife _elephant – becomes "secondary" during rainy season_

Not in area ___/___

Bushmeat source: 1. __"deer"__   2. __monkeys__

Prices (per pound, quarters, etc.) _Small "deer" = $1.50-2.00/quarter;_
water chevrotain = $2.50/quarter because of flavor

Town laws regulating wildlife _do not kill chimpanzee – thought to be_
ancestor; bad luck to bother them – also not allowed to eat hyrax

Species affecting agriculture _cane rat, bush pig, porcupine – also_
monkeys problems, chimps occasionally eat some sugar and bananas.

Person completing this survey __P. Robinson__

Dates: _____January 1982_____

Example 6.11: *Special benefits for rural communities living adjacent to wildlife reserves*

In 1983, the Task Force of the Indian Board for Wildlife recommended that government agencies should recognise the rural areas surrounding wildlife reserves as Special Areas for Eco-Development (SAED) and suggested a list of the various activities and restraints for agencies operating in SAEDS.

Forestry
- Strictly wildlife-orientated forestry operations in buffer zones.
- Restricted community uses of forests in buffer zones.
- Soil conservation in eroded areas.
- Pasture development and afforestation of denuded areas and planning forest management primarily to meet the pasture and firewood needs of local communities.
- Monocultures to be discouraged and efforts to be made to preserve and regenerate natural diversity in forests.

Soil Conservation
- Contour bunding of fields and other soil conservation works in village areas.

Agriculture
- Develop and apply improved dry farming techniques for marginal lands.
- Develop improved seeds and fertiliser regimes.
- Cash crops may be introduced where likely to be more profitable in preference to cereals.

Animal Husbandry
- Gradual reduction in cattle population and improvement of breed through castration of scrub bulls and controlled fertilisation of cows and she-buffaloes in proper health and age with bulls of good breed.
- Establishment of fodder farms where feasible.
- Discourage goat-keeping and in no case sponsor any goat-keeping programme in the SAEDs.

Irrigation
- Take up diversion or diversion cum storage type micro-minor or minor irrigation schemes.
- Support soil conservation of forest and agricultural lands as a part of catchment treatment for major irrigation projects in lower reaches.

Tribal Welfare and Rural Development
- Activities when sponsored through special programmes of these departments must conform to the above items listed for various sectors.
- Promotion of local art and handicraft with captive sale outlets in tourist complexes of well-visited wildlife reserves.

All Agencies
- Preference in employment to local people.

Source: Government of India, 1983

Drawing the line – settlements and war games

'URGENT STOP ARMY INTEND TO USE RESERVE FOR WAR EXERCISES STOP PLANS INCLUDE SIMULATED INVASION COUNTERATTACKS INFANTRY UNITS STOP ROAD 10M WIDTH TO BE BUILT ALLOWING HEAVY TANKS STOP ORIGIN FROM GENERALS STOP NO PERMITS ISSUED AND AGENCY NOT INFORMED STOP INSIST ON CANCELLATION REPEAT CANCELLATION PLANS IMMEDIATELY AS DAMAGE WILDLIFE AND HABITAT OBVIOUS STOP HIGH LEVEL INVOLVEMENT LIKELY STOP REPLY AWAITED REGARDS PARK WARDEN.'

The above cable arrived at headquarters in time to alert the protected area management authority and halt the planned military exercise in an important nature reserve, but it underlines the dangers inherent in allowing military access to reserves.

The manager must realise that when he allows any exploitative use of a protected area he has lost some of his control over that area. He has given away privileges and will be asked for more. Individually, each request may seem small and easily accommodated within the management objectives of the reserve but these uses become cumulative to the point where the integrity of the reserve may be threatened. The manager or his superiors

must have authority to refuse serious incursions. Protected areas are established primarily for protective functions and any use or exploitation should only be allowed if it does not compromise these overriding objectives. Chapter 8 gives guidelines on the compatibility of various types of utilisation but in all cases there must be strict limits.

Destructive war exercises (they do not have to be dangerous – the Zambian army has been 'training' in Blue Lagoon National park for five years with unknown effects on wildlife), uncontrolled human settlements and intensive cultivation other than the simplest planting practised by indigenous peoples have no place in protected natural area management. If in doubt, the manager should always opt for safety and deny further utilisation. Sometimes it may be necessary to refuse certain uses which, though theoretically compatible with the objectives of the area, in practice cannot be controlled successfully or may lead to even heavier demands in the future. This may be no simple matter, especially if the intended users of the protected area carry more political power than the manager. In such cases he must ally himself with additional voices such as appeals to the head of state, alliances with other ministries or seeking the support of NGOs or public media.

Amboseli: a case study in resolving the conflict between man and wildlife (from Western, 1984)

The Amboseli ecosystem in southern Kenya typifies the problems of conserving large mammal communities in Africa. Like many other parks Amboseli's wildlife migrates seasonally beyond the confines of the park boundaries – in this case onto land owned by Masai pastoralists. Traditionally the Masai were subsistence herders, but as their lifestyle changed to a more settled existence they became increasingly unwilling to accept wildlife on their lands since the animals contributed nothing to the local human economy, even though the value of wildlife nationally through tourism was considerable.

The Amboseli basin, fed by permanent springs from Kilimanjaro, is the only source of permanent water in the region. The spring-fed swamps traditionally attracted the Masai and their growing cattle herds during periodic droughts. Wildlife also concentrated around the swamps, making the area a major tourist attraction. The fragile vegetation could not tolerate the dual stress.

Matters came to a head when the Masai, fearing the creation of a national park and exclusion from their traditional grazing rights, lobbied for land tenure to the entire region including the Amboseli basin. Revenues from tourism went only to the Kajiado County Council 150 km away and contributed nothing to the local economy. Wildlife had traditionally served as the Masai's 'second cattle' during droughts but now hunting was banned. Why then should the Masai lose their traditional dry season grazing grounds to benefit the Government, the Council and the tourist? Their own answer was to seek exclusive land rights and to spear much of the wildlife, especially rhinoceros.

Ecological studies showed that both wildlife and livestock migrated in essentially the same fashion between wet and dry season ranges due to water limitations. The dispersal of wildlife over some 5000 sq. km during the rainy season created insurmountable obstacles to conserving the whole ecosystem; some 6000 Masai, 48,000 cattle and 18,000 sheep and goats depended on the same area and could not be relocated elsewhere. Over 80 per cent of the wildlife migrants concentrate each dry season around the 600 sq. km of the basin but this area was inadequate as a self-sustaining national park. It was calculated that the large herbivore population would decline by 40-50 per cent if confined permanently to the basin. Similarly, if the Masai were deprived of the basin's water and swamps their livestock would decline by half.

A water diversion scheme was completed in 1977 whereby water from the springs is piped outside the park boundaries, creating artificial swamps for the Masai herds. This removed the domestic cattle from the park but the wildlife migrants still needed access to Masai lands. A plan was drawn up whereby in return for continued access to the entire ecosystem Amboseli's wildlife could contribute economically to the landowners through a grazing compensation fee (to cover their livestock losses to wildlife migrants), through hunting and cropping on their land and by accommodating tourist campsites and lodges. The net monetary gain of the park per year from continued use of the Masai lands would be approximately $US 500,000 and the benefits from the park to the Masai would ensure them an income 85 per cent greater than they could obtain from livestock alone after full commercial development.

Perhaps the single most successful aspect of the plan has been the demonstration to the Masai ranchers that they can benefit from the park. Over the years, the Masai have shifted increasingly to a cash economy as their per capita livestock holdings have fallen – the result of drought losses and increasing human population. The park has become a source of employment, revenue and social services. An annual compensation fee of $US 30,000 covers the losses the Masai sustain in accommodating the park's wildlife. A wildlife committee meets monthly with the park warden to discuss matters of mutual concern, interest and benefit. The Masai have successfuly negotiated a plan to relocate the tourist campsite on the group ranch where it adds to the ranchers' wildlife income and helps reduce the pressure of visitors in the park. Firewood and road gravel are collected from the ranch, thereby earning the owners additional income and reducing the impact on the park. The newly completed park headquarters is located in the south-eastern corner of the park where it interferes minimally with wildlife and tourism and provides a local community centre with a school and medical facilities.

A direct measure of the improved circumstance in Amboseli since 1977 can be gauged by the increased numbers of wildlife in the ecosystem and especially the park. Elephant had declined from over 600 in the 1960s to less than 480 by 1977, reflecting the poaching levels country-wide. Their numbers have since increased to over 620, with few animals poached. Rhino were virtually exterminated by 1977 largely as a result of spearing by the Masai to show their political dissatisfaction with their prospects in Amboseli. Since then the population has increased to 14 with no animals killed, despite continuing losses elsewhere in Kenya. Other species, especially zebra and wildebeest, have increased substantially due to the exodus of domestic stock, which formerly made up 60 per cent of the liveweight of the basin's animals. Wildlife has redistributed more uniformly through the park following the removal of Masai settlements. The increased numbers and wider distribution should allow higher visitor capacity for a given level of impact. If hunting is also resumed after the temporary national ban imposed in 1977, the income of the ranchers from wildlife in the dispersal areas and from tourist revenue should increase substantially.

The problems of conflicting land use experienced at Amboseli are faced by nearly all African savanna parks and reserves. At Amboseli the 15-year programme has created an integrated use of the ecosystem by including local landowners in the benefits of the park, thereby permitting continued animal migrations beyond its boundaries.

Most parks could support but a fraction of their present biological diversity if their wildife were barricaded from surrounding lands. However, most of the earth's surface will remain rural, a checkerboard of farmland, ranchland, wilderness, etc., all areas that can support wildlife. The Amboseli lesson can be applied to much of the rest of the world – benefit can flow to people from preserving wildlife in the areas outside parks. The challenge that faces conservation is to ensure that wildlife does survive beyond the parks by ensuring that its benefits there exceed its costs.

Example 6.12: Lake Dakataua: a failure to communicate

The example of Lake Dakataua in Papua New Guinea illustrates the problems of establishing protected areas held by local people with traditional land rights. Lake Dakataua is a caldera lake in an area of volcanic activity. Natural features include hot springs, mud flows and dormant volcanoes. The main natural vegetation is lowland rain forest and there is a variety of wildlife including crocodiles.

The area around the lake is sparsely populated. The main village, Bulu Miri, has about 150 inhabitants. The people live mainly by subsistence agriculture, hunting and fishing; shell collecting is also a source of income.

In nearby areas of West New Britain there had been considerable economic development associated with the timber industry and oil palm growing. It was feared that the unique natural environment of th area around the lake might be destroyed unless measures were taken to protect it. In 1975, a park wa proposed to cover 10,350 ha, including the lake and the land around it. Other government department were consulted and raised few objections; there were not thought to be any valuable minerals or othe resources in the area.

At this stage, when it seemed likely that the park would be established, a group of local land-owner started to protest against it. Although the Minister for the Environment and Conservation himself me with local people and left satisfied that all had agreed to the park, there still seem to have been som doubts among the land-owners. Among the questions they asked were:

- Would they or the Government get the entrance fees from visitors to the park?
- For how long would their land be alienated?
- Would the National Parks Board build a road to the park from the nearest town, Talasea?
- Would their traditional rights to hunting be allowed?

The matter is still not resolved and the park has not yet been established.

The Lake Dakataua case exemplifies some of the difficulties in negotiations with customary land-owners. There is the need for general agreement within the group to the transfer of land. There are problems caused if land-owners are absent during the early investigations and meetings. There are the obstacles caused by dissension within the group and by the political aspirations among its members. There is also the difficulty that land-owners may have in understanding the implications of park development and natural resource conservation. The land-owner generally perceives the establishment of a park as a means by which he can get greater benefit from the resources of the area. In addition to the rent or purchase price, there may be income from tourists or from employment in the park. There may also be the opportunity to obtain roads and other government services. However if other types of development, such as a timber project, seem to offer greater monetary rewards and services, then it is inevitable that many rural people from poor and disadvantaged areas will prefer this type of development.

The education and extension role of national parks officers is obviously important in helping to explain the objectives and implications of park development. There is a need for full discussion during investigations and to follow these up when problems arise. Lack of staff and finance have too often been constraints in preventing park investigations and establishment.

Source: Eaton, 1985

7

Communication and Public Relations for Protected Areas

Introduction

In theory, the manager of a protected area could 'go it alone' and protect his 'closed area' from all unnatural disturbances and threats. Although such a policy might be one way to protect an ecosystem, it is unlikely to win public support and without public support no reserve is secure in the long term. Ultimately, the management of resources is *for* people and must be undertaken in a social framework. The survival of a protected area depends heavily on the attitudes of the local people, and public support at both the local and national level is a critical component of management. A vital part of any manager's job is to justify to higher authorities, and to the wider public to which they in turn are responsible, the existence of the protected area, the management policies chosen, and the expenditure incurred in applying such management

Land and water for reserves will only be gazetted if politicians, governors and other decision-makers understand the ecological and economic needs for protected areas, and the genuine benefits arising from them. Government agencies and their administrators are usually more concerned with balance of payments than balance of nature. It is up to the conservation lobby to stimulate their interest and encourage them to promote the benefits of conservation.

In the short term, it may well be enough to convince the leader of a country or local governor that the establishment of a protected area would be a good thing. He simply orders it and it is so. But what about his successor? And what about the general public? How long will they accept the status quo? As pressures for land increase, pro-

tected areas will not survive intact unless the real benefits they confer are appreciated by the whole community.

India, with its large and expanding human population putting increasing pressure on land and natural resources, has realised the need to elicit public support for wildlife conservation and protected areas. First, the Task Force of the Indian Board for Wildlife (Government of India, 1983) assessed the levels of awareness and apathy towards wildlife conservation among different sections of the public and endeavoured to determine the causes. Their findings, outlined below, apply to many countries in the tropics.

- Urban people, upon whom the influences of a depleted or an optimum wilderness are subtle and indirect, are often indifferent to wildlife conservation. Since most decision makers and professionals emerge from this group, lack of concern cripples the support needed for wildlife conservation and protected areas.
- The outlook of rural people is determined by the degree of their dependence upon forests for pasture, firewood, timber and other products. Many communities in the neighbourhood of reserves sustain themselves by eroding marginal land and depleting forest pastures. Their precarious existence may be threatened by enforcement of restrictions in wildlife reserves and this can trigger antagonism towards protected areas.
- The younger generation – both urban and rural – must be viewed as a separate group. Their concern for wildlife will remain largely

25. Widespread public support is a powerful way to influence politicians. Hundreds of young Kenyans
drew attention to the destruction being wrought by illegal poaching. The students made their own
placards and collected 8000 signatures on a petition to the President.
Photo: WWF/Wildlife Clubs of Kenya

undeveloped unless they are exposed to conservation education and interpretation at an impressionable age and made aware of its values and significance.

To achieve long-term support for a protected area programme and to encourage real appreciation of individual reserves, it is, therefore, vital to gain widespread support at all levels of public and institutional sectors (see Example 7.1).

The language, degree of detail, focus and the channel of communication will vary according to the target audience. For instance, it is quite meaningless to quote the scientific names of rare species to land-hungry farmers, counterproductive to bore busy ministers with inessential details, and an ineffective use of time to talk about biological diversity to the army commander who wants to use the reserve for military exercises.

The message must be tailored to fit the audience. This is an important job, requiring professional communicators. At ground level, the manager of any reserve cannot escape involvement in the communications field and must develop his capacities in this direction, even though he was probably selected for quite different abilities. It is the manager who selects the information to be presented and it is he and his staff who have the immediate contact with visitors to the reserve and with neighbouring communities.

Example 7.1 Eliciting public support for wildlife conservation and protected areas – the Indian approach

A. Target groups and their sphere of influence

Politicians

Political Executive (Policy. Final decision and overall control)

Legislators (Legislation. Interaction between electorate and political executive)

Bureaucracy

Planners (Steering of over-all planning process and research allocation)

Administrators & Technocrats (Coordination of programmes and control over resource managers & development agencies)

Resource Managers Wildlife and Forests

Professionals Quality of programmes and their implementation

Enforcement personnel (Programme efficiency)

Public relations personnel (Programme acceptability)

Development Agencies & Resource Users

Development agencies: irrigation power, mining transport etc.(Environmental damage disproportionate to sustainable development benefit)

Tourism (potential threat of over-use of protected areas. promotion of conservation consciousness)

Marginal land users. Forest dwelling communities (while themselves handicapped by low resource productivity. pose immediate and serious threat to protected areas as well as to their own sustaining resource. the land)

Young People (potential future contributors to all spheres)

Other Citizens (Lack of consciousness weakens consumption-discipline. popular support for conservation and viability of non-

B. Ways and means to reach target groups

Audio-visual Aids
(All groups)

Literature
(Student community,
park visitors,
policiticans,
bureaucrats)

Field visits
(All groups including
tourists with appro-
priate intepretation
support)

Parliamentary and
Legislators
Environmental Forums
(politicians)

Environmental Education
(Technical, professional,
administrative students.
Trainees must have courses
as a part of their curricula)

Orientation Course
(In-service
administrators,
technocrats,
professionals

Curricula
(Young people)

Nature Camps
(Young people,
student community
from secondary to
university level)

NGOs
(All citizens,
particularly young
people, policiticans
bureaucrats and communities)

Field Demonstrations
Models of conservation
oriented land use

Effective Enforcements
(Communities, tourists)

Special Areas
for Eco-development
(Communities)

Media
TV, Radio, Press
(All groups)

Post Office
and Other Advertising
(All groups)

Source: Government of India, 1983

Visitor information and interpretation services

The most direct way for the general public to learn about the protected area is for them to see it for themselves. It is crucial that they get a good first impression. It must always be remembered that educating the public is not an end in itself for the protected area, but a means to an end. The reserve needs the support and goodwill of its visitors. They must be made to feel welcome. The way in which the manager addresses the public is through Information and Interpretation Services.

Interpretation in national parks differs from information in that it is not merely a listing of facts but tries to reveal concepts, meanings and the inter-relationships of natural phenomena. Interpretation serves to awaken public awareness of park purposes and policies and strives to develop a concern for protection. It should also educate the visitor to appreciate what the protected area means to the region and the nation. Interpretation should fill the visitor with a greater sense of wonder and curiosity about the natural surroundings and make his or her visit to the area more rewarding.

It is the opportunity of 'first-hand experience' with the 'real thing' that provides the principal distinction between interpretation and education. For example, an interpretative centre in a national park will introduce, clarify, and direct the visitor to the actual resource outside, whereas a museum building in a city generally functions as a destination in itself. A publication titled, 'The Birds of Manu National Park – and Where to Find Them' would clearly be interpretative; whereas, 'The Population Dynamics and Reproduction of Umbrella Birds', in itself, would not.

The objective of the visitor interpretation service should be to provide information, entertainment, stimulation and education in a pleasant and fascinating setting in order to win visitor support for the type of management being applied. It is thus a management tool, influencing behaviour, soliciting support and making the manager's job easier (see Sharpe, 1976).

Most of the visitor information and interpretation service will be presented within the protected area, and the local villages in the reserve's immediate surroundings. It is also important to advertise outside the reserve to attract visitors in the first place. They must know about the reserve, where it is, and what they can do there. The information service covers everything from brochures to film shows but the following types of information will generally need to be included in the protected area information service:

What there is to see and do – visitors will need this information to plan their visit and make best use of their time in relation to their particular interests. This information must also include the seasonal or daily options (e.g. there is a collection of scavengers around a carcase today).

How to see what you want – maps of the reserve and points of interest, with information on how to get there, distances, time, hardships involved, and hazards.

What visitors are looking at – basic information should be presented simply and briefly, but in an interesting fashion so that the visitor gains a greater understanding of what he/she experiences. This is where simple information is translated into interpretation.

How to behave in the reserve – as well as explaining the regulations of what is and is not allowed in the reserve, information should also be given on how to behave so as not to disturb current management operations, other visitors, and the natural features. Visitors should be cautioned not to misuse the reserve facilities, nor to deface physical features. Visitors should be acquainted with the basic etiquette of reserve use – no radios, no vandalism or graffiti, no littering, no collection of fauna or plant materials, no disturbance of wildlife (feeding, chasing, or tampering with nests), keep to designated trails or camp areas, and obey any relevant safety warnings. Visitors should be made aware of the maxim 'take nothing but photos, leave nothing but footprints'.

Why have a reserve at all – answer the basic questions. What is the purpose of protected areas? And why here? Explain the relationship of the protected area to its surrounding lands and its importance in the world system of protected areas.

What is there to attract visitors to come back again – give suggestions for trips of differing durations, centred on different locations, trips with different themes, e.g. wildlife viewing, birdwatching, hiking, camping. Mention noteworthy seasonal happenings, e.g. arrival of migratory birds or calving periods.

How visitors can help – suggest ways in which

impressed or interested visitors can help by becoming supporters of the reserve or of conservation organisations. Provide addresses of local clubs, societies, volunteer organisations, local political leaders and wildlife magazines.

Techniques

There are numerous techniques available to communicate information about the protected area, some of them very simple. All have their particular uses and it is wise to use several methods to get maximum effect. People differ very much in their needs and expectations and it is important to cater for different tastes. The dedicated and experienced animal watcher, for instance, will be happy to put up with considerable hardships and find out information for himself. The challenge to the manager is to attract not just the specialists but a wider audience from among the general public and to stimulate and enhance their appreciation of the area.

Some people prefer to be organised in groups and presented with a standard explanation by a guide, others prefer to find their own way around a trail system with the aid of an explanatory and informative brochure; yet others resent any attempt at organisation and want to 'go it alone'. Some people like to talk, some to listen, some to read information, others to see things. Below is a list of the most widely used methods for communicating with visitors and some hints as to their use.

Brochures and leaflets. These should be as colourful, attractive and interesting as possible. Leaflets should tantalise rather than fulfil. They are for wide distribution in tourist offices and the like. They should lure visitors to the reserve, give information on what can be seen and done there, how to get there and any special preparations required (e.g. bookings, permits, special equipment, clothes or food). The leaflet should outline the conditions and facilities available in and around the reserve and current costs of accommodation, or other expenditures. Brochures (available in several different languages if possible) provide the visitor inside the reserve with basic information to help him or her enjoy and make the most of his visit. This usually includes brief descriptions of the main attractions, a map, and a list of the park regulations. It is useful if the folded brochure fits comfortably into a shirt pocket; then it is more likely to be kept and not discarded as litter.

Specialised guides, keys and checklists. These are often appreciated by visitors with particular interests or those unfamiliar with the area, and sales of such items from park offices may help cover some of the reserve running costs.

Self-guided trails. These are trails of varying lengths, though usually fairly short, where groups or individual visitors stop to view features of interest. Visitors are provided with brochures which give them information about individual sites which are marked in some way, perhaps by a numbered post. Alternatively, the information may be on sign boards along the trail but these are less desirable as they tend to impinge on the natural surroundings and require greater maintenance, unless made of weather-resistant material such as stainless steel. In addition, a brochure can be taken home, shown to other people and thus multiply the education impact of the self-guided trail.

Guided tours. Here, a guide accompanies parties of visitors around a system of routes by foot, horse, boat, bus, or other means, pointing out and discussing natural features along the way. Such a tour has the advantage that the guide can adapt what he says to the particular group of visitors but this obviously requires more manpower than a system of self-guided trails. The method is especially useful with school children and tour groups when the guide may be the schoolteacher or tour leader and not one of the reserve staff. In any case guides must be fluent in the languages of reserve visitors.

Wilderness trails. These are simply well-marked trails for visitors to explore on their own on a 'see and discover' basis. Primitive camping sites and shelters may be provided.

Visitor information centres. These are special buildings in which more detailed information about the reserve can be displayed. Exhibits may include photographs arranged in wall or panel displays, map models of the reserve, stuffed animals or animal remains, diagrams of food chains, etc. Visitor centres are very useful for providing interest for visitors trapped by bad weather, or while they are waiting (e.g. for a tour guide or while a permit is being checked) or who want more information about the reserve. They are useful for showing natural processes, life histories and other features of the reserve that cannot be seen on a short visit, and what happens in the reserve at night or in other seasons. Where necessary, information centres can be enlarged or combined with education centres. Good examples are found in Royal Chitwan National Park in Nepal, Nairobi National Park in Kenya, and O Le Pupu-Pu'e in Western Samoa.

Education centres. These are special buildings capable of mounting more formal educational displays. They usually have facilities to hold classes or discussion sessions and are often equipped with audio-visual equipment for slideshows or films. Permanent ongoing audio-visual presentations may be exhibited in education centres or information centres. Good examples are found in Murchison Falls National Park, Uganda, and Volcan Poas National Park in Costa Rica.

Botanic gardens or animal orphanages. These are interesting sites where visitors can get a closer view of some of the plants or animals found in the

reserve and identify better some of the things they have seen in the wild. They sometimes combine with other functions such as a reserve orphanage, hospital or rehabilitation centre where young or sick animals are being nursed or trained to be eventually returned to the wild. For instance, orang utan rehabilitation stations in reserves in Sumatra and East Malaysia attract many visitors and information centres at such sites can be used to disseminate information about the whole reserve. Botanical plots can also serve as research plots as in the Cibodas Botanic Gardens in Indonesia and botanic gardens on many of the islands of the West Indies.

Informal contact. Reserve staff moving about their normal duties will casually engage visitors in conversation as they meet them, asking how they are enjoying themselves, what they like to see,

26. The establishment of an animal care centre in a protected area tackles two problems together. It enables staff to care for deserted, injured or confiscated wildlife for eventual return to the wild and also serves as an attractive focus for conservation education. The orphanage at Nairobi National Park receives more visitors than the park itself.
Photo: WWF/F. Vollmar

27. This nature trail through montane forest in Morne Trois Pitons National Park in Dominica, West
Indies, stimulated much local use and sparked interest in the recreational values of the park.
Photo: J. Thorsell

and giving relevant current information, e.g. where animals have been sighted recently, lion kills and so on. All reserve staff must, therefore, be fairly proficient in recognising wildlife and knowledgeable about the natural history of the reserve, and may require some training in visitor communication.

Visitor opinion, gathering feedback. Communication is a two-way process. The protected area manager wants to know whether he is getting his message across and what the visiting public think about the reserve, what queries they have (this will shape the content of information services) and whether they have comments, advice, requests or complaints. Feedback comes from direct discus-

sion, invited comments in visitor books and suggestion boxes.

A number of good reference manuals give further details on developing information and interpretative facilities in protected areas (see Sharpe, 1976; Berkmuller, 1981).

Visitor control

To reduce visitor impact on the whole reserve, the management plan will normally identify specific visitor zones for different intensity of use. Provision of good, well-laid-out paths and other visitor facilities, information boards etc., in these selected areas ensures that visitors will be concentrated there. In this way management can often

Example 7.2: Displays and exhibits

Displays and exhibits have advantages as communications media in a protected area:

(a)   they are continuously available;
(b)   they are 'self-pacing';
(c)   they can use original objects and specimens;
(d)   they can be located indoors or outdoors, and can be portable.

Exhibit planning guidelines:

(a)   choose a theme, e.g. tropical rain forest;
(b)   identify the audience and aim to meet its needs;
(c)   define the objectives, e.g. education, entertainment, motivation, or public relations;
(d)   decide what type(s) to build, e.g. panels (text, diagrams, photographs), objects and specimens, dioramas, scale models, live exhibits.

Factors in exhibit design:

a)   location (inside, outside, in visitor centre);
b)   mobility and portability for use in schools, fairs;
c)   durability (and resistance to vandalism);
d)   position (preferably eye level) and viewing distance;
e)   lighting and sunlight's effects on colours;
f)   availability of materials, e.g. glass;
g)   attention-getting title;
h)   brief, readable, provocative labels;
i)   effectiveness of specimens and adequacy of accompanying text;
j)   exhibit sequence, use of partitions;
k)   maintenance and deterioration (if you can't maintain it, don't build it);
l)   use of pesticides and fungicides;
m)   desirability of visitor participation exhibits, e.g. wheel display, guessing games, peep box, electric panels ;
n)   live animal exhibits, e.g. terrariums, aquariums;
o)   plant, rock, and insect collections (must be attractively presented and interpretive);
p)   animal exhibits (obtained from road kills, mounted study skins, bird feeders, plaster casts or tracks, spoor).

Sources: Sharpe, 1976; Berkmuller, 1981.

Example 7.3: Guidelines for developing nature trails in protected areas

A.   *General characteristics:*

A nature trail should be *short* (0.5 to 1.5 km), with a walking time of 30 to 60 minutes.
Ideally, a nature trail is constructed as a *one-way loop* beginning and ending in the same place.
A nature trail is *informative*. Along the trail are signs or labels explaining its features. Signs can contain all the desired information, or simply numbers referring the visitor to an accompanying pamphlet.
A nature trail is *inviting*. It must have a clear, well marked beginning. It should be wide and flat enough to walk in comfort. It should have no steep climbs, muddy places, or physical obstacles.
A nature trail is clean and *well maintained*. Litter cans are often provided at the entrance and at rest stops. Vegetation and debris are regularly removed from the trail.

B. *Developing and constructing a trail:*

Conduct a thorough survey of the area where the trail is to pass. Make a list of all notable natural and historic features (e.g. salt licks, rock outcrops, viewpoints, vegetation, fossils, waterfalls). Mark these features on a sketch map and arrange a trail route to connect them.

Walk the route to check its length and access to noted features and to determine the feasibility of trail construction.

Disturb the natural scene as little as possible. Avoid unnecessary damage during construction by supervising workers carefully.

Clear the walking area of all obstacles along the trail and cut overhanging vegetation to a height of two metres. Avoid cutting large trees, and do not clear all debris down to bare soil. Fill depressions with rock or earth waste.

Build the trail with curves, avoiding straight stretches where possible. A winding trail is more interesting to walk. Avoid designs that 'double back', which may encourage visitors to take short cuts.

Avoid steep hillsides and waterlogged areas. Ensure that drainage runs off, not down, the trail; install water bars and drains. In some areas the trail may need to be raised on a wooden walkway or stepping stones.

At rest stops, provide simple benches.

At stream crossings or deep gorges, it may be necessary to build bridges. Steps may be cut in rock, or a fallen tree may be used for passage if it is wide enough for safety.

Provide a trail entrance sign with basic information (a map and the trail's length). Directional signs may be required at junctions.

C. *Interpreting the landscape along the trail:*

If possible, determine a theme (e.g. 'Vegetation of the Picachos Mountains') for the trail, and give the trail a name (e.g. 'Montane Forest Nature Trail') reflecting that theme. This adds to the interest and appeal of the trail.

Decide between (a) printed labels along the trail and (b) numbered labels referring to a printed leaflet.

At least 12 features, and at most 30, should be identified for interpretation. Information should be accurate, interesting, brief, and easy to understand.

A map must be provided, either on a sign or in a leaflet. Also consider providing a checklist of 'things to see along the trail'. A leaflet, if used, need not be expensive but should include sketches and diagrams and be visually attractive.

Sources: Sharpe, 1976; Berkmuller, 1981; Thorsell, 1984a

confine visitor activities to small areas without visitors feeling restricted or that most of the reserve is being denied them.

Since the whole support for the reserve and the national reserve system ultimately depends on public goodwill, staff should be helpful, courteous and polite at all times even if the visitors are sometimes a nuisance. Protected area staff must always set a good example to visitors and must themselves observe park regulations at all times. Staff should pick up litter even if they are accompanying visitors, and put it in the proper receptacles. Park staff should not feed nor frighten wildlife and should discourage visitors (or tour leaders) from doing so.

Where necessary, staff must be prepared to be firm but courteous with those dropping litter, graffiti artists, and people making too much noise or disturbing wildlife or other visitors. They may have to put out fires made in the wrong places, order removal of tents to proper campsites, or recall visitors from prohibited areas. Sometimes it may be necessary to enforce limits on how many visitors can enter a reserve or part of a reserve. It may even be necessary to periodically close a reserve to visitors in 'unsafe' times (e.g. floods, avalanches, fog, drought), critical wildlife breeding seasons or periods of adverse weather, or to give the staff a chance to repair damaged facilities and clean the area up for another visitor influx.

28. Two examples of visitor centres. The upper photo of the combined museum/visitor centre in Royal Natal National Park, South Africa, illustrates the importance of appropriate architectural design in natural areas. The lower photo from O Le Pupu-Pu'e National Park in Western Samoa is also appropriate for its tropical island setting.
Photos: J. Thorsell

29. The impact of visitors on protected areas may often be negative. Managers must limit visitor use to an appropriate level and establish the necessary controls and zones to safeguard natural values. The photo shows visitors in Galapagos Islands National Park allowed too close to the nesting frigate birds.
Photo: WWF/H. Jungius

Example 7.4: Visitor control in the Galapagos National Park

The Galapagos Islands consist of 13 major islands and many smaller islets and rocks covering a total land area of 7881 sq km. The whole area lies within the Galapagos National Park administered by the Parks Department of Ecuador. The islands' geological history and their long isolation from the mainland of South America have resulted in a unique flora and fauna and make them an ideal natural laboratory for the study of evolution and adaptation.

Visitor use, by both international and domestic visitors, is regarded as an important function of the park. Organised tourism began in 1968 and many thousands of visitors tour the islands annually, attracted by the world famous fauna, the animals' fearlessness, and the dramatic volcanic scenery. To enable large numbers of tourists to visit the area, the park authority has implemented a strict system of visitor controls. Since all visitors must tour the islands by boat they sleep on board and there is no visitor accommodation within the park. The park authority authorises and regulates concessions to tour boat operators. The concessionnaires are controlled as to prices, quality of service, safety and health standards, number and location of visits and boat capacity. Tour boats draw most of their crews from among the islanders and thereby provide employment and contribute to the local economy.

Visitors must be accompanied by park-certified guides. There are two grades of guide: auxiliary guides who can accompany up to twelve tourists; and naturalist guides who must be competent in visitor languages and can accompany larger parties. Guides follow a training course of four to six weeks and are tested on their competence to accompany and inform visitors every three years. Tour boat concession-naires pay a concession fee and each visitor pays an entry fee, income that should be used for park maintenance.

The park authority has established a visitor reception centre at the airport on Baltra Island, the main point of entry, and at the port of Baquierizo Moreno for the few visitors that come by sea. These reception centres provide a link between arriving visitors and concessionnaires so that visitors can select a tour that best suits their interests and finances.

The tourist traffic is supervised and channelled by the park administration to distribute the tourist load among specially-designated Intensive Use Zones or Visitor Sites. The Intensive Use Zones are carefully selected areas, small in total extent, of high visitor interest. In these zones, visitor facilities are provided as necessary, such as boat anchorages and improved trails. To lessen the impact of visitors on the biotic communities, no more than 90 visitors are permitted in any visitor site at any one time. This is achieved by staggering the arrival time of large tour boats and encouraging small operators to visit these areas at off-peak periods. The tour concessionnaires and guides regulate the sites where visitors land to maintain levels of visitor use. Any unauthorised landings can cost the tour operator his concession and the guide his licence.

The sole purpose of land-based visitor facilities is to enable visitors to observe the outstanding natural and scenic features of the park with minimum impact on the resource. On most islands, development is limited to simple landing stages and primitive signed trails. Visitors are not allowed to stray from the paths but can approach close to bird nesting and resting areas along guided trails. Overnight camping is permitted at two sites within the visitor sites of the park; although a 'dry' campsite exists there are no other facilities.

The management authority of Galapagos National Park has evolved a practical and sensible regime of visitor control which allows visitors close access to the island's unique wildlife. By confining visitor use to small areas the park authority is able to minimise disturbance, thereby protecting the park's greatest asset – its wildlife.

Source: Master Plan Parque Nacional Galapagos, 1974

Protected area reference centre/collection

Over the years, park managers and their field staff will collect much information on abundance of wildlife, seasonality of fruiting, flowering, animal breeding, and climatic data. In addition, visiting research workers will produce valuable scientific information, maps, species lists, reports, studies, and papers. Park staff will also need access to a small library of relevant textbooks, fieldguides and other such reference material.

It is very useful if this information is kept securely in a special place where scientists and management authorities have access to it. It is important that such information is kept on file, and that scientists who have worked in the reserve are required to leave copies of useful information and to send their subsequent publications to the protected area manager. As more information is added this data bank becomes more valuable and can help guide future research in the reserve.

The reserve library will hold copies of all the reports pertaining to the reserve, manager's logs, rangers' notebooks, reports and photo documentation. Ideally, original documents should be held in archives in a strong room. In addition, this collection of information may be combined with specimens of plant or animal materials collected in the reserve as reference material. Such a library should be kept for reference only; source material and books should not be lent out for long periods. This is especially important in developing countries where books are difficult to obtain and replace.

Schools and education service

The sooner the reserve manager communicates the conservation message to his potential supporters the sooner it will begin to bear fruit. Moreover, the attitudes of the local people (those most affected by the restrictions of the reserve) will mellow as they begin to appreciate the reserve and its benefits. Using the reserve for teaching purposes is of benefit to both the reserve and the local community and through schools and youth groups the management can extend its message to the younger generation.

Protected area managers should contact local schools directly or through the local education offices to offer facilities for field excursions or classroom lessons about the reserve. Ideally, each reserve should have at least one education officer who is responsible for all arrangements to ensure that school parties arrive in a well-planned manner within the capacity of the reserve, generally avoiding weekends, holidays and other busy periods. Sometimes school visits may be day trips; in other cases, parties may need to stay in dormitories or tents for a longer trip. This may involve the reserve establishing special facilities where organised groups of young people and others can attend appropriate educational courses under the supervision of park staff. These can be simple and quite inexpensive. Sometimes the school's own biology teacher will act as guide and instructor for the visit, but more probably some reserve staff will be involved and will need to be adequately trained. Obviously, the programme arranged will depend on the age and previous experience of the children but extension work with children is most important and worthwhile and may have a powerful effect on their attitudes towards nature and conservation.

30. Group photo of a conservation education programme operating in the Khao Yai National Park, Thailand. It is very important to use parks for education to win support and understanding for the conservation movement, particularly among young people.
Photo: WWF/Association for the Conservation of Wildlife, Thailand

31. A painting competition organised by the Alipore Zoological Gardens as part of Project Tiger helps arouse interest in wildlife among young children in Calcutta, India.
Photo: WWF-India

32. Get them while they're young. World famous ornithologist Salim Ali winning new converts for conservation at a children's wildlife camp in India – an invaluable investment in the future.
Photo: WWF-India

One useful teaching tool which has been found to be suitable for some countries is the production of a teacher's sourcebook such as The Green Book of Fiji, to help the teacher in his or her presentation of a reserve's significant features, both for use in pre-visit classroom sessions and during field excursions to the reserve. This frees park staff from the need to supervise lessons, and results in higher standards of teaching. The park learning experience does not end when the field trip terminates. Often at this point student interest and receptivity to the concepts of conservation and protected areas are heightened. It is appropriate to suggest activities and study topics which prove to be a continuation of the first-hand observations made during the field trip. Students should be encouraged to share information, stories and pictures collected during their trip. They should also be given information about conservation-oriented organisations, magazines and conservation activities that they can pursue at school or at home.

It is vital to develop a local conservation lobby through Natural History Societies, Nature Lover Clubs (as in Indonesia) and the establishment of permanent educational facilities in parks. Young people make keen and enthusiastic supporters for parks and other protected areas. Nature seems to hold an innate fascination for children which they later grow out of unless it can be sustained through the development a more mature interest than their initial sense of wonder.

Local village extension service

Usually the nearest neighbours of the reserve are the greatest potential threat to its integrity but can also be the greatest asset for its protection. Local villagers can make the manager's job difficult, impossible or easy depending on how well or otherwise they accept the principles of the park and are brought to understand how it brings them benefits, not hardships.

Winning the support of the local people at grassroots level and the speed with which this occurs will depend very much on whether local communities do indeed benefit from the park and not just lose access to resources that would otherwise be available to them. Where the benefits accruing to local people are clear and readily-felt, there will be little difficulty in getting local communities to support the park. Where the benefits are not so obvious and the local people still see the park as a restriction on land needs, the manager will have greater difficulty in gaining their cooperation. He will need considerable patience and persuasion, an effective guard force and a major public relations programme.

The manager must take the job of winning friends outside his own protected area boundaries by carrying his message to the surrounding villages. This process of extension work may include posting notices and posters, holding slideshows or film shows in villages, holding discussions with neighbouring land-users or farmers' committees, and giving talks in local schools and to other concerned groups. Nor must the cnvironmental education have to be wrapped in a conservation package. It can be integrated into other types of extension materials. The message to be carried to these villages must achieve various aims:

- explain why it is important to establish protected areas;
- show why this particular area has been selected;
- indicate what benefits derive to the local community and local economy;
- identify alternative sources of land, forest, etc., which villagers may exploit (if applicable), or, in some cases, explain entitlement to compensation payments;
- develop a local sense of pride in the richness of local nature;
- emphasise the Government's determination to make the reserve a success;
- point out that law-breaking for selfish ends is a community offence not just an offence against the government.

Mobile education units are particularly suitable for this sort of extension work. The mobile education unit can consist of no more than a man on foot with posters and colouring books. More generally, however, it implies a vehicle, equipped with a portable generator, slide and film equipment and a staff capable of setting up mobile and impromptu performances in villages and/or schools to show conservation education materials. Such material must be relevant to the country and the particular reserve. It is useful for the park authority to have someone on the staff capable of producing audio-visual material. This sort of training may be given *in situ* by instructors from agencies such as the International Centre for Conservation Education (ICCE) or park staff may be sponsored for extra training at ICCE or elsewhere by international agencies (see Chapter 12).

Mobile unit staff can also hold discussions with village representatives to promote conservation and discuss village grievances. It may also pay the manager to invite village leaders on a conducted tour of the reserve to win over the most influential people in the village. This is done for instance in Khao Yai National Park, Thailand, and in Meru National Park, Kenya.

Example 7.5: Protected areas and people – the Indian approach to conservation education

A Suggested List of Topics for Educational Programmes

Concept of ecosystems, highlighting the inevitable interdependence of all life forms, including man.

How can life support systems, e.g. soil, climate, clean air and water, vegetation, etc., be sustained? Show how man has been a destroyer and how he can be the preserver in the interest of generations yet unborn.

The great diversity of our ecosystems, flora and fauna.

Why we need wildlife conservation and how we can achieve this through a network of protected areas.

Description of some important wildlife reserves and their attributes, particularly 'behind-the-scene characteristics' like humus and soil fertility, water regime, flora and minor and micro-fauna.

Notes on some animals, birds, reptiles, insects etc., explaining their habitats, their behaviour, the benefits they afford to mankind.

Religious and traditional background of conservation, non-violence and compassion towards other life forms, old literature, Aesop and Panchatantra tales.

Suggested Topics for Media Programmes

What is eco-development and why is it important for all people, particularly the rural public? How are wildlife reserves relevant?

How can wildlife reserves be not only compatible but also helpful to reserve-side communities by improving the life support systems?

Conservation means both preservation and wise use of the bounties of nature. In order to conserve our natural heritage, we must have completely protected areas. Explain the core/buffer/multiple-use area concept. Emphasise the need for discipline as an aspect of wise use.

Overall conservation strategy for the country. Need to adopt conservation-orientated land use, including use of forests for timber, firewood, and grazing.

Traditional cultural and religious background of conservation. Animated films and features (including dramas by Field Publicity Units) on Panchatantra tales.

India's rich natural heritage in the form of diverse ecosystems and their rich associations of flora and fauna.

Features and films on important wildlife conservation projects, important wildlife reserves, and some spectacular animals, birds, reptiles and other minor fauna.

Source: Government of India, 1983

33. Mobile Education Units are a very effective means of achieving conservation extension in many developing countries.
Photo: WWF/R. Jeffrey/WLCS Zambia

Publicity and public relations

The protected area management authority must justify its whole programme to the general public and government officials. Similarly, the individual reserve manager must maintain public and government interest in his reserve. Publicity is particularly important for a reserve whose main function is to draw visitors.

The main objective of publicity is to arouse and maintain interest in the reserve's activities and show these off in a good light. For the manager of a protected area, this means general advertisement encouraging visitors to visit the area by such means as leaflets and other inexpensive measures. Advertising can be extended to whatever media are available: radio, television, cinemas, newspapers. It is also useful to generate news items about the reserve: what is happening, interesting events, animal stories, and visitor experiences. These can be placed in a variety of publications, both national and international.

Park managers in some densely-populated areas have realised the importance of public relations and have appointed full-time public relations officers to take charge of all communication affairs. The functions of such an officer could include:

• providing information to the general public on the department's activities through news media; activating sympathetic journalists, etc.;
• informing special interest groups (e.g., visitors, safari operators, hunters, bird groups);

34. Winning the support of leading politicians can create far-reaching results for conservation. The late Mrs Indira Gandhi, as India's Prime Minister, helped transform the face of conservation over a whole sub-continent.
Photo: WWF/Government of India Press Information Bureau

- providing educational materials for schools and teacher training;
- establishing means of internal communication in the department;
- organising in-service training programmes for staff.

The public relations officer will need skill in writing and editing; good contacts among the media and key decision makers; promotional and organisational skills for special events, and a flair for public speaking. His or her job entails determining the messages that the protected area should be communicating, identifying the audiences at which they should be directed and choosing the most appropriate method of communication. In particular, he/she must devote attention to the protected area's rural neighbours. He/she will identify the causes of any local hostility, discuss areas of misunderstanding or distrust; see what can be done to improve real grievances; and try to involve the local people further in management planning so that they receive and appreciate real benefits from the protected area.

Copy production is a time-consuming and difficult business. For protected areas which cannot afford a full-time public relations officer, it is useful to befriend a few sympathetic journalists and encourage them to write pieces about the reserve from time to time. Such pieces will be more interesting if the journalists are familiar with the reserve. It will pay the manager to invite local journalists to visit the reserve themselves and to keep them up to date with newsworthy events. They can also be mobilised to help combat threats to the reserve. Such press support has been very important in safeguarding the Taman Negara in Malaysia, the Silent Valley in India, and Aldabra in the Seychelles.

Park staff themselves should be encouraged to write articles about their park for local conservation magazines and international journals such as Swara, Suara Alam, PARKS Magazine, Tiger Paper, Puma Paper, Vida Silvestre and others.

There are also a number of professional photo-journalists who travel around the world writing articles about colourful and interesting places and experiences. It is usually worthwhile to show hospitality to such people, rather than feel exploited by them. The publicity they generate for the reserves more than pays for the effort needed to accommodate them.

Films can reach an even wider audience and may be very useful for encouraging overseas visitors. Permission to make a film in the reserve should be conditional on the provision of a free copy of the final film, to be used in further extension work.

Committees and dialogue

Another way to help develop better local relations is to establish special committees, to help advise the management authority and/or share decision making responsibilities. Any or all of the following committees may be useful to help in the management of a given protected area.

- Committees with local residents set up specifically to review reserve/village relations and in particular the management of buffer zones and other areas allocated for community use. Such committees can also discuss infringements of park regulations or village grievances, e.g. where wildlife are damaging village crops or stock. Conversely they are a channel through which the reserve management may complain about continuing abuses of reserve regulations by local villagers.
- Inter-departmental committees set up to handle coordination of reserve management activities and requirements with ongoing developments that may affect the reserve, e.g. building of local roads. Such committees generally have members from the local planning authority, tourism, and public works, and may also have non-aligned members to provide technical expertise on certain subjects.
- Advisory committees set up to advise the management authority on technical or scientific matters. In some cases these are set up independently by a particular group of interested parties who wish to have a forum for comment and a representative of the management authority is invited to attend meetings. Alternatively, the authority may only be sent the Minutes and Recommendations of the self-designated committee. In this latter instance, the advice can

often be counter-productive, especially if the management authority feels resentful at the outside committee involving itself in the authority's business. Sometimes advisory committees are constituted at the express request of the management authority to give special advice in a field where it feels its own expertise to be weak and in such circumstances these committees can be very useful. Depending on the issues under discussion, they may be rendered more effective when the members are free agents expressing their own views and not representatives of different interest groups, nor government servants.

Internal newsletter and information service

Many park authorities already produce an internal staff newsletter and regularly post news and information items on staff notice boards. Such an internal news service is good for staff morale yet need not take up much time nor staff resources. Through the newsletter, staff are given up-to-date information on what is going on in the park (and agency), successes and problems, VIPs visiting, visitor totals, wildlife news, and other articles of interest. This is not only interesting in itself but it makes the staff better informed for their discussions with visitors, and generally better equipped to do their own jobs.

Staff who rarely meet in their line of duties can get to know each other better through the newsletter. Guards and other staff members mentioned by name feel that their work is important and that interest is being shown in their activities. Staff can see how their own functions fit into the total picture and what the park management is trying to achieve. The individual staff member takes more pride in his or her own performance and is encouraged to make noteworthy personal achievements. Staff at all levels, including individual guards, should be enouraged to submit their own news items.

Conclusion

Good communication within and from a protected area management authority is an essential component of overall management. it facilitates cooperation, understanding, and appreciation and helps to minimise conflicts and problems. Unfortunately, public relations and other communication skills do not always 'come naturally' and staff may require some training in putting across the conservation message. Effort devoted to conservation education and communication with local communities usually pays off handsomely, even if the immediate dividends are difficult to quantify.

PART C

Managing Protected Areas

The role of tourism and the provision of facilities for tourism in protected areas has been well considered here at Tigertops Lodge in the Royal Chitwan National Park, Nepal.

8

Management of Natural Resources in Protected Areas

Introduction

Management of living resources in natural protected areas involves steering the ecosystem. This requires an understanding of ecological principles, an appreciation of the ecological processes operating in the protected area, and the acceptance of the concept that protected area management is a specialised form of land use.

Ecosystem management is such a technically demanding task and enormous responsibility that many people simply back away from the job and claim that 'Nature knows best'. This passive attitude, however, is also dangerous. Most reserves are already far too small, too isolated and too affected by man's influences – historically, directly, or indirectly – to maintain their original state if simply left alone. Leaving things be may be the easiest and cheapest course to follow but the decision to allow natural processes to continue without interference, i.e. apply a policy of 'benign neglect', is itself a management decision and must be taken with as much consideration as the decision to institute manipulative management.

What management is necessary will be determined by the objectives stipulated for the given area. In most cases, some active management will be required to reach or maintain these objectives. There is almost nothing in Nature that can be called a 'stable environment', even within the large blocks of undisturbed climax rain forest. The elements that managers wish to preserve in protected areas can easily be lost through lack of management simply because the nature of the reserve changes. Sub-climax situations proceed towards climax unless arrested by continuing influences such as cropping, regular burning, landslips and so on. Climax floras age and pass

through collapsing phases before the area becomes recolonised by pioneering plants which again pass through long and complex cycles of succession. By the time mature climax vegetation is reached again, if indeed it is ever allowed to do so, the nature of the soil will have changed and the species composition of the new forest will be different from the old.

All areas continue to change as new species are introduced by wind, animals, man or other agencies. Other species drop out through local extinction, diseases, pests and other ecological factors. By allowing surrounding habitats to be changed, man has enormously affected the remaining undisturbed patches. Because of the ' biological island effect' (see Chapter 3, pages 38-43), they will lose much of their original diversity unless artificial ways of maintaining genetic exchange and immigration with outside populations are developed, or buffers or corridors of similar habitats are established.

Clearly, a good deal of active management is needed to maintain the qualities managers wish to preserve in protected areas. However, it must also be stressed that interference with natural processes is fraught with dangers. Bad management can be worse than no management. It is not necessary to know how a car works to drive it safely but one must know the effects of the different controls on the car's behaviour. So too with ecosystems. It is dangerous to play with the controls until the effects are known. Ecological processes are often unpredictable because of their complex inter-relationships. Although ecological knowledge is growing rapidly, scientists are still so ignorant of the workings of many tropical ecosystems that it is wise to be cautious.

The balance of ecosystems

While no ecosystem is stable on this dynamic planet, some, in the short term, are far more stable than others. One of the basic considerations, from a management point of view, is whether the vegetation is in a climax (mature) or early stage of succession.

Thus protected areas in the two most widespread habitat types found throughout the tropics – rain forests and savannas – require quite different management prescriptions. Whereas savannas are rather unstable ecosystems balanced by climate, fire, wildlife use and human influences, primary rain forest is a climax situation. In order to conserve a savanna area manipulative management – controlled burning, the regulation of animal populations, cutting of vegetation, etc. – is essential. In rain forests, on the other hand, as little interference as possible is generally desirable to maintain the ecological climax and allow regeneration in disturbed areas.

Sometimes management decisions may be crucial in determining whether a unique ecosystem is preserved. For instance, a given protected area may preserve the unique vegetation growing on the side of a volcano; but the vegetation is only a transient stage between the last eruption and a future climax stage when the mountain becomes completely reforested. Allowing the process of natural reforestation to continue may mean loss of unique species. This can only be countered by an active management policy preventing such reforestation. Whether this is an appropriate management policy will depend on the original objectives of the reserve. Was it established to protect this unique flora (i.e. a particular combination of rare species), or to protect the watershed? In the latter case, the greater the forest cover the better. Was the reserve established for the study of the natural processes of vegetation succession, or to provide an attractive setting for visitors? Were the original objectives appropriate or do they need revision?

Take another hypothetical case. An area was originally a hunting reserve where vegetation was cleared to provide open grassy feeding areas to encourage large game. Later, however, the area is declared a nature reserve with the specified objective 'to protect the native wildlife in their natural environment'. After a few years of such protection, it is noticed that the area is becoming reforested and the number of large mammals is dropping. Since the main management objective was to protect the wildlife and their natural habitats, in this case large mammals and early succession stages of vegetation, the manager should apply active management measures such as clearing or burning shrubs and bushes to reopen the grazing areas. Habitat management will probably be restricted to selected areas of the reserve and elsewhere the vegetation will be allowed to evolve naturally towards a climax stage. The matter would have been even clearer if the original objective of the reserve had been phrased 'to protect the characteristic local wildlife, particularly the high density of large mammals, in as natural a habitat as possible'.

Once it is decided that active management is necessary to maintain an area in an early succession stage of vegetation, much consideration should be given to selecting the most suitable means; cutting, burning, grazing, selective ringbarking, etc., are all possible methods. It is safest to test the selected procedure on small-scale experimental plots before applying it over the whole area. Lack of detailed knowledge of species habitat requirements is a major constraint to protecting large mammals.

Maintenance of genetic diversity

Biological diversity is the variety of life forms, the ecological roles they perform and the genetic diversity they contain (see Wilcox, 1984). Genetic diversity is usually taken to mean the variety of different genes, as found within a breeding population, within a whole species or of all species found within a given area. Almost every individual living organism on this planet, apart from clones, possesses some unique genetic combinations so that in a sense genetic erosion or the loss of genetic diversity starts when the first individual plant or animal dies without reproducing. Genetic erosion is a gradual slide but it has steep steps at points where whole 'packages' of genetic qualities

Example 8.1: Managing gorilla habitat

Many animal species are sensitive to the loss of essential habitats. If the aim of management is to conserve a species population then the first need is to establish the species' habitat requirements.

Many large mammals prefer secondary vegetation. For instance gorillas move into areas of disturbed or cleared habitats, in particular the abandoned fields of shifting cultivators. Efforts to establish protected refuges for gorillas will fail unless the preferred habitat is maintained by periodically cutting back the vegetation. In the Virunga Volcanoes National Park, gorillas are found at very high altitudes, probably originally lured upwards by the lush vegetation on newly colonised ashscrees and lava flows. These areas now support forests of mature *Hagenia* woodlands which is sometimes described as the mountain gorillas' natural habitat. However, the *Hagenia* trees are colonisers and show no signs of regeneration. Eventually they will be replaced with some other form of vegetation, perhaps less lush than the original and unsuitable for gorillas.

If we are to conserve the last of these close relatives of man, then it may be necessary to apply active management to preserve their preferred habitat. The first step is to establish study plots in the animals' present range to determine what vegetation changes are occurring and how best to manage these areas for the benefit of the gorillas.

become irretrievably lost. Such danger points, in ascending order, include:

- local loss of a breeding population
- loss of a distinct subspecies
- loss of a species
- loss of a genus
- loss of a block of habitat
- loss of a whole habitat type
- loss of a biological sub-province.

Overall design of protected area systems should attempt to guard against the loss of the larger units such as habitat types. The manager of an individual protected area will be mostly concerned with protecting local populations and as part of this objective, maintaining as full a range of genetic diversity within those populations as possible. It is important to realise that preserving ecosystems is not the same as preserving species, nor is preserving species the same as preserving genes. It is possible to preserve a species but lose genetically distinct populations, a loss which may eventually contribute to the species' extinction.

Breeding populations of wild species are rarely continuous. Even in the same habitat contiguous populations may be genetically distinct, e.g. neighbouring clans of impala antelope in Chirisa Safari Area, Zimbabwe show genetic variation which reflects their breeding system. Most populations consist of large numbers of sub-units or demes which occupy different parts of the habitat, vacating or dying out in those patches where they

are not successful and recolonising from those parts where they are (Levins, 1968). There are sound genetic reasons why most species have evolved mechanisms (their social or dispersal systems) for limiting free genetic exchange. Most species have a system of occasional outbreeding or exchange between inbreeding demes. Such a pattern gives a higher chance of useful genes or combinations of genes being selected and fixed in wild populations than if such mutations were immediately swamped in the total gene pool.

The rate of recruitment of new genes must balance the rate at which genes are lost from the population if there is to be zero genetic erosion. As a general rule, smaller populations are more likely to lose genetic variability than larger populations. Sometimes population numbers may be so reduced that, without active management, the population will become so inbred that it is no longer viable. One way to preserve genetic diversity in small populations is to artificially encourage high rates of genetic exchange with other isolated populations of the same species, for example by exchanging or introducing new individuals (see Chapter 8, pages 164-8).

Although the management authority can and must take active measures to 'help' small, threatened populations, 'prevention is better than cure'. Good reserve design and making reserves as large as possible, and connected or linked by habitat corridors to other reserves, are the best ways to maintain genetic diversity.

Example 8.2: Genetic variability in wild populations: effective population size

Genetic variability plays an important role in the survival of populations. The production, maintenance and loss of genetic variability in species is determined to a significant degree by population size and structure. Populations of small size and simple structure tend to be more susceptible to the loss of genetic variability than large geographically-dispersed and subdivided populations. Loss of genetic variability can diminish the chances of survival of a population in two ways:

- inbreeding depression, which includes factors affecting general viability, reproduction and survival of individuals;
- loss of evolutionary potential, i.e. reduced ability to adapt to a changing environment.

Theoretically, 250 individuals is regarded by some as the minimum number of reproducing individuals needed to maintain genetic variability in an 'ideal population'. In an 'ideal' population (i) the number of reproductive individuals in both sexes is the same (1:1 sex ratio) and (ii) the numbers are the same for each generation.

These conditions are rarely (if ever) fulfilled by natural populations. For instance, many animals are polygynous with just the dominant males breeding. Since only the individuals that breed successfully contribute to the gene pool of the next generation, the size of a population from a genetic standpoint, i.e. the effective population size, may be significantly less than the total number of individuals. For instance, in an isolated colony of moths *Panaxia dominula* studied over a twelve-year period when the population fluctuated between 1300 and 16,000 individuals, the effective population size was estimated to be as low as 500, a fourteenth of the average annual population size (Hartl, 1981).

To maintain genetic diversity in an isolated population normally requires a breeding population several times larger than the minimum 250 described for an 'ideal' population. A population size of 5,000 individuals (Medway and Wells, 1971) would seem more realistic, though few reserves or protected areas are large enough to protect such numbers of some species. If we apply these figures to the orang utan, for instance, then throughout its range only the Gn. Leuser National Park in Sumatra harbours a sufficiently large population. Similarly, an adequate cheetah park in Africa would need to be 10 times larger than Serengeti National Park, Tanzania, and an adequate jaguar park larger than Manu National Park, Peru – options that are clearly not possible. Populations of less than several thousand individuals are unlikely to survive in the long-term without active management.

(Adapted from Wilcox, 1984).

Management of genebanks

Conservation of gene pools of species of value or potential value to mankind is a primary objective of several management categories of protected areas. *In situ* genebanks are areas established with the primary purpose of conserving wild gene pools, or as zones within existing protected areas. Adoption of either alternative will depend on the locations of the gene pools to be conserved and on the social, economic and political practicalities of each situation.

Protected areas established as *in situ* genebanks should have as explicit objectives the maintenance of wild genetic resources and provision of information on and access to those resources by *bona fide* researchers, breeders and *ex situ* genebanks.

If the genebank is part of a protected area with other objectives, the areas required for gene pool conservation should be zoned for gene pool conservation as the primary use. Other uses should be controlled so that they do not conflict with gene pool conservation or should be excluded from the genebank zones altogether (Prescott-Allen 1984).

Each *in situ* genebank should have a list of the species (and populations within that species) it maintains. The list should indicate the locations of the species, including map grid references. Detailed information on gene pools (characteristics, habitats, locations) should be added to the list as research makes it available. As far as possible data on phenology (e.g. time of flowering, fruit ing, and seed maturation) should also be kept. These are valuable aids to germplasm collection and exchange. Ideally, for plants, there should be a herbarium sheet for each species or variety listed (again, giving the precise location). Many genera are taxonomically confusing and the species within them difficult to identify. Herbarium records serve to validate the species list and can save unrewarding trips into the field looking for species that have been misidentified.

There should be an arrangement with the nearest appropriate *ex situ* genebank (this might be in an agricultural research station, a botanical garden, or both) to provide standby storage of germplasm collected in the protected area and to act as a link with the community of genetic resource users. There may also need to be an arrangement with the nearest herbarium to house voucher sheets for the genebank's plant species list. An active partnership with universities and colleges would be extremely valuable. Species lists could be compiled and herbarium specimens collected at very low cost if they were done as directed studies and thesis topics, as could more advanced research on gene pools.

Managing rare and endangered animals

Management to ensure the survival of rare and endangered species is a major worldwide preoccupation of nature conservation and many protected areas were, and continue to be, established with this need in mind. Clearly the conservation of species populations may demand different strategies from those appropriate for the protection of ecosystems.

Where there is a firm objective to manage a protected area for the protection of specific rare or endangered animals the manager's task is not unlike that of a rancher managing his domestic herds except that he is managing for an ecological carrying capacity and not a maximum harvest. The manager will need to have a measure of the species' ecological requirements and year-round needs. He must monitor the size and the age structure of the population and its general health and determine whether the population is stable, declining, or increasing (for methods see Mosby, 1963; Caughley, 1977; Riney, 1982). If the population is of satisfactory size for the carrying capacity of the habitat and is stable or rising, he can maintain the current schedule of management and leave well alone. But where, despite vigorous protection of the vegetation and physical environment, populations start declining to dangerously low levels the manager must look for causes and in particular identify the factors limiting the population.

Many species in nature show seasonal and annual fluctuations in numbers but over a longer timespan these fluctuations oscillate around a stable equilibrium level. This indicates that there are factors in the ecosystem which tend to limit the growth of natural populations. These limiting factors can be of two types: direct factors such as predation, starvation or disease, and indirect factors such as climatic fluctuations, habitat destruction or habitat succession.

In a natural situation, species populations dip, crash and may become locally extinct but there is a good chance of recolonisation from elsewhere. With small populations or vulnerable populations of rare species restricted to small areas, such as reserves, there may be no opportunity for natural recovery and the manager must sometimes interfere to prevent such population crashes and possible extinctions. For instance, wildfires in the Galapagos in 1985 threatened the survival of giant tortoises so a management decision was taken to airlift tortoises to safety and use helicopters to fight the fire. In China, where the bamboo crop has failed, pandas are being given artificial provisions and there is now a project to plant bamboo. In drought conditions in Africa in 1984, park authorities were able to save some of the threatened wildlife by providing extra water and food.

We cannot affect climate but we can alleviate its effects. We can control other factors which may limit populations – food availability, predation levels, etc. However, before the manager can act to protect or increase the population level of a rare or endangered species he must first understand something of its ecology, particularly its critical habitat requirements and population dynamics, i.e. which factors are limiting for that species in that environment. The ultimate factors regulating the population's size are not necessarily those factors which are causing the largest or most obvious mortality losses.

If the manager believes that a population is

35. This rare, slow-breeding Indris, restricted to parts of N.E. Madagascar, faces the threat of extinction due to rapid destruction of its forest habitat. Conservation of such vulnerable animals requires special attention to individual species' needs and should be based on detailed studies of the species' ecology and behaviour.
Photo: WWF/J.J. Petter

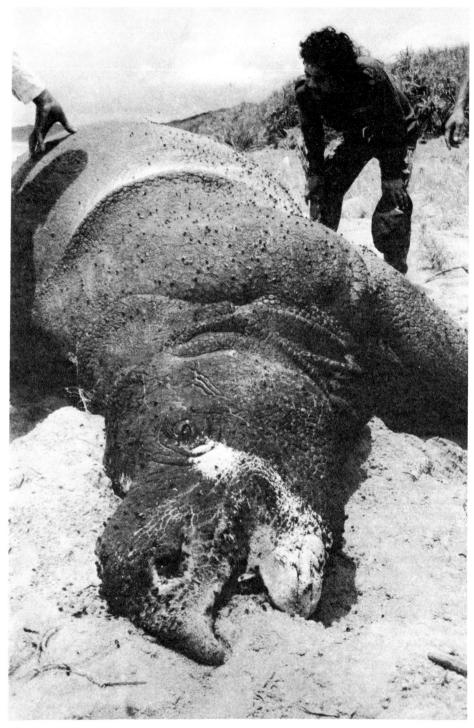

36. The death of at least six out of the estimated 60 Javan rhinos in Ujong Kulon National Park, Indonesia, due to a mystery disease in 1981/2, highlights the grave risk of containing an entire world population of a species in a single small protected area. The Asian Rhino Specialist Group of the Species Survival Commission has recommended establishing a second population of this species. Photo: WWF/Wahiju

declining but is in doubt what to do, then he should seek expert advice. Given suitable habitat and good management most species will recover relatively quickly, even from fairly low levels. There are some species, however, whose breeding behaviour or social behaviour have evolved in circumstances of high density and are maladapted for low-density living. These include some communal nesting species such as turtles and megapodes (mound builders) which employ a breeding strategy of locally swamping their possible predators. This strategy simply collapses when populations fall below critical levels and the local predators can find and remove every egg laid. Similar problems occur with communal mating species such as some pheasants and birds of paradise where several potential breeders must congregate together to elicit proper courtship behaviour. Such species populations may need quick management help in the form of a sudden injection of new numbers.

Generally, however, simply introducing new animals into declining populations is seldom a satisfactory solution. This is like treating the symptoms rather than the disease. It is more important to identify the causes of the decline and try to treat them, so the population can recover by itself.

There are three main factors causing an animal species to become rare or in danger of extinction:

- loss and destruction of vital parts of its habitat;
- unusually high mortality (either natural or induced) or low reproduction;
- climatic, geological and evolutionary changes.

All these causes may act concurrently.
The following management measures can be considered to help a declining or dangerously small population of a species of special interest:

- Stopping habitat alteration, which is a primary cause of wildlife extinctions. In practice, this means enforcing conservation laws, renouncing logging concessions, and controlling tree felling, collection of other forest produce, forest fires, and clearing and burning new farm land. In certain cases, the habitat may require restoration by artificial means, i.e. seeding, planting or other propagation methods of vital food plants, clearing and maintenance of grazing grounds.
- Extending or increasing protection to migration corridors, breeding sites, or roosts (e.g. provision of nest boxes).
- Developing habitat management. This includes all forms of manipulation of the vegetation to make it more suitable for the species in question. For grazers and browsers, this might mean preventing woodlands from reaching climax or even maintaining cleared or burned areas of grassland as feeding areas. It can include planting or removing particular plants. In Sarawak, Malaysia, for example, a method called 'liberation thinning' was proposed whereby large timber trees in reserves were to be ring-barked to kill them so that the smaller fruit trees which provide the bulk of the food for the arboreal animals would be 'liberated', enabling them to grow faster and be more productive (Proud and Hutchinson, 1980).

- Actively protecting the endangered species. This involves improving patrols, controlling illegal hunting and trapping, and adopting special intensive anti-poaching measures, e.g. actually guarding animals by day and enclosing them at night as had to be done with the introduced white rhinos in Kenya's Meru National Park.
- Reducing predation of the young by physically excluding potential predators, e.g. by fencing turtle nests to prevent egg predation by monitor lizards and wild pigs.
- Headstarting. This can include artificial hatching of eggs and rearing of young to reduce early mortalities, but there may be difficulties in releasing the young again as many species need to imprint on either their parents or their birthplace. This method has been successfully applied to megapode nesting areas in Sulawesi (see Example 10.7) and crocodiles in Zimbabwe.
- Provisioning. Providing extra food, water, minerals at salt licks and shelters, or by planting favourite food plants is often quite effective and is usually only necessary for a short period or critical part of the year. Problems may arise if this results in causing unnatural concentrations of animals which render them vulnerable to predation or disease. It may also cause local damage to the vegetation, as has occurred at many park waterholes in Africa.
- Controlling or eliminating exotic or non-indigenous animals which may severely disturb and compete with the indigenous community. Such introduced animals are a major cause of island extinctions. Reducing competitors is a rather drastic action but may be justifiable if the competitor in question is an exotic or feral species or present in unnaturally high numbers or to save a

threatened ecotonal species. The control of the introduced Kikuyu grass and other exotic species in Hawaii Volcanoes National Park is an example where such action is needed.

- Controlling or (better) eliminating feral animals (i.e. domestic animals that have run wild) as they may kill, compete or interbreed with wildlife (e.g. the goats on the Galapagos Islands and cats on Kiribati).
- Reducing the levels of predators. This is justifiable only if the predators are exotics. Indeed the local predators are often the most threatened species of the ecosystem. Usually predators are actually helping to maintain optimal density and good health in a prey species by removing sick animals from the population. Overkilling of wolves in Alaska resulted in a drop, not an increase, in the numbers of their main prey, the caribou.
- Controlling disease. High mortality, whether caused by disease, predation, hunting or poaching, (except for commercial reasons) has rarely led to extinction of a wildlife species. Even an epizootic like rinderpest, which severely ravaged the populations of African buffalo at the turn of the century, did not cause the species to become endangered. However, epizootics may become an acute threat to a species already rare or endangered, particularly when the disease originates in a population of a species sharing the habitat with the rare species.
- Relocating part of a population. Where suitable habitats are available, part of the population of an endangered species should be moved there to avoid the risks of having only one, or a few, populations of a particular species. Where possible, this risk should be spread internationally to avoid extinctions due to political unrest.

- Restocking. This can be used to re-establish a population in areas where it has become extinct or is very rare by relocating individuals from wild stock elsewhere or releasing captive-bred animals. Before boosting populations by restocking the manager must first discover why the original population was dwindling. There is no point in raising the population level if the habitat cannot support greater numbers.
- Breeding in captivity, or from seed and sperm banks. This can be a last means to save a species from extinction. Captive-bred individuals can subsequently be re-introduced in protected, appropriate habitats. The success stories of the NeNe goose (Hawaii), Arabian oryx (Oman) and white rhinoceros of Natal are well known. Captive propagation should be carried out in a safe place, for instance in zoos of good reputation or institutions especially equipped for propagating endangered species. Captive breeding may also be done on site, in the species' own habitat, under rigorous protection. There may be some problems in capturing wild animals for breeding stock, e.g. shock, stress, and mortality during immobilisation and transportation. The animals' physiology and behaviour may also change in captivity and adversely affect breeding success. Some of the problems of restocking and reintroduction are dealt with in more detail below.
- Creating new legislation. This may be necessary when existing laws are no longer appropriate to guarantee survival of the species. Other measures could include adding the species to the protected species list, thus prohibiting hunting and trapping; establishing new sanctuaries or up-grading the status of existing reserves.

Example 8.3: *Managing the available area to enhance survival prospects for the species of interest*

There are numerous steps that a reserve manager can take to favour particular species or habitats. These include: creating the desired habitat or mixture of habitats by preventing fires, by instituting fire rotation, or by other means; maintaining permanent water sources in an arid environment; periodically introducing additional individuals of the particular species of interest; introducing, or regularly adding, prey species, pollinators, or other species which enhance the species of interest; eliminating competing species; and culling the species of interest so as to optimise the sex ratio or age structure.

The more effort and expense devoted to management, the smaller the area in which a given species can be accommodated. An effective population of several hundred lions may require thousands of square kilometres under natural conditions; perhaps only hundreds of square kilometres if deer are periodically released for food, as is now being done for the last Indian lions in the Gir forest; and only one square kilometre under zoo conditions. Conversely, the smaller the area of a reserve, the more effort and expense of management will be required to maintain a given species or ecosystem.

Three caveats should be added about managing under-sized reserves. First, management is expensive, and the expense may be required indefinitely. Culling and transfers of large mammals account for a substantial fraction of the budget of South African reserves. These on-going management expenses should be compared with the one-time costs of more land acquisition that would render these management costs unnecessary. Secondly, for most species we simply do not know enough to manage for them. Finally, managing for individual species may be a tenable strategy in a reserve established with the aim of protecting a few particular species, but is a hopeless strategy in a reserve where the objectives include protecting a whole ecosystem with many key species and thousands of constituent species.

Source: Diamond, 1984

Protecting island reserves

Islands have several inherent advantages as reserves because they have clear boundaries, have already developed a balance between their size and species number, cannot be easily encroached upon and are relatively independent ecological units.

They also have a number of disadvantages. Islands do not contain and cannot protect anything like as wide a range of species as a piece of comparable habitat of similar size on the adjacent mainland. Islands show rather fast species turnover, i.e. the species composition of the island changes so the particular species of interest for which the reserve was established may be lost through natural processes. Moreover, deliberate and unintentional introductions of man's commensals and other species can be disastrous to island floras and faunas. The islands of Hawaii have lost more than half of their original endemic species due to incautious introductions of other animals and plants.

Small islands or isolated continent-sized islands, such as Madagascar and Australia, or isolated water bodies, e.g. Lakes Malawi and Tanganyika, are often the homes of rare endemic species and archaic or primitive forms. These species have radiated to fill the available niches and have survived because of the failure of more advanced species to reach the island, reduced niche competition and the general absence or small size of predators on small islands. Under such circumstances, the introduction of just two domestic cats can be a disaster. The spread of an Australian bird-eating tree snake is another example which resulted in the decimation of the six endemic bird species on the island of Guam.

Islands may be useful as isolated 'pens' where rare species facing extinction on the mainland can be released in the absence of competitors and predators and given high levels of protection in the hope that the population can be nurtured back to a higher level. This technique has been used very successfully to save the rare kakapo, New Zealand's ground-living parrot, and the Kri Kri ibex released on several islands near Crete. Such experiments have considerable hazards, however, and like all manipulative management should be attempted only after serious ecological investigation.

In practice, the general management of island reserves is relatively simple and is best illustrated in the management techniques developed for measures taken to protect the Galapagos National Park (see Example 7.4). The following general guidelines are offered for island reserves:

- Whenever possible, the entire island should be included in the reserve.
- Ideally no residents should live in the reserve. If possible, no staff should live there either, but they should visit and patrol on a regular basis.
- Very strict regulations should be enforced to prevent the introduction of exotic animals or plants. If introduced species have already reached the island and are a threat to the original species, they should be eradicated.
- Where the entire population of a species, or valuable subspecies, occurs on a small island, or is confined to one continuous habitat patch on a larger island, it is advisable to transfer part of the population to a second suitable site to avoid the risk of an epidemic or natural disaster.

37. The plight of Africa's black rhinos is now well documented and the species is effectively extinct outside certain protected areas. Even here, in the crater of the Ngorongoro Conservation Area in Tanzania, the population has dropped from 109 to 16 in the past 20 years.
Photo: J. Thorsell

8. Nusambier Island, Irian Jaya, Indonesia – a rare example of an uninhabited, unspoiled island. Such islands are highly vulnerable and require very careful conservation.
Photo: WWF/Ronald Petocz

39. The famous Coco de Mer is a rare plant confined to one group of islands in the Seychelles. It is an example of a threatened island endemic facing loss of habitat and competition from introduced species. Conservation of this species will require special attention and artificial propagation. Photo: Christian Zuber

decimating the population, i.e. 'don't have all your eggs in one basket'.

- If possible, ensure that there is some natural or semi-natural habitat on the mainland closest to the island to act as a colonising source for well dispersed species. Where there is no such habitat left on the nearby mainland, the island may suffer from species losses unless immigrants are introduced artificially.
- Efforts must be made to prevent fishermen and others camping on the island. Islands in the tropics are highly susceptible to fire, vegetation removal and disturbance of nesting birds.
- Survey the marine or aquatic potential around the island. If the surrounding waters have high conservation value, they should be included in the reserve, or as a buffer, to increase the overall use and benefits of the reserve. (For further guidelines on the management of coastal and marine areas see Salm and Clark, 1984).

Management of over-abundant populations

Theoretically, populations in the wild should not become over-abundant or if they do periodically, natural checks on population numbers (limited resources, climate, disease, predation or dispersal), should act to control population size. Unfortunately, few ecosystems have escaped the influence of man or are large enough to allow such mechanisms to operate effectively. This is especially true in the case of large mammals in protected areas, since even the largest reserves may not include all the year-round needs for all the populations confined within their borders (see Riney, 1982; Ferrar, 1983).

Some protected areas have become fenced 'islands' while others are surrounded by agricultural lands or other man-modified habitats where the presence of many wild animals, and particularly large mammals, is intolerable. Fences around protected areas or other factors that prevent or inhibit animals from leaving an area can lead to unusually high densities of some species and lead to problems such as overgrazing. While elephants are becoming increasingly scarce throughout Africa, in some protected areas they are so numerous that they are destroying their own environment. With natural balances no longer effective, the protected area manager has no alternative but to cull or otherwise remove part of the elephant population. (For the classic case of this problem as experienced in Ruaha National Park in Tanzania, see Barnes, 1983).

Apart from destroying their own habitat, increasing numbers of one species may have deleterious effects on the habitats of other species, or on other management objectives within the protected area. Species like elephant, for example, may change the physiognomic character of the vegetation, converting savanna woodlands to open grassland within a few years. Such habitat modification may lead to the loss of habitat-sensitive species, such as roan antelope (see Example 8.11). Similarly, where predation levels have been artificially reduced, certain prey species may increase to the detriment of other rarer species. Thus, in Ujung Kulon National Park in Java, Indonesia, the wild ox or banteng has become increasingly numerous since the local extinction of the tiger by hunting some twenty years ago. Where there were formerly about 200 banteng (Hoogerwerf, 1970), there may now be over a thousand. Such a number may pose an added threat to the rare Javan rhinoceros with which the banteng shares many foods and parasites. The large number of wild cattle probably also affects the rate of tree regeneration and alters the vegetation of the reserve. Since one of the primary objectives of Ujung Kulon is to protect the Javan rhinoceros, this situation needs careful monitoring and perhaps management to reduce the number of banteng.

What can the manager do when he thinks that a species in a protected area is too numerous? First, he can seek expert advice to check whether the situation merits action. Populations naturally show highs and lows – the physical condition and age structure of the population tells much about its health, and whether the population is declining, stable or on the increase. Secondly, he can decide on suitable control measures, again with expert involvement. He should take note of methods used to deal with similar problems elsewhere and, if possible, run a trial on a small scale before more widespread application.

Generally the methods of control will fit into one of the following three categories:

- *Culling,* by capture or killing, of selected individuals or selected groups of individuals. Killing should be performed by expert marksmen in a humane fashion and all culling should cause as little disturbance as possible to other wildlife and visitors. Culling is the most direct form of population control with an exact number of selected individuals being removed. Culling is common practice in African parks and reserves.

If it is decided to control the numbers of a particular population, then the reasons for the decision should be spelled out. Controlling animal populations, especially if it involves killing, is a highly emotive issue and may evoke considerable public debate which can be obviated by frank explanation of the reasons why action is being taken. To minimise public reaction, the killing should be as discreet as possible, i.e. cull in remote areas; close the park during the cull; cull during the off-season.

The decision to control animal numbers in national parks or other reserves should be based entirely on ecological considerations. If the manager decides to cull, he should then, and only then, consider how best to dispose of any useful products which might result. If products are to be marketed, as in many African countries, they should be of as high a standard of preparation as can be achieved under field conditions. This calls for considerable skills and organising ability, especially when salvaging perishable products such as meat and skins.

Managers should minimise capital outlay on equipment for culling activities except where harvesting is to be on a sustained basis as heavy investment may influence later decisions on whether to cull, decisions that should depend on ecological considerations alone.

- *Live-trapping and removal.* If practicable this method is preferable to killing excess animals. It enables the manager to control more precisely which animals are to be removed. It has the advantage that captured animals can be released into other areas of suitable habitat where they may be poorly represented or utilised to stock captive breeding projects or zoos or even be used for domestication, e.g. Asian elephant. Various forms of traps have been devised for live trapping. There are numerous other capture techniques including immobilisation with dart guns but this requires the services of an expert. Thousands of large mammals have been relocated using such methods in Natal, Namibia and Zimbabwe.

- *Biological control.* In theory, biological control is an attractive option but, in fact, it is fraught with problems. It may be a useful tool in the control or eradication of exotic species (see below) but is of rather limited value in protected areas where, as a general rule, anything involving the introduction of more exotic species should be avoided.

Control of problem animals originating from protected areas

As important as the control of over-abundant species may be within a protected area, often a greater problem is the control of problem animals that move out of the area onto neighbouring lands and come into conflict with legitimate human interests. Elephant, lion, tiger, hippopotamus, crocodile, puma, jaguar, spectacled bear, and many monkey species may be attractive elements of the fauna within a protected area, but their garden and stock raiding activities outside are generally intolerable, especially to poor neighbouring communities, unless these communities can be compensated in some way for the losses they suffer. It is sometimes possible to have highly profitable hunting schemes around protected areas to control problem animals but this is not a universally good formula.

Sometimes species may leave the reserves because these cannot provide for all the species'

needs. Elephants, for example, may need access to distant mineral sources, tigers and Cape hunting dogs have large home ranges which extend beyond the reserve boundaries, and condors soar over enormous areas to find their prey. Similarly, individuals of territorial species may disperse outside the reserve to find new ranges. Sometimes management can solve the problem. Elephants can be provided with artificial mineral sources (salt licks), and prey of the tiger can be increased by enlarging the open grazing areas.

Good knowledge of the species' needs is important if appropriate measures are to be taken. Elephant corridors have been tried in Thailand and Sri Lanka to permit seasonal movements between vital feeding areas. If such measures are impossible or inappropriate, then the management authority must resort to alternative control measures.

Example 8.4: *Controlling predation by lions dispersing from parks in Zululand*

Species like lion are an asset within a park but often become serious pests when they leave its borders. In Zululand, the parks authorities were forced to pay out large sums of money in compensation when lions left the parks and preyed on villagers' livestock.

Adult lions are generally sedentary in behaviour, occupying well-established territories. Those animals that had to be destroyed while raiding livestock were mostly young, well-grown individuals, with males outnumbering females. These young sub-adults leave the parental home range and often wander considerable distances. Many perish but those that survive establish their own territories in suitable habitats; in this way the species is able to colonise vacant areas. Dispersing individuals facilitate genetic exchange between otherwise isolated sub-populations.

The Zululand parks authorities have been able to effectively curb predation on livestock outside the parks by deliberately shooting a high proportion of young, well-grown lions, particularly males, inside the parks. Clearly this strategy has had the effect of eliminating individuals before they reached the age at which some of them at least would have been expected to disperse. Vacant territories are not readily available within the parks so that most dispersing individuals would have ended up in village farming areas where there is little suitable prey other than livestock.

Lion and other large predators are generally intolerable in stock raising areas, where problem animal control is costly but necessary. By observing which segment of the lion population was responsible for most stock raiding, and by appreciating their significance as dispersing individuals, the Zululand park authorities were able to take practical action to reduce the problem considerably. Such action makes good economic sense and does much to remove a point of serious friction between a park and its neighbours.

Before taking expensive and time-consuming control measures, one should be sure that the reported damage has indeed been inflicted by wildlife. In assessing the damage, look for tracks, tusk and claw marks, droppings, the way the damage has been inflicted (kill technique, broken trunk or branches) and which part of the crop or animal has been eaten.

For mammals, some of the following control measures may be useful:

Fencing. Fences erected between the protected area and agricultural lands help keep wildlife inside the reserve and domestic animals out. Construction costs are often prohibitive, however, and fences require maintenance and repair. They must be of solid construction, of sufficient height and they should be visible. A netted or interlocking structure is necessary. Wire strands, while adequate for use with domestic animals, are generally unsuitable for containing wildlife – especially for species which travel at high speed – as animals can become impaled or be strangled by the wires. Wire fencing has been used successfully for deer, wild boars and other species but conventional fences are usually no real barrier for elephants.

Grating. A grid across entrance roads, in combination with a fence, has proved an efficient barrier for most wildlife species.

Electric fencing. This is generally cheaper to erect and less dangerous than a fixed fence but may be weaker and break if struck by a fast-moving animal. Electric fences can be moved easily and are useful as temporary barriers, e.g. to contain animals that are being driven from one area to another. Electric fencing has proved effective in protecting oil palm and other plantations against elephants in West Malaysia, Kenya and Malawi and are used as veterinary barriers in Zimbabwe. However, it is one thing to encircle a plantation and another to surround a whole reserve, and there are other problems to be considered.

- A power supply must be applied over many hundreds of metres. Solar powered units can be used in open areas.
- Broken strands of wire are a threat to wildlife.
- Wires are easily earthed, especially on wet ground or where overgrown with vegetation.
- Fences and powerpoints are regularly hit by lightning in some lightning-prone areas. Replacement of units or erection of an overhead earthed conductor wire add considerably to overall costs.
- The long wire strands may prove irresistible to local people for domestic use or even to make snares for poaching.

40. Effective wildlife fences, like this one in McIlwaine Recreation Park, Zimbabwe, should be of netted, rather than strand, construction. A strip of vegetation has been cleared along the perimeter so that animals can see the fence and not charge blindly into it.
Photo: WWF

Canals, moats, ditches. Ditch construction is less expensive than fencing, but requires more maintenance. Elephant trenches (3 m wide and 2 m deep) have been found useful in West Malaysia and Africa, where they are as much a psychological as a physical barrier. Trenches in Royal Chitwan National Park, Nepal, have proved effective at containing Indian rhinoceros within the park. Canals around the Padang Sugihan Wildlife Reserve in Sumatra, Indonesia, are effective barriers to elephants in swampy terrain.

Buffer zones. Such zones are the best solution. Size and location are important (see Chapter 5). It is sometimes possible to reduce the tendency of wildlife to come out of a protected area by encircling the reserve with unattractive buffer zones planted with species that are not very palatable to wildlife or domestic stock but are useful to local communities. Examples are tea plantations, pine or *Agathis* plantations, *Eucalyptus*, teak, Kamiri nuts (*Aleurites moluccana*), sisal and many others.

Chasing and scaring. Chasing animals away from crops may be efficient for short periods, for example when crops are ripening. Chasing can be done in various ways: drumming, shooting, rattles, shots in the air, firecrackers, propane or acetylene cannons, fires, etc. The responsible wildlife officer and his staff may assist farmers in chasing wildlife off farmlands.

Shooting. When the measures noted above prove ineffective or cannot be implemented for financial or technical reasons, the manager must consider elimination of the problem animals. In principle, shooting can be a selective control measure. Hunting or shooting of protected animals turned pest outside the reserve boundaries should be done by park staff or as a special operation under their control.

Trapping. Certain species of animals are more suited to being trapped than shot, e.g. small, cryptic, nocturnal, shy or arboreal species. A large variety of live traps, kill traps, snap traps and leg traps have been developed to control wild animal damage. Traps are placed on animal trails or at the entrance to burrows. Larger carnivores have been trapped for relocation using baited, steel cage traps placed on regularly-used trails.

The problem with trapping is that species or individuals other than the troublemakers may be caught. Live traps are usually more selective (depending on the bait) than kill traps. Never use non-humane snares, or leg or foot snares or traps which trigger and injure the animal when stepped upon – they cause great suffering. Even if they are checked regularly, an animal can be trapped in the interim period.

Poisoning. This method is regularly used by farmers in agricultural areas to reduce populations of various pest species but there are serious drawbacks to the use of most commercial poisons. Many poisons are non-selective but even selective poisons, once they are in the foodchain, can affect non-target species, e.g. birds of prey. If poisons are used they must be strictly controlled to avoid all undesirable side-effects.

Other animal control measures such as anti-fertility compounds, repellents and fumigants are commercially available but are generally expensive and inappropriate for widespread use in the tropics.

Compensation schemes. As a last resort, the management authority may have to evolve some form of compensation scheme to reimburse local villagers for losses incurred through wild animal damage. At the Gir Wildlife Sanctuary in India, home of the last population of Asiatic lions, natural prey species are scarce and the lions take a number of domestic cattle each year. Here, the Indian authorities pay compensation for stock lost. A similar system is in effect in Kenya. Such

41. Repairing of rhino fencing at the Royal Chitwan National Park in Nepal. In the absence of natural boundaries, such physical barriers have proved a cost-effective management tool, reducing both rhino outbreaks and human incursions into the park.
Photo: WWF/Mark Boulton

schemes are expensive, however, and open to abuse. The Game Department in West Malaysia has had particular success with its policy of making it clear to land owners that it is up to the owners themselves to protect their land against possible wildlife damage and not the responsibility of the government.

Example 8.5: The elephant problem

Conflicts between man and elephants are widespread in Africa and tropical Asia. Expanding human populations and extensive land clearance for agriculture have compressed the elephants' ranges, leaving a few pocketed herds in isolated blocks of forest, often too small to provide an adequate year-round supply of food, water and shelter. Increasingly, wild elephants are reported raiding and destroying crops and coming into conflict with local communities. Possible solutions include:

Live capture

Immobilisation is the best method for capturing individual problem elephants. Modern drugs have a considerable safety margin for this species. This technique requires qualified personnel for capture and after-care (experienced elephant trackers, expert marksman with dartgun, veterinarian). Groups of elephant are probably better caught using bomas (kraals) and traditional elephant capture techniques.

Moving captured animals may be a problem. In Asia, domestic elephants with their mahouts can be used to guide elephants freshly revived after immobilisation. Trucks and tractors can be used where access is easy but loading wild elephants can be troublesome and may require the guidance of tame elephants or special equipment. Helicopters have been used in Rwanda to airlift young immobilised elephants to the Akagera National Park. During transport animals must be kept under sedation and held tightly with strong jute ropes (not chains).

Translocation

Relocation of elephants, though attractive from a conservation point of view, is logistically difficult, especially when adults are involved. Inevitably it causes stress. It is better to move a whole herd if possible. The older elephants' experience of food gathering, seasonal movements, etc., is important to the survival of the herd. Care must be taken not to separate calves from their mothers.

Taming and training

Asian elephants can be readily trained and sold to offset some of the costs of the capture operation or kept to work in the park, e.g. hauling logs, transporting tourists, etc. Only younger elephants (less than 210 cm high at the shoulder) are suitable for taming. Older, aggressive or sick animals should not be selected. Elephant training courses are organised in Thailand.

Driving

A line of beaters, tame elephants or vehicles can drive elephant herds to a new area. Animals should be driven to the centre of the new sanctuary, not just to the borders. Elephant driving requires good planning and coordination. Progress is usually slow and it is difficult to keep the herd together; some animals may break away. Drums, firecrackers, buzzing helicopters and all other sudden noises should not be used as they tend to stampede the animals.

Creating special reserves

This is complex and costly. Suitable areas of adequate size are scarce, especially in densely-populated Asia. Translocated elephants with their destructive feeding habits may soon modify and degrade the habitat of any 'new' sanctuary.

Elephant corridors

Ideally, reserve boundaries should incorporate the whole range of the local elephant population, especially the wet season dispersal areas, the areas where animals concentrate in the dry season and any well-used routes between. Some countries have designated special elephant corridors to protect natural lands along elephant migration routes, e.g. Thailand, Sri Lanka.

Buffers

When agricultural or forestry projects are planned adjacent to parks, crops should be selected that are not attractive to elephants. This excludes most human food crops. Cultivations or plantations bordering reserves should be well maintained as elephants are more likely to venture into poorly-weeded and overgrown areas.

A 'laissez-faire' policy

If the park authority decides to do nothing about the elephant problem and 'let nature take its course', there is a danger that farmers will shoot and maim animals. Moreover, elephant populations living in isolated protected sanctuaries may 'eat themselves (and other wildlife) out of food'. On the other hand, isolated populations may eventually die out naturally if not managed.

Extermination

Extermination of problem animals is a last resort. Animals should be killed as humanely as possible by well-trained park staff or marksmen under their supervision. Elephant control should never be left to local police or the army.

Sources: Olivier, 1977; Child, 1985

Rehabilitation of captive animals

Rehabilitation is the process by which animals are returned from captive life to wild living in a natural environment. The animals concerned may have been bred in captivity or taken into captivity because they were sick, injured, orphaned, rescued, or were pets or zoo animals.

Rehabilitation projects have attracted a lot of attention in recent years. However, in terms of the numbers of animals successfully returned to the wild, rehabilitation projects play an insignificant role in species conservation. (There have been certain notable exceptions, e.g. Arabian oryx). Rehabilitation does, however, generate a lot of emotion and interest. It is the sad wildlife stories that make the news, not the slow erosion of populations. Animals continue to require rehabilitation for humanitarian, political, propaganda and sometimes genuine conservation reasons and the following guidelines should help avoid some of the possible pitfalls.

In general, conservationists should concentrate on tackling the causes of species loss rather than becoming sidetracked by the often attractive and praiseworthy efforts of animal welfare groups who wish to tackle the displaced animal problem. Such rehabilitation projects do, however, generate interest and publicity which may provide considerable benefits to the conservation movement. Rehabilitation stations can often be useful focal points for education centres.

Where rehabilitation is considered, the following factors should be kept in mind:

- *Reasons for decline*. Avoid masking the cause of a declining species population by reintroducing or restocking without first looking for the reason for the original decline, i.e. 'treating the symptoms but not the disease' (see Example 8.6).
- *Difficulties and costs*. Rehabilitation means handling, transporting and providing care, food, medication and shelter for the animals concerned. This is logistically costly and time

consuming. It can overtax the time, manpower, and budget of a protected area and distract management from more important but perhaps less exciting matters. The real benefits of any rehabilitation project must be weighed against these costs. In general, protected area authorities should leave the funding and running of rehabilitation projects to voluntary agencies.

- *Behavioural problems*. Releasing strange animals into wild populations can cause social problems. The ease with which a rehabilitant animal can be released into a wild population depends very much on the social system of the species concerned. Social animals tend to have rather closed groupings, and often guard their territories jealously, e.g. black rhinoceros, and many cats. They may attack or kill the released animals. Gibbons, for instance, live in small family groups (a monogamous pair plus their offspring) and defend their territory against neighbouring gibbons. Released gibbons are immediately attacked, and even when the animals are paired as duetting couples before release, they are usually unable to hold their own against the resident groups. It is only feasible to release gibbons in areas where there are no wild gibbons left or where there are real gaps in the territory map. In most social species, sexually maturing and young females are the most likely age/sex class to be accepted and may quickly find a wild mate and establish themselves.

Before any reintroductions are made into wild populations, it is vital to establish that there is room for them, i.e. that the wild population is below the carrying capacity of the habitat. If the wild population is already overcrowded, adding new animals will simply exacerbate the problem, causing increased social stress in the wild population. In orang utans, for instance, there appears to be a severe drop in breeding rate whenever the population becomes overcrowded or disturbed by the presence of too many displaced homeless individuals (MacKinnon, 1974).

In some species, such as gorillas, young animals may be adopted by wild groups. With other species such as chimpanzees or lions, they are more likely to be killed. Naive experimentation is usually a recipe for tragedy. Rehabilitation should only be undertaken when the behaviour of the species is well understood and there is a good chance that the rehabilitant will be assimilated successfully into the wild population.

- *Learning problems*. Most higher animals have to undergo considerable learning in their juvenile stages to behave competently as adults: to learn what is edible, what is dangerous or a potential predator, and where different wild resources can be found. Releasing a naive captive-reared animal, or even a displaced wild-born animal, can be very dangerous for the animal concerned.

Usually, it is almost impossible to duplicate this learning process in captivity. The young of some species (e.g. most primates and lions) may need several years schooling in semi-wild conditions before they can be safely released. Animal species which rely more on 'instinct' than learning can be rehabilitated more easily.

- *The human factor*. Particular problems and dangers occur if the animals to be released have become fixated on humans. Animals in captivity often become dependent on their human foster parents to the extent that they count on them for food, company or as playmates and even see them as suitable breeding partners. A playful sunbear running towards unknowing villagers will usually not survive the game. Such animals often become dangerous to people and have to be destroyed.

- *Diseases*. If reintroductions are being considered remember that the rehabilitants may have picked up zoonoses or diseases from their human contacts, or from other animals during their captivity. These diseases will be 'foreign' to the wild population which may have no resistance against them.

Great care must be taken to medically screen animals before release. Animals should also be kept in quarantine for an appropriate period prior to release. Zoonoses pose a two way threat and regular health checks must be carried out on both the animals and the people involved in the projects.

42. Release of captive animals into the wild can be both difficult and dangerous. Through regular contact with humans, these young rehabilitant orang utans could pick up human diseases and communicate them to the wild orang utan population. Although rehabilitation projects attract valuable publicity and support for conservation, the actual releases are of little value in helping to save the species.
Photo: WWF/Georg Gerster

Example 8.6: Bali starling project

The Bali Barat National Park in Indonesia is the last home of the rare and endemic Bali starling. There are now only about 200 individuals left in the wild yet the bird is quite common in international zoos and breeds readily in captivity. Several American zoos therefore decided to breed a surplus stock of 200 birds to be returned to Bali for release in the park. However, the International Council for Bird Protection (ICBP) have requested that these birds are not released in Bali Barat for a number of reasons. First, it was feared that the released birds might carry undetected diseases from the zoos into the wild population which has no immunity to them. Secondly, it would be difficult to assess how successful the operation had been, i.e. in a few years how many of the starling population would be original releases, how many the offspring of ex-captive birds and how many wild stock.

However, the main reason for the ICBP's advice was the fact that the releases would obscure the effects of management. That the wild population has dropped so low means that there is something wrong with either the habitat or its management. ICBP recommend detailed studies of the bird's biology to identify shortcomings in the habitat condition or protective management. Only after the causes for the decline have been identified and corrected should reintroductions be considered.

Introductions, reintroductions and translocations

Translocations can be classified into two categories: introductions into areas outside the historical distribution of the species, when the species would be considered an exotic; and reintroductions within the species' distribution range either as reintroductions to areas where the species has died out, or translocations to boost falling populations.

Translocation

Translocation is considered in three main circumstances : first, where land development is about to destroy wildlife habitat and translocation is seen as a possible way to prevent the wastage of valuable wildlife resources; secondly, where a wild population is not faring well and the manager wishes to boost its numbers and thirdly, when a manager decides to split a population to reduce the risk of losing the entire population.

As a general rule, if a management decision has been made to augment a population of animals, rather than release animals that have been held for a long time in captivity, it is better to capture wild animals and transfer them to new homes. Such operations from habitats that are about to be destroyed can save significant numbers of animals and the captives are released before they become fixated on their captors or pick up human diseases. They are already wise in the ways of their environment and need little rehabilitation before release. If a whole social unit can be caught and transferred together, this causes less social disruption.

Care should, of course, be taken to choose a suitable release point, preferably one where the resident population is low and needs boosting or has died out but conditions are now favourable for reintroductions. Translocation operations of this kind include the well-known Operation Noah's Ark to rescue a wide range of wildlife when the Kariba Dam was built (Child, 1968); the elephant operation in Sri Lanka where a herd was moved to Wilpattu National Park; and the even larger 'Operation Ganesha' in Sumatra, Indonesia, where over 230 wild elephants were herded 40 km to a new reserve. Natal, Namibia and Zimbabwe have considerable experience in translocation operations and each year move thousands of head of large mammals, including buffalo and several species of antelope.

Example 8.7: Guidelines for the introduction and translocation of animals

The following recommendations concerning introduction, reintroduction, translocation and rehabilitation were devised for primate species in South America but are applicable to other animal groups elsewhere.

- Introduction projects should be avoided wherever possible because they may have deleterious effects on the local ecology, and suitability of habitat for the introduced animals is difficult to evaluate. As a conservation tool, introduction should be considered only as a last resort, if at all.
- Translocation and reintroduction projects should be considered only where the habitat at the release sites is intact, where adequate protective measures are in effect, and where the species in question has disappeared locally for reasons unrelated to habitat suitability (e.g. overhunting).
- Wherever possible, only intact social groups should be used for translocation and reintroduction projects. Otherwise efforts should be made to establish cohesive groupings prior to release.
- In all cases of translocation and reintroduction, animals should be provisioned in their new habitat for as long as necessary to supplement natural foods. Provision of shelters may also be desirable.
- Where reintroduction has been deemed appropriate, translocation of recently-caught wild animals is preferable to the use of animals born and/or reared in captivity.
- In cases where the survival of wild populations seems unlikely, it is important that captive breeding colonies are established to ensure that at least some representatives of the species survive. Institutions involved should realise that, in many cases, maintenance of captive colonies may become an end in itself, with reintroduction no longer a viable alternative. Nevertheless, in the event that reintroduction does become possible at some future date, captive colonies should be provided with as diverse an environment as possible so that a maximum of behavioural variability can be maintained and rehabilitation facilitated.

Source: Konstant and Mittermeier, 1982

Example 8.8: A successful reintroduction: golden lion tamarins in the Poco das Antas Reserve, Brazil

The golden lion tamarin *Leontopithecus rosalia* is regarded as a critically endangered species with no more than 400 individuals now left in the wild. This monkey has always been restricted to the coastal lowlands of the state of Rio de Janeiro where forest destruction has resulted in the almost total disappearance of the animal's natural habitat. Although a wild population estimated at 75-100 animals exists in the Poco das Antas Biological Reserve, much of the area is not suitable habitat for the lion tamarin, which depends on mature trees for holes in which to shelter at night. Other threats to the reserve monkeys include poaching, disturbance from a road and a railroad cut through the reserve, and a new dam which will flood part of the area.

To increase the chances of survival of the golden lion tamarin in the wild, World Wildlife Fund are working with the Brazilian Forestry Department and the Rio de Janeiro Primate Centre to reintroduce individuals from captive colonies in the USA. Fifteen captive-bred animals were released into the Poco das Antas Reserve at a site where there were no resident wild tamarins. Of these releases, five animals have disappeared or died (one due to snakebite) but the remaining ten cative-born animals have settled in well and an infant has been born to one of the released females.

In another trial, a family group of six wild golden lion tamarins were translocated successfully to the reserve from a patch of forest that was being destroyed. The success of this venture is important because future conservation efforts outside the reserve may require moving animals from forests scheduled for felling to protected areas. Moving individual animals may also be desirable to facilitate genetic exchange between small populations.

Work to improve the 5018 ha reserve for tamarins includes planting seedlings of native trees and liming to correct soil acidity in degraded areas. Other management measures include increasing the number of guards, fencing the reserve and the development of firebreaks to prevent the spread of wildfires.

Source: Kleiman, 1984.

43. This leopard in Kenya is being moved from an area where it was killing domestic animals to a protected area. Translocation of carnivores is a convenient solution to this problem. Such animals may, however, have problems in adapting to the release area, especially if there is already a large population of resident carnivores.
Photo: WWF/Judith Rudnai

44. Managers must expect local extinctions of populations in small or isolated reserves. These can only be countered by artificial reintroductions. Here, a group of the rare Liechtenstein's hartebeests await reintroduction into the Gonare Zhou National Park, Zimbabwe. Note the woven plastic and nylon netting of the release compound. Animals are not able to see through the netting and few animals challenge the structure while being held prior to release in a new area.
Photo: Zimbabwe Department of National Parks and Wildlife Management

45. A white rhino is captured for translocation. The conservation of much of Africa's big game is now dependent on such active management. Tens of thousands of animals have been captured and moved to maintain isolated populations.
Photo: WWF/J.H. Blower/J. Allan Cash

Introductions

Introductions may be particularly useful in stocking new or artificially altered habitats; for example where dams or irrigation projects have created new lakes and swamps, or where reforestation projects have created new but faunally-impoverished habitats.

Many of the constraints described for releasing rehabilitant animals in wild populations also apply to translocating and reintroducing species.

Exotics

Exotic plants and animals are unwelcome and dangerous additions in protected natural areas. There are endless examples of exotic species becoming terrible pests in their new homes and often outcompeting and replacing native species as well. Much of the original fauna and flora of Hawaii has been lost as a result of ill-considered releases. The disastrous introductions of rabbits and prickly pears into Australia are other well-documented cases. The message is clear: exotic species should not be introduced into new habitats unless under exceptional circumstances. However, in some categories of multiple-use protected areas, or in special circumstances in other protected areas, exotics may sometimes play an important and useful role (e.g., species introduced into multiple-use areas for economic or utilisation purposes; stabilisation of erosion-prone areas, biological control of other exotic or pest species).

If for any reason the introduction of an exotic is

contemplated the following points should be kept in mind:

- Do not introduce species which are potential pests, e.g. known to feed on domestic stock or crops, known carriers of dangerous diseases, species with a high capacity to disperse and reproduce, or close ecological equivalents of local species.
- Avoid introduction of an exotic species if a local species will do just as well, e.g. for shade trees. Similarly, do not use exotic flowering or ornamental plants in flowerbeds around park buildings.

- Take care that the exotic can be controlled or exterminated if necessary.
- Make trial introductions in small isolated areas where the species can be exterminated if the trials are unsatisfactory.
- Essential exotics, e.g. vegetables grown for staff consumption, draught and pack animals for management purposes, should be as few as possible and located outside the protected area or limited to development areas wherever practicable.
- Avoid introducing any secondary species or diseases with the exotic.

Control of Exotic Species

The presence of exotic or alien species in a protected area is generally contrary to the management objectives of that area. Unless the exotic has been deliberately introduced to help management or is of such long standing that it is in balance with the ecosystem or of interest in its own right, it is best to attempt to eradicate or control the exotic species. For instance, there are now programmes to eradicate feral cats which prey on native birds in the Galapagos Islands and in the reserves of Kiribati.

For removal of exotic animals, hunting and trapping are usually the most effective methods. In Brazil's Brasilia National Park, for example, rangers carry loaded rifles and shoot all dogs on sight. Since the park is near a major urban centre it is completely fenced to discourage squatters but dogs dig under the barrier. Poisoning campaigns to eliminate domestic dogs have also been carried out in Ethiopia's Bale Mountains National Park.

For plants, cutting or ring-barking is often used. Sometimes careful and selective use of herbicides may be necessary. For example, the *Acacia ara-*

bica bushes planted as a fire break around a fire-managed grazing ground in Baluran National Park, Java, are now invading the grazing area and all management attempts to curb this encroachment have so far failed. In this case, it may be necessary to use a selective weed-killer, even though such poisons should generally not be used in protected areas if there are other alternative methods.

All the methods suggested on pages 155-6 for dealing with overnumerous animal species can also be applied for the control of exotic species.

Biological controls can sometimes be effective as with the introduction of myxomatosis into the rabbit populations in Australia and other countries and the introduction of the moth *Cactoblastis cactorum* to attack the prickly pear *Opuntia* and other cacti which are serious pests in Australia and southern Africa. But these require specialised knowledge and great care must always be taken to ensure that the measures employed against the target species will not be harmful to native animals or plants.

Restoration of vegetation

There are many areas where the original vegetation has been destroyed by natural or artificial means and where it is desirable to restore the habitat to a condition as close to the original as possible.

Natural succession will depend upon the availability of parent seed. Colonising species usually

disperse their seeds widely, employing wind, water or animals as dispersal agents; they readily colonise cleared land. What is more difficult is encouraging the regeneration of climax species. There may be some regeneration from seed dispersed naturally from adjacent forest blocks but elsewhere it may be necessary to use artificial

46. Mangrove forests can be restored artificially by simply implanting the viviparous seeds of several species in the mud. The example shown is a plantation of *Rhizophora* successfully generated near the village of Tanjung Benoa, Bali, Indonesia.
Photo: WWF/N.V. Polunin

propagation and plant seedlings.

In any area in the tropics cleared of forest cover and left open for some time, the soil will have become greatly degraded by erosion and leaching. Where areas have been burned regularly and the surface organic material destroyed, the soil will often be acid. In such areas it is very difficult to restore forest cover.

Various methods have been employed to establish forest cover in open grasslands: seeding from aircraft; planting of small seedlings; and planting of sticks of coppiceable secondary forest trees. Sticks are preferable to seedlings. Planted when a metre in height, they grow quickly and soon shade out the grass beneath. They are also less susceptible to fire and lack of water. The area must be protected from fire and this may involve the planting or construction of firebreaks. The young trees may also need protection from browsing herbivores (e.g. erection of deer fences).

The first stage in returning secondary grassland to forest is to prevent further burning and to establish a shade tree-cover to kill the grass. Preferred coloniser species would be fast-growing, fire-tolerant species which fix nitrogen in their roots and thus help to build up a soil layer. Care should be taken that the stocking density of the nitrogen-fixers is not so great as to exclude other colonisers that may be useful in other ways, e.g. by attracting birds or bats to the area. Coloniser species should be short-lived. They will eventually be replaced by larger, slower-growing tree species whose seedlings and saplings can survive in the shade of the young forest and will ultimately form a climax forest.

If the first tree cover has a mixture of planted fast-growing legumes and natural secondary forest species, it will soon provide enough cover and food to attract birds, monkeys, bats and other dispersal agents from the surrounding forest areas and these will introduce (via defecation) the seeds of their favourite fruits. Such natural regeneration may lead to a new forest with a high density of fruiting trees, making the area particularly attractive to animals.

Exotic species should only be used for reforestation where the primary objectives are soil protection or forestry production and where the exotic species is clearly superior for these purposes to a local one. Exotic species may also be useful to form a buffer zone which is unattractive to local wildlife and discourages them from crossing into neighbouring agricultural land.

Sometimes the manager will want to achieve exactly the reverse process in habitats where woody plants have suppressed grasses. The obvious management prescriptions of burning or increased grazing often in fact have the effect of increasing woody cover (see Example 8.11). Severe management in the form of cutting may be needed, but clearing such woody plants may prove very difficult where seeds are still in the soil or the plant can reproduce vegetatively from roots beneath the ground, e.g. bamboo, acacia bushes.

One solution which was used successfully to create artificial grazing grounds in Ujung Kulon Reserve, Java, was to allow villagers to clear and cultivate areas for several years, then stop cultivating and reseed with selected grass species. The 'taungya' system of reforestation commonly used in Burma is somewhat similar, except that tree seed is sown at appropriate spacing together with the agricultural crop and cultivation is normally only permitted for one to two years after which the cultivators move elsewhere. They are paid for the number of surviving tree seedlings, whose further care is the responsibility of the Forest Department.

Fire as a management tool

Natural fires, due to lightning, spontaneous combustion, volcanism etc., and fires set by man have had a prolonged and marked influence on the vegetation in many parts of the tropics.

Many of the spectacular wildlife vistas and large densities of ungulates seen in tropical savannas are a consequence of fire. Fire prevents forest regeneration and maintains open grassland, and the ungulates feed on the fresh grass. Fires arising from natural causes are generally rare and irregular in occurrence. Many habitats that show the effects of regular burning are, or have been in the past, largely affected by man. For instance, the savannas of Southeast Asia are man-created. These fire climax vegetations and fire-shaped mosaics are of great biological interest, but maintaining them requires regular burning.

Fire may sometimes be used deliberately within

Example 8.9: Some possible effects of prescribed burning on five ecological processes

Ecological Process	Effects
Natural succession	• Curtailment of natural succession and ecosystem evolution • Vegetation pattern reflects pattern of burns, the mosaic containing different successional stages • Creation of bare areas which facilitates invasion of weed and exotic species • Local breakdown of ecological balance between species • Progressive reduction of species' diversity depending on fire tolerance • Progressive increase in uniformity with fewer ecosystems and specialised niches • Migration and concentration of herbivores in areas with a flush of new, nutritious plant growth
Organic production and decomposition	• Loss of biomass • Reduced primary production and energy capture due to leaf loss • Reduced secondary production at least until new flush of plant growth • Diversion of photosynthate to plant shoots • Reduction of organic turnover by decomposition
Nutrient circulation	• Loss of elements by windblow of ash, smoke and volatization • Diminution and simplification of nutrient cycle • Reduced retention of nutrient capital in organic matter • Reduced significance of litter layers in decomposition • Enhanced loss of elements by surface run off and leaching • Changed rate of nitrogen fixation
Water circulation	• Reduction in interception of precipitation • Increase in through fall • Reduction in transpiration • Increase in surface run-off • Reduction in moisture in upper soil layers due to greater evaporation • Increase in soil moisture and higher water table • Increase in water discharge
Soil development	• Increase in soil erosion with loss of vegetation cover • Reduction in soil breakdown by organic acids with loss of organic matter • Formation of a base rich soil surface layer • Increase in pH of soil surface layer affecting micro-organisms (e.g. nitrifiers) • Darkening of soil with charcoal and loss of vegetation resulting in higher soil temperature • Death and decomposition of plant roots • Increase in nutrient loss by leaching • Possible progressive long term decline in soil nutrient capital • Increased salinity with loss of trees and raised water table

Source: Ovington, 1984

a protected area to maintain some artificial grazing areas in otherwise forested regions; such grazing grounds support a slightly higher density of ungulates and are more accessible for wildlife viewing. Fire has many uses:

• It is a fast way of clearing scrub vegetation before replanting: early season burning of grassland is a standard way of reducing the risk of more dangerous and destructive fires later in the season.

• Burned strips act as firebreaks to reduce the potential spread of wild fires.

Fire is a powerful management tool but a very dangerous one. It must be used with great care and expertise. Too-frequent burning, especially at the wrong time of year in areas of low rainfall and poor soils, can have the opposite effect to that desired by suppressing perennial grasses and favouring bush encroachment and thicket formation. The relative effects of fire vary with climate, soil fertility and moisture, other local characteristics, the season in which burns take place, their frequency, and the weather conditions during the burns, including ambient temperature and wind velocity. Too-frequent burning may lead to less suitable grass species dominating the flora such as the coarse *Imperata cylindrica* grass of tropical Asia, which is now a major problem. A burning regime which in one part of a country can lead to the elimination of woody vegetation in favour of perennial grassland, elsewhere in the same country may suppress the grasses in favour of woody plants, scrub encroachment and accelerated soil erosion.

Careful observation of the effects of fires under known conditions and following known burning practices will provide information on the general effects of different burning strategies in various habitat types. Example 8.9 lists some of the possible effects of burning on ecological processes.

Some general guidelines on the use of fire as a management tool in a protected area are:

• Do not burn in periods of extreme drought.
• Do not burn in very windy conditions when fire can get out of hand or spread to unscheduled habitat.
• Ensure wildlife will not be trapped by fires.
• Burn small areas at a time – do not start longer firelines than you can control.
• Cut, rather than burn, wherever feasible.
• Know the fire ecology and fire history of the area and monitor and record all burns.

Grazing by domestic animals as a management tool

Grazing of domestic stock is generally incompatible with the aims of a protected area. In most cases to allow it would be to condone the introduction of an exotic or exotics which have not evolved with the natural environment. For example, in many parts of Africa, like the arid regions of Botswana, native species are either solitary and sedentary or gregarious and highly mobile. The introduction of cattle under most management regimes has resulted in a sedentary gregarious species that has a marked influence on the local habitats and competes seriously with wild herbivores.

Sometimes grazing by domestic stock may be permitted in a protected area as a temporary expedient in times of natural catastrophe such as drought. This can have two serious consequences. It encourages pastoralists with access to such 'emergency' grazing to overstock the range; and it accentuates the stresses on wild browsing and grazing animals, which are also likely to be short of resources because of the drought. This, in turn, compounds the pressures on the habitat. Example 8.10 lists some of the effects of grazing by domestic stock on ecological processes.

Example 8.10: Some effects of grazing by domestic stock on five ecological processes

Ecological process	Effects
Natural succession	• Modification of natural succession by treading and selective grazing leading to dominance of unpalatable species • Invasion of weed and exotic species • Reduction of palatable tree, shrub and perennial species and expansion of grassland particularly of annual species • Increased competition with native herbivores • Excretion of dung and urine making vegetation unacceptable to native species • Disturbance of native animal species by domestic grazing

Organic production and decomposition	• Primary production diverted to ground level with loss of trees and shrubs • Reduction in total biomass and possibly energy capture • Decrease in biomass of native animals • Natural decomposition process circumvented by grazing animal cycle • More of primary production diverted to large herbivores • Increased herbage intake leading to less litter and lower rates of decomposition
Nutrient circulation	• Reduction in nutrient pool with fewer nutrients in vegetation • Local and uneven re-allocation of nutrients according to distribution of faeces and urine • Increased rate of nutrient circulation • Replacement of slow cycling through soil organisms by more rapid, plant-animal cycling pools • Initial stages of decomposition in rumen and gut of grazing animals • Loss of nutrient capital with removal in animal products (meat, milk, hides)
Water circulation	• Increased surface run-off • Reduction in interception and transpiration • Soil surface layers drier • Increase in evaporation from soil surface with loss of vegetation cover
Soil development	• Localised overgrazing resulting in soil erosion • Increased exposure of soil especially where animals congregate • Increased salinity with loss of trees and shrubs • Increased soil compaction due to treading

Source: Ovington, 1984

Under certain circumstances, grazing or browsing by domestic stock may be permitted in certain categories of protected areas but this should be carefully controlled in terms of well-defined management objectives.

• Grazing may be useful for maintaining a desirable level of ecological succession. Grazing by domestic animals can help maintain open grassland to attract and encourage wild ungulates. This is less laborious than cutting and less dangerous than burning, but also harder to control and may lead to elimination of the desired species of grasses.
• There may sometimes be strong socio-economic reasons for allowing some grazing rights inside some categories of protected area.
• Grazing by domestic livestock may help to preserve a specific flora and associated fauna that is limited to heavily-grazed pasture. In Great Britain, several rare plants, butterflies and other species are confined to grazed chalk downs. Originally these communities evolved when deer and hares were the main grazing agents but now the pastures are maintained by sheep grazing. Remove the sheep to form a nature reserve and the species managers are trying to save will be lost.
• Grazing domestic stock, which are dipped to kill ticks, can be used to curb unnaturally high tick populations in parks.

If grazing is considered in a protected area, the principal points to be kept in mind are:

• The manager must maintain absolute control over grazing rights. As soon as the desired level is reached, the manager must have the authority to stop the practice. No sense of traditional grazing rights must be allowed to develop. Mkomazi Game Reserve in Tanzania, for example, has been overrun by pastoralists after they had been allowed an initial 'foot in the door'.
• There may be dangers of spreading disease and parasites from domestic stock to wild populations. Ungulate diseases and parasites are generally rather broad in their specificity.

- Grazing should not be permitted if the domestic stock actually disturb or displace wild ungulates.
- No such grazing should be permitted if the activites of stockherders cannot also be controlled; such herdsmen should not be allowed to hunt, light fires, burn land to improve the short-term grazing, or to be accompanied by dogs.
- The effects of grazing by domestic livestock should be carefully monitored to ensure that the protected area does not lose any of its original values due to the presence of the stock.

Harvesting of plant products in protected areas

Various degrees of harvesting of plant products may be allowed within protected areas depending upon the category of the reserves and their specific objectives. Such harvesting can range from collection of seeds for storage and *ex situ* propagation to agroforestry, and varying degrees of use between these two extremes.

Any bulk harvesting will have permanent effects on the continued productivity of the forest. Fallen leaves and dead wood, for example, should not be removed from a Category I or II reserve as they contain vital nutrients which will be recycled into the ecosystem and dead wood is also an important microhabitat. Some tropical forests stand on very poor soils and are highly dependent on the recycling of minerals from decaying litter. Even very modest harvesting of dead wood and leaves could cause a real decrease in the forest productivity. Yet other forests can sustain quite substantial harvesting of living and dead materials.

Different types of harvesting are listed below in increasing order of the disturbance they cause to the natural ecosystem:

47. Illegal grazing in Amboseli National Park in Kenya has been a continuing management issue between the park authorities and the local Masai. Impacts have been severe yet a fully satisfactor solution to the problem has not been found.
Photo: J. Thorsell

- Collection of botanical specimens for identification
- Collection of seeds or tubers for *ex situ* propagation
- Collection of fruits for human consumption
- Collection of medicinal herbs
- Harvesting of dead wood for fires
- Cutting of thatch
- Cutting of fodder for domestic animals
- Collection of ornamental plants (ferns, orchids, aroids, etc.)
- Harvesting of bamboo and rattan
- Cutting of poles for construction
- Selective non-mechanical harvesting of timber hauled by hand or animal
- Selective harvesting of timber mechanically
- Agroforestry

Deciding on what level of harvesting is permissible, and when, in a given reserve will depend on the management objectives of the area and the damage or threat posed by the activity. Many of these activities would not be allowed in most protected areas except as a management activity. Where harvesting is allowed, it must be:

- carefully controlled;
- kept within prescribed zones;
- restricted to limited timespans or to certain seasons, e.g. so as not to disturb breeding animals;
- kept within fixed quotas;
- controlled by an effective system to check these activities, and to suspend them all together should the ecological interests of the area so dictate.

Example 8.11: Overgrazing by domestic cattle in the Nxai Pan National Park, Botswana

Nxai Pan is an old lake bed on the north-western fringe of the extensive Makadikadi saline system in north-central Botswana. This is an important wet season grazing area, attracting spectacular concentrations of game of a variety of species. Overgrazing, by cattle in particular, has grossly modified the vegetation to the west of the pan, altering it from lightly wooded grassland to dense thicket in the space of 17 years. This has resulted in the local disappearance of roan antelope and springbok, and to a reduction of wildebeest, in the areas affected by this bush encroachment.

Heavy grazing by cattle began in 1949 as part of the Colonial Development Corporation's beef production scheme in Botswana, which survived for less than a decade, leaving behind it widespread habitat deterioration. In the Nxai Pan area, the heavy grazing pressure was reduced to a low level after a few years as the programme faltered, but from 1956 heavy grazing occurred again when large numbers of cattle were moved through the area to export markets in Zambia and Katanga.

By 1966, the vegetation comprised a dense thicket, locally impenetrable to species such as gemsbok, and through which a route had to be bulldozed to permit the passage of cattle. The scrub consisted of a number of species with fire-sensitive forms showing the characteristic ground level coppice caused by fires burning back the aerial stems without damaging the roots. These then produce new stems after each successive fire.

Examination of the vegetation suggests there were two thresholds in the transformation of the vegetation from grassland to thicket. Heavy grazing during the Colonial Development Corporation scheme led to suppression of grass vigour and permitted the establishment of the thicket-forming species; but there was still adequate grass for fires of sufficient intensity to kill off the stems. The second threshold followed closely after the stock route through the area was opened up and the new wave of heavy grazing further reduced the grass cover. Significant fires were no longer possible and the stems grew out, possibly further contributing to the decline of the sward by 'shading out' the grass that survived.

Similar vegetation thresholds are found elsewhere in Botswana, also due to the mismanagement of domestic livestock, leading to the invasion by woody plants of previously open, well-grassed habitats.

Sources: Child, 1968; Paris and Child, 1973

Hunting in and around protected areas

Hunting is clearly one of the main management objectives in areas specifically designated as hunting reserves. It may also be allowed in a few multiple-use reserves but is generally prohibited in other types of protected areas. Whether hunting should be allowed on land or buffer zones adjacent to a reserve will depend very much on the individual situation. In some circumstances, this would be disastrous exposure of the protected populations to highly unnatural levels of disturbance and mortality, sometimes eliminating them from the reserve or at best rendering the hunted species very shy and difficult to see. In other circumstancess, a hunting reserve may be a useful extension of the protected habitat for the wildlife and a useful source of local employment, revenue, meat, and other useful products. Controlled hunting by either locals or sportsmen may also be useful in eliminating animals which leave reserves to raid neighbouring agricultural crops for food or as compensation for the damage such animals cause.

In some national parks, hunting is allowed as a means to reduce numbers of alien species. Examples include the hunting of feral pigs and goats in Hawaii Volcanoes National Park and deer and elk in some New Zealand national parks.

The successful and profitable running of a hunting reserve is highly technical and outside the scope of this handbook (useful references include: Leopold, 1933; Caughley, 1977; Van Lavieren, 1983). Such reserves must have satisfactory measures for:

- determining the methods of hunting;
- delimiting the area in which hunting is permitted;
- controlling the number of licensed hunters using the area;
- limiting the hunting period;
- setting balanced quotas and bag limits;
- optimising off-take;
- controlling the quota of harvestable animals;
- controlling the age/sex classes of animals hunted: e.g. hunting of females may be prohibited;
- monitoring off-take for numbers, quality and hunter effort;
- controlling the types of firearms and ammunition used;
- having trained staff to dispatch injured animals;
- instituting safeguards to prevent accidents to hunters or staff;
- protecting protected species in the hunting area;
- providing facilities for the cleaning of trophies and for the storage and utilisation of carcases;
- collecting revenues – licence fees and kill or bag taxes.

Wildlife farming and utilisation

The development of commercial breeding of wildlife species (through rearing and farming methods) can help take utilisation pressure off wild populations, and can even prove a benefit to them (by way of returned animals). Moreover, such commercial enterprises can help to justify the continued protection of the wild populations on which the industry is ultimately dependent. Example 8.12 indicates a number of ways in which a crocodile industry can be effectively controlled.

The amazing recovery of the vicuna is a classic example of the conservation benefits of such utilisation. The vicuna was nearly driven to extinction by over-exploitation but was saved by international conservation efforts to the point where vicuna can once again be harvested to bring benefits to local people (see Example 8.13).

In some categories of protected areas, it is possible to include objectives specifically aimed at managing populations of wild species with the aim of allowing collection for rearing and farming stock. However, there may be dangers in encouraging legitimate trade in wildlife species if protection of the wild populations is still inadequate especially if it is not possible to control the trade or distinguish products from reared or wild specimens. On the other hand, a legitimate trade often encourages regulation and hence the better conservation of wild populations. The following points should be considered:

- Develop a system whereby there is a net gain to the wild population. In exchange for permits to remove from the wild either breeding stock or eggs and young for captive rearing projects, the farming/rearing agency must agree to make available for release into the wild an agreed number of animals or percentage of reared stock, should this be deemed desirable by the management authority.

- Link farming and utilisation closely to adequate protection of wild populations. Maintain close links both spatially and in terms of formal cooperation between the protection of the wild population and the licensed wildlife farming/rearing agency.

- Develop a control system that makes it difficult for wild stock to be poached and traded as farmed animals. Methods can include application of upper size limits and supervised marking of captive stock. This is particularly important for species listed under the Convention for the International Trade in Endangered Species of Fauna and Flora (CITES), particularly Category I, for which authenticated documentation indicating captive-bred material must be provided by the national management authority.

- Avoid creating a legal loophole by which an illicit trade can develop under the aegis of a legitimate trade. In South Africa, for instance, farmers have developed effective methods of ranching and breeding white rhinoceros. It would be possible to start a very profitable legitimate trade in farmed rhinoceros horn (these can be harvested without killing the animal which grows a new horn). However, in the interests of stamping out poaching of wild rhino this possibility has not been exploited and there is a total ban on any export of rhino products.

Management for the maintenance of hydrological regimes

The role of vegetation cover in maintaining hydrological regimes is of extreme importance. Water is vital to human survival, human agriculture, and human industry. In many cases the protection of water sources is the most valuable use that can be made of upland catchments. Guidelines for selecting such hydrological protection reserves have been given in Chapter 3.

Hydrological reserves protect the water-generating capacity of a catchment, by controlling soil erosion, and preventing siltation of waterways, dams, canals and irrigation channels. They also function to reduce the incidence and scale of flooding and provide waterflow during dry periods.

In most cases, the best management for a hydrological reserve or a reserve serving a major water catchment function is to protect and maintain a thick cover of the original vegetation. Where this is not possible, or where the original vegetation cover has already been destroyed, replanting may be necessary. The following points should be considered:

- Rate of soil erosion is more closely related to the ground vegetation than to the upper storey cover. Thick grass or scrub gives better soil protection than a tree crop with bare understorey, such as is often found in teak plantations. Tree leaves focus rainfall into heavier spouts and droplets which can cause more severe erosion than the rainfall itself. Natural forests act as good protection because of the undergrowth and especially the layers of leaf litter that protect the soil.

- The potential for sheet erosion (caused by surface water passing over the ground) and gulley erosion (where draining water creates or widens the drainage channels) increase with gradient and length of slope. On steep slopes, it is vital to maintain a thick ground cover.

- Highest erosion losses occur where bare soil is exposed to rain or flowing water. This is most severe when land is cultivated or burned annually. Erosion levels can be as much as a hundred times greater on burned areas than on ground with natural vegetation cover (MacKinnon, 1983).

- The 'sponge' effect of natural vegetation cover is due to root penetration increasing soil porosity so that water is absorbed and run-off is slower. This vegetation cover is most needed to slow run-off and prevent erosion on lower slopes and in the wet tropics tree cover is much better for achieving this than grass or shrubs.

- In drier parts of the tropics, high water losses due to the transpiration of trees and other woody plants may be undesirable. In many parts of Africa, a ground cover of grasses and sedges in the upper drainage of tributaries is much preferred for hydrological protection.

- Water channels should be as convoluted as possible with check dams, gabions, bolsters, etc., if necessary, to retard drainage, maintain high water tables and catch sedimentation.

Example 8.12: Schematic representation of activities needed to organise and control a crocodile export industry

The level of checks and controls that are needed to regulate a wildlife industry, permitting a legal trade but prohibiting an illegal trade is extremely complex. In the example given, the management agency must set harvest quotas; check that these are adhered to; witness the kill to mark legal skins; remove returned animals to the wild; and distinguish legal from illegal material at each stage in the rearing and export process. Having a maximum size limit for exported skins is a vital control to discourage the shooting of the adult wild breeding population.

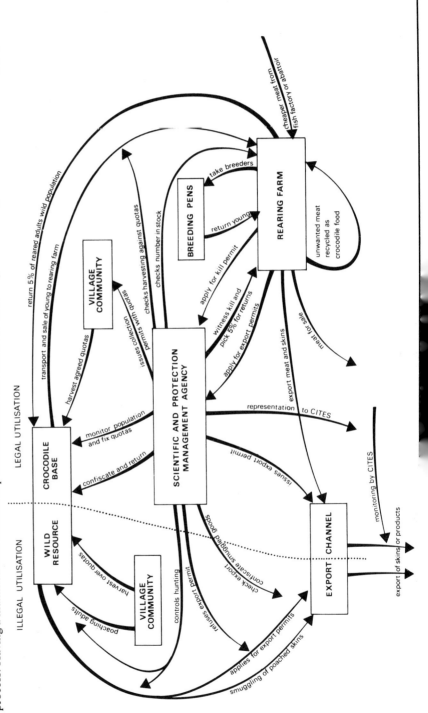

Example 8.13: Vicuna: from endangered species to harvestable resource

The rescue of the vicuna in the Pampa Galeras National Reserve, Peru, is a classic, though controversial, example of how conservation can be profitably integrated to meet regional needs. The flow chart shows the range of benefits that have been developed since 1964 when negotiations with local communities first began at a time when the vicuna was on the edge of extinction.

Pampa Galeras National Vicuna Reserve, Peru: simplified schematic model or flow chart

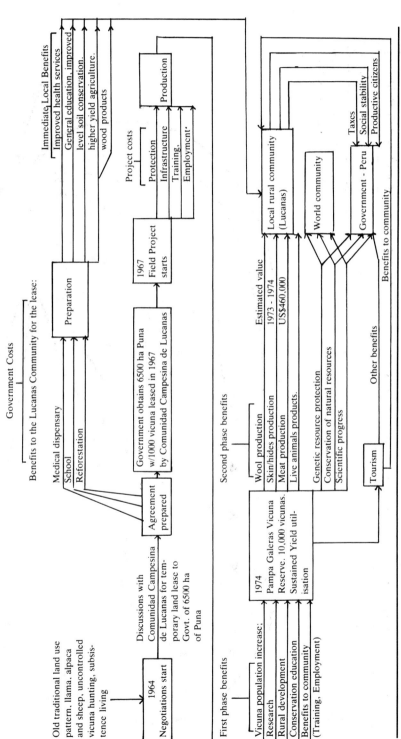

Source: A. Dalfelt, 1976

Ditches, drains and artificial canals or erosion gullies can change the water table and modify the natural vegetation.

- Burning under tree cover is almost as likely to cause erosion as burning vegetation in open areas. Cultivation of land under tree cover, however, can actually increase soil porosity and thus decrease erosion depending on slope and soil-type.
- Logging roads (and other poorly aligned and constructed roads) cause very high levels of gulley erosion in logged forests with otherwise good vegetation cover. Even selective logging should not be permitted in important water catchments.
- Settlers inside important catchments should not be allowed to burn vegetation to cultivate land. They should be translocated to new areas in the interests of the wider community. Strictly-controlled grazing alone is usually less harmful than burning, provided this does not reach levels of overgrazing leading to impoverishment of the sward, and hoof erosion.

Protection of aesthetic values and geological sites

Some of the values for which the protected area is created can be very subtle in form – an atmosphere of wildness, beautiful views which may extend beyond the boundaries of the protected area, silence, or a pristine waterfall. Such values may be destroyed quite inadvertently by various developments. A distant concrete tower or a line of electricity pylons can destroy a whole panorama. The sound of overhead aircraft or tourists with radios can break the spell of tranquil silence. A garish signboard or a pile of litter can ruin the pleasure of experiencing unspoiled nature. The magic of a cave of stalactites is broken by crude graffiti or the chipped traces of souvenir collectors.

The manager of a protected area must identify which features he wants to preserve and take the appropriate action to protect them. In some cases, he may wish to close access to certain features, such as waterfalls, geysers, mud spouts, or archaeological ruins and allow visitor viewing only from a distance.

The management authority must take care not to destroy the wild aspects and scenery of the protected area with its own roads, buildings and other structures and must lobby other agencies to prevent developments that threaten reserve values. It may be possible to enhance views by clearing natural vegetation or constructing lookout platforms in suitable places.

It may be necessary to employ a professional geologist to identify features of geophysical interest (e.g. fossil beds, petrified forests, etc.) and advise measures for their protection. Fossil sites and some dynamic geological features such as mud volcanoes, hot springs, fumaroles, glaciers, sand dunes, or deltas, may be particularly vulnerable. A geologist can also be consulted on the advisability of construction works in the protected area. Fox (1984) gives a cautionary tale of what damage a well-intentioned park staff can cause to a protected area through ignorance of the geology of the area.

Directing research activities for the benefit of management

Research is an important aspect of good management of protected areas and some guidelines on useful types of research for management purposes are presented in Chapter 9, pages 203-8 and Example 9.8. In addition, research *per se* is a legitimate activity in protected areas and can usually be compatible with most protected area objectives. However, it is important for the management authority to have a clear policy of what research it will allow and on what terms. If this is stated clearly at the outset, it can avoid later fric-

tion with the scientific research community. Some suggested guidelines are:

- Each research project should be approved by both the relevant national scientific institute and the management authority of the protected area.
- When approving research, the protected area manager must check that the project is compatible with the objectives of the reserve. The authority may request slight modifications to

the project to make it more relevant to management needs, or to better complement other research projects in the area.

- Researchers should submit periodic written progress reports and occasional verbal presentations of their findings to the protected area staff.
- On completion of the study, the researcher should submit a full final report on his studies, with a compulsory section on the relevance of the findings to management of the protected area.
- Each researcher must be required to send the management authority copies of all scientific and other publications that arise from his research in the protected area and these should give due acknowledgement to the assistance of the reserve management and (where relevant) staff.
- Collection of materials in reserves for identification, study or analysis must require the specific permission of the management authority who may request duplicate specimens and identifications to be deposited at the pro-

tected area or at a national museum. Material to be taken abroad should require a special permit from the relevant national scientific institute which again may insist on duplicate specimens being left in the country or the return of valuable material after examination.

- Researchers should be required to leave copies or summaries of their original qualitative and quantitative data for the files of the protected area, on the assurance that these will be used only for management purposes and will not be quoted in publications for an agreed period or until the researcher himself releases the information.
- The protected area management authority must retain control over all activities in the protected area. This may mean that the reserve manager must give prior approval of researchers' travel and work schedules or he may, for management reasons, place restrictions on such activities. The same rules should apply to departmental research scientists who may not be directly under the manager's command.

The need for inventory and monitoring

A manager wants to answer two types of questions about the species in the reserve:

What species communities occur within the protected area, where and in what numbers? (inventory)

What are population trends over time? (monitoring)

A distinction must be made between these two objectives. The methods used are also quite different. Both involve making sample counts but employ different criteria.

A useful inventory for management purposes can be as simple as a habitat map based on aerial photography with ground checks, augmented by information on the distribution of important species. Data should be collected on those species which are ecologically dominant forms, endangered species or species whose numbers reflect important ecological processes. Even crude indications of the numbers of these species will add to the value of the inventory. An inventory can be completed during a single visit and its accuracy will increase as more new areas are sampled, rather than by resampling the same area.

Changes in the distribution and abundance of species are of major significance to management. These are usually determined by periodically measuring similar samples, i.e. by recording trends over time. It is also possible to judge whether populations are increasing, stable or decreasing from data collected on a single visit using techniques as outlined by Riney (1982). For the results of periodic sampling to be meaningful, the sampling techniques and the sample areas should be the same throughout. If there is likely to be seasonal variation, care should be taken to repeat samples at the same time of year. For instance, ungulates may move seasonally or may be less visible at certain times because the grass is longer, so the annual census should always be made in the same month and at the same localities every year.

Highly precise numbers are seldom important except where populations are to be managed intensively, as for example when culling an elephant population. Whereas conservationists often make a great play on the numbers of rare species, from a management point of view it is much more important to know the trend of species populations. Is the population stable, increasing or declining? The answer will determine management policy.

Monitoring biological resources should be a basic routine activity in protected area management. It is the principal way in which the management can check the condition of the environment and identify trends or changes and so gauge the effectiveness of its actions. Often this is an unplanned and subjective procedure but it is easy to collect useful biological information in a simple, systematic and scientific manner. Useful sampling methods can be found in specific books and papers on monitoring techniques (see Mosby, 1963; Giles, 1971; Ferrar, 1983; MacDonald and Grimsdell, 1983; Van Lavieren, 1983 and Riney, 1982).

It will soon become obvious, however, that the job of monitoring fully a large wilderness area including hundreds or thousands of living species is impossible. The manager has to be very selective and restrict observations to a few indicator species or key phenomena which reflect broader trends, and to other measurements that give an indication of the general biological condition of the environment.

It is almost impossible, for example, to measure the populations of many small plants and invertebrates, but it is known that most are closely tied to particular habitat types, which can be recognised from certain common or conspicuous indicator species. By monitoring the extent and condition of the respective habitat types, it can be determined if any changes are likely in the populations of associated species. Without identifying a single species (it is only necessary to distinguish sampled forms), it is possible to make estimates of species richness both of plants and invertebrates using species discovery curves. If, for instance, it is found that over a ten-year period the area of a certain habitat type has shrunk by 30 per cent but that measurements of species richness of plants and insects have not changed, it can be assumed that all the original species associated in that habitat type are still present, even though the population of each species has declined. Conversely, it might be found that the area of habitat has stayed the same but species discovery curves indicate that there has been a considerable loss of species richness. In this case, it can be assumed that the commoner species have probably increased in numbers but that many rarer species have been lost.

Monitoring usually aims at recording three different features of biological resources.

- Trends in population numbers of key plant and animal species over time, including historical evidence where possible
- The measurement of reproductive success or productivity of species
- Assessing the quality or condition of species and habitats

A number of useful techniques have been developed to census populations. Plants are easier to count than animals because they remain stationary. Some methods involve direct sighting and counting from set observation posts, or while walking along census trails, from boats along rivers, from moving vehicles or aerial surveys. Other methods use indirect signs such as tracks, droppings, pellet counts, nests, and vocalisations (Van Lavieren, 1983; Mosby, 1963; Caughley, 1977).

Measuring reproductive success involves estimating the proportion of the breeding population, the mean number of offspring produced per breeding individual, and the proportion of offspring surviving. Productivity includes reproduction but also takes into account the increases in size of the individuals of the population. It covers the overall turnover of the population.

Measuring the quality and condition of species involves estimating such parameters as size, weight, fat deposits, age/sex structure of the population, and incidence of disease. Measuring the quality and condition of habitats can involve examining soil loss and water run-off patterns, measuring total biological productivity or assessing species composition. Measures of overall species richness can be very revealing. In forests, it is useful to document the size and structure of the trees (e.g. diameter at breast height). New methods enable a botanist to describe the forest trees as 'trees of the future', 'trees of the present', or 'trees of the past', which reveals much about the forest's condition – whether it is growing, stable or senescent (Halle *et al.*, 1978). Similarly, for animals it is sometimes possible to deduce much about population condition and trends (whether declining, stable or increasing) from a one-time sample of the age/sex structure and physical condition of the population (see Riney, 1982).

With advice from scientists and ecologists, the manager should be able to include a number of useful monitoring activities in the routine duties of the work force, as well as special seasonal or annual censuses, counts or other activities. He can seek advice on more sophisticated methods of sampling and analysis of results, but many trends

Example 8.14: ***Age structures of population*** *(examination of the age/sex structure of a wildlife population gives the manager valuable information on its condition)*

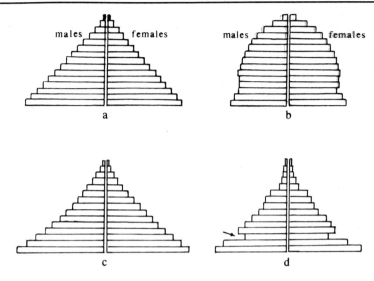

a) Stationary population: natality and mortality constant
b) Regressive population: declining natality
c) Progressive population: increasing natality
d) The marked age-class has suffered excessive mortality
   (epidemics, natural calamity)

Source: Riney, 1982

can be recognised by plotting simple histograms against a time scale. When erratic noncyclic trends appear, this is a signal of ecological imbalance and is usually the time to call in experts to see if the changes are serious and to advise on any appropriate revisions in management practices.

Management trials and experiments

Active manipulation of ecosystems is not only permissible but in many cases vital for the successful management of many types of protected area. Habitat manipulation, such as the provision of grass or grains for migratory wildfowl, is particularly appropriate in Category IV wildlife refuges. It is worth repeating a number of general principles that should be followed in implementing such management:

Before applying a new form of management on a wider scale, it is wise to run a small trial first. Select a non-critical area for running the trial. This need not necessarily be in the reserve; provided the environmental factors are sufficiently similar to those where the eventual application is planned.

- Choose a control area as similar as possible in every way to the trial area to compare the effects of the management.
- If the test involves any introduction of species, the trial area should be isolated from similar habitat so that the introduced species can be contained and eradicated if they should prove unsuitable.
- Keep accurate records of methods and results and test the results using appropriate statistics before applying an apparently successful strategy elsewhere.

If the results look favourable, the next step is to cost the management activity in terms of manpower, materials, and transport, and consider the possible risks and indirect consequences of introducing the practice. Time-and-motion studies may be useful to decide between alternative management practices.

Management trials may often be conducted by outside scientists. In this case, the manager should be consulted and have the right to comment upon or to veto the experiments. What may be interesting science may be out of line with management objectives.

9

Planning for Protected Areas

Introduction

Good planning is central to good protected area management, but it is merely a management tool and not an end in itself. It is an on-going process involving the formulation, submission and approval of management objectives, how these are to be attained and standards against which to measure their achievement. Good planning leads to good management; poor planning, or lack of planning, impedes successful management. There is no value in plans, however beautifully presented, that are impractical or do not result in effective action.

The first step in planning must be the formulation of clear, sensible objectives, within the policy framework of the protected area management authority. The plan must then outline the actions needed to achieve these objectives, specify the cost of implementation and justify these costs for budgetary approval. After implementation, the results are evaluated and the process begins anew with the preparation of follow-up plans. This process may be repeated at different levels of detail and to cover different time-spans. Planning may involve the production of a long-term national or regional conservation strategy for a system of protected areas or, on a much smaller scale, a single management operation in one protected area. These different levels of planning will be discussed from the general to the particular.

National strategies for conservation

The *World Conservation Strategy* (WCS) outlines the ways in which conservation objectives should be integrated into broader land-use plans and development projects in order to obtain more benefit and sustained yields from the world's renewable natural resources. One of the first steps is the preparation by each country or state of its own National Conservation Strategy (NCS).

The National Conservation Strategy should summarise the total renewable natural resources of the country in terms of ecosystems, genetic resources, natural production systems (forests, wildlife, fisheries), water catchments and hydrological regimes, aesthetic and geological features, cultural sites and recreation potential. The Strat-

egy should evaluate current and potential benefits derived from these resources and any existing or potential threats to these benefits. It should also identify how the nation wishes to use its natural resources and design patterns of land use that will safeguard their availability and generally maximise the long-term benefits within the limits imposed by the country's specific needs for living space, agricultural land, forest products, fisheries, energy and industry. A major part of this Strategy should be the decision to designate or maintain a national system of protected areas, preferably including several categories with different management objectives. A sample Table of Contents for a typical NCS is presented in Example 9.1.

Example 9.1: *Sample table of contents for a typical National Conservation Strategy (Vietnam)*

Preface
Executive Summary

PART I - INTRODUCTION

I.1. The setting for the production of a NCS for Vietnam
I.2. Conservation for sustainable development

PART II - THE CURRENT SITUATION

II.1. Environmental Profile of Socialist Republic of Vietnam

a) Geographical setting	i) Agricultural production
b) Landform and soils	j) Industrial production
c) Climate	k) Energy resources
d) Natural vegetation	l) Mineral resources
e) Wild genetic resources	m) Human population
f) Fisheries	n) Workforce
g) Environmental impacts of war	o) Cultural aspects
h) Land-use	p) Standard of living
	q) Education

II.2. The development context of Vietnam
II.3. Conservation needs in relation to development in Vietnam

Maintenance of Ecological Processes and Life-support Systems

a) Forest life-support system	d) Freshwater life-support system
b) Midlands life-support system	e) Estuarine and coastal life-support system
c) Cropland life-support system	f) Deep sea life-support system

Preservation of Genetic Diversity

a) Development of protected areas	d) Control of trade
b) Protected species	e) *Ex situ* conservation
c) Hunting regulations	

Sustained utilisation of resources
Maintenance of environmental quality for human life
Attainment of a balanced state

II.4. International implications
a) Management and utilisation of migrant species
b) Management of shared transfrontier resources
c) Management of resources of international concern
d) Management of transfrontier watersheds
e) Control and organisation of international trade
f) Participation in international cooperative efforts
g) Access to foreign aid and technical assistance
h) Preservation of cultural heritage

II.5. The obstacles to conservation

PART III - THE STRATEGY

III.1. Purposes of the National Conservation Strategy
    a) Goal
    b) The strategic aim
    c) Objectives

III.2. Operational principles to be used in the implementation of the National Conservation Strategy
III.3. Summary of issues and cross-sectoral actions needed
III.4. Vehicles for priority conservation action

    Organisations involved in the NCS
    a) National board of environmental coordination
    b) Ministries
    c) Government committees and institutions
    d) Non-governmental organisations

    Policy matters
    Planning
    Legislation and organisation
    Education, public awareness and training
    Information and research
    The need for international arrangements
    Specific projects
    Public participation

II.5. Internal responsibilities
II.6. External agency involvement

ART IV - IMPLEMENTATION

V.1. Schedules for action

ART V - METHODS FOR MONITORING PROGRESS AND MAINTAINING THE NCS

.1 Monitoring
.2. Maintaining the NCS
.3. Launching the NCS
.4. Eliciting public participation

PPENDICES

urce: Government of Vietnam/IUCN, 1985

Systems planning for protected areas

The next step, which may be included within the National Conservation Strategy or may be a separate exercise, is the preparation of a plan for a National System of Protected Areas. The systems plan is the design of a total reserve system giving protective coverage to the full range of ecosystems and species communities found in the particular country. This plan should be based on the principles outlined in Chapter 3 on the Selection of Protected Areas. It should aim to evaluate existing and proposed protected areas, and assess their overall suitability for inclusion in the different categories of protected areas. On the basis of this appraisal, proposals can be made as to which areas should be developed as protected areas and in what priority.

Ideally, the resulting national system of protected areas will be a balanced and representative sample of the natural ecosystems of the country. Each reserve should be large enough to survive independently as an ecological unit so that if it is well planned and managed it can continue to provide useful benefits to future generations.

The National Protected Areas Systems Plan will initially be a draft proposal and may include alternatives and guidance to help decison-makers make final selections. It will need considerable discussion and review by the regions concerned and the other government departments involved in its implementation. The draft evolves to an approved plan as the selection process progresses and certain areas are chosen in preference to others. Many decisions will rest with the protected area management authority itself. For instance, where the national plan requires the inclusion of one example of a certain habitat type in the reserve system and only two such areas exist, the management authority may initially investigate the larger area as it covers a wider altitudinal range and is less populated. However, subsequent ground surveys may reveal that the smaller area is much richer in species and the authority will then request this area in preference to the first. Such feasibility or suitability surveys are an important feature of systems planning.

Eventually the National Protected Area Systems Plan becomes an approved policy document and the process of applying for and acquiring new protected areas, or revising the boundaries of existing reserves, carries the plan towards the realisation of a complete reserve system. Examples of countries where system plans have been prepared include Brazil, Costa Rica, Indonesia, Kenya and Oman. (Examples of the methods used are given in Chapters 2 and 3.)

Planning of feasibility studies

Feasibility studies and other preliminary surveys are a vital step between large-scale national planning and the actual development of reserves on the ground. The need for such studies will soon become clear to anyone engaged in planning national systems. Of fundamental importance are specific answers to such questions as the following: Where is more detailed information needed before a definite proposal can be made for a protected area? What are the area's specific values, the most suitable boundaries, and to which category of protected areas should it be assigned?

To be successful, the feasibility study must itself be well prepared. It should have definite objectives. All available background information must be collected and studied *before* the survey. Enough time, trained personnel and suitable equipment must be allocated to do the job properly. It is useless to undertake such surveys in a casual way without proper objectives or sufficient time. Far too many reports contain statements like: 'The forested hills looked rather interesting but unfortunately we did not have time to visit them.' – 'The villagers claim there are huge waterfalls on the other side of the mountain but we could not verify this.' – 'The coastal areas may also be of interest but we did not have snorkelling equipment nor funds to rent a boat.' The limited resources available for conservation in the tropics require that the job be done right the first time.

The objectives of feasibility studies vary considerably but stating them clearly will greatly improve the efficiency of the survey over the 'general look around' approach. Examples of clear feasibility objectives could be:

- Assess the suitability of the 'V' mountains for development as a National Park.
- Survey the province of 'W' for sites of touristic interest and potential for recreation development.

- Survey the southern boundaries of the 'X' reserve to make recommendations for its revised alignment and the location of buffer zones.
- Survey the mangrove forests along the east coast of 'Y' province to select the most suitable examples for reserve development.
- Examine the rates of stream flow and levels of erosion in the 'Z' district and make recommendations on the extent of forest cover required to protect the catchment.

The following steps should be included in a feasibility survey:

- List the objectives of the survey.
- Assign the objectives to be achieved at specific localities with approximate length of time needed at each location. Allow time to collect data from local informants, e.g. village heads, residents, local department offices.
- Design travel itinerary.
- Allow for contingencies. Delays may occur due to breakdowns of public transport, blocked roads, floods, lack of expected facilities, absence of key informants, etc.
- Prepare a budget and list of equipment needed for the field survey.
- Gather relevant background information: maps, aerial photos, inter-departmental reports and those published by other agencies, such as land-use plans, irrigation plans, communication networks, and resettlement programmes.
- Arrange permits, travel budgets, vouchers, letters of introduction.

- Execute survey. Make sure that the time allowed for execution is sufficient to achieve the objectives (e.g., consider seasonal climate).
- On return, allow time for collation of data and preparation of the report.
- Budget for report reproduction and distribution and allow time for follow-up discussions with concerned parties.

The Feasibility Report should answer as concisely as possible the questions posed in the objectives. The report should not be cluttered with all the disjointed bits of information that may have been collected by the survey team. It should, however, quote the types of information collected, where they are deposited and their sources, and list key local people who may be useful future contacts.

There is no need for feasibility reports to include long lists of the team members and the itinerary of the survey. A route map or list of localities visited is sufficient. The head office may require a detailed itinerary to confirm that the team did their job properly but this should be filed separately as a field trip report and not included in the final feasibility report.

Clarity, brevity and attractive presentation are the keys to successful reporting. Extensive lists of Latin names, long wordy descriptions and discussions give a very shallow impression of hard work. The decision makers who need the report will not have time to look at a lengthy document and in skipping through it may miss the vital points.

Management plans

Introduction

It is now accepted as a basic principle of protected area management, that every protected area should have a management plan. The management plan guides and controls the management of protected area resources, the uses of the area, and the development of facilities needed to support that management and use. It facilitates all development activities and all management actions to be implemented in an area.

Central to such a plan is a statement of goals and measurable objectives to guide the management of the area. These goals and objectives form the framework for determining what actions to take, when they will be taken, and the budget and personnel needed to implement them. A management plan is a valuable tool for identifying management needs, setting priorities and organising the approach to the future.

A management plan provides this guidance for a specified period of time, typically five years. Annual operations plans are developed during the implementation phase using the longer-term management plan as a guide. The management plan is always subject to modification as new information is obtained, particularly regarding feedback on the effectiveness of the actions taken in the annual operations plan.

By identifying the management steps necessary

for the protected area, and the resources needed to take them, the management plan helps the manager to allocate, and make best use of, his limited staff, funding, equipment and materials. Where such resources are inadequate to achieve the management objectives, the plan can be used to document these deficiencies and list the protected area's needs. In this way the plan becomes a valuable fund-raising tool to seek needed support both internally and from outside assistance programmes.

A management plan can also serve as a communication tool to gain the understanding and support of both the general public and relevant government officials. Such understanding is important for gaining the cooperation of local peoples and the political support needed for adequate funding.

Finally, the management planning process can be important training for management personnel. Involvement in the planning process exposes staff to the full range of management needs which leads to a fuller understanding of their role. The management plan aids this process by providing continuity over time and facilitates consistency during staff transfers.

A word on terminology is in order here. Many managers and planners may be more familiar with the term 'master plan' for what is described here as a 'management plan'. The two terms are essentially synonymous. The term management plan is preferred, for the simple reason that 'master plan' implies a comprehensive and complete document, one that is static and covers all possible situations. What is needed, however, is a flexible plan that can be modified to reflect new information and changing needs. The term 'management plan' embodies these characteristics and identifies its orientation to managers and management.

Those working on a planning team should attempt to keep the plan as simple as possible, particularly at the start, in keeping with real-life limitations on funding, staffing, staff expertise, degree of national development, and the like. The simpler the plan, the easier it will be to develop and implement. It will take less time to prepare, it will cost less, it will be more flexible to change, it will be easier to read and understand, and it will require fewer staff with lower levels of training – all of which are important factors to consider in a developing country. Complexity of detail and sophistication of approach will evolve naturally as the plan is regularly updated and as increased support, based on measurable progress, becomes available.

What the Management Plan should not be (but often is) is a compendium of all existing biological information and scientific descriptions about a given reserve. The three main target audiences – planners, reserve managers and local government – are probably not scientists and will only be confused by lengthy technical descriptions or lists of scientific names. The fault arises because it is often a scientist who prepares the management plan without due consideration of how the plan is to be used.

Management Plans should be published in the official language(s) of the country. Many excellent plans prepared by foreign experts in their own language have never been implemented because they were never translated and did not always involve local managers in their preparation.

A brief, clear and good looking 'Executive Summary' of the management plan can also be produced for the general public, decision-makers and potential funding sources.

In instances where the data base is inadequate or when a complete management plan is not required, it is possible to abbreviate the planning process by preparing interim management guidelines which serve as a holding action until a full plan can be prepared. They are an acceptable, and perhaps even a necessary, step in the early stages of an area's development.

The protected area management plan process

Although planning methodology can be complex, the basic steps in an idealised procedure are outlined below. The 16 steps listed cover the full range of possible factors to be considered. Needs, limitations and priorities will vary widely with each situation and the management planner must tailor the process to meet his particular circumstances.

Although the planning process is summarised as a list of ordinate steps, it will often be necessary to consider some steps simultaneously, and to review earlier decisions as new information becomes available. Similarly, it is recognised that existing developments in parks may influence decision making. In addition, non-technical factors such as budgets, institutional limitations, and considerations of a political nature may affect the time scheduling of the plan. These factors can only be dealt with at a higher executive level where matters related to the programming of the park system are considered.

As a final caveat, it should be noted that the following steps display a thought process, a means

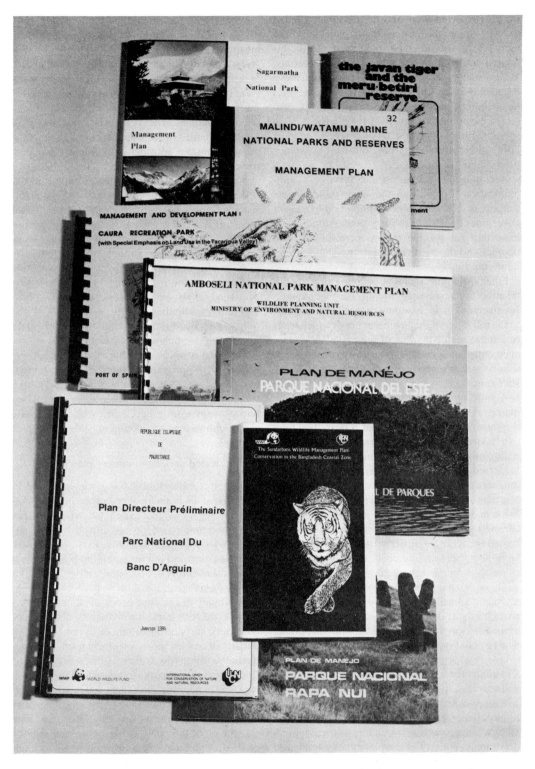

48. The production of clear management plans is a key activity for effective management of
     protected areas.
     Photo: IUCN

of organising a future based on an assessment of the present. It is not, therefore, the nomenclature or the exact order which is important but the process by which one evaluates and addresses the management problems of a protected area. The generalised approach discussed here is based largely on the manual prepared by Miller (1978). For more detail of what to do at each step, the reader is referred to this original work.

Step 1. Form the Planning Team. Although a plan can be prepared by one individual, it is most often a team exercise involving a core group of three to six individuals. It is useful if the team members have a mix of capabilities in the methodology of planning, ecology, sociology, economics, and various other resource sciences. If such individuals are not available from within the agency, they may be hired as consultants, borrowed from regional institutions or universities or requested through outside assistance programmes.

In addition to these specialists, the preparation of a management plan also requires the participation of those who now manage the park as well as those who will use the park or who will be affected by the plan. To be truly effective, the planning process must be responsive to the needs of the managers in the field since they are ultimately responsible for its implementation. If the planning function is centralised at the headquarters office, field managers should still have an integral role in management plan preparation, perhaps through short-term attachments to the planning team. Most importantly, the park warden should be a member of the planning team because of his knowledge of the park and his role in implementing the plan. The warden is perhaps best able to assist the planning team in finding practical approaches and solutions to management problems in his park.

The full range of both technically trained and non-technical personnel should be involved in the planning process. In practical terms this means that the planning team should involve personnel from all levels of management, and consult with scientists, experts on tourism, educators, concessionnaires, and people living in and around the protected area.

Step 2. Gather Basic Background Information. The next step is a review of all resource material available on the protected area. This includes the enabling legislation, data on biophysical features, cultural resources, and socio-economic data. This information can be collected from various sources including a literature review, office files, and interviews with knowledgeable people. A base map and reference file system are prepared at this stage.

Step 3. Field Inventory. Planning usually requires fieldwork to gather new information, to check and update existing data, and to view the area with new perspectives. The purpose is to develop the information base needed to make informed management decisions. Generally, a review is made of environmental resources and visitor use. Attention is also given to archaeological sites and contemporary cultures, regional economics, poaching, transportation networks, and attitudes of local people. Particular attention is devoted to critical environmental areas and potential development sites. The warden and his staff, being most familiar with the area, play a key role in accumulating the necessary data.

It is important to remember that you are collecting information in order to identify the most important management needs, not as an end in itself. Collect only that information which is most pertinent to your management task. Any gaps can be identified in the next step.

Step 4. Assess Limitations and Assets. Limitations of an environmental, economic, political, administrative or legal nature should be recognised and analysed at this point. Senior management at headquarters play a critical role in defining these limitations, and identifying key problems of the site. A review of programmes outlined in the national plan regional or district development plans should be done at this stage, although the absence of such plans should not deter one from proceeding. Aim to ensure that options to be developed in later stages will be realistic in the light of current limitations. Assets should be recognised and analysed to make effective use of them.

Step 5. Review Regional Inter-relationships. A protected area must be integrated as an essential element in the regional land-use pattern. The planning team must attempt to review the potential effects of development outside protected area borders as well as the effects of the protected area on the region. The special arrangements that may be required with adjacent inhabitants are outlined here, as are the roles of buffer zones and key regional decision makers.

Step 6. State the Objectives of the Area. With the above steps completed, it will be possible to spell out in detail the values and objectives of the area in relation to its particular set of resources, to the region, and to the country as a whole. Senior management should review the plan at this point to ensure that all factors have been considered and that the objectives identified are appropriate to a particular protected area.

Step 7. Divide the Area into Management Zones. Most protected areas will be zoned for different objectives and uses. These can range from zones for intensive tourism development, to dispersed recreation zones, to controlled resource production zones, or full protection zones. Different management practices allowed or prohibited in each zone should be itemised. A standardised zoning scheme should be developed for all categories of protected areas in the country.

Step 8. Review Boundaries of the Area. Few protected areas have ideal ecological boundaries. With the resource inventory, management objectives, regional integration review, and zoning stages of the plan in place, the team should now consider boundary modifications.

Step 9. Design the Management Programmes. Once the zoning concept has provided the basis for what is to be done where, the task now is to answer the questions How? and Who?. This action-oriented component is the heart of the plan and addresses the four major programmes of protected area management:

49. Consulting with local people is a key element in the planning process. Members of Kenya's Wildlife Planning Unit are seen here discussing management issues with local chiefs next to the Masai Mara Reserve.
Photo: J. Thorsell

Example 9.2: Management objectives

This is a crucial section of the plan which must be given serious thought and be carefully worded. Too often the management of protected areas is unclear because the stated objectives are too vague, e.g. 'the conservation of nature' or 'preservation in perpetuity of native wildlife'. Even such apparently precise objectives as 'conservation of orang utans' is far too vague. Consider the four different objectives below, each of which gives a quite different direction to management:

- Give maximum benefit to a population of orang utans; or
- offer recreational viewing of wild orang utans to visitors; or
- facilitate research into orangutan behaviour; or
- preserve the natural ecosystem of the orang utan.

In all four cases, the management is directed towards the conservation of orang utans, but in the first case the orangutans are clearly the first priority. The reserve may be managed to favour the orang utans, possibly at the expense of other species, and visitors could be excluded if their presence conflicts with the welfare of the orang utan population. In the second case, the primary concern is clearly the visitors. Considerable facilities for visitor access into the forest, accommodation, clearing of viewing areas, building of towers, attracting animals to special feeding sites, would all be justified. In the third case, the emphasis is on research. This would probably preclude visitors or release of rehabilitant orang utans in the area as these might disturb the behaviour of the wild population and render the research invalid. Management would, however, accommodate the construction of research facilities, study trails, etc. In the last case, the emphasis is clearly placed on the whole rain forest ecosystem and management would be directed to reducing all disturbance and preserving the natural habitat.

Fig. 9.1: Zoning of a small, intensively used protected area

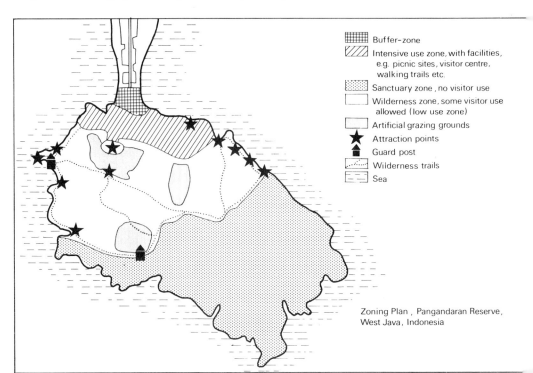

Buffer-zone
Intensive use zone, with facilities, e.g. picnic sites, visitor centre, walking trails etc.
Sanctuary zone, no visitor use
Wilderness zone, some visitor use allowed (low use zone)
Artificial grazing grounds
Attraction points
Guard post
Wilderness trails
Sea

Zoning Plan, Pangandaran Reserve, West Java, Indonesia

Source: Blower & Wind (1977)

Example 9.3: Types of management zones

Management zones are the most common tool of protected area managers for separating areas of conficting uses and in managing areas for multiple uses. There is no universal set of zones; various designations have been used. The following examples illustrate the variety which can be found in the management plans for different parks.

- *Lake Malawi National Park* has four zones inside the park boundary: (a) a 'special area' (the water portion of the park) with the stress on protection and research; (b) a 'wilderness recreation zone' in which motorised transport is banned; (c) a 'general outdoor recreation zone' for heavy use, with recreation facilities and accommodations; (d) a 'natural environment zone' (a buffer between Zones b and c, with some developed facilities). In addition, the park lies within a conservation area with five management zones for tourism, village settlements, controlled fishing, cultivation, and reforestation.

- *Amboseli National Park* has three zones: (a) an 'intensive use zone' (small areas for park and visitor facilities); (b) an 'extensive use' zone (the main viewing area, where off-road driving is banned and roads are the only facilities); (c) a 'low use' zone (completely undeveloped) constituting 54 per cent of the park.

- *Lake Manyara National Park* has three zones: (a) a 'strict natural' zone, with sensitive environmental conditions (wetlands, hot springs); (b) a 'natural' zone, comprising most of the rest of the park; (c) a 'recreation' zone with facilities and headquarters.

- *Selous Game Reserve* has four sectors and 48 hunting blocks with different permitted activities.

- *The Rio Platano Biosphere Reserve* in Honduras has three management zones: (a) a 'cultural zone' which is inhabited by indigenous populations and is extensively utilised and altered; (b) a 'natural zone' which is largely unused by reserve inhabitants and is in a fairly pristine state; (c) a 'buffer zone' which surrounds the reserve and will be used for manipulative experiments and demonstration plots for appropriate land-use practices.

Source: Thorsell, 1984

- Resource management and protection. This management programme focuses on issues relating to the protection of the biological and physical resources of the area.

- Human use. This programme deals with all aspects of use by people including traditional use, recreation, interpretation, and extension, and the facilities and developments necessary for these purposes.

- Research and monitoring. The management of protected area resources frequently requires an understanding of specific ecological processes. One important aspect of management involves the design and development of research programmes to meet these needs. Similarly, a monitoring programme is needed to detect problems as they arise and gauge progress in meeting the management objectives of the area.

- Administration. The operational, manpower, and financial resources needed to run the protected area are outlined. Headquarters facilities, vehicles, equipment, and maintenance requirements are some issues of concern here.

Step 10. Prepare Integrated Development Options. This step in the management planning process summarises all the physical facilities that must be developed to accomplish the various management programmes. The team may wish to present various development options, including the engineering and construction implications.

Step 11. Outline Financial Implications. No plan can be evaluated without costing the planning proposals, at least as general estimates. In some cases, the economic justifications will need intensive treatment in a cost/benefit analysis. In any case, the planning team must now present the cost estimates of their proposals.

Step 12. Prepare and Distribute a Draft Plan. Before proceeding further, the team should seek comment and feedback on their proposals. A rough first draft of a plan should be compiled and distributed to the range of actors who are the key to the plan's success, both within and outside the agency if public involvement is desirable.

Step 13. Analyse and Evaluate the Plan. After digesting input from all concerned parties, the team is now in a position to narrow its options. A final review of all development proposals is made and approved by senior management.

Step 14. Design Schedules and Priorities. As the plan is now finalised and ready to put in motion, the team decides on the timing and priorities of each event. It is important that a formal approval page is then presented to the Director for his signature.

Step 15. Prepare and Publish the Finalised Plan. With authorised approval from the Director, the plan is produced, published and distributed in a form suitable to reach a general audience. Copies of the document should be given to political leaders, ministry officials, and related government departments, regional councils, international agencies, scientific personnel involved in research and monitoring, and to appropriate public interest groups.

Step 16. Monitor and Revise the Plan. Plans soon need revision as new information becomes available and basic conditions change. Thus a five-year planning horizon is often used as a realistic time-span for a management plan. As a final step the plan should be reviewed at intervals. You need not wait five years for review. Reviews may take place more frequently, but, in each case, always planning five years into the future.

The management plan document

A number of different styles and formats have been used in different countries for the content and organisation of a management plan document. Based on the above process, however, five chapters usually reflect the work that results:

(1) National and Regional Background
(2) Description and Inventory of the Area
(3) Management Considerations and Objectives
(4) Management Programmes
(5) Development Programme.

Examples of protected area management plans adhering to the process followed above and the outline presented below can be found in plans produced by many countries, including Brazil, Chile, Costa Rica, Ecuador, Kenya, Liberia Panama, Peru and Thailand.

(1) *National and Regional Background.* The preliminary chapter sets the stage for the Plan by providing an overview of the area within the national and regional context. The reserve is viewed from the perspective of national conservation objectives and biogeographic representation. The regional economy, surrounding land uses and communication networks are reviewed briefly.

(2) *Description and Inventory of the Protected Area.* The descriptive section will be based on information about the landform, geology, soil types, climate, biological aspects, socio-economic and historical background of the area. However, these data must be interpreted and summarised in a conservation context. For instance, the information we need to know about the soil types is not their makeup and properties but how they affect the native flora, drainage, erosion, and agricultural potential. Only directly relevant information should be reproduced in the Management Plan. Other data collected by the planning team should be filed in technical data files for the relevant reserve or put in a second volume of Appendices.

The descriptive section is purely informative; avoid including evaluations or recommendations. These should go into subsequent sections.

(3) *Management Considerations.* This section moves from description and inventory to evaluation and projection. It is here that the crucial definition of the management objectives for the area is given. Special limitations and constraints are identified and an overall evaluation of the significance of the area is given. The zoning plan for the area is also presented.

(4) *Management Programmes.* As noted under *Step 9*, this is the action-oriented component of the Plan that addresses the four pro

grammes of protected area management: Resource Management, Human Use, Research and Monitoring, and Administration.

(5) *Development Programmes.* All building and equipment requirements are presented here along with a summary of all financial and personnel implications of the Plan. A development schedule indicating priorities and scheduling concludes the section.

These five chapters will be followed by appendices which summarise data used in support of the plan. These appendices will typically include:

- details of legal establishment of the particular protected area
- complete reference list of all relevant publications
- species checklists
- pertinent climatic and socio-economic data
- supporting maps and air photos

Finally, decision makers are busy people; they want to be presented with evaluated suggestions, not with raw facts. It is advisable to present the pertinent conclusions in a very brief, pithy summary at the beginning of the plan so that a busy official can quickly grasp the whole picture without having to read further.

Annual operational plans – action plans

In many countries, the manager is required to submit a plan of his anticipated activities and budgetary requirements for the forthcoming twelve months. His first optimistic draft may need subsequent revision but once his operational plan is approved, it will guide and regulate his management activities and options for that year. The routine maintenance activities of most reserves are predictable and can be planned well in advance, but in view of the unpredictable nature of natural systems the action plan (and budget) must be sufficiently flexible to accommodate unexpected contingencies.

Annual Operation Plans (AOP) should be based on the Management Plan but will inevitably diverge from it in minor ways as a result of delays (or more rarely completion ahead of schedule) of planned activities, and having to deal with some new and unanticipated developments.

Good planning enables the manager to do what is needed when it is needed but successful implementation depends on many factors, some of them outside the manager's control – purchase of equipment, recruitment of key staff, release of budgets, climatic factors, and others. Some of the activities planned for completion in the year can be delayed or even postponed without undue problems, others may not. It may not matter if the signboards are repaired one month later than planned but it does matter if the annual nest count of some seasonally breeding birds is a month late.

Different protected area agencies have different formats for Annual Operation Plans. In general, an AOP provides the following information:

- Brief description of the area and its resources, regional setting, and public use.
- Major management problems.
- Limitations on effective management (e.g. administrative support, personnel, equipment).
- Availability and condition of existing infrastructure and equipment.
- List of personnel with positions, training, distribution in the field; include organisational diagram indicating chain of command.
- Statement of progress made in implementing management plan or previous AOP.
- Work to be carried out in coming year, listed under four headings: resources, visitor use, research, administration.
- Tools and supplies needed to carry out planned work, with suggested priorities.
- Personnel needed to carry out planned work, with suggested training levels and staffing changes.
- Budget summarising all costs and suggesting outside sources of funding.
- Assistance from central office needed.
- Time chart showing schedule for all activities and distribution of work load over the year.

When the AOP is in draft form, the regional supervisor should review it before sending it to the Director for approval. A year after its submission, a progress review is made and the next AOP is suitably revised (Barborak, *et al.*, 1982).

The following procedures may be helpful in the preparation of an AOP:

- List activities planned for the year in the Management Plan, plus any tasks still outstanding from the previous year, and any newly-arisen needs and priorities for management action.
- Classify these activities with symbols indicating urgency or priority; indicate those which are vital and must be completed, those that are necessary but not so urgent, and those that are desirable if time, funds and manpower are available but, if necessary, could be postponed until later.
- Put dates against activities that must be executed within a certain time period.
- Indicate activities that are dependent on the prior completion of other activities and indicate which activities they must follow. Quite complex chains of dependency may result, which may reduce the flexibility of the plan but will

Example 9.4: Management zones

Zoning is the process of applying different management objectives and regulations to different parts or zones of a protected area. Clearly only those that are applicable to a particular reserve, i.e. its stated management objectives, should be considered. The following types of zones are in use in various protected areas:

Sanctuary Zone: where no visitors are allowed, restrictions may be placed on the types of scientific research conducted and only those management measures essential for protection (e.g. firefighting, monitoring reserve condition, pursuit of poachers) are permitted.

Wilderness Zone: where limited visitor use is permitted but management is primarily aimed at maintaining undisturbed nature, or a desired balance, or the natural *status quo*. Recreation management is limited to the provision of rough trails and sometimes primitive campsites.

Semi-intensive Visitor Use Zone: where management is concerned with giving visitors an optimum view of nature. The impact of roads, constructions and other facilities is kept to a minimum and a natural aspect is maintained but measures may be taken to improve wildlife viewing, e.g. unobtrusive hides, watchtowers, or salt-licks.

Wildlife Management Zone: where specific manipulation is permissible to favour selected species, e.g. fencing turtle nesting areas from predators, clearing water weeds to encourage certain fish or maintaining grazing areas to boost ungulate populations.

Intensive Use Zone: where high human impact is expected and recreational and administrative objectives exceed the protection of nature. Such zones are generally very small in total area and may be sub-classified according to function into:

- Special Use Zone: where administrative buildings, service areas, car parks, high intensity visitor recreation, organised camping sites, staff quarters, public works installations, communication towers and other special facilities have to be accommodated.
- Recovery Zone: where damaged or newly-added areas of land may need special management, e.g. replanting to help bring them back into a near natural condition.
- Fishing Zone: where sport fishing is permitted.
- Historic Sites: special sites within the protected area with historic interest, e.g. megalithic remains, prehistoric cave paintings.
- Traditional Use Zone: where people living in a traditional way and in balance with a natural ecosystem are permitted to continue using the reserve.

Buffer Zone: where management is aimed at reducing the friction between neighbouring incompatible land-uses, such as strict nature reserves and agricultural settlement, and in which various types of harvesting may be permitted, e.g. firewood collection, sport hunting, production of plant materials.

allow the manager to assign realistic priorities to his activities.

- Plan out the activities on a bar chart. Start with the vital activities and put lines to indicate time limits. Gradually fill up the chart with bars so that the most important activities are fitted in first and dependent activities are in sequence. Within the time scales allotted for the various activities try to spread the workload fairly evenly over the year. Keep in mind the need to have some free manpower at all times for emergencies. Some seasons may need more emergency manpower than others (e.g. the dry season in a fireprone reserve). Visitor cycles and other activities may be seasonal or only possible at specific times of year.

- Once the activities are arranged on the bar chart, this can be used to guide management activities throughout the year and the manager can start preparing sections or individual work schedules.

- The protected area manager may also find it useful to prepare a graph of expected expenditure throughout the year to accompany the bar charts. Since most government agencies are very strict on financial control, the manager can check his expenditure at any time and ensure that management activities are completed according to schedule and within their budget allocation.

Site plans

Specially prepared plans may be needed to guide specific operations at specific locations. These include site plans, engineering specifications or architect's designs for buildings, or draft layouts of information for wall displays in education centres. Some, such as architectural designs, may be prepared by outside specialists but the reserve manager should be consulted from the start and, if possible, have final approval. The following principles and hints may be useful in making and evaluating site plans:

- Man-made structures should interfere as little as possible with the natural ecosystem. Examples of bad siting include roads that block the flow of streams and thereby cause erosion on hillsides, structures which frighten wildlife from waterholes, and effluent drains that pollute natural waterways.

- Structures must be as unobtrusive as possible. They should not dominate their natural surroundings nor detract from the intrinsic natural values of the area. They should be made of local materials whenever possible: stone, timber, bamboo, mud-brick, etc. Avoid alien materials such as asbestos sheeting, breeze blocks, etc. and garish colour schemes. Buildings should be in local styles and blend with their surroundings. If possible, buildings should be screened by natural bluffs or groves of trees.

   If a visitors' lodge is sited on a ridge with a commanding view over the whole area, the building will be visible from many aspects.

However, if it is sited below the horizon and is single-storeyed and sombrely coloured, it will be far less obtrusive.

- Suitable siting of buildings depends on functional considerations; it is not enough to consider only their strategic aspects. For example, guards will not inhabit posts unless they are serviced by reasonable access and water is available. These considerations may seem obvious but there are many examples where money has been wasted on uninhabited and uninhabitable guardposts, and on watchtowers located where there is nothing to watch.

- Before buildings are sited, some thought should be given to their accessibility and the flow of users. Tourist facilities should be separated from the administrative and workshop areas of a park headquarters if the two aspects are not to interfere with each other. It is better to service a group of buildings with a circular one-way flow road with a parking area set to one side than to have two-way traffic blocking the focal area of activity. Similarly, in an information centre, exhibits and panels should be arranged in a sequential order which draws visitors in a one-way flow around the room to the exit.

- Roads and paths should be unobtrusive. Whenever possible, they should use the cover of dips in the land, trees, hills, and other features. They should flow with the land contours rather than cut across them. They should be designed to minimise erosion and therefore be of slight gradient with adequate drainage.

• Although roads may be built to bring visitors close to animals, they should avoid sensitive areas such as the breeding areas of waterbirds. They should employ bends or raised 'humps' to control speed. Bends are also good for approaching wildlife and roads should be wide enough (or have special parking places) so that cars can pull off to view wildlife without obstructing other traffic.

50. Poor siting of park buildings can lead to unsightly scarring of the landscape. The gulley erosion seen in this photo will soon spread to threaten the buildings themselves.
Photo: WWF/P. Jackson

Fig. 9.2: *Siting roads (graded tracks) in parks and reserves*

WRONG: poor profile, impeded drainage, road surface below ground-level, shade from high vegetation slows drying after heavy showers

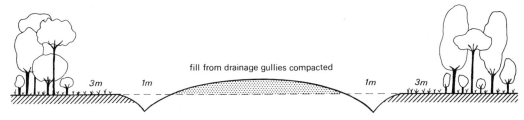

fill from drainage gullies compacted

RIGHT: good profile, side gullies and cleared vegetation keep road surface dry

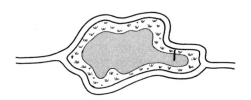

WRONG: wildlife viewing road around a waterhole

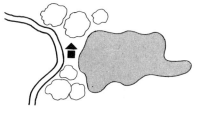

RIGHT: road leading to watchtower at edge of waterhole

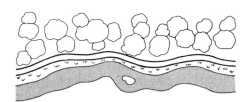

WRONG: road following river course for long stretches

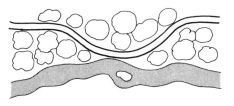

RIGHT: road lead to river at certain view-points

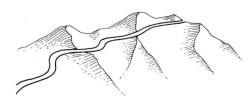

WRONG: road across mountain crest scars the landscape

RIGHT: road follows lower slopes

Source: Van Lavieren, 1983

Example 9.5: Site evaluation checklist

The following checklist provides design guidelines for evaluating the appropriateness and adequacy of specific site developments.

* Everything must have a purpose (relation of park to surroundings, relation of facility to use area and zones, relation of facilities in the site, relation to overall objectives of park master plan). Eliminate superfluous elements; where feasible, locate facilities on perimeters.
* Design for people. Recognise the optimal sociological use-limits of the site, as well as safety and convenience factors.
* Design within the constraints of the resource. Recognise the optimal environmental capacity of the site and potential impacts. Use the facility as a positive control in directing use; allow only day-use facilities in some areas.
* Satisfy both form and function. Balance economic, human, and resource values. Recognise design elements of exposure, dominance, texture, motif, form, and colour. Whenever possible use local building materials. Design with quality, utility and simplicity and build in local style. Landscape as appropriate to make buildings less obtrusive.
* Provide facilities suited to the function of the place, the scale of the place, and the personalities of the users.
* Recognise technical requirements (size, quantity, standards, orientation to weather and sun, convenience of access, utility costs).
* Ensure efficient and safe operating use. Where possible design for year-round use.
* Investigate the long-term implications of providing facilities: such as changing demands and technology, and continuing maintenance. Discourage undesirable uses.
* If budgets are limited, start with simple but well-built camps of bamboo, thatch, etc., which can be replaced with more permanent buildings later.

Source: Thorsell, 1984

Example 9.6: Planning access trails

In planning trails, the following considerations should be borne in mind;

* Review the technical aspects of trail construction with experts (i.e. alignment, excavations, constructions).
* Be sure that the trail serves the purpose for which it is meant.
* Locate trails in such a way that the park features and scenery can be enjoyed, avoiding serious disturbance to the natural setting. Location, alignment and grade should be selected considering both technical (soil type, bedrock, excavation, slope, drainage) and aesthetic criteria (scenic beauty, features of interest).
* Make an inventory of landscapes and natural features from aerial photographs, combined with reconnaissance surveys on the ground; make a landscape assessment.
* Select, where possible, slopes of gradient not more than 15%-17%; trail construction on such slopes requires minimum excavation, scouring of soil, stabilisation and drainage. Excavation of trails on slopes exceeding 70% should be avoided, as it requires costly stabilisation work on the inside slope.
* Angle across the slope to reduce the risk of erosion and to avoid steep gradients.
* When 'switchbacks' are required, use, where possible, the configuration of the terrain. Avoid too narrow angles and, to prevent short-cutting and 'multiple trailing', try to make loops invisible.
* Assess expected visitor impact, list fragile features, and mark stretches where slope stabilisation, drainage or other erosion control measures are required.
* Use existing trails, where possible, but close unsuitable existing trails.
* List the facilities to be provided (resting places, shelters, benches, litter bins, sign posts, steps, culverts, bridges, picnic sites, interpretive panels, safety barriers such as rails or fences on bluffs).

- Work out a schedule of patrolling and litter collection and disposal.
- Design an interpretive programme using themes, locations, designs, and techniques appropriate to the trail.
- Calculate construction and maintenance costs, estimate labour requirements.
- Establish a maintenance schedule.

Planning research programmes for protected areas

Man's influence on the planet is already too great to imagine that any wilderness is totally 'natural' or stable. Protecting anything of Nature, whether it be a single important species or a whole representative ecosystem, requires management intervention to ensure that the appropriate environment is maintained. To manage nature with any degree of efficiency and safety, the manager must first know and understand a great deal more about the way in which the various ecosystems operate.

Six basic areas can be identified where the manager will require accurate, scientifically-collected, biological information before he can draw up a comprehensive plan for the long-term management of a protected area.

- Inventory. What plants, animals and other natural resources are present?
- Quantification. What numbers of each species are present and how are they distributed in space and time?
- Ecological relationships. Who eats what? Competes with what? What depends on what?
- Species needs. As much information as possible should be gathered on the particular habitat requirements, shelter, food, minerals, and water needs of species of special management significance.
- Dynamics of change. Studies are needed on colonisation of disturbed areas, seral succession of plant communities, changes of river flow, evolution of swamps, invasion by new species, and population trends within species.
- Predictive manipulation of ecosystems. Where the natural processes of change are contrary to the objectives of management, the manager will want to prevent change or affect its direction. To do this he will need special knowledge of the direct and indirect, short-term and long-term effects of different management options.

Apart from biological research, the manager of the protected area needs to encourage the collection of information on the effects of his reserve on the local economy and society. Some, or all, of the above information, may already be available as a result of previous or ongoing research. Whether or not this is so, one of the first tasks of the manager should be to suggest a social research programme identifying the particular research needs in his reserve, giving some indication of priority or urgency and even suggestions on who might conduct such research. With his own research priorities in mind, the manager can decide which research activities to actively encourage, which to aid and which to allow if they do not interfere with other management activities.

Although some proposed projects may appear purely academic and have no immediately obvious management value, they should not be discouraged unless they conflict with reserve objectives, tie up valuable resources or interfere with current management practice, as their findings may prove of value later. In determining his research priorities, the manager must be largely influenced by the nature of the particular reserve, its designated function, management objectives, the complexity of its biology and the amount of knowledge already available to him through previous and ongoing research. Each research programme will contain some of the elements listed in Example 9.8, which indicates the particular relevance of certain projects to management of natural systems, and the need for external assistance for such research.

Having defined where more information is needed, the manager should see how much of this can be accomplished by his own staff through routine surveys and reporting, regular monitoring activities or special operations. He may be able to appoint an ecologist to his staff as research officer to undertake some of the programme and coordinate the rest. Requests should be made to local universities and national scientific institutes to undertake further elements of the programme. Help should also be sought from international foundations, universities, museums, and granting agencies. Close cooperation should be maintained between the management authority and the national scientific authority on all research matters. In cases where a protected area falls within the terms of Unesco's Man and Biosphere (MAB) programme, considerable advantages can be obtained through cooperation with the national MAB Committee.

Research plans have been prepared for a number of protected areas including Morne Trois Pitons National Park in Dominica and the Galapagos National Park in Ecuador (see Example 9.7).

Example 9.7: Research programme for Galapagos National Park, Ecuador

The 1974 management plan for the Galapagos National Park, Ecuador, outlines the main research topics to be developed in the park. Scientific investigation in the National Park is managed by the Charles Darwin Research Station in accordance with the agreement to this effect between the Government of Ecuador and the Darwin Foundation. The National Park Committee considers applications from scientific institutions and park officials supervise the activities of the research station and of researchers in the park. The research terrain for each scientific mission is determined according to protection imperatives and research needs.

Support is given especially for research necessary to promote the continuous integrity of the Galapagos ecosystems and to develop and improve management techniques. Research on the socio-economic development of the Province is also encouraged with the aim of harmonising the demands of the provincial population with the conservation needs of the park and eliminating pressure for consumption of the archipelago's resources.

One of the most important objectives of the Galapagos National Park is to allow scientific research there. The national park administration will facilitate pure research on topics such as organic adaptation and evolution, and volcanic processes. The scientific world as an important user of the park is expected to contribute to the maintenance of the resource, especially through the Research Station and in the training of technical personnel in natural sciences and wildlife management.

The management plan identifies research on the following topics as important and sometimes indispensable for the development of management techniques:

- Monitoring biological communities by means of plant and animal censuses. Such research is carried out primarily in critical areas such as Intensive Use Zones, islands affected by introduced plants or animals and areas adjacent to colonised zones. Regular censuses should be made of colonies and nesting areas of Hawaiian petrels, flamingoes, albatrosses, penguins, cormorants, fur seals, sea-lions, native rats and all reptiles. The research station plans the monitoring programme and analyses the data.
- Research on the population dynamics of certain threatened species (land iguanas, snakes, petrels). Important studies have been conducted on such species as marine iguanas, mockingbirds and Galapagos finches.
- Detailed studies of the population dynamics of introduced organisms and development of improved programmes for eradicating them. Study of introduced predators, rodents and certain plants, e.g. avocado, guayaba, lantana, pasto elefante.
- Environmental monitoring for contaminants originating outside the archipelago (chlorinated hydrocarbons in seabird eggs, heavy metals in predatory fish).
- Synoptic study of offshore zones (flora and fauna) within the park. Regular sampling of permanent quadrats in the littoral and sub-littoral zones to detect possible changes.
- Studies of tourism impact.
- Assessment of water resources and volcanic hazards.

Source: Government of Ecuador, 1974

51. Research activities in protected areas provide management with valuable information on the ecology and population dynamics of species the park was established to protect. A tiger in Royal Chitwan National Park, Nepal, is examined before being fitted with a radio collar.
Photo: WWF/John Blower

Example 9.8: ***Summary of research needs of relevance to protected area management***

	Management Relevance	Outside Execution
1. Qualitative Inventory	Reserve selection Identification of management objectives Information service	Professional tax-onomist needed
2. Quantitative Inventory	Information Planning and Reserve Management Monitoring	Professionals, student volunteers all useful
3. Vegetation Mapping	Monitoring Habitat management Determining manage-ment priorities	Specialised botan-ist: could be research student
4. Seral Succession Studies	Determining needs for habitat management	Specialised botan-ist: could be research student
5. Synecological Studies	Planning suitable management of wild-life and habitat	Professional ecolo-gist or research student
6. Autecological Studies	Improving management or protection of special species Habitat requirements	Professional ecolo-gist or research student
7. Special Problem Studies	Solving emergency or special management problems	Specialists or consultants
8. Consequences of Management *	Evaluating management effectiveness Planning management action	Ecologists or experienced land managers
9. Socio-economic Studies	Relations with surrounding lands Economic justification Visitor use	Agronomists, econ-omists, sociolog-ists, anthro-pologists

* high priority for research and monitoring by protected area authority, itself under supervision of staff ecologist

Staff Execution	Sponsorship	Comments
Preliminary surveys and some collecting possible	Museums Management authority	Generally low priority for management authority apart from selection phase
Patrol and survey data can build up useful picture of species abundance	Management authority	Should be part of routine monitoring
Only if crude or superficial cover-age required	Management authority or research grant	Great variation of detail possible but most areas should have some form of vegetation map
Long-term monitoring highly relevant	Management authority or research grant	Particularly important in reserves with large areas of subclimax vegetation or unstable land form.
Long-term routine monitoring data relevant	Management authority or research grant	General ecological description should exist for each reserve
Can collect routine data	Management authority or research grant	Particularly needed where species conservation is of high priority
Useful where long-term observation needed	Commissioned by management authority or external aid	As relevant
Long-term monitoring by staff useful. Management records essential	Commissioned by management authority	Can be integrated into regional Environmental Impact Assessment Programme
Defining problems, basic data collect-ion (e.g. numbers, costs, harvests etc.)	Management authority, local univers-ities	High priority for suitable projects by local universities or local government

52. Charles Darwin Research Station, Galapagos. The development of modest research facilities in
    protected areas can attract overseas research interests, bring funds into the reserves, and help to
    build up a better information base for management decisions.
    Photo: WWF/H. Jungius

10

Implementing Management

Introduction

This chapter reviews the implementation of the management and operation plans, and includes the various activities involved in protecting, developing and administering a protected area once it has been established. These tasks involve a knowledge of what has to be done and how best to do it. Human and financial resources are always limited so must be used efficiently. There is often a need to seek extra voluntary help wherever it can be found without prejudice to the protected area or its objectives.

Management is the actual execution of activities carried out to meet the objectives of the protected area. It does not occur spontaneously – it needs to be consciously designed and then implemented to provide the benefits for which the area was established. Implementation is often the weakest phase in the whole process of planning, establishing and operating protected areas.

The reserve warden or manager is the person responsible for implementation. He is guided in the management of the protected area both by the area's legal status or criteria of protection and by the stated management objectives in the management plan. The management plan will also outline the manager's duties. The annual operation plan details the routine maintenance and other

activities planned for the year ahead. The warden's main job is to organise the staff, budget and equipment available to manage the park and implement these plans as efficiently as possible.

While the approved plans determine the warden's duties for much of the year, they only go so far. Nature is full of surprises: the unexpected and the unplanned frequently occur. Often the warden has to improvise and act boldly, sometimes on the basis of little information and in a crisis situation not of his making (e.g. elephants on the rampage or an outbreak of rabies among vampire bats roosting in the park). He can, of course, draw on expert advice but the ultimate management decisions are his. An unscheduled operation should be well-documented, detailing the reasons for following a certain policy and how this fits in with the guidelines and stated objectives of the reserve. If the operation is a success all is well: if it fails, then it is possible to analyse the decisions taken, determine where mistakes were made, and apply what has been learned the next time.

Implementation of management responsibilities requires a commitment by the manager and his staff to pursue the stated objectives of the area. The actions involved in implementation are discussed below.

Allocation of duties and staff selection

The warden may be in the lucky position of selecting his own staff but more often he 'inherits' them. He must assess their strengths and weaknesses

and allocate them to the jobs for which they are best qualified. If the reserve has a large staff, this task may fall to a specialist manpower officer. In

53. The ultimate evidence of staff dedication – a monument erected in memory of 25 guards who gave
    their lives in defence of Virunga National Park in Zaire.
    Photo: WWF/F. Vollmar

both cases the ultimate responsibility for staff
performance is the warden's and he should
attempt to have personal contact with all his staff
and be involved in the selection of key personnel.

In allocating staff to positions and duties, the
warden will have to take into account a number of
factors:

- the level of training and education, skills and
  abilities of the various staff members;
- work aptitude, ability to follow orders, and ability to assume responsibility;
- capacity to improvise in new situations;
- trustworthiness, honesty and personal courage;
- personal relationships (ability or otherwise to
  work together with other staff members);
- past work performance and seniority in service;
- status in the local community and their relationships with key personages (village heads,
  officers in other government divisions, and to
  headquarter staff);

- marital status and dependants, home ties,
  family;
- personal appearance and image.

On the basis of this information, the warden must
allocate duties without favouritism. If the permanent work force is too small to fulfil all the duties
outlined in the year's plan, he must organise new
recruitment, hire local labour, sub-contract or use
volunteer helpers.

Each staff member should be given concise,
written terms of reference (a job description)
which outline his or her status and duty station,
routine duties and whether he or she is liable to be
requested to perform additional special duties.
These terms of reference must specify to whom
each staff member is responsible and where and
when each should report.

The importance of having clear terms of reference cannot be stressed too strongly. Some
reserves are inefficient because staff do not do

anything unless given specific orders and/or extra pay. Sometimes staff may resent, or even refuse to perform, tasks they consider as not part of their job; elsewhere staff may regularly be absent from their duty stations for personal reasons, or to undertake other paid activities quite unrelated to the job. Managers should avoid all of these problems by clearly outlining the duties of individual staff members at the start. Routine duties should be embodied in monthly work schedules or rosters and a copy given to every staff member, so each individual knows exactly what tasks he is expected to perform, when and where. Example terms of reference and work roster are given (Example 10.1).

The warden or superintendent must build up a structure of control and command if none exists. He must establish and underline his channels of authority. Ultimately, he is in charge and must have responsibility for everything that happens in the reserve, good or bad. He must keep this in mind when he chooses subordinate officers as they, in turn, will delegate the actual execution of routine tasks to junior staff. Each staff member must fully understand what he is responsible for, and to whom he is responsible. Staff may be responsible to different officers for different aspects of their duties. These relationships can be usefully shown on a chart (see Fig. 10.1).

Example 10.1: Examples of guards' terms of reference and work roster (Indonesia)

a) *Guards' Terms of Reference*

Heads of Duty Stations	3: Duty Stations: One each at Parey, Dua Saudara and Batuangus
	Duties:
	Responsible for the guards and guard posts of a) Parey, b) Dua Saudara and Pinangunian and c) Batuangus respectively. Liaison between guards and regional head. Leaders of guard patrols and operations. Keeping patrol notes and regularly reporting to regional head. Arrest of poachers, timber thieves or ladang makers in reserve.

b) *Work Roster for Guard*

Name : Edy
Level : Day staff
Duty stations : Batuangus

Each week:

Occupy guard post Batuangus
Perform basic maintenance to post
1 coast trip to Remesun   Patrols to be unpredictable, i.e.
1 sea trip to Remesun   varied days of week and times
1 boundary trip to Pinangunian   of day/night including Sunday

Each month:

1 trip to Parey, report to regional head
1 trip to Manado, report to provincial head
4 days wildlife surveys along prescribed survey trails

Each year:

Participate in 10-day annual survey, censusing animal populations
2 x clear all survey trails in duty area
1 x clean boundary trail, report damage to boards and poles, replace damaged items when supplied from Manado
Participate in one week annual training session.

Fig. 10.1: Schematic diagram of staff requirements of a typical national park

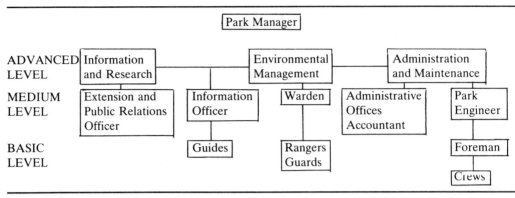

Adapted from: Miller, 1973

Staff may be recruited locally by the warden from the local community, or posted to the reserve from outside the region, having been recruited by the regional or headquarters office. Both methods have their advantages and drawbacks; the most effective recruitment policy may be a balance between the two.

Local recruitment has the following advantages:

- The warden often knows local applicants personally and can generally select the best members of the community for his purpose, often those who have shown themselves to be well-motivated, hardworking and trustworthy when hired as local labour.
- Local villagers are familiar with the area, bring much useful local knowledge and contact into the park management and are not afraid of the wild areas where they must work.
- If the warden is to be held responsible for the performance of his team, it is often best for him to choose its members himself.
- Generating local employment creates good relations with the local communities, relations that are essential to the ultimate success of the reserve.
- Local men are more willing to stay in guard posts and their families are more likely to accompany them.

Disadvantages of local recruitment are:

- Local villagers generally do not have the levels of education or training required for any but the most junior jobs in the reserve. However, they can be given extra training and encouraged to work their way up through the service.

- Local staff employees may tend to be more lenient on violations of park integrity by other locals (poachers, wood gatherers, etc.).
- Local staff may inherit or be involved in long-standing local divisions, feuds and jealousies.
- The loyalties of the recruiting officer may be stronger towards his family or tribe than his department and new recruits may be drawn almost exclusively from one family or group. This is not such a problem if that group is well accepted locally.

Advantages of central or regional recruitment are:

- There is a much wider pool from which to select staff.
- Selection can be made for higher levels of education and training.
- Staff can be posted to areas where they have no previous relationships nor loyalties.
- In the event of any trouble with local people, they can be moved again to a new posting.

The disadvantages of central recruitment are:

- Staff may have little sympathy for or empathy with the local people whose trust and support must be won. They may well belong to a different ethnic group, tribe or religion and be opposed and resented for that reason.
- They will have no prior knowledge of the area they have to manage and may be reluctant to explore it properly.
- High school recruits from urban areas may be suitable for some desk jobs but are often quite unsuitable for guard force work in remote

regions. They may feel they are too well-qualified for fieldwork and see themselves as administrators rather than fieldworkers.

• Because work in nature conservation is neither well paid nor glamorous, it does not always attract the best graduates from high school and university. Some candidates may turn to nature conservation after failing to get better jobs elsewhere. This can mean a poor quality of recruitment and low work morale.

In conclusion, it is generally preferable to recruit locally for guards. It is also wise policy to move guards between duty stations every few years. This broadens their work experience and avoids a situation where their loyalties to the local community may become greater than their allegiance to the park authority. Senior staff are generally best recruited on a country-wide basis.

All park employees should be recruited for an initial six-month probationary period. Those who work well should be placed on the regular government payroll as soon as possible; this gives them job security and improves morale and work performance.

There should be standard, printed staff record cards for all members of the agency, recording date of recruitment, personal data on education, previous employment, family, medical history, leave, transfers, salary, etc. Cards go with the employee on transfer to another station.

Specialised tasks, such as building offices and guardposts, are often sub-contracted to local builders. If the warden is in charge of contracting the work he should be guided by previous experiences with local contractors, and look for workmanship of a high standard, offered at a fair price within his budget. Contracting local workmen brings benefits to the communities neighbouring the protected area. Moreover, local contractors, building in local style with local materials, are preferable from an aesthetic point of view and likely to be less expensive since they should not incur high transport costs. Costs to the reserve may be further reduced if the management can purchase and transport the building materials and the contractor is responsible only for providing his specialised labour. However, government tender procedures may preclude such an arrangement.

Example 10.2: Roles required to fulfil the functions of park management

1. *Management*

The *park manager* is the director of a given park unit. He or she is leader of the team made up of staff members of the park and on loan from the regional and national offices or other institutions, and must integrate, coordinate and stimulate them to achieve the objectives for which the manager is held responsible. The manager must deal with other agency directors as well as local leaders, and must present and defend the image and programmes of the park.

2. *Protection and Resource Management*

The *park ranger* (guard) is responsible for the management and protection of park resources and park visitors. The ranger works with scientists to design and implement the necessary resource management activities. The ranger deals directly with the visiting public, introducing them to the park and guiding them to enjoy their activities in ways compatible with overall park policy. The ranger spends a great deal of time in the interior of the park where he controls and monitors the resources, applies park laws and policies and tends to park visitors.

3. *Ecology**

The *park ecologist* is responsible for the investigations related to management problems and the park interpretation programme. He represents the natural resources found in the park and guides the management programme in relation to the adequate treatment of the park's natural values. He spends a great deal of time in the field analysing resource problems, consulting other members of the staff, and advising the manager on aspects related to overall resource management. He or she coordinates, integrates and directs all cooperative science and monitoring activities within the park.

* Where a park features predominately cultural resources, an archaeologist or historian may fill the role of the ecologist.

4. *Interpretation/Education*

The *park interpreter* (naturalist or guide) is responsible for the interpretative and educational aspects of the park programme. He or she 'interprets' the values and features of the park and presents them to the park visitor in formal and informal ways and in a language and manner which can be understood and appreciated at all levels. Where possible, a team of interpreters can be organised as guides for park visitors and relieve the park ranger of this role. Or, in certain cases, the ranger and the interpreter can combine their roles.

5. *Administration and Accounting*

The *administrative officer*, and the specialists in accounting, are responsible for the overall operational aspects of the park as specified in the management and development plan. They work closely under the manager, report to him on the progress of all physical, institutional and personnel development activities, and the overall personnel and budgetary status of the park.

6. *Maintenance*

The *maintenance specialist* (park engineer) is responsible for the proper functioning and upkeep of the various buildings, grounds, roads, trails, and other installations and facilities of the entire park. During such periods when physical developments are being designed and constructed in the park, the park engineer works in close collaboration with contractors and architects.

7. *Sociology*

The *park sociologist* (recreation specialist) is responsible for the investigations related to the users of the park. He represents the recreationists, tourists and other users, and guides the management programme in relation to the treatment of park users. He spends a great deal of time in the field analysing park users, consulting other members of the staff on recreation, tourism and user problems, and in advising the manager on aspects related to overall user management. In many cases, the sociologist will also address issues dealing with interactions with local people residing near the park.

8. *Economics*

The *park economist* is responsible for the investigations related to the allocation and utilisation of the park's resources by the various types of park users. He represents the aspects of resource allocation and guides the management programme in relation to the adequate understanding of resource and user management. He spends most of his time gathering and analysing information on park resources, user behaviour and preferences, ecological constraints and budgets, and guides the manager on alternative plans of action to meet the goals of the park.

9. *Botany, Zoology, Geology, Anthropology, Archaeology, History, Marine Biology, Oceanography, etc.*

The *park botanist, zoologist, geologist anthropologist, archaeologist, historian, marine biologist, oceanographer*, or expert in other specialised fields related to the specific resources of a given park, are responsible for the investigation of particular aspects of the park which are required for support of the park management and interpretation programmes. They spend the majority of their time in the field working directly on the problem(s) to be studied, and guide the major programme functions and the manager on aspects related to park management and monitoring, and the effects of internal and external impacts and human use.

10. *Law and Resource Policy*

The *park law and policy specialist* is responsible for the investigation and support of the legal and policy aspects of the park management and development programme. He or she guides the major programme functions and the manager in the legal and policy aspects of park management, and works directly on controversial issues related to the overall park programme.

11. *Land Tenure and Acquisition*

The *land tenure* and *acquisition* specialist is responsible for the study and analysis of land use within and around park boundaries. He or she works in connection with the creation of new parks and with the annexation of park areas, and guides the manager and major programme functions on the feasibility and methodology for acquiring lands for park management.

12. *Public Relations/Extension*

The *public relations specialist* is responsible for drafting and issuing information to the general public, primarily outside the parks, on the overall park programme. He or she prepares materials for publications for general distribution, and aids in the design of speeches and materials which project the image of the park and the park programme to other agencies, the media and the public. He or she prepares programmes and materials for fund raising to support the park. He or she is responsible for the maintenance of open and clear channels of communication within the park, between the park and regional and national offices, with other agencies, institutes and the public.

13. *Planning*

The *park planner* is responsible for coordinating the preparation and periodic updating of management and development plans for each park, for the park systems plan and for the park department's strategy. He or she advises and assists park managers in the preparation of management plans for park areas, and works with engineers and architects in the design and control of physical development. He or she is responsible to monitor the development of human and institutional capacity. He or she is responsible for coordinating the park system and strategy plans and advises the park department director and managers on progress and problems, and suggests alternative courses of action.

14. *Landscape Architecture, Architecture, and Civil Engineering*

The *park landscape architect, architect* and *engineer* are responsible for the design and construction of park facilities and infrastructure. They must work directly in the field and produce installations compatible with the environment. The engineer responsible for maintenance may combine roles with the engineer responsible for physical development where appropriate. The critical point, however, is the role of continuous long-term maintenance versus short-term construction activities. Both functions must be covered.

15. *Art, Exhibits, and Museum Technique*

The *artist, exhibit designer* and *museum technique specialist* are responsible for the design and construction of exhibits and materials on the resources, heritage and values of the park, to serve for interpretation and education. In collaboration with the public relations officer, they assist in the preparation of materials for park extension activities and fund raising.

Source: Adapted from Miller, 1973

Management of staff

Since a protected area is usually too large for one man to supervise everything himself, the manager must delegate routine affairs to his staff. The efficiency of the staff and the way in which they are managed will be reflected in the way in which the whole reserve is run. The manager of each protected area must build up a disciplined, efficient, well-motivated and loyal staff. The following points are important:

• *Discipline*. Management of a reserve requires similar, if less rigorous levels of discipline to those required by police, armed forces or surgical operation teams. The management team should have a clear hierarchy of authority. Officers in charge of operations must have absolute authority over that operation and their subordinates must be trained to obey and implement orders. The success of the operation may depend on prompt action in response to orders, e.g. apprehension of poachers. Officers caught abusing their position should be disciplined, demoted or dismissed.

- *Encourage high standards of personal appearance*. This is part of the development of pride in the reserve and in the job. Park staff should be supplied with simple, practical uniforms, which should be standard to the whole conservation service of a country. All park staff from the warden downwards should wear uniform when on duty, with appropriate badges of rank. Visitors will draw meaningful conclusions from the way the staff appear and carry themselves. Pride in appearance and uniform, however, should not go so far that staff are afraid to get their hands dirty. Many of the duties involved in reserve management involve hard physical work, dirt and sweat. Similarly, a gleaming unscratched landcruiser may symbolise good care and pride but also may point to unnecessary expenditure on a car clearly not being used for park patrols.

- *Maintaining morale and team spirit*. The manager should encourage activities that promote high morale and team spirit among his staff, such as regular off-duty activities, sports, outings, interest groups, and social events. The manager should show an interest in the staff's families and their welfare. In the rush to take conservation education to outside villages, the management must not forget to show films and slide shows to its own staff and families. Most important, the manager must take a deep interest in all aspects of staff work. Give praise for good performances, encouragement where it is needed and a reprimand when work is poor. Emphasise to the staff that their job is worthwhile and why. Each conservation service and large protected area should have its own internal newsletter and regular posting of news on a staff notice board.

Staff members should be encouraged to learn more about the reserve and its wildlife and to undertake personal interest projects or studies in different elements of reserve biology, the socio-economic aspects of protected areas, or management. The protected area manager should always support the staff in public, even when they are in the wrong. Discipline should be a private affair. If the manager is loyal to the staff they will be loyal in return.

The manager should seek the advice of staff and hold regular meetings with them. Staff members often have good ideas, being both closer to the local community and to the day-to-day running of the reserve. It is good for them to feel that they contribute to reserve policy. It is also useful for senior field staff to attend annual conferences with colleagues from other protected areas. These are a valuable forum for exchange of ideas and discussion of common problems, and help alleviate the feelings of isolation and neglect which tend to develop when personnel spend long periods on their own in isolated field stations. Most meetings should be of an informal nature, held either at headquarters or different field locations.

- *Staff welfare*. Whenever possible, the protected area authority should provide medical and educational facilities for the staff and their families. There is often a problem of how to man remote guard posts which are unsuitable for families. This can sometimes be achieved through a rotational system, with men spending, say, two weeks on outpost duty and then being relieved and spending one to two weeks at park headquarters with their families. There is also the problem of where to site staff quarters; if they are based at headquarters they form a small town which is unsightly, causes much disturbance, and is a constant source of problems for the Chief Warden or Park Manager. It is, therefore, generally preferable that staff are quartered outside the park where they are less restricted, are able to cultivate and also to keep domestic livestock if they so wish.

- *Rewards and incentives*. Good performance will be encouraged by the development of a fair system of incentives and punishments. There should be real rewards for good work, such as public commendation, transfers to popular postings, speedy promotion, inclusion on the regular government payroll, increased responsibility, opportunities to travel, study, or attend conferences, extra leave and, at the daily level, words of appreciation. Promotion should not be automatic with seniority but dependent on ability and proficiency of performance. Poor performance should not be allowed to pass unnoticed. Sometimes punishment is necessary – demotion, loss of special privileges, unpopular postings or job assignments, or dismissal. There are subtle and fair ways of 'punishing' someone for poor performance without being brutal or arousing hostility.

Example 10.3: Awards for protected area personnel

There is a range of awards given by international agencies to individuals for exceptional work in the field of protected area management. Deserving conservationists are eligible for any one of the following marks of recognition:

The J. Paul Getty Wildlife Conservation Prize

The 'Nobel Prize of Conservation', the Getty Prize is awarded each year for outstanding achievement in wildlife and habitat conservation of international significance. The $US 50,000 prize is administered by World Wildlife Fund-US the winner being selected by an international jury. Candidates for the Prize are evaluated for their contributions in various fields, including the conservation of rare or endangered species and their habitats, the conservation of ecosystems, the increase in public awareness of the importance of the natural world, the establishment of conservation legislation, or the foundation of an organisation or society of unusual importance to wildlife conservation.

World Wildlife Fund Gold Medal

This award is WWF's highest, presented for highly meritorious and strictly personal services to the conservation of wildlife and natural resources.

World Wildlife Fund Members of Honour

Appointees are selected from among persons of great distinction in conservation or fields related to conservation.

World Wildlife Fund Award for Conservation Merit

In 1981, WWF International instituted a new conservation award to honour people who receive no headlines for their behind-the-scenes work, yet who make substantial contributions to conservation. An inscribed scroll is presented to the winner.

The Order of the Golden Ark

The Order of the Golden Ark was created by His Royal Highness Prince Bernhard of the Netherlands, Founder-President of World Wildlife Fund, to mark outstanding service to the conservation of wildlife and the natural environment.

The IUCN/CNPPA Fred M. Packard International Parks Merit Award

Founded as the 'Valor Award' to honour parks personnel for acts of unusual courage involving a high degree of personal risk in the face of danger, the award was changed in 1982 to the 'Fred M. Packard International Parks Merit Award' – the 'Parks Merit Award' for short – to expand its scope and to honour the individual who started the award and established its endowment fund. This is the only award which is directly related to IUCN's Commission on National Parks and Protected Areas activities and which has the objective of recognising protected area professionals.

The award includes a cash prize, usually of $US 500, and a certificate. Nominations can be accepted for any individual (or group of individuals) who has carried out his duties in the service of protected areas above and beyond the call of duty.

The Peter Scott Merit Award

Periodically, the Species Survival Commission of IUCN wishes to recognise a particularly significant and noteworthy contribution to the conservation of wild fauna and flora, especially (but not limited to) endangered and threatened taxa and those subject to exploitation by man. The recipient of the award may be one or more individuals, an organisation, or an institution. The award consists of a certificate and citation together with such other tangible recognition as may be deemed appropriate.

Reporting

The establishment of good channels and routines for reporting is basic to effective administration. It ensures that work is indeed done when it should be; builds up a valuable source of systematically-documented information; protects the reportee and establishes evidence when it is needed; and keeps senior staff supplied with up-to-date information. Examination of the various types of reports plays a crucial role in evaluation of performance and progress.

Reporting may take many forms, including submission of handwritten notebooks, photographic documentation, verbal reports, radio reporting, formal written reports, personnel evaluation, and library and equipment ledgers. While good reporting is essential, it is worth stressing that reporting is not an end in itself. Reporting should not consume too much valuable staff time. Reports should be brief, and judged on their clarity, accuracy, timeliness and content, not on their thickness or the beauty of their duplication. Even so, a report is only as valuable as the audience it reaches. In many cases, the design and use of standard reporting forms will speed up the time spent on writing and reading reports and make the information readily available for enumeration and evaluation (see Example 10.4).

Example 10.4: Some tips on report writing

Who will read it? A report is not a literary effort. Its purpose is to communicate ideas, facts, and opinions. Keep in mind the target audience and outline the relevant points, then start writing.

Get attention quickly. 'Background material' on the first page is usually well known. Summarise briefly or leave it out. State the report's purpose in a few words, itemise, and then come to grips with the facts.

Make it objective. People are seldom interested in what the writer thinks, and would rather read what he knows. Don't write reports with the idea of making an impression. Let the report sell itself.

Practise restraint. The report need not be stuffy, but it should take a conservative approach to the problem under consideration. Avoid extravagant statements, unless supported by facts.

Spell it out. The typical executive is too busy to take time digging out pertinent information from a deluge of words. List facts in 1-2-3 order, set off with headings.

Document the report. One of the best ways to make a report inviting to read is to use attachments rather than incorporating the data in the report itself. Refer to exhibits by number for easy reference.

Break it up. Long paragraphs are difficult to follow. Restrict paragraphs to a few lines, and provide key paragraphs so that the reader will know what it is all about.

Emphasise each important point. To make doubly sure the reader does not lose the thread of the argument, indent and underscore key points.

Present it well. A good report invites reading. Don't crowd a lot of words into a little space. Leave wide margins on the right for notations. Make plenty of copies.

Summarise the main points and conclusions. Conclude the report with a brief summary of its points, and if desirable offer recommendations. If they are rejected, don't be disappointed. Only those responsible for the entire operation have the overall perspective needed to make important policy decisions.

Inspection and supervision

However good and well-motivated the staff of the protected area, efficiency and work performance will improve if an effective system of supervision and inspection is established. Headquarters staff should make regular inspection visits to the protected area to consult with, and encourage, the warden and his staff. The warden and his staff should visit and participate in the activities of their sections and each section must have senior officers checking on and advising the guard force. Inspectors should give constructive criticisms and praise where merited. They should get to know their juniors personally as this is good for morale.

Inspection visits which are advertised well in advance have little real value. It is much more useful if the inspector can turn up unannounced and join the staff on a typical work day, seeing the type of problems they face and how they go about their work. This enables him to see the constraints of the job and to become aware of any lack of equipment, etc. The senior officers chosen to carry out inspections should themselves be of high calibre, experienced and competent in the duties they are overseeing. They are not there to ingratiate themselves with junior staff nor to belittle the local section heads. It is no use sending a normally desk-bound town-bred officer to comment on the efficiency of reserve guards if he cannot keep up with patrols. Inspectors must be people who can command respect. Most staff actually like to be evaluated, learn from constructive criticism, and enjoy praise for good work.

Especially noteworthy performances should be recognised in staff newsletters, and medals for many years service, and valour, can prove a strong incentive. Staff found abusing their position for self-profit must be suspended immediately.

Maintenance of physical structures and stores

The maintenance of physical structures – cleaning, repairing, repainting, rethatching of buildings, repair of hides, watchtowers, bridges, fences, notice boards, boundary markers, cleaning of ditches and drains, and maintenance of paths and roads – should all be part of the routine duties of the reserve staff. Maintenance work should be allocated a substantial part of the annual budget, be allowed for in work schedules, and be specified in staff job descriptions. The first rule of good maintenance is 'don't build it if you can't maintain it'. Far too often budgets are raised for a contractor to erect a new structure but no follow-up budget is requested for maintenance. In some cases, routine maintenance may extend as far as clearing up litter discarded by visitors and cleaning off graffiti and other unwelcome signs of man.

All structures have an estimated life expectancy and budgets should allow for their renewal and repair. Managers and Inspectors should be empowered to declare items unsafe or beyond repair and order them demolished. Unwanted or dangerous physical structures should be dismantled and removed under routine maintenance. Rotting buildings and tree hides are not only an eyesore, they are dangerous.

The protected area manager is responsible for supervising a maintenance programme, estimating costs, and scheduling maintenance efforts.

- *Housekeeping* is a basic daily activity and involves simply keeping things clean and orderly. Examples are washing vehicles at the end of each day, keeping toilet facilities clean, sweeping offices, and cleaning windows.
- *Preventative maintenance* involves regular inspections and testing of equipment. Regular shutdowns of equipment are often necessary for performing routine checks to locate potential breakdowns before they occur. Keep a schedule of maintenance requirements, and a record of maintenance inspections.
- *Breakdown maintenance* is required because of unscheduled events such as accidents, storm damage, or vandalism.
- *No maintenance* usually results in total deterioration and waste of the investment in facilities and equipment.

One problem in tropical countries is that the standards of decoration and fittings in buildings expected by overseas tourists may be quite beyond the guards' own appreciation. To a guard who has never experienced better accommodation than a simple hut, a piece of corrugated iron roughly tacked over a roof hole may seem an adequate repair. He may need training to understand the standards required, which will vary according to the function of the structure, from a luxury class tourist lodge to a hostel dormitory and the staff quarters. The manager and the inspectors between them must ensure that effective standards are achieved. However, even these officers often have erroneous ideas of what foreign visitors want. Many tourists actually prefer the novelty of local styles and materials rather than the airless concrete boxes sometimes provided.

Visitors pay attention to the standards of the buildings and other structures in the reserve. If the management authority cannot maintain a simple bridge, what sort of a job are they doing in maintaining the rest of the park?

Stores maintenance and inventory

Most protected areas services have to operate under considerable budgetary restraints. Once major items of equipment are acquired, it can be particularly difficult to replace them, so it is unfortunate if such equipment is then lost or wasted through lack of maintenance.

Operation, maintenance and replacement costs for all equipment must be allowed for: it is a common fault to budget only for purchase of new items. In addition, equipment donated to individual reserves or divisions through aid agencies or conservation charities must be regarded as part of the reserve equipment, listed in the inventory and maintained. This may require an extra maintenance budget.

Many items of equipment need special care and attention. Vehicles need regular servicing. Electronic equipment must be kept dry and as cool as possible to prevent decay (not easy in the tropics). Typewriters rust, tents rot unless dried and aired, and rubber boats will be eaten by rats unless properly stored. It is not enough to have a store room in which to dump everything. Keep an inventory of all equipment and establish proper maintenance schedules.

Cost-effectiveness aims to minimise waste in the form of loss of investment through negligence, inefficiency, unnecessary purchase, and inoperative equipment.

Efficiency of operation depends on equipment being kept in good working condition, being readily located on station where it is needed (there is no point in the reserve boat being tied up in harbour 40 km away), and being stored where it can be found quickly and brought into operation as needed.

The inventory is a list of all equipment on site,

specifying its exact location, who is responsible for its maintenance or use and its current condition. In most protected areas, most equipment will be issued to individual staff or on loan to individual offices. There will be special stores, such as boathouses, garages, and radio houses, for specific items. There is generally a field store at headquarters or at other posts for small items of equipment.

Items in fieldstores must be listed and signed out to staff with due authorisation. It is a good idea for one member of staff at each duty station to be designated as station stores officer. The storemaster is responsible for checking equipment out and back into the store and chasing up overdue items. Ideally, the condition of the item should be noted each time it is issued and returned. Similar control should be applied to books and libraries.

Maintenance schedules must be kept for all items that need regular attention: oiling, servicing, and cleaning. The stores officer must see that regular maintenance schedules are kept. This may need considerable planning. For example, servicing of a regularly-used boat engine must be fitted into the operation schedule for the boat.

Some items of equipment such as camera equipment and delicate electronics should be kept in special containers, such as airtight boxes with dry silica gel (the gel will need drying out at regular intervals), an air conditioned room or a heated cupboard. Such preparations may seem time-consuming or expensive but extend the life and usefulness of equipment.

Once a year the equipment inventory should be reviewed. This annual inventory summarises all equipment, its location and condition and the frequency of use of each item, its appropriateness for certain tasks and any particular problems or advantages experienced.

Such an inventory guides maintenance needs and budgeting and indicates which items need renewing or major repairs. It is an opportunity to recover mislaid equipment. Apart from its value in planning further equipment purchases, the annual inventory shows the cost-effectiveness and usefulness of the equipment in hand. The purchasing officer can quickly see what equipment is much in demand and should be duplicated, what is rarely used, what is inadequate and cannot cope with the workload, and what is not effective because it breaks down too often, cannot stand up to the local conditions, or is not suitable for the job. The inventory allows the authority to pin point replacement needs.

In conclusion, it is worth restating that a

organised maintenance programme means simply looking after your investment properly. Regular maintenance extends the useful life of the facilities or equipment and makes for better and safer working conditions. Staff will take better care of equipment that is properly serviced. Finally, well-maintained buildings, facilities and equipment make a good impression on the visiting public.

Patrolling

Patrolling is one of the basic and most important functions of the guard force of a protected area. Patrolling can be done on foot, on horseback, by vehicles, boats, helicopters, small planes, or other forms of transport, by one man with a notebook, or a whole armed squad. Patrolling involves routine inspections inside the reserve, checking the boundaries and sometimes patrols outside the protected area, and visiting local villages. Modern radio communications equipment has greatly facilitated patrol work and most park systems today place heavy reliance on radios in patrolling operations.

The main function of patrols is to ensure that the reserve regulations are being observed; that strict sanctuary areas are not being trespassed; that visitors have proper permits and do not break park regulations; that only authorised personnel are active in restricted zones; and that there is no illegal hunting, logging or clearing of land for agriculture in the reserve. In addition, regular patrols can monitor changes within the reserve and collect valuable data on the availability of water, on flowering and fruiting seasons, and animal populations and breeding. This can be done with very little training or scientific background.

In the Tangkoko-Batuangus Reserve in Sulawesi, Indonesia, for example, locally recruited junior guards with only the lowest educational standards were able to achieve a very high level of reliability in recording biological information during regular monthly patrols. Patrol routes were allocated and divided into numbered sections. At the end of each section of 500 m the guards, working in pairs, stopped to write details of all sightings of wildlife and fresh tracks within that section. Patrols also recorded any trees in fruit along the patrol path. Over a two-year period, these records built up a remarkably detailed picture of the distribution and seasonal variations of biological resources over the whole reserve. Such biological records can be a valuable aid to monitoring the effectiveness of management. Similarly, analysis of law enforcement data as was done for the Chirisa Safari Area, Zimbabwe (Conway, 1984)

allows for better deployment of patrols, the collation of intelligence and an assessment of the patrols' effectiveness in curbing poaching.

Patrolling can be part of in-service training and serves as visible advertisement to visitors and local people that the reserve staff are active and interested in maintaining the integrity of the reserve. Local people are not likely to show much respect for the reserve if the staff do not patrol it.

The number of men in patrols, the frequency of patrols and how intensively an area should be patrolled will all vary according to local conditions and may differ according to seasons (e.g., more frequent patrolling of turtle nesting beaches during the breeding season). Some general principles of patrolling activities are given in Example 10.5. (For pratical hints, see also Corfield, 1984.)

Patrolling inside forests is sometimes a case of not seeing the wood for the trees. It may be easier to get a clear picture of who is collecting forest produce by sitting on a bare hillside outside the reserve and watching the forest from a distance. Regular aerial surveys and photographs or even satellite imagery will show where new clearings are being made, and the whereabouts of poachers' camps and fires. Foot patrols can be despatched to the area to apprehend the offenders. Similarly, a man stationed in a village quickly learns who regularly goes into the forest and to do what. This is a good reason to site guardposts in villages. Apart from the more obvious advantages of accessibility to services, much useful intelligence information can be gleaned from cooperation with the local police and district officers as well as from informers.

Guards stationed in different parts of the reserve must be instructed as to what area to patrol. They must also be familiar with that area and know how often to carry out routine patrols and which localities require most attention. Patrol rosters should be prepared by the warden's office.

It is often useful to plan for patrols to meet at set points. Patrols might meet half way between their respective guardposts to exchange news and information, and coordinate further movements and

54. Rangers on patrol in the Serengeti National Park, Tanzania. The rangers are the foundation of good protected area management. A disciplined, properly equipped, well-motivated and well-supported guard force is an essential element in successful protection of conservation areas. Photo: Guy Dussaule

Example 10.5: Some hints on organising guard patrols

- Patrols should consist of at least two men, to give mutual support, to summon help in case of accident or illness and to corroborate one another's evidence.
- Patrols should be unpredictable, conducted at irregular intervals, on differing routes, over holiday periods as well as normal working days, at night as well as by day, or whenever law-breakers may be active.
- If law-breakers are likely to be armed, then patrols should also be armed. If guards are armed, they should be trained in how to use and maintain weapons. Firearms must be well-maintained and strictly controlled.
- Patrols must cover the whole area of the reserve and not just patrol the boundaries. The outer wall of a forest may look in good condition yet hide a honeycomb of clearings behind the crest of the hill. Poachers in grasslands can be equally 'invisible' unless patrols are thorough.
- Guards should be moved around regularly between posts. Also the details making up each patrol must be changed frequently. This provides variety of work experience and prevents guards becoming too familiar, and perhaps too lenient, with local people.
- Patrols should be thoroughly briefed and debriefed.
- Each guard should be provided with a notebook and pencil. Patrols should note evidence of crimes and names of offenders. The patrol's log can be submitted as evidence in court cases.
- Patrols should also record biological data of interest to the reserve management.

55. Rangers on border partrol in Manas Wildlife Sanctuary in Assam. Trained elephants are the ideal method of transport in many parks in Asia.
Photo: J. Thorsell

other activities, such as tracking down poachers.

It is very important that accurate notes be kept by all patrols, not just of criminal activities and offenders apprehended, but also of biological data (see above). The information must be summarised every month or quarter and reported through the appropriate channels. This infor- mation is extremely valuable as it shows trends in the extent of use and abuse of the reserve. The warden's office should maintain 'ongoing maps' recording signs and other evidence of crimes. This facilitates more efficient and effective deployment of patrols.

In-service training

Senior staff should be trained in both the theoretical and practical aspects of their work at national or regional schools. Protected area planning and management is a highly technical science bringing together the theory of several quite diverse disciplines – ecology, forestry, agro-forestry, geography, wildlife management, education, public relations, landscape architecture, land-use planning, hydrology, estate management, tourism, social sciences, economics, personnel management, and general business management. It has become increasingly apparent that development of these abilities requires specialised training courses. National and regional schools and numerous specialised seminars are now available. Schools such as the College of African Wildlife Management, Tanzania, the Ecole de Faune in Cameroon, Centro de Instruccion de Guardparques, Argentina, Indonesia's School of Environmental Conservation Management, and the Tropical Agricultural Research and Training Center in Costa Rica, are examples of field training institutions.

Guards and rangers are the foundation of any

reserve. They are the most important, but often most ignored, unit in the whole conservation department. In-service training programmes must be developed particularly for these personnel. The best training is actual field experience, and the reserve manager should realise that in organising his workforce he is also training his staff.

New staff should be teamed with experienced hands so that they benefit from their valuable know-how. The manager should keep notes of each staff member's particular abilities and work experience. It is prudent to rotate staff from time to time so that they learn most of the different aspects of reserve management and are familiar with the whole area. Varied duties will not only improve individual performance but will give the manager more flexibility in rearranging staff in the event of transfers and absences. Rotation of duties allows everyone to get to know the other staff, helps them to work better as a team, and facilitates the mounting of non-routine operations.

Supervisors must fully understand and be able to perform themselves the jobs they are now supervising. This is not just a matter of efficiency but of morale. Workmen respond better to a boss who has done his stint.

It is worthwhile holding periodic refresher courses or training exercises and time should be set aside for this purpose. Such exercises can be enjoyable, good for personnel relations and morale-boosting, as well as valuable training.

In addition, many of the routine tasks that have to be done – regular checking of buildings, repairs, painting and maintenance, annual surveys and counts, cutting of new survey trails, measuring and mapping of trails, site plans for new developments, preparation of new information materials, discussion groups with local village representatives, demarcation of buffer-zones, and many other useful activities, can be performed as training exercises. As such, manpower can be temporarily increased by accepting junior staff for the training course from other reserves which lack similar programmes.

Where there are several widely scattered parks and reserves, a possible solution for training junior field staff (guards, rangers, etc.) is through one or more small mobile training teams. These consist of two or three instructors with their own vehicle and teaching aids (audio-visual equipment, etc.) who can give basic training and refresher courses in each area in turn, in collaboration with the Chief Warden and his senior staff. Such a scheme has several advantages:

- It is possible to select the best instructors and employ them full-time on training, free of other duties.
- The scheme provides uniformity of training throughout the agency.
- Feedback to the training team from field staff in the areas visited would promote exchange of ideas on common problems.
- It allows the Chief Warden and other senior staff in the parks/reserves to spend less time on training staff though they will, of course, still participate in training courses.
- The training team, based at headquarters but spending much of the time visiting out-stations, could be a valuable source of information to the Head of Department/Director-General on current problems in the field.

Concession services

The means by which facilities, food and accommodation services are provided for visitors to protected areas will vary depending on government policy. The choice lies between self-operation by the protected area agency or through a contractual arrangement with a private operator, usually termed the concessionaire. In situations where a protected area is not used in significant numbers by visitors because of its remoteness or seasonality, there may be no choice but for governments initially to subsidise provision of facilities.

The major concern, whatever system is used, is control over the quality of service that is provided. Visitors invariably assume that the responsibility for visitor services rests with the protected area agency and seldom realise that a private concessionaire is responsible. Quality of structure, types of building materials, location and size of facilities will all influence the visitors' impression of the park and should be specified by the park authority. Other considerations are length of lease, specific contractual arrangements, profit margins and method of financing.

56. Teaching manuals are an effective way of improving in-service training

Land control is another important variable in determining the appropriate concession system. In some countries (e.g., Papua New Guinea) virtually no land within the national parks is owned by the administrative agency while in most other countries all land in parks is publicly owned.

General government policies on the balance of public or private enterprise will have an overriding effect on the visitor services provided in protected areas. This, in turn, is affected by the stage of a country's development and its social policies. Unless there is a highly developed commercial ethic in a country, government should probably supply service facilities in a reserve. It is difficult for a private concessionaire to accept strict controls when there is an obvious demand for more visitor facilities. The case of the overdevelopment of several parks and reserves in Kenya (Amboseli, Masai Mara) is a reflection of these pressures.

Public (government) provision of services

There are few countries in which governments both supply and operate visitor facilities in their entirety. An exception is South Africa which plans, constructs and operates all its visitor service facilities, adhering to a policy of complete government control on all such services, with no leasing arrangements available to any private operators or concessionaires.

Most countries, however, operate a dual system, with visitor facilities provided by both public and private sectors. Sometimes a government must step in because the services provided by private concessionaires are too few and too expensive to meet the needs of most park visitors.

An outstanding example is Japan where visitors to national parks increased dramatically during the 1960s. This growth, accompanied by a dire shortage of inexpensive facilities and a tendency by private operators to offer increasingly luxurious and expensive facilities, led to the introduction in 1961 of the 'National Vacation Village' system to increase the numbers of facilities available to young people and families and to disperse the park users within the parks. By 1972, there were 21 villages accommodating 150-400 persons per village. Facilities include park shelters for day visitors, overnight accommodation, swimming pools, ski areas, camping grounds, nature trails, etc. These villages are supported entirely from public funds, with the revenue-producing facilities financed on government loans so that such capital funds are eventually recovered.

The main advantages of government management, ownership and operation of visitor service facilities are:

- Quality of goods and service can be given a high priority (perhaps a higher priority than profits).
- Complete control in all staffing and personnel matters.
- Complete control over all financial transactions.
- Tight control of stocks and records.
- Control of visitor use and movement so that disturbance to wildlife is minimised.

Disadvantages of the public approach are:

- The large capital investment which may be required to construct facilities and equipment may not be available from government sources.
- Staff personnel matters can consume an inordinate amount of time, sometimes to the detriment of other management activities.
- There may be difficulties in securing a qualified and experienced concession manager, as well as qualified staff.
- When profit motivation is not critical to the operation, there may be inefficient employment of staff.

Ideally, public (government) control should provide an acceptable level of visitor service facilities with the optimum financial return to the government agency. Moreover, there persists a feeling, even in many developed countries, that all returns from visitor services in a public park should accrue to the public purse, rather than to a private operator holding a preferential contract. This may be an oversimplification of the situation, where many operational factors are not evident, despite a 'captive' market and a preferential contractual arrangement.

The key to successful public operation of visitor services appears to rest to a large degree with the employment of a well-qualified *on site* manager. Control and efficiency of operation are of a much higher order with a competent manager who is 'on the firing line'. Contractual arrangements may allow the manager a bonus on gross or net profits, or similar incentives to encourage a well-run operation, while insisting on a good quality of service.

Private concessionaires

In many countries, private individuals or companies are allowed to construct and provide visitor services in protected areas that receive significant numbers of visitors. These services include accommodation, food, transportation, fuel supplies, and gift or curio shops. Concession leases are granted under varying terms depending on the type of service provided. Contracts range from 1 to 30 years in relation to the capital investment of the private operator.

The selection of an appropriate concession operator is an important responsibility of the management agency. It will be based on the operator's proven ability to manage the selected facility with evidence to demonstrate that he is sympathetic to the primary values of the park. If a tendering process is used, a full financial prospectus may also be required.

The concessionaire must be given adequate time to earn a reasonable return on his investment. The financial return to government is normally based on a system of franchise fees which comprise a flat annual fee plus a percentage of gross receipts. The concessionaire's contract is renewed at the expiration of the original contract, assuming services have been satisfactory. If such facilities and services are no longer required, the buildings, structures, fixtures and all improvements become the property of government with the contractor being reimbursed for the value of such buildings and equipment (at current values).

The major advantages of a private concession in the management, ownership and operation of visitor service facilities are:

- Capital investment is the responsibility of the operator, relieving government of such financial obligation.
- It is essential that profits are realised, ensuring on-site management for optimum returns on the investment.
- Service staff are closely supervised and controlled.
- Much emphasis is placed on efficiency and cost control in labour and service.
- If one concessionaire operates a number of facilities, there may be a better opportunity to realise savings on purchase of goods and saleable products.
- All personnel matters are the responsibility of the operator.

Some of the major disadvantages of the private concession or leasing approach are:

- Profit motivation may lead to inferior goods and services.
- It may be difficult to control quality of service to the public, while the public assumes the operation is government-operated.
- Leasing or granting concession rights may result in political pressures to increase the type and availability of certain services not deemed appropriate for the park.

However, if the concessionaire does prove unsatisfactory the management authority has the option to refuse to renew, or even to withdraw, the lease.

Non-profit concession services

Another common method of providing visitor services is through a 'trust' arrangement. A trust operates as a non-profit organisation with no formal relationship to the public or private sector. The National Trusts of Zimbabwe, Barbados and the Bahamas and the King Mahendra Trust in Nepal are some well-known examples.

These trusts may own lands, buildings, and even entire villages. Donors provide an endowment for maintenance and are often allowed to retain residence rights on a portion of the property. Visitor fees augment the current upkeep of properties along with members' subscriptions, legacies and gifts to the general fund.

Caution must be exercised by a trust in accepting land and/or buildings from an individual donor. The agency accepting the gift must receive full control of the donation to allow optimum public use of the site and avoid restrictions or other constraints to the public. The essential element is one of control. What at first may appear to be a highly desirable donation of land from a private donor may not be as attractive a gift if too many restrictions are attached to its use.

In conclusion, the role of government is seen as a social one while that of the private concessionaire is essentially economic. Precisely how these two roles can be meshed to implement proper public use of the protected area must be viewed within the total social and political context of the country concerned.

Controlling resource utilisation

In protected areas where various types of harvesting or utilisation are permitted, strict controls must be instituted to ensure that the resource being used and the other objectives of the protected area are not compromised. Generally there will need to be a quota system to limit use, a permit system to control entry, and a system of checks on both. In addition, some sort of agreement or policy is necessary to govern harvesting, as well as the other activities of harvesters and other resource users.

Harvesting of wild populations is limited by the productive capacity of the population to sustain the harvest and (perhaps more important) the

ability of a competent management authority to restrict the harvest to this level. In practice, the harvestable proportion in naturally-regulated systems is rather low. High harvests can usually only be achieved by manipulating the system, such as by manipulating the habitat or reducing the mortality factors of the species in question (for fuller details see Caughley, 1977). Setting optimal levels for a harvest or annual off-take can be a complex process.

The main problem with quotas is that they are sometimes regarded as targets that have to be reached to ensure that the quota will be the same or higher next year. This can create a vicious circle

57. Collection of tern eggs in the Seychelles. Strict controls must be applied to all forms of wildli[f]
utilisation if harvesting is to be sustained.
Photo: WWF/Christian Zuber

with harvesters working harder and harder to collect the allowed quota, driving the resource to lower and lower levels, eventually to their own disadvantage. Quotas should be set annually and monitored.

Theoretically, it should be possible to set a quota for the harvested species which guarantees that its numbers do not fall below an agreed lower limit. Such would be the case in a hunting reserve where it was decided that at least five hundred breeding stock of a given game species, at a certain male to female ratio, must be left at the end of each season. The next year's quota could then be the number of animals in excess of this minimum. In reality one can and usually does harvest with no very precise idea of absolute population size but with an accurate index to population trends. The off-take must then be monitored for numbers and quality. Where the population of the species being harvested cannot be assessed, the manager must rely on applying a conservative quota and watching for signs of overharvesting. If there are no such signs the quota may be gradually increased.

It is generally best to start with a low quota; it can always be increased but a population that has been overharvested cannot always recover. Even if the quota is set at a low 'safe' level it should be carefully monitored so as to avoid over-harvesting which can be both ecologically and economically damaging to the enterprise. Common signs that a quota is too high and that a population is being overharvested are:

- Loss or obvious reduction in the numbers of the population
- Increasing distances travelled to find the resource
- Increasing unit effort needed to collect the resource
- Falling harvests
- Decreasing mean condition, size or age of individuals in the harvested population

These factors should be monitored to ensure that quotas can be reduced or a complete ban imposed if needed. Even where a population could in theory be harvested at a sustained level, if there is no management capacity to control the harvesting, a complete ban is required.

Permit systems

Example 10.6 highlights the problems of overharvesting communal resources. A wise farmer kills only so many of his chickens and leaves enough eggs to replenish his stock. He knows it is in his own interest to limit today's harvest to ensure tomorrow's. The same holds true for communal resources. The community using the resource must be convinced that it is in their interests to control the level of harvesting within sustainable limits. In practice this will not work if individual harvesters exploit for short-term self-interest at the expense of the community and, in the long-run, themselves.

Many traditional societies already have local rules controlling the use of communal resources and these can sometimes be adapted to control use of resources in reserves. The main advantage of such local systems and tribal laws is that they are familiar to the local people rather than seen as edicts imposed by an outsider, in this case the management authority. The authority should seek to incoporate such local traditions into its own control system as this makes regulation easier. Although there should be consultation with local community councils about levels of harvesting, and how it is controlled, the ultimate responsibility for regulation should remain with the management authority.

Any formula for control of communal harvesting of products in conservation buffer zones or protected areas should consider the following points:

- Try to introduce a territorial element into harvesting so that a given area is designated as being for the sole use of people from one village, who will defend their privilege against outsiders.
- Try to ensure that every resident household is able to benefit fairly; otherwise those left out will not respect harvesting limits. However, to avoid creating an attractive zone which draws more people, harvesting rights should be granted only to original households and their descendants.
- Encourage those who have harvesting rights to appoint a management committee to decide on cropping and planting schemes, quotas and labour requirements.
- The committee must arrange with harvesters a fair system of labour inputs. Villagers may be requested to provide an agreed quota of work-days themselves, provide substitute labour, or make a financial payment to the management committee to hire labour.
- Harvestable quotas should be decided by the committee with approval by the protected area management authority.

Example 10.6: Bird egg harvest in Indonesia

The reverse quota system has been operated successfully in Sulawesi, Indonesia, where villagers harvest the eggs of the maleo bird, a megapode which lays its large eggs in the sand at communal breeding sites where they are incubated by natural heat. Since a maleo egg is six times the volume of a chicken's egg and a very rich source of protein, it is well worth evolving a system where the eggs can be harvested on a sustained-yield basis. But wherever these breeding areas are utilised by villagers as a communal resource, the collectors almost invariably overharvest and eventually cause local extinction of the bird. However, if fresh eggs are collected and reburied in a cage they can be protected from human disturbance and natural predators, such as pigs and monitor lizards, and have an 80 per cent hatching success. By burying a set minimum number of maleo eggs within simple protective cages at known laying sites, it is possible to guarantee a certain number of young birds for release into the wild population each year. Any excess eggs can then be harvested. With slight experimentation with the numbers of birds for release, it should be possible to devise an optimal harvesting system for this resource.

Source: MacKinnon, 1981b

- The management committee should keep records of all materials harvested, and be responsible for marketing any cash products and arranging fair disposal of products, such as house poles, roofing materials, or meat.

The closed shop principle involved in such a formula is necessary to stabilise use of the buffer zone and to avoid attracting extra newcomers into the area.

Law enforcement

As discussed in Chapter 4, pages 56-64, it is important that the protected area management either has it own law enforcement officers and/or develops a very close working relationship with the national law enforcement agency to control abuses against protected areas. The most important link in the ultimate success of conservation activities is the person who has the task of enforcing protection laws and regulation. This is the guard – sometimes called a wildlife or game guard, ranger, scout or conservation officer. Guards should be familiar with the rules and regulations of the protected areas and with the rules and regulations of the Hunting Regulations and Wildlife Act relevant to their daily duties.

It is best if guards possess real handling power, e.g. to arrest law breakers. In some countries, this power is uniquely reserved for the police force, which is often not the most efficient body to curb illegal activities in conservation areas. Guards should have the power to confiscate arms, tools, logs, cattle and illegally-collected produce such as animals, eggs, plants, flowers, rattan or trapped animals.

It is vital to establish clear procedures for handling those apprehended for illegal activities in reserves. Without proper procedures criminals may escape prosecution and guards may even find themselves facing legal proceedings for improper arrest or confiscation. In more lawless areas, lack of clear procedures may result in guards being injured or killed. The level of training and equipping of guards to apprehend offenders will vary considerably from one country or type of reserve to another. In some countries, merely warning offenders and documenting reserve abuses may be adequate, whereas in some states the apprehension of poachers has become a mini-war with poachers equipped with fast transport and modern weapons and showing no hesitation in opening fire on reserve staff. Clearly the staff in such a situation need very special training and high levels of discipline and motivation. Since guards are in the front line of action, all guards must be aware of the proper procedures for:

- Arrest or apprehension of persons engaged in illegal acts inside a protected area.

- Documentation of illegal activities for court proceedings (if needed), including what to record, evidence in the form of confiscated articles, photographs, signed statements, and reports to local district officers.
- Confiscation of items prohibited within protected areas or needed as evidence to testify to

an illegal act (e.g. animal carcases).
- Simple legal procedures in delivering arrested persons into the hands of the law and filing charges.
- Basic principles of public relations as applied to local people (see Chapter 7).

58. Reserve guards pose with a massive haul of poachers' snares and spears collected during a routine anti-poaching exercise in the Hlane Wildlife Sanctuary in Swaziland.
Photo: WWF/Michael Ibstedt

Encroachment of human settlements and shifting cultivation

This is the major management problem in many of the parks and reserves in the tropics where expanding human populations need more land for agriculture. Ambiguous conservation laws and ineffective law enforcement organisations aggravate the problem.

Illegal agriculture and settlement in reserves must be stopped very early, before the problem grows out of hand. Such incidents must be handled with great tact. Eviction or displacement of illegal agriculturalists can evoke bad publicity detrimental to the conservation agency's cause. The following guidelines may prove useful in such circumstances.

- Ascertain why the land has been settled. Is it land speculation by people who already have enough land to support themselves and their stock? Are the offenders clearing the land for themselves or for some distant speculator to whom they may be in debt? If the settlement is greed-motivated land speculation, proceed quickly to eject the people and rehabilitate the cleared land.

  If the agriculture is clearly a matter of survival for needy, landless people, they must be translocated elsewhere. This usually takes time so some temporary land use must be agreed. Such a compromise should at least hold the *status quo* and prevent further damage until a solution is found.
- It is better to persuade squatters to move out of a protected area voluntarily rather than force them out. If the settlement is of long standing, this may mean finding them alternative legal land-holdings, employment or some other incentive and this usually costs money. Where translocation needs are anticipated, budgets and new lands can be allocated but sometimes this is impossible. Protected area managers must take firm action to protect areas from new settlers. Often protected areas are invaded by land-hungry settlers because they are less well guarded than other lands.
- Unless there has been some alternative provision made for evicted or translocated people, they will tend to drift back. It is also wise to remove dwellings and apply better protection, or the vacated lands simply attract other settlers.
- Avoid adverse publicity. Discourage press coverage of relocation of landless, needy people which portrays the action of a heartless

agency putting, the interests of wildlife before those of people. With good press relations, the conservation department can point out how the people were knowingly at fault but the agency and government are helping them to find more suitable homes in less environmentally sensitive locations.

A technique which has been tried in Ethiopia and Indonesia is to send a team from local government to explain to the farmers that their clearings are illegal, not environmentally sound, or on land needed for other purposes. Under threats of more serious action later, the farmers sign letters admitting their illegal occupancy of the land and agree to leave voluntarily as soon as they have harvested their crops. In practice, this method has not been very successful; later inspections sometimes find more permanent perennial crops, a more permanent dwelling and a new occupant who claims to know nothing of the earlier agreement. The method could be useful but needs vigilance of application. If the farmers do not leave as agreed, the management authority, having first warned them fairly, is in a much better legal and media position if it has to forcibly evict them.

Illegal logging

Unless the world demand for tropical hardwood decreases, it is unlikely that any primaeval tropical moist forest outside parks and reserves will escape the chainsaw. Consequently, illegal fellings inside protected areas will probably continue to be a major threat to parks and nature reserves in forested regions.

Collecting forest produce

This problem arose originally in areas where the establishment of parks and reserves excluded local people from collecting forest produce for subsistence. More recently, there has been an increase in the trend to collect forest produce for commercial gain, e.g. orchids, rattan.

Poaching and trapping of wildlife

Poaching and trapping of wild animals for trade, meat, skins, feathers, horns, antlers or ivory is a threat to the survival of many species. In view of the increasing demand for these products, it is unlikely that the illegal market for them will subside in the near future, unless effective national

59. Despite their primitive weapons, poachers have caused massive destruction of wildlife in some parts of Africa. These Waliangulu poachers use their poisoned arrows to devastating effect.
Photo: IUCN/Kenya Information Services

laws and international conventions can be enforced more effectively.

Poachers and timber thieves have to be tracked down, identified or arrested and 'persuaded' through legal action to cease their activities inside protected areas. It is sometimes necessary to do some detective work to identify the real source of the problem. Sometimes the perpetrators are not free agents but are sponsored by, or working under orders for, a boss who never goes near the protected area himself. Tackling the sponsors and their marketing facilities may be an easier way to stop these crimes than chasing the thieves through the bush.

Livestock grazing

Overgrazing of rangelands, as a result of poor management (overstocking, fires, erosion) has forced pastoralists in most arid and semi-arid tropical regions of the world to either reduce their herds voluntarily – by both intentional slaughter or natural mortality – or move herds to areas where grazing is still available. Unfortunately, parks and reserves are often the last resort for these people, causing headaches to the park warden and his staff. The problem is now extending to some parts of the humid tropics.

It is not easy to arrest or prosecute a cow and generally unsatisfactory to bring to court a herdsman for not having adequate control of his free-ranging stock. Moreover, it is generally impossible and undesirable to fence the whole protected area. Killing or confiscating domestic animals found in reserves can lead to retroactive legal proceedings and the creation of great ill-will (remember the reserve is vulnerable to the malcontent's fire).

The most effective policy is to round up and impound stray domestic animals found in the reserve, charge grazing and herding fees for the animals' return and fine the owner.

Arson

Out-of-control fires inside reserves are one of the most difficult, and devastating, problems for the manager of protected areas. Sometimes arson is a purely malicious act by someone with a grudge against the reserve, but more often it is connected with the need to obtain grazing for pastoralists' stock, with collecting honey or to facilitate poaching. Accidental fires often arise from those camping in reserves or spread from burned agricultural lands. As a rule, arson must be dealt with very severely to discourage further deliberate burning.

In all law enforcement matters, the management authority should try to develop the image of a humanitarian but firm agency, sympathetic and understanding of the needs of local people but uncompromising in its determination to protect the integrity of the protected area.

11

Evaluating the Effectiveness of Management

Introduction

Up to this point this handbook has suggested principles for the selection, classification, protection, management, development and use of protected areas. To complete the cycle, a manager also needs an approach for deciding whether the actions taken are effective.

Evaluating the effectiveness of management should be a conscious process aimed at judging the progress made towards achieving the specified short-term and long-term management objectives for a protected area, or the system of protected areas. Moreover, it should be a recognised phase in the overall management process. Such stock-taking is an important phase in the continuum of management.

Successful economic activity is judged by profitability over time, but the extent of the profit or loss can often be predicted. By gauging cash flow and by making timely adjustments, it may be possible to influence the overall success of the venture. This is accepted financial practice. The same principles apply when evaluating the outcome of protected area management activities with a view to ensuring that they are socio-economically acceptable, politically feasible, and ecologically desirable. In addition to simple units of barter such as dollars and cents, the monitoring of the effectiveness of land management is concerned with human attitudes and reactions, and with ecological processes and their responses to various forms of manipulation. Precision and objectivity may thus be difficult and it may be necessary to rely on trends, and relative values, rather than on finite measurements.

Approaches to evaluating the effectiveness of management will vary with circumstances, but it is prudent to ensure that all management programmes have sufficient resources to enable the manager, his superiors and his sponsors to judge the effectiveness and appropriateness of his actions. This obvious fact has sometimes been overlooked with the result that a great deal of money and effort have been misdirected, sometimes over decades.

One example of such misdirected management was the attempted elimination by hunting of the large wild vertebrate hosts of the tsetse fly *Glossina* in parts of Africa. Tsetse flies are the vectors of human sleeping sickness and can be equally fatal for livestock. Several African countries have attempted to control the disease by eliminating the flies' host species. In Botswana and Zimbabwe, these expensive hunting operations continued for 20 and 40 years respectively, yet analysis of the hunting returns demonstrated that none of the main hosts of the tsetse were reduced in numbers (Child, *et al.*, 1970). Earlier evaluation of the effectiveness of this sort of management could have saved much expense and effort.

The real value of continuously evaluating a management programme is that it allows the programme to learn and build on its own experience, and to adjust so as to achieve its goals as efficiently as possible. With the numerous dynamic ecological and socio-economic variables likely to influence the outcome of land management, especially where this involves the protection of complex natural systems, it is very important that these evaluations should provide the manager with ongoing direction that will enable him to adapt his actions.

It is equally important that the programme is sufficiently flexible so as to be able to respond. Such feedback is essential and is applicable to different levels of the management process ranging from the setting of policy objectives, through planning to the implementation of management strategies. In addition, the evaluation process itself provides a psychological motive for high performance and good management.

Pragmatically, there are several major benefits to be derived from conscious evaluation of the effectiveness of management:

- to ascertain if policy and management plan objectives are being achieved and if they are in fact realistic;
- to judge whether the human and financial resources provided for this purpose are sufficient to attain the expected results;
- to report progress to higher authority, including those supporting the management programme and those interested in its implementation;
- to provide an insight into the benefits being derived from a protected area at the local, regional and national levels;
- to help prepare future management programmes;
- to help evaluate the contribution of the protected area to the national and international conservation objectives;
- to help improve the art of conservation management.

Evaluation of the effectiveness of management is difficult or impossible unless this can be measured against well-defined management objectives. Unless a manager knows what is to be expected through management, he has no means of determining how well he and his programme or the sub-units of this programme are performing.

A recurring theme in this handbook is the importance of clearly-defined objectives at the policy, planning and operational levels. Without such goals effective direction becomes problematic and a question of individual judgement and interpretation or personal inclination. This Chapter reiterates the need for defining objectives to achieve effective, efficient and appropriate action.

Various approaches can be used for evaluating the effectiveness of management.

Self evaluation

All routine reports should contain aspects of evaluation – a comment on the success and effectiveness of the activities being reported, the appropriateness of the methods used and suggestions for improvement. Individual staff should be encouraged to evaluate their own performance and the manager of the protected area must evaluate his own performance as well as that of the whole staff. Guidelines for this technique are offered in Example 11.1.

Evaluation by headquarters

Headquarters staff will form their own evaluation of the functioning of the reserve based on the reports they receive and the opinions and comments of visitors to Headquarters, inspectors, visits to the protected area, auditors checking expenditures, and others. Headquarters will evaluate progress in the reserve against the planned expected outputs or achievements and can also effect comparison with other protected areas to get a good idea of how each is doing.

Independent assessment by outside experts

The effectiveness of management in a particular protected area, or system of such areas, can be assessed by a panel of knowledgeable outsiders who are not directly associated with the programme. This procedure can have the advantage of providing an unbiased independent evaluation of progress in a number of areas, thus providing a set of standards against which to measure individual performances. However, it may sometimes be insensitive to local circumstances.

One advantage of this approach, which may be purely coincidental, is that it may raise the morale of a protected area manager and his staff, especially if they feel neglected by their central administration, as it provides an independent audience with whom management actions and their outcome can be discussed and justified. If correctly structured, this type of assessment by outside professionals can be useful both to higher authority and the actual personnel involved in different facets of management, such as research monitoring and law enforcement. The assessors will not only review the methods adopted and their appropriateness to local circumstances, but may make helpful recommendations derived from their own experiences elsewhere.

If this method is adopted, there are pitfalls that should be avoided. Any appeal for outside support against the 'establishment' is likely to be counter-productive and damaging to the protected area authority as a whole, unless it is very carefully orchestrated. It is important when appealing for outside support to ensure that this brings no discredit to the organisation, as otherwise such actions can undermine corporate loyalties and morale, especially where pressure groups within an agency appear to be criticising the policies and objectives of the agency in public. While every member of staff should be able to question and contribute to the orderly evolution of management policies and procedures, it is self-defeating to permit disgruntled or ill-disciplined individuals to destroy progress based on agreed objectives.

Example 11.1: *Questionnaire for rating the effectiveness of the protected area manager*

Are the area manager and staff sufficiently familiar with their area that they can readily notice significant changes in resources?

Have existing problem areas been identified and action taken to correct them?

Are environmental impacts being minimised during projects or activities?

Are on-the-ground activities being conducted in a manner compatible with the objectives of the area?

Have special efforts been made to ensure that public use does not damage the area's resources?

Have special studies or monitoring programmes been identified and programmed?

Is a large-scale base map available for the area?

When in the field do management personnel carry adequate reference material to aid in the performance of their job?

Is an annual work plan used to guide the operation of the area?

Do managerial staff organise their work activities to ensure that the objective of the work plan will be realised?

Do management procedures provide a system of checks and balances to ensure that on-the-ground work is accomplished according to plans and specifications?

Are safety training and accident prevention given high priority in all activities?

Are important documents of value to management retained on file?

Is a management plan for the area available? If not, is one in preparation?

Does the area manager use the experience and training of key staff in problem solving and making important decisions?

Does the area manager delegate authority to selected staff in order to spend more time on higher-level work?

Does the area manager make himself readily available to, and maintain good working relations with, employees at all levels?

Is outstanding work performance duly recognised in employees' work performance ratings? Does poor performance result in appropriate action?

Does the area manager exemplify a proper work ethic, attitude, and deportment?

Are training opportunities made available to employees to improve job satisfaction so that they may have opportunities to qualify for positions of higher responsibility or pay?

Do employees have written job descriptions, so that they understand their duties?

Do duty assignments reflect employee qualifications?

Are jobs planned to use personnel effectively?

Are the rangers and guards smartly turned out and well disciplined?

Are stores and equipment properly accounted for and maintained?

Are all personnel receiving the pay and allowances due them on a regular monthly basis?

Are field staff provided with basic necessary equipment (boots, blankets, poncho, mosquito net, etc.)?

Does the manager have a good relationship with local government officials, chiefs, headmen, and local people?

Adapted from: Deshler, 1982

Local advisory committee

The formation of a local 'Protected Area Advisory Committee', as described in Chapter 7, pages 139-140, can be helpful in evaluating the effectiveness of management in some tropical countries. The committee may involve local personalities, protected area users, concessionnaires, members of other land use agencies or neighbouring communities. Regular meetings are essential and are a useful means of promoting local understanding. There is, however, always a danger that such committees tend to reflect personal or local vested interests, or that they become too enmeshed with the day-to-day administration of

an area and cease to remain objective in evaluating the effectiveness of overall management.

Direct response from visitors

This is not a very rigorous means of evaluating an overall management and development programme, but it can yield immediate responses to certain types of questions. An experienced manager should have little difficulty in distilling useful suggestions from the wide range of comments he receives. Informal interviews, questionnaires distributed to visitors, a suggestion box or a book inviting reactions and comments, all provide valuable feedback on how visitors see the area.

Comparing expenditures and budgets

The effectiveness of operation management in terms of budget expenditure is relatively easy to calculate. How efficiently was the budget utilised? The percentage of available budget (the commitment) actually used (delivered in services, purchasing and construction) is sometimes called the 'percentage of delivery'. This figure avoids the question of how effective was the delivery but provides an approach to gauging the efficiency of the planning and execution of management recommendations, and this makes for more efficient planning in the future.

Where delivery proceeds closely to the planned schedule and budgeting for anticipated costs is accurate, delivery should approach 100 per cent. Where delivery is low, this means that items were overcosted, requirements were overestimated or that management execution, purchasing or other uses of the available financial resources were slow or inefficient. The items for which delivery was low can be examined in detail to see why they were not on target. Were there uncontrollable delays that prevented the timely expenditures? Was planning unrealistic in its expectations? Which items should be given more or less budget next year?

Evaluating progress in terms of time schedules

Just as actual expenditure can be compared with projected budget allocations so actual activities and construction can be evaluated against the operational plan. Did the surveys take place on time? If not, why not? Were all planned constructions finished? Were they on schedule or late? Why? Was the total of routine patrols up to prescription?

Such analysis highlights weaknesses in the management, points out where understaffing or lack of equipment is critical and helps improve planning for next year. The knowledge that he will be expected to account fully for progress and expenditures at the end of the year keeps the manager on his toes, pushing things along.

Assessing attainment of goals

Sometimes the objectives of management are poorly defined and too vague to assess, e.g. a) 'conserve the natural ecosystem', b) 'save the rhinoceros' or c) 'develop visitor use of the reserve'. In such cases, it is not easy to judge success. For this reason, it is useful to lay down specific targets or identify success indicators when making management plans. Progress towards the objectives of management can then be measured against expectations. More precise and measurable objectives for the above examples might be:

a) To prevent any further erosion of the area by shifting cultivators, involving:

- the phasing out within three years of firewood collection and hunting of wildlife in the reserve by local villagers.
- the loss of no more major mammal species from the reserve during the period of the plan.
- the existence at the end of the planning period of a fully operational trained staff of 20 persons able to run the reserve without further technical assistance.

b) To achieve at least a 5 per cent increase in the rhino population over the five-year period, involving:

- the establishment of a protective network of four guard posts manned by 12 trained guards to be fully operational by the end of the planning period.
- the total eradication of rhino poaching.
- the improvement and rehabilitation of rhino habitats.

c) To gradually increase visitors to more than 4000 per year by the end of five years, involving:

- guest lodge to be profitable and requiring no further subsidy after 3 years.

0. The success or inadequacy of management is revealed by monitoring the numbers and condition of those species which it aims to protect. It is usually not possible to predict exactly what management is needed to conserve species. The best policy is to apply what management seems appropriate, then monitor effects on populations and make modifications as required.
Photo: WWF/IUCN/Willi Dolder

- completion, by the end of the third year, of an information centre complete with displays.
- opening, by the end of the third year, of 50 km of wilderness trail including a self-guided trail with information brochures.

These are examples of specific targets outlined as management objectives and against which progress can be measured. Where progress is way ahead or way behind these targets the management authority must find out why. Were the targets unrealistic? Has development been unreasonably slow? Have other conditions such as the political situation, world economy, diseases or other unexpected factors influenced the outcome?

Evaluating cost-effectiveness

Have we got our money's worth (or effort's worth) out of the management applied to the protected area? This is a difficult question to answer. In normal business or development, effectiveness is measured in material production or the amount of profit. Achievement can be translated into monetary equivalents and compared with the investments made. Cost-effectiveness is a measure of gain per effort compared with gains that could be expected from the same effort in alternative directions.

Some aspects of protected area management such as various types of production, utilisation, or some recreational developments can be evaluated in a purely economic manner. If the costs of providing firewood for villagers in reserve buffer zones is greater than the price at which such products could be purchased from elsewhere, then clearly that aspect of reserve management has not proved cost-effective.

It is not so easy to assess the value of protective functions but some can be evaluated in purely economic terms. An absolute monetary value, for example, could be calculated for the hydrological function of a reserve that protects the water supply of an irrigation system or a hydro-electric development (see also Examples 5.2 and 5.3).

Where precise estimates cannot be made, it is sometimes useful to at least have a rough idea of the value placed on the protective functions being safeguarded. For example, if the government has decided that the area should be retained as a protected area instead of developed for production, then, in theory, the value of its protection function should be greater than that of the most profitable alternative use. If a particular reserve could have been converted into agricultural land with an expected yield of $US 20 per hectare per year then this value could be scaled up to give a minimal annual evaluation of the protective function. Given such an 'opportunity cost' the protective function can be weighed against this alternative land use.

The land-use values of most reserves estimated in this way are so great, and so much greater than subsequent investment in protective management, that comparison of the figures to justify management expense are futile. As a general rule, any management that succeeds in achieving its management objectives is certainly cost effective. A more relevant question is 'given the limited resources available can management be made more effective?'

Where management is clearly failing to reach its objectives, it is not being cost-effective and the greater sacrifice of taking the land out of unrestricted production is wasted. Whether management could be more effective centres on two questions: 'Are the right aspects being addressed? (i.e. Are energies being applied in the right direction?)' and 'Are the most appropriate techniques being used?' The manager must check to see where efforts are wasted or inadequate. He should identify areas of wastage such as overstaffing, unnecessary purchases, idle equipment, and futile, unproductive or unnecessary activities.

Managers must also consider comparing the costs of the current programme with alternative and perhaps cheaper, techniques to reach the same objectives. Comparisons can be made with other reserves with similar objectives but using different methods. A view should also be kept on other countries to copy better, cheaper or more effective techniques. Time-and-motion studies may be relevant to check the efficiency of some operations.

The use of checklists in evaluating management

The use of an evaluation checklist provides a systematic method for obtaining a relatively objective evaluation of the effectiveness of the administration and management of a protected area. Since management effectiveness is measured against the objectives of the particular category of protected area, any checklist must be derived from these objectives. When related to the policy and management plan for a specific protected area, the checklist has the benefit of standardising the approach to all levels of management and time frames, e.g. as a basis for monthly, quarterly or annual reports. Such checklists are also of use to Headquarters for comparing progress between different protected areas.

Periodic evaluations of this type are useful to the individual officer for assessing his own performance over the reporting period and for informing his colleagues and superiors of the progress he has achieved. They are also an insurance for the individual and his team against allegations, by higher authority, that they are misdirecting their efforts, as unless a periodic report brings a return order from Headquarters for corrective measures, they are entitled to assume the tacit approval of their actions. This in turn obliges supervisory personnel at different levels in the hierarchy to evaluate the progress of their subordinates' work at regular intervals, providing the basic machinery for the continual reassessment of the effectiveness of the management programme and its various components. They are then in a position to initiate corrective action and meet their obligations to report to the national authority for protected areas, so that the nation can be informed as to the state of protection of its natural heritage.

The list below has been used by IUCN's CNPPA to indicate the type of questions that a protected area manager should consider in evaluating the effectiveness of the management of his area.

1. *Clearly defined specific objectives to guide management*, this area:
   a) has written objectives specific to the area.
   b) has only broad objectives.
   c) lacks specific objectives at present.

2. *Legislation*, this area:
   a) is fully protected by the national or provincial legislation and has a compatible set of regulations specific to the area.
   b) is protected by national legislation but does not have a set of regulations specific to the area.
   c) is inadequately protected by national legislation and lacks local regulations.
   d) is sufficiently protected by national legislation and does not require local regulations.

3. *Basic resources information*, this area has the following:
   a) Inventory of mammals
   b) inventory of birds
   c) inventory of other vertebrates
   d) complete inventory of plants
   e) partial inventory of plants
   f) vegetation map
   g) inventory of invertebrates
   h) geological map
   i) soil map
   j) climatic data
   k) hydrological data
   l) topographic map
   m) aerial photographs
   n) bibliography of publications

4. *Basic ecological information*, this area has the following:
   a) studies of wildlife population dynamics
   b) studies of population status and trends of key species
   c) information on relationships between wildlife and the habitat
   d) studies of predator-prey relationships
   e) information on the carrying capacity of the habitat for key species
   f) information on disease reservoirs among the wildlife
   g) studies on ecological succession
   h) information on fire history and its effects

5. *Watershed management*, this area, (check more than one if necessary):
   a) protects a watershed or watersheds considered to contribute to the welfare of downstream human populations (e.g. drinking water, irrigation, flood control).
   b) protects a watershed or watersheds considered to contribute to downstream

ecological process (e.g. estuarine and coastal fisheries).

c) because of its importance to human welfare, is left unmanipulated (in a natural state).

d) is lightly manipulated, through natural means (e.g. fire control, reforestation).

e) is manipulated through engineering works (checkdams, streams channelisation, terracing).

6. *Genetic resources*, this area:

a) has a number of species of plants/animals of potential or actual benefit to humanity and these receive special attention in management decisions.

b) probably has a number of species of plants/animals of potential or actual benefit to humanity, but there is little available data about them so they receive little special attention.

c) has little data available but genetic resources are still given special consideration in management decisions.

d) is managed on the basis of overall intrinsic values of nature so genetic resources are not given specific attention.

e) is managed to preserve biological diversity and genetic conservation incidental to this.

7. *Management plan*, this area:

a) has an approved management plan which is being implemented and monitored.

b) has a management plan but it has not been accepted/approved/implemented.

c) has a management plan in preparation.

d) lacks a management plan at present.

e) lacks a management plan and local circumstances do not call for one at this time.

8. *Zoning*, this area:

a) has a zoning plan which effectively controls human impact and development relative to carrying capacity.

b) has a zoning plan which partially controls human impact and development relative to carrying capacity.

c) does not yet have a zoning plan, but such a plan is being prepared.

d) does not have a zoning plan.

e) does not have a zoning plan, nor is a plan required at present.

9. *Boundaries*, this area:

a) has physically and narratively demarcated boundaries which effectively define the area.

b) has demarcated boundaries in certain key areas and this is felt adequate.

c) has some boundaries demarcated, but these are felt insufficient.

d) lacks demarcation of boundaries.

e) lacks or partially lacks formal demarcation of boundaries but this is deemed appropriate for the current situation.

10. *Ecologically sufficient boundaries*, this area:

a) encloses an entire ecosystem, so is fully self-sufficient.

b) comprises the upper part of a watershed, but has no control over the lower parts.

c) comprises the lower part of a watershed, but has no control over the upper parts.

d) comprises only a fragment of a total ecosystem, requiring intensive management to maintain natural functioning.

11. *Protection of natural resources*, this area:

a) is fully and effectively protected from resource exploitation.

b) is protected at a level appropriate to area objectives.

c) is used only by local people for their own needs.

d) suffers from illegal harvesting of vegetation, illegal grazing, or poaching of animals.

e) permits exploitation of selected resources.

12. *Research*, this area at this time:

a) has a strong, well-integrated programme of basic and applied research which provides support to the management objectives.

b) has only basic, academic research which provides indirect input to improved management.

c) has *ad hoc* research which may provide support to management objectives.

d) has no research, either basic or applied.

e) has no on-going or planned research programme and local circumstances do not call for one at this time.

13. *Formal education*, this area:

a) has adequate educational facilities or

extension programmes and is well used
by local/national educational institutions.
b) is used by local/national educational
institutions for planned, supervised field
trips but there are few local facilities.
c) is used by students for informal,
unsupervised field trips.
d) is seldom used for educational purposes.

14. *Informal education*, this area has the following visitor facilities:
a) Leaflets
b) Maps
c) Marked trails
d) Signs
e) Guide service
f) Information centre
g) Audio-visual programmes
h) Public transportation
i) Hides

15. *Tourism*, this area:
a) is important for tourism and has all necessary facilities for present levels of visitor use.
b) receives so many tourists that the reserve
staff has little time for other management activities.
c) receives many tourists, but facilities are
inadequate.
d) is of only minor importance for tourism
at present.
e) does not include tourism as an objective.

16. *Political support* (check more than one if
necessary):
a) the central government has made a commitment to attain the conservation
objectives of the area.
b) the regional government has made a
commitment to attain the conservation
objectives of the area.
c) the local people support the protection
of the area.
d) lack of political support is a major
problem.
e) insufficient support (or active opposition) by local people is a major
problem.

17. *Local participation*, this area:
a) has a local advisory committee or otherwise involves local people in decision-
making.

b) involves at least some officials of local
government.
c) involves local people only informally.
d) does not involve local people at all.

18. *Benefits to local people*, this area:
a) brings *real* benefits to the local people in
terms of watershed protection, employment opportunities, buffer zone
development, economic subsidy, or
other related developments.
b) brings some benefits to the local people.
c) brings virtually no benefits to the local
people.

19. *Budget*, this area:
a) has sufficient budget to attain its objectives as stated in management plan.
b) receives a budget which is insufficient to
allow the management plan to be fully
implemented.
c) receives a budget which allows only basic
maintenance and staffing.
d) lacks a budget.

20. *Maintenance*, this area:
a) has a budget for maintenance and this is
sufficient to keep equipment/facilities in
reasonable working order.
b) has a budget for maintenance but this is
insufficient to keep equipment/facilities
in reasonable working order.
c) does not have any budget for maintenance but maintenance of equipment/
facilities is still acceptable.
d) has no budget for maintenance and
equipment/facilities suffering as a result.

21. *Personnel and training*, this area:
a) has sufficient trained personnel to attain
the specified management objectives.
b) lacks sufficient personnel and access to
training programmes.
c) has no personnel or training
opportunities.

22. *Equipment*, this area:
a) is sufficiently well equipped to attain its
management objectives.
b) needs more vehicles/boats.
c) needs more uniforms/equipment for
rangers.
d) needs more housing/guard-posts/head-
quarters buildings.

244 Managing Protected Areas in the Tropics

e) needs more survey equipment

f) needs more medical/first aid equipment.

g) needs more communication equipment.

h) needs more office equipment.

23. *Role of external support*, this area (check more than one if necessary):

a) is sufficiently well managed and funded that no outside support has been requested.

b) has received/is receiving external support.

c) receives additional support from within the country.

d) needs outside support, which is being sought.

e) needs outside support but such support is not being sought.

f) has voluntary workers/honorary officers helping in management projects.

12

International Cooperation

The need for international assistance

Of the 118 nations classified by the UN as 'developing' most are in the tropics and less than half have properly constituted national parks. Nevertheless, some tropical countries possess parks which are among the finest in the world, with well-established, professionally staffed organisations to administer them. Such countries need neither external assistance nor advice: on the contrary, they could usefully teach others much in the field of resource management. Unfortunately, these nations are in a minority and the majority, especially among the least developed countries, either have no parks as yet or have areas which do not conform to internationally accepted criteria.

This may be due to a variety of reasons: lack of suitable areas or the lack of trained personnel to run them; political instability and consequent security problems in the remoter areas which have the best potential for national parks; lack of government recognition of the need for parks or low priority in comparison with other development needs, such as irrigation schemes, schools, or hospitals.

The international conservation community understands the problems of tropical countries and is often prepared to provide effective assistance where needed. Mechanisms must be developed for the fair sharing of costs and benefits associated with protected area management, both among nations and between protected areas and adjacent communities. The World Heritage Convention implemented by Unesco is one way of sharing the costs but has a very limited budget and covers only relatively few areas. Areas which are really worthy of development as national parks are part of an international heritage as well as being of value to the country concerned, and it must be recognised that the poorest countries cannot reasonably be expected to develop parks to the requisite standard without substantial external support.

Some countries which now have national parks and the qualified staff to manage them may sometimes need occasional support and assistance in certain specialised fields such as research, interpretive programmes, legislation, preparation of management plans, or the planning of marine parks. Such needs can best be met by short-term projects or consultancies, preferably employing suitably-qualified people from neighbouring countries or consultants with past experience in the region. Assistance and funding can be requested from many sources: multilateral organisations, such as United Nations Development Programme (UNDP); non-governmental organisations with international programmes; international bilateral assistance organisations; national governmental agencies with international programmes; volunteer organisations; international banks and other sources such as corporations and trusts.

Types of assistance

The need for international assistance varies considerably from country to country. It is usually available in one of the following five categories:

Supplies and equipment

In some countries the most serious limitation to effective management of protected areas is simply the lack of supplies and equipment. Purchases of overseas technical equipment are difficult for many government departments and locally purchased items may be two or three times their original cost. Donations of equipment can sometimes be cleared duty free by the recipient department or project. Care must be taken to ensure that such equipment is appropriate for local use and that provision is made for maintenance.

Technical assistance and specialised consultancies

Temporarily-assigned experts or consultants are frequently engaged to review government projects and policies or prepare special plans and reports. There are some dangers, however, in countries developing too great a reliance on overseas experts. First, the foreign experts sometimes fail to adapt their ideas and standards to the particular culture and economic level of the country concerned. There is much energy wasted on the production of excellent reports and plans (including many national park management plans) that are too technically advanced for implementation in the country concerned, have not involved the managers in their preparation, or which are never translated nor locally assimilated. There is also the problem of never developing local expertise so long as there is someone else to do the job. Developing countries should not place excessive reliance on international assistance which can dry up at any moment in a major world recession. They must develop their own competence for basic operational tasks. To this end, it is essential that all foreign consultants are supplied with enthusiastic local counterparts who can absorb technical skills by working with the expert.

There will always be a need for real specialists (e.g. elephant control experts) at the international level and developed countries make even more use of such foreign experts than do developing countries.

Experts are also often brought in by park directors to get plans or policies passed by the central government, since such projects are sometimes given greater credence and acceptability simply because they were produced by 'special consultants'. This is just a matter of human psychology – 'The grass always seems greener on the other side of the hill' – but it is sometimes a valid justification for international assistance nonetheless.

Training programmes

Building up technical knowhow depends on training. Counterparts can learn skills and techniques during their working assignments with visiting experts but this rarely gives them the range of theoretical and practical training needed to fulfil the wide range of functions involved in management of protected areas. It is necessary also to have more formal training opportunities. International assistance has been provided for a number of training schemes including:

- Providing help in establishing regional training centres. Regional training schools have been established in Turrialba, Costa Rica; Dehra Dun, India; Ciawi, Indonesia; Mweka, Tanzania; and Garoua, Cameroon. The Bariloche school in Argentina provides training primarily for staff from the Argentine National Park Administration but a few non-Argentinians have attended the two-year ranger course. These schools offer excellent broad training programmes for senior and middle management staff. Not only do they provide valuable training at the field level but they are also a useful forum for exchange of ideas and views from individuals working with similar problems throughout the region, though the protected areas for which they are responsible may cover very different habitats.
- Providing overseas instructors for local training schools and courses. The cheapest way to teach new techniques to a large number of people in a country is to train them locally, importing instructors as necessary.
- Providing overseas fellowships and scholarships for individual students to undertake training abroad. Where specialised knowledge is needed by only a few people, this is cheaper than organising local training. Many universities in developed countries, e.g. University College (London, UK), Lincoln College (Christchurch, New Zealand), University of

Example 12.1: A workshop on wheels – CATIE's Mobile Parks Seminar

Modelled after the U.S. National Park Service (USNPS) International Parks Seminar, the mobile wildlands workshop organised by the Centro Agronomical Tropical de Investigacion y Ensenanza (CATIE) has been modified to address the socio-economic realities of Central America and the unique characteristics of the tropical ecosystems of the region. Every two or three years, the seminar with its twenty or so participants visits several Mesoamerican nations for a first-hand look at their national parks, wildlife refuges, biosphere reserves, multiple-use areas.

The trip is facilitated by the Wildlands and Watershed Unit of the Tropical Agricultural Research and Training Center in Turrialba, Costa Rica. Outside specialists from other Latin American and Northern American agencies back up the CATIE staff and each country visited is expected to provide logistical support and technical assistance. Course participants are presented with myriad opportunities for interactive learning experiences and conservation agencies are challenged to present the best possible image that professional and financial resources will permit. Discussions have not only benefited course participants but also park personnel who, when visited by the seminar, have gained new perspectives on difficult resource management problems. Sharing of ideas is strongly promoted and regional communication networks have been strengthened as a direct result of these mobile seminars. In an area as mutually dependent and ecologically linked as Central America, a united conservation voice is imperative if long-term environmental stability is to be achieved. Perhaps more than any other training exercise in the region, the Mobile Parks Seminar fosters that cooperation.

Michigan (Ann Arbor, U.S.A.), and others have relevant higher degree courses.
- Providing funds for study tours and international seminars. Senior staff who cannot be released from their important duties for too long can often benefit greatly by attending special study tours or international seminars, e.g. Australian Summer School of National Park Management and the annual International Seminar on National Parks and Equivalent Reserves held in North America or CATIE's Seminar in Central America.

Execution of projects

International assistance is sometimes sought to help execute special projects or operations. This is very useful if the operation is a specific one or if, during participation, the local staff learn how to perform similar follow-up projects themselves. For example, a veterinary scientist was lent by the Government of Namibia to supervise the darting and translocation of a herd of elephants in Sri Lanka where his considerable experience in such operations greatly contributed to the success of the project.

Maintaining long-term experts to help run or supervise protected areas is rather costly and can undermine the country's own capabilities. Alternatively, the employment of overseas volunteer workers from such agencies as British VSO, Canadian CUSO, and U.S. Peace Corps, can provide useful and well-motivated personnel who are often able to develop good rapport with the technical officers and labourer levels of project execution.

Research assistance

Foreign scientists, when partnered by local counterparts, can contribute to the development of improved management techniques. Protected areas in the tropics provide scientific laboratories of great interest to many temperate world researchers and such research is an area where international cooperation is common. Each country must make an effort to pioneer its own management methodology, as well as liaise and compare findings with researchers in other countries, if it is to make the best use of its renewable living resources and protected areas.

Sources of help: technical assistance agencies and organisations

In many tropical countries the main international agencies involved in conservation, wildlife management and national parks during the last two decades have been UNDP/FAO and WWF/IUCN. The development and implementation of a national system of parks and protected areas in Indonesia is an example of their joint cooperation. Elsewhere, UNDP/FAO have allocated funds, personnel and equipment for wildlife management projects and rural development projects which have a conservation component (e.g. agroforestry schemes and buffer zone developments). In South America, FAO has provided expert technical advisers to work with local counterparts in developing park system plans in Brazil and Chile.

Identifying the most appropriate agency

Depending on the scope of the project and the sort of help requested, assistance may be obtained from a wide range and variety of aid agencies. Useful summaries of organisations able to help with expertise and resources are given in Quigg (1978), and Chapter 14 of McNeely and Miller (1984).

The various aid agencies generally have their own particular field of specialisation and, especially in the case of donor countries, may also have geographical priorities, which restrict their activities to certain regions or countries. There is also very considerable variation in funding capabilities. For example, a small private foundation may be able to assist to the extent of only a few hundred dollars whereas UNDP-funded projects typically range from $US 100,000 or so to a million dollars or more, with a duration of from one to several years. The World Bank, on the other hand, is not normally involved in projects of less than about $US 10 million. The information which follows covers potential donors and should enable an administrator or park manager to identify the most promising sources of possible assistance to meet his particular needs. Contact addresses are given in the Appendix.

United Nations agencies

FAO, Unesco and UNEP are the three United Nations agencies most concerned with environmental affairs.

FAO

The United Nations Food and Agricultural Organisation is the UN agency responsible for the execution of protected area management projects funded from UN sources, primarily from the United Nations Development Programme (UNDP). The protected area manager or protected area authority must process any request for FAO assistance through established channels of the government ministry to which the management authority belongs (usually Forestry or Agriculture) and this ministry in turn must convince the ministry responsible for finance and economic planning to include it in the nation's requests for UNDP funding. Initiatives for seeking assistance are taken in the country concerned and are a matter of negotiation between the Ministry of Finance and Economic Planning, the local UNDP representative and the FAO representative.

Examples of projects provided under such assistance include:

- Assistance to Brazil's Forestry Development Institute on Strategic Wildland Planning
- Uganda National Park Rehabilitation Project
- National Parks Development Programme in Indonesia
- Provision of teaching personnel for the Ecole pour la formation de spécialistes de la faune in Cameroon.

Unesco

The United Nations Educational, Scientific and Cultural Organisation, through the World Heritage Convention and the Man and the Biosphere (MAB) Programme, has given direct support to many protected areas. World Heritage Funds are given as grants for research, technical assistance, training and equipment.

Assistance under the MAB programme should be requested through the national MAB committee. Requests for assistance under the World Heritage Convention should be directed to the World Heritage Committee in Paris.

Examples:

- Contributed to Wildland and Watershed Management Training Workshop for Central American Park Administrators

- Equipment and training for Simien National Park, Ethiopia
- Management plan for the Ngorongoro Conservation Area in Tanzania

UNEP

The United Nations Environment Programme, through regional programmes and entrusted donations, provides an information service on environmental issues, holds conferences, provides fellowships, produces publications, executes some projects and supports other agencies such the Secretariat of the Convention on International Trade in Endangered Species of Wild Fauna and Flora (CITES). UNEP's mandate is to be catalytic rather than active in project management and implementation and it works closely with IUCN on a number of projects. UNEP programmes of particular relevance to the management of protected areas are the Regional Seas Programme, the Programme on Desertification Problems, and the Global Environment Monitoring System (GEMS), one part of which is the IUCN Conservation Monitoring Centre – including the Protected Areas Data Unit (PADU) – at Cambridge, UK.

Other multinational organisations

Several organisations, such as the Colombo Plan, the Organisation of American States (OAS), and the European Economic Community (EEC), can provide funds (usually on a much more modest scale than does the UN) for specific projects, fellowships, etc., but funding may be available only for developing countries in certain geographical regions. For example, the Colombo Plan is restricted to South and Southeast Asia while the South Pacific Commission is concerned solely with maintaining and improving the quality of life of the Pacific Island countries.

Examples:

- Turtle conservation in Irian Jaya, Indonesia (Council of Europe)
- Equipment for Uganda National Parks (EEC)
- Training fellowships for Afghanistan and Nepal wildland managers (Colombo Plan)
- Wildlife research in Central America (Organisation of American States)
- Regional Conferences and Training Courses on National Parks in the Pacific (South Pacific Commission)

Non-governmental organisations (NGOs) with international programmes

Of the NGOs, IUCN and WWF have been by far the most active in tropical countries, supporting field projects throughout the world to establish and manage national parks and protected areas. Countries with major programmes have included China, Costa Rica, Ecuador, India, Indonesia, Kenya, Madagascar, Mali, Tanzania, and Zambia. Project proposals should be submitted to IUCN and WWF headquarters in Gland, Switzerland.

WWF-International currently funds about 350 projects worldwide each year. WWF-US has been actively involved with the design, preparation of management plans, and operation of protected areas in Latin America. Frankfurt Zoological Society, New York Zoological Society, The Nature Conservancy (USA.), and African Wildlife Foundation have provided substantial help to many tropical countries, especially in Africa. Many of the other non-governmental organisations have only very limited funds and usually allocate these in the form of grants to individual researchers for specific projects. Some agencies may, however, be prepared to provide instructors, fellowships or partial costs for training courses in protected area management or wildlife management.

Examples:

- Provision of instructor and part costs for courses on primate conservation and management in India (Smithsonian Institution)
- Assistance in establishing wildlife clubs in Africa (African Wildlife Foundation)
- Teaching aids and booklets for environmental education for grade schools in Costa Rica (Rare Animal Relief Effort)

Such organisations may respond well to approaches from national non-governmental organisations which work with the park authority.

The U.S. Nature Conservancy also has an important international programme which concentrates on assisting government agencies and local conservationists to protect a variety of magnificent biological resources in the Caribbean and Central America.

Bilateral assistance

Many bilateral organisations have economic and

social development as their main objectives of development aid. Support for protected areas should, therefore, be presented as part of rural development projects, watershed projects, desertification programmes, projects for minority groups, and so on. Most donor agencies concentrate their aid in a limited number of countries which often have a resident representative who can give informal advice before requests are presented through the appropriate national ministry. Assistance from bilateral sources is normally provided for projects above a certain minimum size and may include almost any type of expense (investments, training scholarships), though operations or running costs are harder to obtain.

Examples:

- The Kenya Wildlife Planning Unit (CIDA, Canada)
- Funds to hire an instructor for College of African Wildlife Management in Mweka, Tanzania (DANIDA, Denmark),
- Mahaweli Scheme, Sri Lanka (USAID),
- Ciawi Conservation School, Indonesia (DGIS, Netherlands)

National government agencies with international programmes

Canada, Australia, New Zealand and the USA all have excellent systems of protected areas run by well-qualified staff. Staff members from the management authorities concerned are able to offer advice, technical assistance, training and management evaluation to tropical countries. Programmes may involve secondment of staff from the donor agency and overseas training for selected staff from the recipient country. The International Affairs Division of the United States National Parks Service has been particularly active in supporting parks management efforts throughout the world (Milne, 1981; Wetterberg, 1984).

Examples:

- Technical assistance to Dominica on Environmental Interpretation, legislation and park planning (Parks Canada)
- Establishment and planning of National Parks in Saudi Arabia (USNPS).
- Support to Cook Islands and Papua New Guinea with secondment of staff to national parks agencies (Australia National Park and Wildlife Service)

- Establishment and management of national parks in Nepal and Western Samoa (New Zealand National Parks)
- Biological inventory programme in Paraguay (U.S. Fish and Wildlife Service).

Volunteer organisations

Although not directly involved with the funding of the projects, many countries have volunteer organisations which will provide personnel for implementation of protected area projects. In most areas, the mother agency provides the living and medical expenses of the volunteers, though sometimes the host government may be expected to pay them modest salaries. The normal length of service is one to three years and the volunteers serve at the request of the host country institutions. These volunteers generally assume mid- to low-level positions and work with a national counterpart. Often volunteer organisations are able to provide the long-term continuity to protected area projects that other organisations cannot.

Examples:

- Volunteers to prepare management plan and implement management in Wildlife Sanctuaries, Sarawak (VSO, Great Britain; CUSO, Canada)
- Volunteers to repair radio equipment in East African national parks (African Wildlife Foundation)
- Paraguay Natural Resource Conservation Project with 25 volunteers working with 60 host country counterparts in the areas of national parks planning, biological inventory, deforestation and environmental education (U.S. Peace Corps)

International banks

Every year large amounts of money are channelled to the tropical countries through the international banks, especially the World Bank in the form of development loans which have to be repaid by the borrower nation. At present, very little of this money is used for conservation related projects. This is partly because conservation seldom receives the priority it deserves from government decision makers and the donor agencies themselves but also because protected area administrations fail to formulate requests correctly or channel them to the appropriate aid agencies. Increasingly, however, the major fund

Example 12.2: The role of the U.S. National Parks Service in international assistance

The National Parks Service (NPS) is required by administrative actions (U.S. bilateral environmental and economic agreements) and Congressional mandates (conventions, treaties, and acts) to provide information, technical assistance, training, and advice to various nations which are in the process of establishing national park systems.

These activities are undertaken by the International Affairs Division which lends technical expertise at both the conceptual and field level in designing a 'National Plan for Conservation Units' to facilitate the selection of biologically representative protected areas.

This assistance is global in scope, although treaties, conventions and bilateral agreements tend to concentrate activities in specific countries and regions. Activities are generally conducted in response to unsolicited requests and may come from any country. Countries in which NPS has been directly involved include: Argentina, Brazil, Chile, Colombia, Costa Rica, Jordan, Panama, Paraguay, Taiwan and Venezuela. In addition to its relations with government counterpart agencies, the NPS also maintains working relationships with a wide variety of international and non-governmental organisations and IUCN.

The NPS is frequently requested to lend its expertise to multidisciplinary counterpart teams preparing management plans for individual national parks. A few recent examples include: Ecuador's Machalilla National Park, Trinidad and Tobago's Caroni Swamp Wildlife Sanctuary and Panama's Soberania National Park. The Service is currently providing training assistance and advisory services in the design of facilities and infrastructure in national parks in China, India, Saudi Arabia and Sri Lanka.

The Park Service has a long history of providing training in matters related to protected area design and management, environmental monitoring, habitat preservation, and environmental interpretation. Through the running of its summer seminar on national parks, it has provided training to over 3000 foreign park professionals in the last decade, including the majority of national park system directors worldwide.

---

ng agencies are becoming aware that conservation is an integral part of development and that prevention of environmental degradation is better, and cheaper, than curing it. The World Bank, the major funder of large-scale developments worldwide, now insists that all Bank-financed projects should have a readily-identifiable environmental component. The Bank finds that it is less expensive to incorporate environmental and health safeguards into project planning (usually no more than 3 to 5 per cent of the total project cost) than it is to ignore them and have to take remedial action later (Goodland, 1984).

World Bank projects are prepared by potential borrowers (member governments) often with the help of consultants. The Bank incorporates necessary environmental safeguards into each stage of the project cycle, from initial identification to final evaluation, and consults closely with the national ministry of environmental affairs and other concerned agencies.

Although the Bank carefully appraises each project before any commitments are made, it largely relies on the borrowing government for the details and project quality. It is, therefore, essential that the government's environmental or wildlife agency actively assist the implementing ministry in project design (see Example 12.3).

The problem of managing natural resources and environmental systems is a matter of growing concern, especially in many of the Bank's tropical member countries. Tropical countries are inherently more susceptible to environmental degradation, and ecological stress, can ill afford the expensive measures necessary to repair environmental degradation and tend to have burgeoning populations whose needs for fuel, food and shelter strain the environment's carrying capacity more than in temperate countries. Many developing countries are now adopting the preventive management approach.

Over the past decade, the World Bank has financed approximately 30 projects in 21 countries which have significant wildland conservation components. Such conservation components in Bank projects may vary from 100 per cent of project costs to zero but with significant benefit to the habitat and wildlife. Kenya's Wildlife and Tourism Project (1976) was entirely devoted to wildlife conservation, with more than $US 36 million allocated for seven national parks, anti-poaching measures, wildlife studies and training of personnel. In contrast, manipulation of Zambia's Kafue hydroproject cost nothing extra to the borrowing government but was designed to replicate seasonal flooding of the Kafue flats, important grazing land for wildlife including the endemic Lechwe antelope *Kobus leche*. Similarly, in Sudan's Rahad irrigation scheme the design of a canal was altered to avoid an important wildlife migratory route, yet no additional costs were incurred. One of the most cost-effective measures is expected in Indonesia's 1980 Irrigation XV loan of $US 54 million (Example 12.4).

Other sources

Corporations, national trusts, private foundations, non-governmental organisations, and Rotary Clubs are examples of other sources of support.

Sources of funding for protected area management are available to most countries from the private sector, either at home or abroad. In the case of countries which have major industries based on natural resources, it would seem appropriate that these industries should contribute to conservation, perhaps through a modest tax levied on the export value of timber, oil, minerals, exported wildlife, etc. (Blower, 1984). To secure private funds, the project manager must present sound projects in a format acceptable to the potential donor. There may be advantages in establishing a reputable national trust to solicit and control such donations.

Example 12.3: The World Bank project cycle

Project Stage	Environmental Input
1. *Identification*	
Selection by Bank and borrowers of feasible projects that support national and sectorial development strategies. Projects are incorporated into the lending programme of the Bank for a particular country.	Economic and sector work containing environmental analysis and natural resource assessments improve the mix of projects. Environmental reconnaissance mission by Bank or consultants determine work needed.
2. *Preparation*	
Borrowing country or agency examines technical, institutional, economic and financial aspects of proposed project. Bank provides guidance, and perhaps financial assistance for preparation (one to two years).	Pre-feasibility and feasibility studies address all major environmental aspects and integrate them into project design.
3. *Appraisal*	
Bank staff review and report on all aspects of the project: technical, institutional, economic, and financial (3-5 weeks in the field).	Details design includes preventive measures for potentially adverse environmental impacts.
The appraisal report serves as the basis for negotiations with the borrower.	Operational Evaluation Department reviews appraisal report.

4. *Negotiations*

Discussions with the borrower on the measures needed to ensure success for the project. The agreements reached are embodied in loan documents presented to the Executive Directors of the Bank for approval and signature.

Environmental agreements are reached during negotiations. The loan document may include covenants.

5. *Implementation and Supervision*

The borrower is responsible for implementation of the project. The Bank is responsible for supervising that implementation, through progress reports from the borrower and periodic field visits.

Environmental measures are implemented during construction. Supervision ensures that such measures function adequately. Adjustment to environmental measures made when necessary.

6. *Evaluation*

Evaluation follows the final disbursement of Bank funds for the project. The Operations Evaluation Department of the Bank reviews the completion report (PCR) of the Bank's Projects staff, and prepares its own audit of the project, often by reviewing materials at headquarters, and on-site where needed.

Environmental problems and mitigatory measures implemented are examined in this post evaluation. The accuracy of pre-project problem identification and the efficacy of mitigatory measures are evaluated. The results serve as 'feedback' for future work.

Source: Baum, 1982

Preparation and submission of requests

Requests for assistance should be properly prepared and presented and submitted through the correct channels. The following is an outline of the steps required:

The Problem. Identify the problem; confirm that it cannot be satisfactorily resolved through exclusive use of local resources, and that external assistance is needed and justified in relation to other alternative priorities and government policies.

Donor Agencies. Identify appropriate donor agency and, subject to clearances, make an informal approach either to the local representative or by letter, briefly outlining the problem, the assistance required and enquiring whether the agency concerned can help;

- *Project Proposal.* Having found a possible donor agency which is at least prepared to consider your request, prepare a formal project proposal including all relevant background information, description of the problems, the assistance required, the form it should take, and its estimated cost and proposed timing. Most of the larger donor agencies, e.g. The World Bank, have their own prescribed format for submission of project proposals, and may appoint a team of specialists to help prepare the proposal.
- *Submission of Proposal.* Submit the project proposal through the appropriate governmental or other channels, including any official endorsements which may be required.

Example 12.4: *Integrated development: a national park developed with international assistance*

The Dumoga Bone National Park, located midway along the northern arm of the island of Sulawesi, Indonesia, includes some 278,700 ha of primary tropical rain forest with an altitudinal range from 100 to 2000 m above sea level. The park was first identified as an area of high conservation value in 1977 and its subsequent development has been closely related to World Bank funding of the Dumoga Valley Irrigation Schemes. This is one of the first instances where a major development funding agency has fully recognised protected area conservation as an integral part of development.

Twenty years ago, the Dumoga Valley was almost completely covered in forest. Then the construction of the Dumoga Valley highway opened up the area to a wave of new settlement and more farmers moved into the valley on sponsored government transmigration schemes. The main agriculture in the valley is rice cultivation which depends on two major irrigation schemes. As new migrants moved into the area and original settlers sold their land to the newcomers and cleared new lands, more and more forest was cleared even in the catchment areas on which the irrigation schemes depend. Maintenance roads built along the canals facilitated access to the forest borders and accelerated encroachment of the catchment area, reducing the potential water flow from feeder rivers and increasing the likelihood of siltation of the vital irrigation canals.

Concern about deforestation of the watershed area in the Dumoga basin culminated in an agreement between the Government of Indonesia and the World Bank to allocate considerable financial support, as part of the irrigation loan, towards the development and protection of the watershed area proposed as the Dumoga Bone National Park. Forest protection programmes began in 1980 with the recruitment of forest guards and the appointment of a WWF consultant to prepare a management plan for the park. World Bank provided funds mainly to establish and demarcate park boundaries, hire guards, develop a management plan and provide necessary infrastructure and equipment. For less than 1 per cent of the cost of the total project, this conservation investment protects the World Bank's $US 54 million investment in a valuable irrigation scheme by helping to minimise siltation and the resulting high maintenance costs and by helping to ensure a steady year-round flow of water.

Apart from its water catchment role, the park also preserves much of Sulawesi's unique flora and fauna including many endemic birds. The park has been developed on model lines with buildings in local materials and of local design and is expected to draw increasing numbers of tourists and local visitors. It is becoming an increasingly important centre for research. A land-use plan is being prepared by the local university and Dumoga achieved international recognition when it was chosen for Project Wallace in 1985, a major year-long scientific expedition mounted to celebrate the 150th anniversary of the Royal Entomological Society.

Source: Sumardja, *et al.*, 1984.

Counterpart contributions

When requesting external assistance it is important to remember that few agencies or foundations are prepared to cover the cost of a project in its entirety, and that the recipient country is normally expected to provide a substantial counterpart contribution in the form of personnel and services, and sometimes in cash. Typically, the donor agency will meet the cost of experts, overseas training, imported equipment and other foreign currency costs, but will expect the country or organisation requesting assistance to cover all local costs such as salaries of local personnel, construction of buildings and maintenance of vehicles and other equipment. In order to avoid delay in execution of the project, it is, therefore, essential to ensure that the necessary counterpart budget is available in good time.

International and regional cooperation and conventions

Regional cooperation

It is worth considering the possibilities for long-term institutional links between national parks services in more developed countries and counterparts in countries in a less advanced development stage, on similar lines to the involvement of the New Zealand Parks Service in the Sagarmatha National Park, Nepal. Such links can provide opportunities for training, interchange of personnel and the gradual establishment of a close relationship between the two organisations which can be of lasting benefit to both. Instead of short projects with intensive inputs of expertise and equipment for two or three years and then a complete break, this type of cooperation allows more gradual phasing out of sustained support and involvement. Such support can be funded under bilateral aid programmes and need not be any drain on the usually hard-pressed budget of the park services involved.

Cooperation between countries on a regional basis is particularly valuable and should be encouraged. This could, for example, take the form of exchanges of personnel, working attachments to parks departments, study tours, liaison visits by management level personnel and periodic mobile seminars involving visits to parks and reserves, hosted in rotation by the countries concerned. Such activities could be funded under the United Nations Programme for Technical Cooperation between Developing Countries (TCDC).

One of the most effective ways that neighbouring countries can assist each other in protected areas programmes is to develop transfrontier reserves across their mutual borders, with all parties benefiting from the larger size of the total protected area but having to protect only part of the boundary. Agreement for such reserves might include technical cooperation, sharing of knowledge and data, as well as legal agreements not to harbour poachers.

International commitments and conventions

National participation in bilateral or multilateral agreements relating to protected areas may also involve the protected area manager in legal processes. International conventions, treaties or agreements, to which a country is a party, may require that it reframe and implement its domestic protected area legislation.

The scope and focus of international conventions may vary. Some may be 'universal' in nature, without geographic limitations (e.g. CITES). These are open for acceptance by all nations. Other conventions may be regional in scope or restricted in some other way so that only certain nations can qualify. In addition, the substantive focus of areas may vary. Some conventions focus on protected areas, others focus on protected species.

The park manager should become familiar with relevant agreements to which his country adheres. The domestic implementation of these treaties may impose legal constraints on the management of protected areas or species within them or, alternatively, may commit the country to undertake actions which can be extremely helpful in attracting additional financial, technical and legal resources to the area.

Adherence to international treaties represents a major legal and moral base of support for the manager because:

- An obligation entered into through an international agreement becomes a solemn legal obligation upon which adequate national implementing legislation can be based. This may be of particular importance for certain federal states where matters such as wildlife and conservation fall under the jurisdiction of individual states or provinces. In such cases the conclusion of an international agreement may automatically give competence to the federal authorities for implementation, resulting in an overall coordination of conservation measures which otherwise would not have been constitutionally possible.
- A treaty establishes the same obligations for all parties. States are, therefore, often more ready to accept certain constraints and expenditures when they know that other States have accepted the same.
- Protected areas included in an international network are required for the preservation of the habitat of migratory species or other shared living resources. This has an obvious international dimension.
- Treaties may provide for better international cooperation especially through improved mutual information systems on the best means to achieve common objectives.

61. The use of international arrangements can help spread the burden borne by national agencies.
    CITES has limited the level of illegal wildlife trade, and thus reduced the pressure of poaching in
    many protected areas.
    Photo: Michael Kahn

A brief description follows of the major conventions concerned with terrestrial protected areas. A basic reference work has recently been prepared by Lyster (1985) and only essential details are included here.

Global Protected Area Conventions

Convention concerning the Protection of the World Cultural and Natural Heritage

This Convention was adopted in 1972 by the General Conference of Unesco, and entered into force in 1975. The objective of the Convention is to ensure support by the international community for world heritage sites (natural or man-made) which are recognised as being held in trust by nations for mankind. Natural and cultural sites identified by states and recorded on a World Heritage List by decision of a committee are provided special protection with the possibility of financial and technical assistance through a World Heritage Fund.

By December 1985, 88 countries were party to the Convention and the World Heritage List included 61 natural properties in 29 countries. World Heritage Sites are an additional designation that is only given to a select number of a country's most outstanding protected areas. The map (Fig. 12.1) indicates the location of all World Heritage Sites.

States having designated cultural or natural sites on the World Heritage List must take specified measures for their conservation. Obligations under the Convention also include the payment of compulsory dues amounting to one per cent of the annual dues to Unesco. The Secretariat of the Convention is provided by Unesco. Technical advice on the natural sites is provided by IUCN and technical advice on cultural sites is provided by the International Council for Monuments and Sites (ICOMOS). Member States of Unesco may become Parties by depositing an instrument of ratification or acceptance, and all other states by depositing an instrument of accession, with Unesco.

Convention on International Trade in Endangered Species of Wild Fauna and Flora (CITES)

This Convention was adopted in 1973 by a diplomatic conference held in Washington, D.C., USA. The Convention entered into force in 1975 and now has 90 contracting parties. The aim of the Convention is to establish worldwide controls over trade in endangered wildlife and wildlife products – in recognition of the fact that unrestricted commercial exploitation is one of the major threats to the survival of species. More than 2000 endangered species of wild animals and plants are listed in three Appendices to the Convention. Each Party to the Convention has designated national management authorities and scientific authorities in charge of administering the licensing system, in direct cooperation with their foreign counterparts. CITES provides countries with up-to-date information, and with a direct communications network linking national enforcement agencies. Technical assistance is available for the training of personnel, and identification aids and other materials are made available to facilitate implementation of the Convention.

Convention on the Conservation of Migratory Species of Wild Animals

This Convention was adopted in 1979 at a diplomatic conference held in Bonn, Federal Republic of Germany. The Convention entered into force in 1983 and by 1985 there were 19 contracting parties. The purpose of the Convention is to provide a framework mechanism for international cooperation for the conservation and management of migratory species, and to identify endangered migratory species in need of urgent conservation measures at national level. The Convention will promote financial, technical and training assistance in support of conservation efforts made by developing countries and urges international and national organisations to give priority in their aid programmes to the management and conservation of migratory species and their habitats in developing countries to better enable such countries to implement the Convention.

Convention on Wetlands of International Importance especially as Waterfowl Habitat (RAMSAR)

The objectives of the Wetlands Convention, sometimes also known as the Ramsar Convention, adopted in 1971, are to stem the loss of wetlands and ensure their conservation for their importance in ecological processes as well as their rich fauna and flora. In order to achieve these objectives, the Convention provides for general obligations for Contracting Parties relating to the conservation of wetlands throughout the territory and for specific obligations pertaining to wetlands which have been included on a List of Wetlands of International Importance.

By 1985, some 300 sites covering in excess of 20 million ha have been designated for the list of wetland sites of international significance in terms of ecology, botany, zoology, limnology or hydrology. Placing an area on the Ramsar list has had considerable impact upon the conservation of the area and upon public recognition of the global importance of the site.

Regional conventions providing for protected areas

Africa

The African Convention on the Conservation of Nature and Natural Resources was adopted in 1968. (A revised Convention is expected for the 1986 Organisation of African Unity (OAU) meeting). Recognition was given to the need for:

- controls in trade of species and their products as well as hunting regulations and habitat conservation;
- the establishment of national conservation agencies to deal with the implementation of the convention;
- conservation education.

Western hemisphere

The 1940 Convention on Nature Protection and Wildlife Preservation in the Western Hemisphere provides that the Contracting Parties' explore at once the possibility of establishing in their territories, national parks, national reserves, nature monuments and strict wilderness areas'. It also provides for contracting governments in the Americas to cooperate among themselves in promoting its objectives, to lend assistance to one another and to enter into agreements to increase the effectiveness of this cooperation. On the basis of the principles of the treaty, most of the states in the region have taken important conservation

Fig. 12.1: Distribution of natural world heritage sites (1985)

Key

Central/South America

1. Everglades National Park (U.S. – Florida)
2. Tikal National Park (Guatemala)
3. Rio Platano Biosphere Reserve (Honduras)
4. La Amistad/Talamanca Reserves (Costa Rica)
5. Darien National Park (Panama)
6. Galapagos Islands National Park (Ecuador)
7. Sangay National Park (Ecuador)
8. Huascaran National Park (Peru)
9. Machu Picchu Historic Sancturay (Peru)
10. Iguazu National Park (Argentina)
11. Los Glaciares National Park (Argentina)

Africa

12. Ichkeul National Park (Tunisia)
13. Tassili N'Ajjer (Algeria)
14. Djoudj National Bird Sanctuary (Senegal)
15. Niokolo-Koba National Park (Senegal)
16. Comoé National Park (Ivory Coast)
17. Tai National Park (Ivory Coast)
18. Mount Nimba Strict Nature Reserve (Ivory Coast)
19. Garamba National Park (Zaire)
20. Virunga National Park (Zaire)
21. Salonga National Park (Zaire)
22. Kahuzi-Biega National Park (Zaire)
23. Simien National Park (Ethopia)
24. Serengeti National Park (Tanzania)
25. Ngorongoro Conservation Area (Tanzania)
26. Selous Game Reserve (Tanzania)
27. Aldabra Atoll (Seychelles)
28. Vallée de Mai Nature Reserve (Seychelles)
29. Lake Malawi National Park (Malawi)
30. Mana Pools National Park (Zimbabwe)

Indomalaya/Australia

31. Royal Chitwan National Park (Nepal)
32. Sagarmatha National Park (Nepal)
33. Manas Wildlife Sanctuary (India)
34. Kaziranga National Park (India)
35. Keoladeo National Park (India)
36. Kakuda National Park (Australia)
37. Great Barrier Reef Marine Park (Australia)

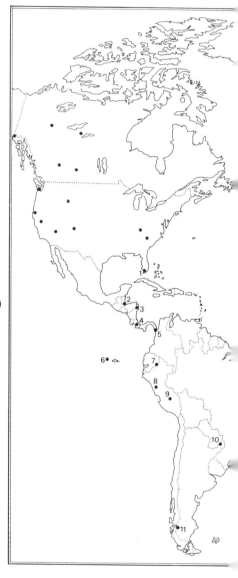

steps, including the establishment and management of protected areas.

South Pacific

The Convention on Conservation of Nature in the South Pacific was adopted in 1976 and will come into force in 1986. It encourages the creation of national parks and national reserves intended to safeguard representative samples of natural ecosystems as well as superlative scenery, striking geological formations and regions or objects of aesthetic interest or historic, cultural or scientific value.

Vicuna Convention

Following the serious depletion of wild populations of vicuna, the 1969 Convention for the Conservation of Vicuna was concluded by the States within the species' range – Argentina, Bolivia, Chile, Ecuador and Peru. Conservation measures taken, including the establishment of protected areas, resulted in steadily increasing numbers of vicuna, with the largest concentrations now occurring in the Pampa Galeras National Vicuna Reserve in Peru.

The role of IUCN and the CNPPA

The International Union for Conservation of Nature and Natural Resources (IUCN) is the largest and most representative partnership of conservation, environment and wildlife interest groups in the world. Founded in 1948, the Union includes 58 State members, 123 ministries or other government agencies and 350 major national and international non-governmental organisations and citizens' groups – a total of 537 members in 116 countries. This unique mix of policy makers, administrators and activists helps solve common conservation problems. It also provides an independent forum for conservation debate.

The Union works in close partnership with the United Nations Environment Programme (UNEP) and Unesco and advises the World Wildlife Fund (WWF) on conservation priorities, prepares programmes and manages over 300 conservation field projects in 70 countries. The Fund itself was established in 1961 to mobilise moral and financial support for safeguarding the living world and is among the closest of IUCN's many partners in conservation.

IUCN, primarily through its Commission on National Parks and Protected Areas (CNPPA), has been deeply involved with national parks from its very beginnings. This involvement has included:

- Establishing the Commission on National Parks in 1960. Now enlarged to become the Commission on National Parks and Protected Areas (CNPPA), this body has a current membership of 316 senior park professionals from 124 countries.
- Establishing a system of biogeographic

provinces of the world (Udvardy, 1975), now widely used for assessing protected area coverage and suggesting regions for priority attention.

- Publishing lists and directories of protected areas. The Protected Area Data Unit (PADU) was established in 1981 to computerise the data held by IUCN and to promote greater applications of the data.
- Publishing basic conceptual papers dealing with protected area matters such as regional system reviews, legislation guidelines and threats to the world's protected areas (see Example 12.5).
- Publishing the quarterly journal *Parks* which provides informative articles on protected area management problems and solutions.
- Cooperating closely with United Nations agencies involved in protected area matters (FAO, UNEP, Unesco), at both planning and field levels. This includes providing technical evaluations of natural sites nominated for the World Heritage List to Unesco's World Heritage Committee and acting as the Secretariat for the Convention on Conservation of Wetlands of International Importance especially as Waterfowl Habitat.
- Holding meetings in various parts of the world to promote protected areas. CNPPA holds two working sessions per year, rotating among the biogeographic realms. IUCN has organised major international meetings on protected areas, including the First World Conference on National Parks in Seattle, Washington, 1962, the Second World Conference on National Parks in Grand Teton, Wyoming, 1972, th

15ᵀᴴ GENERAL ASSEMBLY
INTERNATIONAL UNION FOR CONSERVATION
OF NATURE AND NATURAL RESOURCES.

CONSERVATION ET SOCIETE
STRATEGIE MONDIALE DE LA CONSERVATION A L'OEUVRE.

62. IUCN in assembly. IUCN serves its international membership, providing a wide range of global services through the functions of its various Commissions and the planning of its Secretariat. Photo: Green & Hahn

International Conference on Marine Parks and Reserves, Tokyo, 1975, and the World Congress on National Parks, Bali, Indonesia, October, 1982.

• Supporting field projects, especially in developing countries, aimed at establishing and managing national parks and protected areas. Funded primarily by the World Wildlife Fund, some 1500 projects involving the expenditure of over $US 40 million had been implemented in support of protected areas by 1983.

A closing note

Nature conservation is a global concern and cannot be neatly compartmentalised by international frontiers. Those engaged in the huge task of establishing, planning and managing protected areas must take a broad view of what they are doing. Success and failure should be viewed in the wide framework of a world effort and need to be measured over the long time-span of several generations.

Few countries are even holding their own in the conservation effort. The world becomes a poorer place for wild living resources each year. The funds and manpower available are restricted, political will is not always sufficient and the odds to be faced often appear insurmountable. But there are genuine grounds for hope. There have been some spectacular successes and it is encouraging to see the growing list of national organisations, parks authorities and outstanding individuals who are doing a competent job.

As protected areas become the last remaining natural habitats, they will become even more val-

Example 12.5: *Publicising threats to protected areas: IUCN's list of the world's most threatened protected areas (1984)*

By publishing the list below, IUCN focused attention on the threats facing eleven protected areas, eight of them in the tropics. The attendant publicity helped some park authorities to address threats to their protected areas and raised public support for corrective actions.

Site	Country	Threats
Araguaia National Park	Brazil	Construction of 60 km road through middle of park. Squatters invade with 30,000 domestic livestock in dry season.
Juan Fernandez National Park	Chile	Introduced animals (domestic and wild) causing serious erosion, alien plants overwhelming natural species, logging.
Krkonose National Park	Czechoslovakia	Acid rain pollution, half of park forest affected, 1000 ha already dead.
Kutai National Park	Indonesia	Extensive forest fire, logging, oil and mineral exploitation and associated roads. Human settlement.
Tai National Park	Ivory Coast	Illegal settlement, mining, poaching, insufficient management resources.
Manu National Park	Peru	Roads, settlement, prospecting, canal construction.
Mt. Apo National Park	Philippines	Human settlement, logging, removal of vegetation. Declassification of 32,000 ha for agricultural development.
Ngorongoro Conservation Area	Tanzania	Poaching black rhino. Wildfires. Overgrazing by domestic stock, insufficient management resources.
John Pennekamp Coral Reef State Park and Key Largo National Marine Sanctuary	USA.	Water pollution from dredging, landfilling and sewage. Damage by boats, fishermen and shell collectors. Condominium development.
Durmitor National Park	Yugoslavia	Hydro dam proposal, pollution from lead processing plant.
Garamba National Park	Zaire	Poaching, world's last northern white rhino (15 animals) threatened with extinction. Elephant population reduced by two-thirds in last 7 years.

Source: IUCN, 1985a

uable and an even more important part of forms of social and economic development which are sustainable. The responsibility of protected area managers as the custodians of the wild heritage of all mankind will certainly grow. To the extent that this responsibility is understood and appreciated by the public and government decision-makers, resources for conservation can similarly be expected to grow.

As all protected area managers know, conservation is a worthwhile and positive effort from which no country can afford to withdraw. Each part of the tropics contains unique features and features of high biotic value and importance. Each country must pull its own weight if we are not to lose an irreplaceable heritage for mankind.

But high levels of international cooperation are also needed to achieve more lasting results. Countries with few resources need to cooperate effectively with their neighbours to ensure that knowledge is shared productively. Technologically advanced countries should share their know-how with those less fortunate. There must be a pooling of resources and mutual support of programmes. International conservation programmes need to be integrated with regional, national and provincial programmes and conservation must be closely integrated with other components of each country's development.

Such concerted effort is a huge task requiring a major commitment in people and resources. It is also a complex task that needs many skills – biologists, geologists, planners, administrators, sociologists, economists, law enforcement officers, and many others – all brought to focus to reach common objectives.

IUCN has prepared this book in the hope that it will help and encourage the managers of protected areas throughout the tropics. This audience shares, through its communal responsibilities, the fate of most of our planet's living species, and can together have a major effect on the health of the planet our children will inherit and the variety of biological options that our grandchildren can use for their future welfare.

Enough of words – read this book in the evenings, and spend your days putting action onto the ground. There's a world to be saved for the benefit of people and wildlife alike. The protected areas of the tropics deserve our concerted stewardship and our full commitment.

PART D

Bibliography

Reference Library, College of African Wildlife Management, Mweka, Tanzania
Photo: Mweka

Bibliography

(* Denotes key references that should be available to all park managers)

AMBIO (1979). Theme issue on Environmental Development. 3(2-3): 1-96. Royal Swedish Academy of Sciences.

Armstrong, G.J. and Starling, J. (1982). Implementing Management. Paper presented to Managing Protected Areas Workshop, World National Parks Congress, Bali, Indonesia.

Asibey, E.O.A. (1974). Wildlife as a Source of Protein in Africa South of the Sahara. *Biological Conservation* 6(1): 32-39.

Atmosoedarjo, S., Daryadi, L., MacKinnon, J. and Hillegers, P. (1984). National Parks and Rural Communities. In: McNeely, J.A. and Miller, K.R. (Eds), *National Parks, Conservation and Development: The Role of Protected Areas in Sustaining Society*. IUCN/Smithsonian Institution Press, Washington, D.C.

Australian Conservation Foundation (1980). *The Value of National Parks to the Community*. A.C.F. Hawthorn, Victoria. 223pp.

Ayensu, E.S. (1981). Biology in the Humid Tropics of Africa. In: Ayensu, E.S. and Marton-Lefevre, J. (Eds), *Proceedings of the Symposium on the State of Biology in Africa*. ICSU and Unesco. Pp. 22-36.

Barborak, J., MacFarland, C. and Morales, R. (1982). The Operational Plan: A Useful Tool for Improving Management of Protected Wildlands. Invited paper, Managing Protected Areas Workshop, World National Parks Congress, Bali, Indonesia.

Barnes, R.F.W. (1983). The Elephant Problem in Ruaha National Park, Tanzania. *Biological Conservation* 26: 127-148.

Baum, W.C. (1982). *The Project Cycle*. The World Bank, Washington, D.C. 25 pp.

Bell, R.H.V. (1983). Decision making in Wildlife Management with Reference to the Problem of Overpopulation. In: Owen-Smith, R.N. (Ed.), *Management of Large Mammals in African Conservation Areas*. Proceedings of Symposium held in Pretoria, 1982.

Bell, R.H.V. (1984). Notes on Elephant-Woodland Interactions. In: Cumming, D.H.M. and Jackson, Peter, *The Status and Conservation of Africa's Elephants and Rhinos*. Proceedings of the Joint Meeting of IUCN/SSC African Elephant and African Rhino Specialist Groups, Hwange, Zimbabwe.

*Berkmuller, K. (1981). *Guidelines and Techniques for Environmental Interpretation*. University of Michigan, Ann Arbor.

Berkmuller, K. (1984). *Environmental Education about the Rain Forest*. IUCN, Gland, Switzerland. (English and Spanish)

Betancourt, J.A., Hanson,D and Wild, K. (1979). Honduras' La Tigre: Public Benefits through Conservation. *Parks* 4(2).

Blower, J. (1984). National Parks for Developing Countries. In: McNeely, J.A. and Miller, K.R. (Eds), *National Parks, Conservation, and Development: The Role of Protected Areas in Sustaining Society*. IUCN/Smithsonian Institution Press, Washington, D.C.

Blower, J.H., and Wind, J. (1977). *Penanjung Pangandaron Reserve Management Plan* 1977/82. FAO FO/INS 73/013, Field Report 1, p.27.

Bothe, M. (Ed.) (1980). *Trends in Environmental Policy and Law*. IUCN, Gland, Switzerland.

Breslin, P. and Chapin, M. (1984). Conservation Kuna-style. *Grassroots Development* 8(2): 26-35

Brownrigg, L.A. (1985). Native cultures and protected areas: Management options. In: McNeely, J.A. and Pitt, D. (Eds), *Culture and Conservation: The human dimension in environmental planning*. Croom Helm, London. Pp. 33-44

Brusard, Peter F. (1982). The Role of Field Stations in the Preservation of Biological Diversity. *Bioscience* 32(5): 327-330.

Burhenne, W.E. (1970). The African Convention for the Conservation of Nature and Natural Resources. *Biological Conservation* 2(2): 105-114.

Byrne, John E. (1979). *Literature Review and Synthesis of Information on Pacific Island Ecosystems*. Fish and Wildlife Service, U.S. Department of Interior, Washington, D.C.

Campbell, A.C. (1973). The National Park and Reserve System in Botswana. *Biological Conservation* 5(1): 7-14.

Caughley, G. (1977). *Analysis of Vertebrate Populations*. John Wiley and Sons, New York. 481 pp.

Child, G. (1984). FAO and Protected Area Management: Where Do We Go From Here? In: McNeely, J.A. and Miller, K.R. (Eds), *National Parks, Conservation, and Development: The Role of Protected Areas in Sustaining Society*. IUCN/Smithsonian Institution Press, Washington, D.C.

Child, G.F.T. (1968). An Ecological Survey of North-eastern Botswana. FAO Report No. TA 2563. 155 pp.

Child, G.F.T. (1970). Wildlife Utilization and Management in Botswana. *Biological Conservation* 3(1): 18-22.

Child, G.F.T. (1977). Problems and Progress in Nature Conservation in Rhodesia. *Koedoe* (Suppl.) 1977: 116-137.

Child G.F.T. (1983). Elephant Culling and Carcass Recovery within the Parks and Wildlife Estate in Zimbabwe. Dept. of National Parks and Wildlife Management Report. Mimeo. 22 pp.

Child, G.F.T. (1984). Managing Wildlife for People in Zimbabwe. In: McNeely, J.A. and Miller, K.R. (Eds), *National Parks, Conservation, and Development: The Role of Protected Areas in Sustaining Society*. IUCN/Smithsonian Institution Press, Washington, D.C.

Child, G.F.T. (1985). An evaluation of elephant problems associated with the Accelerated Mahaweli Development Programme in Sri Lanka. FAO.

*Christiansen, M.I. (1977). *Park Planning Handbook*. John Wiley and Sons, New York.

Clad, J.C. (1982). Conservation and Indigenous Peoples: A Study of Convergent Interests. Invited paper, Managing Protected Areas Workshop, World National Parks Congress, Bali, Indonesia.

Clarke, William C. (1976). Maintenance of agriculture and human habitats within the tropical forest ecosystem. *Human Ecology* 4(3): 217-259.

CNPPA/IUCN (1976). The biosphere reserve and its relationship to national and international conservation efforts. Report to Unesco. IUCN, Gland, Switzerland. Mimeo.

Cobb, S. 1979. Are the Right People Being Trained the Wrong Way? *Wildlife News* 14(3).

Conway, A.J. (1984). Antipoaching measures in Chirisa Safari Area, Zimbabwe. In: Cumming D.H.M. and Jackson, Peter (Eds), *The Status and Conservation of Africa's Elephants and Rhinos* Proceedings of the Joint Meeting of IUCN/SSC African Elephant and African Rhino Specialis Groups, Hwange, Zimbabwe.

*Corfield, T. (1985). *The Wilderness Guardian*. David Sheldrick Foundation. Nairobi.

Croft, T. A. (1981). Lake Malawi National Park: A Case Study in Conservation Planning. *Parks* 6(3)

Croze, H. (1984). Monitoring Within and Outside Protected Areas. In: McNeely, J.A. and Miller K.R. (Eds), *National Parks, Conservation, and Development: The Role of Protected Areas in Sustaining Society*. IUCN/Smithsonian Institution Press, Washington, D.C.

Cumming, D.H.M. (1981). The management of elephant and other large mammals in Zimbabwe. In Jewell, P.A., Holt, S. and Hart, D. (Eds), *Problems in Management of Locally Abundant Wild Mammals*. Academic Press, London. Pp.91-118.

Curry-Lindahl, K. (1974). Conservation Problems and Progress in Northern and Southern Africa *Environmental Conservation* 1(4): 263-270.

Dahl, Arthur R. (1980). Regional Ecosystems Survey of the South Pacific Area. Technical Paper No 19, SPC, New Caledonia.

Dalfelt, A. (1976). Some Data Related to Costs and Benefits of National Parks in Latin America

CATIE, Costa Rica. Mimeo report. 66 pp.

Dalfelt, A. (1984). The Role and Constraints of International Development Agencies in Promoting Effective Management of Protected Areas. In: McNeely, J.A. and Miller, K.R. (Eds), *National Parks, Conservation, and Development: The Role of Protected Areas in Sustaining Society.* IUCN/ Smithsonian Institution Press, Washington, D.C.

Darling, Sir Frank Fraser (1980). National Parks ... a matter of survival. *Parks* 4(4): 16

Darlington, P.J. Jr. (1957). *Zoogeography: The Geographical Distribution of Animals.* J. Wiley and Sons, New York.

*Dasmann, R.F., Milton, J.P. and Freeman, P. (1973). *Ecological Principles for Economic Development.* J. Wiley Ltd., London. 252 pp.

Dasmann, R. F. (1980). Ecodevelopment – an ecological perspective. *Tropical ecology and development*, pp. 1331-1335. Intern. Soc. Tropical Ecology, Kuala Lumpur.

Dasmann, R. F. (1984). The Relationship Between Protected Areas and Indigenous Peoples. In: McNeely, J.A. and Miller, K.R. (Eds), *National Parks, Conservation, and Development: The Role of Protected Areas in Sustaining Society.* IUCN/Smithsonian Institution Press, Washington, D.C.

de Alwis, L. (1984). River Basin Development and Protected Areas in Sri Lanka. In: McNeely, J.A. and Miller, K.R. (Eds), *National Parks, Conservation, and Development: The Role of Protected Areas in Sustaining Society.* IUCN/Smithsonian Institution Press, Washington, D.C.

DeKadt, E. (1976). *Tourism: Passport to Development?* Oxford University Press, Oxford.

de Klemm, C. (1984). Protecting Wild Genetic Resources for the Future: The Need for a World Treaty. In: McNeely, J.A. and Miller, K.R. (Eds), *National Parks, Conservation, and Development: The Role of Protected Areas in Sustaining Society.* IUCN/Smithsonian Institution Press, Washington, D.C.

Deshler, W.O., (1982). A systematic approach to effective management of protected areas. Background paper to Managing Protected Areas Workshop, World Congress on National Parks, Bali, Indonesia.

DeVos, A. (1969). The Need for Nature Reserves in East Africa. *Biological Conservation* 1(2): 130-134.

Diamond, J.M. (1975). The island dilemma: lessons of modern biogeographic studies for the design of natural reserves. *Biological Conservation* 7: 129-146.

Diamond, J.M. (1980). Patchy distributions of some tropical birds.in Soulé, M.E. and Wilcox, B.A. (Eds), *Conservation Biology*, Sinauer Associates, Sunderland, Massachusetts. Pp. 57-74.

Diamond, J.M. (1984). Biological Principles Relevant to Protected Area Design in the New Guinea Region. In: McNeely, J.A. and Miller, K.R. (Eds), *National Parks, Conservation, and Development: The Role of Protected Areas in Sustaining Society.* IUCN/Smithsonian Institution Press, Washington, D.C.

Dickinson, R.E. (1981). Effects of tropical deforestation on climate. In: *Blowing in the Wind: Deforestation and Long-range Implications.* Studies in Third World Societies, No. 14. College of William and Mary, Williamsburg.

Dorst, Jean (1974). Parks and Reserves on Islands. In: Sir Hugh Elliott (Ed.) *Second World Conference on National Parks.* IUCN, Gland, Switzerland. Pp. 267-276.

Douglas-Hamilton, I. (1984). Antipoaching: Lessons from Uganda. In: Cumming, D.H.M. and Jackson, Peter (Eds), *The Status and Conservation of Africa's Elephants and Rhinos.* Proceedings of the Joint Meeting of IUCN/SSC African Elephant and African Rhino Specialist Groups, Hwange, Zimbabwe. Pp. 78-91.

Duncan, P. and Esser, J. (1982). The use of fauna and flora as a contribution to environmentally sound development in the Sahel. IUCN, Gland, Switzerland.

Dunlop, Richard C. and Singh, Birendra B. (1978). *A National Parks and Reserves System for Fiji.* The National Trust for Fiji. 117pp.

Dupuy, A.R. (1984). *Les gardiens de la vie sauvage.* WWF/IUCN, Gland, Switzerland.

Dwyer, P.D. (1974). The Price of Protein: five hundred hours of hunting in the New Guinea Highlands. *Oceania* 44: 278-293.

Eaton, P. (1985). Land Tenure and Conservation: Protected Areas in the South Pacific. South Pacific Regional Environment Programme. Noumea.

Ehrlich, Paul R. (1982). Human Carrying Capacity, Extinction, and Nature Reserves. *Bioscience* 32(5): 321-326.

Eidsvik, H.K. (1978). Involving the Public in Planning: Canada. *Parks* 3(1):3-5.

Eidsvik, H.K. (1980). National Parks and Other Protected Areas: Some Reflections on the Past and Prescriptions for the Future. *Environmental Conservation* 7(3).

Eisenberg, J.F. (1980). The density and biomass of tropical mammals. In: Soulé, M.E. and Wilcox, B.A. (Eds), *Conservation Biology*, Sinauer Associates, Sunderland, Massachusetts. Pp. 35-55.

Elliott, Sir Hugh (1973). Past, Present and Future Conservation Status of Pacific Islands. In: Costin, A.B. and Groves, R.H. (Eds), *Nature Conservation in the Pacific*. Australian National University, Canberra. Pp. 217-227.

*Elliott, Sir Hugh (Ed.) (1974). *Second World Conference on National Parks*. IUCN, Gland, Switzerland. 504 pp. (English, French, Spanish editions).

*Fazio, James R. and Gilbert, Douglas, L. (1981). *Public Relations and Communications for Natural Resources Managers*. Kendall/Hunt Publishing Co, Iowa.

Ferrar, A.A. (Ed.) (1983). Guidelines for the Management of Large Mammals in African Conservation Areas. South African National Scientific Programme Report 69. Pretoria.

Field, C.R. (1979). Game ranching in Africa. *Applied Ecology* 4: 63-101.

*Forster, R. (1973). Planning for man and nature in national parks. IUCN Publication New Series 26. IUCN, Gland, Switzerland.

Fox, A.M. (1984). People and Their Park. An Example of Free Running Socio-ecological Succession. In: McNeely, J.A. and Miller, K.R. (Eds), *National Parks, Conservation, and Development: The Role of Protected Areas in Sustaining Society*. IUCN/Smithsonian Institution Press, Washington. D.C.

*Frankel, O.M. and Soulé, Michael E. (1981). *Conservation and Evolution*. Cambridge University Press, New York. 327 pp.

Fryer, G. (1972). Conservation of the Great Lakes of East Africa: A Lesson and a Warning. *Biological Conservation* 4(4): 256-262.

Garcia, Jose Rafael (1984). Waterfalls, hydropower, and water for industry: Contributions from Canaima National Park. In: McNeely, J.A. and Miller, K.R. (Eds), *National Parks, Conservation and Development: The role of protected areas in sustaining society*. IUCN/Smithsonian Institution Press, Washington D.C. Pp. 588-591.

Gardner, J.E. and Nelson, J.G. (1981). Lake Malawi National Park: A Case Study in Conservation Planning. *Parks* 6(3).

Garratt, K.J. (1981). *Sagarmatha National Park Management Plan*. Dept. of Lands and Survey, New Zealand, for the National Parks and Wildlife Conservation Office, Kathmandu, Nepal.

Garratt, Keith (1984). The relationship between adjacent lands and protected areas: Issues of concern for the protected area manager. In: McNeely, J.A. and Miller, K.R. (Eds), *National Parks, Conservation, and Development: The role of protected areas in sustaining society*. Smithsonian Institution Press, Washington D.C.. Pp. 65-71.

Giles, R.H. (1971). *Wildlife Management Techniques*. The Wildlife Society, Washington, D.C. 633 pp.

Goeden, G.B. (1979). Biogeographic theory as a management tool. *Environmental Conservation* 6 27-32.

Gomez-Pompa, A., Vasquez-Yanes, C. and Guevara, S. (1972). The Tropical Rain Forest: a non renewable resource. *Science* 177: 762-765.

Goodland, R. (1984). The World Bank, Environment, and Protected Areas. In: McNeely, J.A. and Miller, K.R. (Eds), *National Parks, Conservation, and Development: The Role of Protected Areas in Sustaining Society*. IUCN/Smithsonian Institution Press, Washington, D.C.

Government of Ecuador.Unesco/FAO (1974). *Plan Maestro para la Proteccion y Uso del Parque Nacional Galapagos*. Quito.

Government of India (1972). Project Tiger: A planning proposal for preservation of tiger (*Panthera tigris tigris* Linn.) in India. Report of Task Force, Indian Board for Wildlife, Dept. of Environment, New Delhi. 114 pp.

Government of India (1983). Eliciting Public Support for Wildlife Conservation. Report of the Task Force, Indian Board for Wildlife, Dept. of Environment, New Delhi.

Government of Vietnam/IUCN (1985). *Vietnam National Conservation Strategy* (draft). Prepared by the Committee of Natural Resources (Programme 52-02) with assistance from the International Union for Conservation of Nature and Natural Resources (IUCN), Gland, Switzerland. 97 pp.

*Grater, R.K. (1976). *The Interpreter's Handbook*. Southwest Parks and Monuments Association, Arizona.

Green, K. (1980). An assessment of the Poco das Antas Reserve, Brazil, and prospects for survival of the golden lion tamarin, *Leontopithecus rosalia rosalia*. Unpublished report to WWF.

Guppy, N. (1984). Tropical Deforestation: A Global View. *Foreign Affairs 62(4): 928-965.*

Gwynne, M.D. (1982). The Global Environment Monitoring System of UNEP. *Environmental Conservation* 9(1): 35-41.

Gwynne, M.D. and Croze, H. (1975). East African habitat monitoring practice: a review of methods and application. Proceedings International Livestock Centre for Africa (ILCA) Seminar on Evaluation and Mapping of Tropical African Rangelands, Bamako, 1975: 95-142.

Hales, D. F. (1980). Does the World Heritage Convention Really Work? *Parks* 4(4).

Halffter, G. (1981). The Mapimi Biosphere Reserve: Local Participation in Conservation and Development. *Ambio* 10(2-3).

Halle, F., Oldeman, R.A.A. and Tomlinson, P.B. (1978). *Tropical trees and forests: an architectural analysis*. Springer, Berlin.

Harcourt, A.H. (1981). Can Uganda's Gorillas Survive? – A Survey of the Bwindi Forest Reserve. *Biological Conservation* 19(4): 269-282.

Harrison, J., Miller, K.R. and McNeely, J.A. (1984). The World Coverage of Protected Areas: Development Goals and Environmental Needs. In: McNeely, J.A. and Miller, K.R. (Eds), *National Parks, Conservation and Development: The Role of Protected Areas in Sustaining Society*. IUCN/ Smithsonian Institution Press, Washington, D.C.

Hartl, D.L. (1981). *A Primer of Population Genetics*. Sinauer Associates, Sunderland, Massachusetts. 191 pp.

Henderson-Sellers, A. (1981). The Effects of Land Clearance and Agricultural Practices on Climate. In: *Blowing in the Wind: Deforestation and Long-range Implications*. Studies in Third World Societies, No. 14, College of William and Mary, Williamsburg. Pp. 443-486.

Hoogerwerf, A. (1970). *Ujung Kulon, the land of the last Javan rhinoceros*. Brill, Leiden.

Hoose, P.M. (1981). *Building an Ark: Tools for the Preservation of Natural Diversity Through Land Protection*. Island Press, Covelo, California. 212 pp.

Huntley, B.J. (1978). Ecosystem Conservation in Southern Africa. In: Werger, M.J.A. (Ed.), *Biogeography and Ecology of Southern Africa*. Junk Publishers, The Hague. Pp. 1333-1384.

Hutton, A. (1985). Butterfly Farming in Papua New Guinea. *Oryx* XIX: 158-162.

IBRD (1981). *Economic Development and Tribal Peoples: Human Ecologic Considerations*. International Bank for Reconstruction and Development (World Bank), Washington, D.C.

IUCN (1962). *First World Conference on National Parks*, Seattle. U.S. Dept. of the Interior, Washington, D.C.

IUCN (1976). *Proceedings of a Regional Meeting on the Creation of a Coordinated System of National parks and Reserves in Eastern Africa*. IUCN, Morges, Switzerland.

IUCN (1978). *Categories, objectives and criteria for protected areas*. IUCN, Gland, Switzerland. 26 pp.

IUCN (1979). *The Biosphere Reserve and its Relationship to other Protected Areas*. IUCN, Gland, Switzerland.

IUCN. 1980. *World Conservation Strategy: Living Resource Conservation for Sustainable Development*. IUCN/UNEP/WWF, Gland, Switzerland. 48 pp.

IUCN (1981a). *Draft Action Plan for the Conservation of Nature in the ASEAN Region*. Prepared for the Interim Coordinator ASEAN Expert Group on the Environment by IUCN (first draft 20 February 1981). Gland, Switzerland.

IUCN (1981b). *Conserving the Natural Heritage of Latin America and the Caribbean*. IUCN, Gland, Switzerland.

IUCN (1982). *IUCN Directory of Neotropical Protected Areas*. IUCN, Gland, Switzerland.

IUCN (1984a). *The Bali Declaration*. In: McNeely, J.A. and Miller, K.R. (Eds), *National Parks, Conservation and Development: The Role of Protected Areas in Sustaining Society*. IUCN/Smithsonian Institution Press, Washington, D.C.

IUCN (1984b). Categories, Objectives and Criteria for Protected Areas. In: McNeely, J.A. and Miller, K.R. (Eds), *National Parks, Conservation and Development: The Role of Protected Areas in Sustaining Society*. IUCN/Smithsonian Institution Press, Washington, D.C.

IUCN (1985a). Threatened Natural Areas, Plants and Animals of the World. *Parks* 10(1): 15-17.
*IUCN (1985b). *1985 United Nations List of National Parks and Protected Areas*. IUCN, Gland, Switzerland and Cambridge, UK.
Island Resources Foundation (1981). Economic Impact Analysis for the Virgin Islands National Park. US Dept. of the Interior, National Park Service, Washington D.C.
Jewell, P.A., Holt, S. and Hart, D. (Eds) (1981). Problems in Management of Locally Abundant Wild Mammals. Academic Press, New York.
Johns, A.D. (1981). The effects of selective logging on the social structure of resident primates. *Malaysian Applied Biology* 10(2): 221-226.
Johnson, B. and Blake, R.O. (1979). *The Environmental and Bilateral Aid*. International Institute for Economic Development (IIED), London/ Washington. 58 pp.
Johnson, H. and Johnson, J.M. (1977). *Environmental Policies in Developing Countries*. Erich Schmidt Verlag, Berlin.
Jorge Padua, M.T., and Tresinari Bernardes Quintao, A. (1984). A system of national parks and biological reserves in the Brazilian Amazon. In: McNeely, J.A. and Miller, (Eds), *National Parks, Conservation and Development: The Role of Protected Areas in Sustaining Society*. IUCN/Smithsonian Institution Press, Washington, D.C.
Kavanagh, M. (1984). Planning Considerations for a System of National Parks and Wildlife Sanctuaries in Sarawak. Talk given to Angkatan Zaman Mansang (AZAM) Kuching.
Kayanja, F. and Douglas-Hamilton, I. (1984). The Impact of the Unexpected on the Uganda National Parks. In: McNeely, J.A. and Miller, K.R. (Eds), *National Parks, Conservation, and Development: The Role of Protected Areas in Sustaining Society*. IUCN/Smithsonian Institution Press, Washington, D.C.
Kleiman, D.G. (1984). An Ecological Study and Reintroduction Programme for the Golden Lion Tamarin *Leontopithecus rosalia* in the Poco das Antas Biological Reserve, Rio de Janeiro, Brazil. Progress Report to WWF-US.
Knox, M. (1981). *The Green Book of Fiji*. A Teacher's Handbook on the Conservation of Nature in Fiji. The National Trust for Fiji.
Kombe, A.D.C. (1984). The Role of Protected Areas in Catchment Conservation in Malawi. In McNeely, J.A. and Miller, K.R. (Eds), *National Parks, Conservation, and Development*. IUCN Smithsonian Institution Press, Washington, D.C.
Konstant, W.R. and Mittermeier, R.A. (1982). Introduction, reintroduction and translocation o' Neotropical primates: Past experiences and future possibilities. *International Zoo Yearbook* 22 69-77.
Krishnamurthy, K. and Jeyaseelan, M.J.P. (1980). The impact of the Pichavaram mangrove ecosysten upon coastal natural resources: A case study from southern India. Asian Symposium on Mangrove Environments: Research and Management. Kuala Lumpur.
Kwapena, N. (1984). Wildlife Management by the People. In: McNeely, J.A. and Miller, K.R. (Eds) *National Parks, Conservation, and Development: The Role of Protected Areas in Sustaining Society* IUCN/Smithsonian Institution Press, Washington, D.C.
Lamprey, H.F. (1975). *The Distribution of Protected Areas in Relation to the Needs of Biotic Com munity Conservation in Eastern Africa*. IUCN Occasional Paper No. 16. Morges, Switzerland.
Lanly, J.P. (1982). Tropical Forest Resources. FAO Forestry Paper 30. FAO, Rome.
*Lausche, B.J. (1980). *Guidelines for Protected Areas Legislation*, IUCN, Gland, Switzerland.
Laws, R.M. (1970). Elephants as agents of habitat and landscape change in East Africa. *Oikos* 21: 1-15
Lawson, G.W. (1972). The Case for Conservation in Ghana. *Biological Conservation* 4(4): 292-300.
Leopold, A. (1933). *Game Management*. Charles Scribner and Sons, New York.
Levins, R. (1968). *Evolution in Changing Environments*. Princeton University Press, Princeton, New Jersey.
Lovejoy, T.E. (1980). Discontinuous Wilderness: Minimum Areas for Conservation. *Parks* 5(2): 13-15
Lovejoy, T.E., Bierregaard, R.O., Rankin, J.M. and Schubart, H.O.R. (1983). Ecological dynamics of tropical forest fragments. In: Sutton, S.L., Whitmore, T.C. and Chadwick, A.C. *Tropical Rainfores. Ecology and Management*. Blackwell Scientific Publications. Oxford.
Lucas, G. and Synge, H. (Compilers) (1978). *The IUCN Plant Red Data Book*. Unwin Brothers, UK
Lucas, Grenville L. (1984). The Survival of Species Genetic Diversity. In: McNeely, J.A. and Mille

K.R. (Eds), *National Parks, Conservation, and Development: The Role of Protected Areas in Sustaining Society*. IUCN/Smithsonian Institution Press, Washington, D.C.

Lucas, P.H.C. (1984). How Protected Areas Can Help Meet Society's Evolving Needs. In: McNeely, J.A. and Miller, K.R. (Eds), *National Parks, Conservation, and Development: The Role of Protected Areas in Sustaining Society*. IUCN/Smithsonian Institution Press, Washington, D.C.

Lusigi, Walter J. (1978). Planning human activities on protected naturalecosystems. *Dissertationes Botanicae* 48. J. Cramer, Vaduz, Germany. 233pp.

Lusigi, W.J. (1981). New Approaches to Wildlife Conservation in Kenya. *Ambio* 10 (2-3).

Lusigi, W. (1984a). Future Directions for the Afrotropical Realm. In: McNeely, J.A. and Miller, K.R. (Eds), *National Parks, Conservation and Development: The Role of Protected Areas in Sustaining Society*. IUCN/Smithsonian Institution Press, Washington, D.C.

Lusigi, W. (1984b). Major Trends in National Parks and Protected Areas Management in Africa. In: *Proceedings of the Twenty-Second Working Session of CNPPA, Victoria Falls, Zimbabwe*. May, 1983.

Lyster, S. (1985). *International Wildlife Law*. Grotius, London.

MacArthur, R.H. and Wilson, E.O. (1967). *The Theory of Island Biogeography*. Princeton University Press, Princeton, New Jersey. 203 pp.

MacArthur, R.H. (1972). *Geographical Ecology: Patterns in the Distribution of Species*. Harper and Row, New York.

MacDonald, I. and Grimsdell, J. (1983). What causes change? Getting at the facts. The role of ecological monitoring. In: *South African. National Scientific Programme Report 69*. CSIR, Pretoria, South Africa. Pp.77-95.

MacFarland, C., Morales, R. and Barborak, J.R. (1984). Establishment, Planning and Implementation of a National Wildlands System in Costa Rica. In: McNeely, J.A. and Miller, K.R. (Eds), *National Parks, Conservation, and Development: The Role of Protected Areas in Sustaining Society*. IUCN/Smithsonian Institution Press, Washington, D.C.

MacKinnon, J. (1974). The Behaviour and Ecology of Wild Orangutans. *Animal Behaviour* 22: 3-74.

MacKinnon, J. (1981a). Guidelines for the Development of Conservation Buffer Zones and Enclaves. Nature Conservation Workshop PPA/WWF/FAO, Bogor, Indonesia.

MacKinnon, J. (1981b). Methods for the Conservation of Maleo Birds *Macrocephalon maleo* on the Island of Sulawesi, Indonesia. *Biological Conservation* 20: 183-193.

MacKinnon, J. (1981 and 1982) (8 volumes). National Conservation Plan for Indonesia. FO/INS/78/061 Field Reports 19 and 34, FAO, Bogor.

MacKinnon, J.R. (1983). Irrigation and watershed protection in Indonesia. Report to the World Bank.

Marsh, C.W. and Wilson, W.L. (1981). A Survey of Primates in Peninsular Malaysian Forests. Final Report for the Malaysian Primates Research Programme, Universiti Kebangsaan Malaysia and University of Cambridge, UK.

McEachern, John and Towle, Edward L. (1974). *Ecological Guidelines for Island Development*. IUCN Publications New Series No. 30: 1-65.

McNeely, J.A., and Miller, K.R. (Eds) (1984). *National Parks, Conservation and Development: The Role of Protected Areas in Sustaining Society*. IUCN/Smithsonian Institution Press, Washington D.C. 825 pp.

McNeely, J.A. and Pitt, D. (Eds) (1985). *Culture and Conservation: The human dimension in environmental planning*. Croom Helm, London. 308 pp.

Mani, M.S. (Ed.) (1974). *Ecology and Biogeography in India*. Junk Publishers, The Hague.

Medhurst, G. and Good, R. (1984). Fire and Pest Species: A Case Study of Kosciusko National Park. In: McNeely, J.A. and Miller, K.R. (Eds), *National Parks, Conservation, and Development: The Role of Protected Areas in Sustaining Society*. IUCN/Smithsonian Institution Press, Washington, D.C.

Medway, Lord (1971). Importance of Taman Negara in the Conservation of Mammals. *Malay Nature Journal* 24: 212-4.

Medway, Lord and Wells, D.R. (1971). Diversity and density of birds and mammals at Kuala Lompat, Pahang. *Malay Nature Journal* 24: 238-247.

Medway, Lord (1978). The tropical forests as a source of animal genetic resources. In: *Proceedings of Eighth World Forestry Congress*. FAO, Rome.

Meganck, R. and Goebel, J.M. (1979). Shifting Cultivation: Problem for Parks in Latin America. *Parks* 4(2).

Miller, K.R. (1973). Development and Training of Personnel – the Foundation of National Park Programs in the Future. In: Elliott, H. (Ed.), *Second World Conference on National Parks*. IUCN (1974). Pp. 326-347.

Miller, K.R. (1975). Guidelines for the management and development of national parks and reserves in the American Humid Tropics. *Proceedings IUCN Meeting on the Use of Ecological Guidelines for Development in the American Humid Tropics*, Caracas, 20-22 February 1974. IUCN. Pp. 94-105.

*Miller, K.R. (1978). *Planning National Parks For Ecodevelopment*, University of Michigan, Ann Arbor.

Miller K.R. (1984a). The Natural Protected Areas of the World. In: McNeely, J.A. and Miller, K.R. (Eds), *National Parks, Conservation, and Development: The Role of Protected Areas in Sustaining Society*. IUCN/Smithsonian Institution Press, Washington, D.C.

Miller K.R. (1984b). The Bali Action Plan: A Framework for the Future of Protected Areas. In: McNeely, J.A. and Miller, K.R. (Eds), *National Parks, Conservation, and Development: The Role of Protected Areas in Sustaining Society*. IUCN/Smithsonian Institution Press, Washington, D.C.

Milne, Robert C. (1981). International Cooperation: Enlightened Self-Interest. *Parks and Recreation* 16(8): 59-62.

Milton, J. and Binney, G. (1980). Ecological Planning in the Nepalese Terai: A report of conflicts between Wildlife Conservation and Agricultural Land Use in Padampur Panchyat. *Threshold*. Washington, D.C.

Mishra, H.R. and Shah, B.B. (1981). *Kingdom of Hope: A review of a decade of Nature Conservation in Nepal*. HMG/Department of National Parks and Wildlife, Kathmandu.

Mishra, H.R. (1984). A Delicate Balance: Tigers, Rhinoceros, Tourists and Park Management vs. The Needs of the Local People in Royal Chitwan National Park, Nepal. In: McNeely, J.A. and Miller, K.R. (Eds), *National Parks, Conservation and Development: The Role of Protected Areas in Sustaining Society*. IUCN/Smithsonian Institution Press, Washington D.C.

*Moore, A.W. (1984). Operations Manual for a Protected Area System. Guidelines for Developing Countries. FAO Conservation Guide 9, FAO, Rome.

Mosby, H.S. (Ed.) (1963). *Wildlife Investigational Techniques*. (2nd edition). The Wildlife Society. Washington, D.C.

Mosha, G.T. and Thorsell, J.W. (1984). Training Protected Area Personnel: Lessons From the College of African Wildlife Management, Tanzania. In: McNeely, J.A. and Miller, K.R. (Eds), *National Parks, Conservation, and Development: The Role of Protected Areas in Sustaining Society*. IUCN Smithsonian Institution Press, Washington, D.C.

Mosley, J.G. (1978). Regional Parks, National Parks and Wilderness Areas – A Framework for Recreation and Conservation. *Land for Leisure*. Royal Australian Institute of Parks and Recreation. Canberra, Australia. Pp. 14-24.

Mossman, Rex (in Press). *Managing Protected Areas in the South Pacific Region: A Training Manual* South Pacific Commission, New Caledonia.

Myers, N. (1972). National Parks in Savannah Africa. *Science* 178: 1255-1263.

Myers, N. (1973). Tsavo National Park, Kenya, and its Elephants: An Interim Appraisal. *Biological Conservation* 5(2): 123-132.

*Myers, Norman (1979). *The Sinking Ark*. Pergamon, Oxford.

Myers, N. (1980). The Present Status and Future Prospects of Tropical Moist Forests. *Environmental Conservation* 7(2): 101-114.

Newby, J.E. (1984). The Role of Protected Areas in Saving the Sahel. In: McNeely, J.A. and Miller, K.R. (Eds), *National Parks, Conservation and Development: The Role of Protected Areas in Sustaining Society*. IUCN/Smithsonian Institute Press, Washington, D.C.

Nietschmann, B. (1982). Indigenous Island Peoples, Living Resources and Protected Areas. In McNeely, J.A. and Miller, K.R. (Eds), *National Parks, Conservation and Development: The Role of Protected Areas in Sustaining Society*. IUCN/Smithsonian Institute Press, Washington, D.C.

Norton-Griffiths, M. (1978). *Counting Animals*. (2nd Edition). African Wildlife Leadership Foundation, Nairobi.

*Odum, E.P. (1971). *Fundamentals of Ecology*. (3rd Edition). W.B. Saunders, London.

Olembo, R. (1984). UNEP and Protected Areas. In: McNeely, J.A. and Miller, K.R. (Eds), *National Parks, Conservation, and Development: The Role of Protected Areas in Sustaining Society*. IUCN/Smithsonian Institution Press, Washington, D.C.

Olivier, R.C.D. (1977). A study of pocketed elephant herds in Sri Lanka. Mimeo. Cambridge. 8pp.

Organization of American States (1972-74). *Proceedings of the Second and Third International Seminars on Natural Areas and Tourism*. Chubut, Argentina.

Organization of American States (1978). Final Report on Conservation of Major Terrestrial Ecosystem of the Western Hemisphere. San José, Costa Rica.

Ovington, J. Derrick. (1984). Ecological Processes and National Park Management. In: McNeely, J.A. and Miller, K.R. (Eds), *National Parks, Conservation, and Development: The Role of Protected Areas in Sustaining Society*. IUCN/Smithsonian Institution Press, Washington, D.C.

Owen, J.S. (1969). Development and Consolidation of Tanzania National Parks. *Biological Conservation* (2): 156-158.

Owen-Smith, R.N. (Ed.) (1983). Management of Large Mammals in African Conservation Areas. *Proceedings of Symposium held in Pretoria Centre for Resource Ecology, Witwatersrand University, South Africa*. Haulm, Pretoria.

Panwar, H.S. (1980). Conservation-oriented development for communities in forested regions of India. *Tropical Ecology and Development*. Proceedings of the Vth International Symposium on Tropical Ecology, Kuala Lumpur, April, 1979. Pp. 467-474.

Panwar, H.S. (1984). What To Do When You've Succeeded: Project Tiger Ten Years Later. In: McNeely, J.A. and Miller, K.R. (Eds), *National Parks, Conservation, and Development: The Role of Protected Areas in Sustaining Society*. IUCN/Smithsonian Institution Press, Washington, D.C.

Paris, R. and Child, G. (1973). The Importance of Pans to Wildlife in the Kalahari and the Effects of Human Settlement on these Areas. *Journal of South African Wildlife Management Association* 3(1): 1-8.

Pennington, H. (1982). *A Living Trust: Tanzanian Attitudes Toward Wildlife and Conservation*. Yale University Press, New Haven, Conn.

Pielou, E.C. (1979). *Biogeography*. J. Wiley and Sons (Wiley-Intersciences), New York.

Polunin, N., and Eidsvik, H.K. (1979). Ecological principles for the establishment and management of national parks and equivalent reserves. *Environmental Conservation* 6(1).

Ponce Salazar, A. and Huber, R. Jr. (1982). Ecuador's Active Conservation Programme. *Parks* 6 (4): 7-1O.

*Poore, D. (1976). *Ecological guidelines for development in tropical rainforests*. IUCN, Gland, Switzerland. 39 pp.

Prance, G.T. (l982). *Biological Diversification in the Tropics*. Columbia University Press, New York.

Prescott-Allen, R. and Prescott-Allen, C. (1981). *In situ conservation of crop genetic resources*. IBPGR and IUCN.

Prescott- Allen, R. and Prescott-Allen, C. (1983). *Genes from the Wild*. Earthscan, London. 101 pp.

Prescott-Allen, R. and Prescott-Allen, C. (1984). Park Your Genes: Protected Areas as *In Situ* Genebanks for the Maintenance of Wild Genetic Resources. In: McNeely, J.A. and Miller, K.R. (Eds), *National Parks, Conservation, and Development: The Role of Protected Areas in Sustaining Society*. IUCN/Smithsonian Institution Press, Washington, D.C.

Proud, K.R.S. and Hutchinson, J.D. (1980). Management of Natural Reseves to Maintain Faunal Diversity: A Potential Use for Forest Silviculture. *Tropical Ecology and Development 1980*: 247-255.

Putney, Allen D. (1980). Overview of Conservation in the Caribbean Region. In: Sabot, Kenneth (Ed.). *Transactions of the Forty-fifth North American Wildlife and Natural Resources Conference*. Wildlife Management Institute, Washington, D.C. Pp. 460-467.

Quigg, P.W. (1978). *Protecting Natural Areas: An Introduction to the Creation of National Parks and Reserves*. National Audubon Society/International Series Number Three. Washington, D.C.

Randall, R.E. (1978). *Theories and Techniques in Vegetation Analaysis*, Oxford University Press, Oxford. 61pp.

Ranjitsinh, M.K. (1979). Forest destruction in Asia and the south Pacific. *Ambio* Vol. VIII, No. 5.

Rao, K. (1985). Legislative and Organisational Support for Protected Areas in India. In: Thorsell, J.W.

(Ed.), *Conserving Asia's Natural Heritage*. IUCN, Gland, Switzerland.

Rappaport, R.A. (1967). *Pigs for the Ancestors: Ritual in the Ecology of a New Guinea People*. Yale University Press, New Haven, Conn.

Ratcliffe, D. (Ed.) (1977). *A Nature Conservation Review*. Vol.1. Cambridge University Press.

Riney, T. (1982). *The Study and Management of Large Mammals*. J. Wiley and Sons, New York.

Roome, N.J. (1984). Evaluation in Nature Conservation Decision Making. *Environmental Conservation* 11(3): 247-252.

Roth, H.H. and Merz, G. (1980). Management and Research Needs for Conservation Areas in Tropical Rainforests in West and Central African Areas. Unpub. manuscript.

Saavedra, C.J. and Freese, C.H. (1985). Biological Priorities for Conservation in the Tropical Andes. WWF-US. Unpublished report. Washington. October. 56 pp. and appendices.

Saharia, V.B. (1984). Human Dimensions in Wildlife Management: The Indian Experience. In: McNeely, J.A. and Miller, K.R. (Eds), *National Parks, Conservation, and Development: The Role of Protected Areas in Sustaining Society*. IUCN/Smithsonian Institution Press, Washington, D.C.

Salazar, A.P. (1984). Ecuadorian Strategy for the Conservation of Wildlands and Wildlife. In: McNeely, J.A. and Miller, K.R. (Eds), *National Parks, Conservation, and Development: The Role of Protected Areas in Sustaining Society*. IUCN/Smithsonian Institution Press, Washington.

Sale, J.B. (1981). *The Importance and Values of Wild Plants and Animals in Africa*. IUCN, Gland, Switzerland. 44p.

*Salm, R.V. and Clark, J.R. (1984). *Marine and Coastal Protected Areas: A Guide for Planners and Managers*. IUCN, Gland, Switzerland.

Sayer, J.A. (1977). Conservation of Large Mammals in the Republic of Mali. *Biological Conservation* 12(4): 245-263.

Sayer, J.A. (1981). Tourism or Conservation in the National Parks of Benin. *Parks* 5(4).

Schaffer, M.L. (1981). Minimum population sizes for species conservation. *Bioscience* 31:131-134.

Schonfeld, C.A., and Hendee, J.C. (1978). *Wildlife Management in the Wilderness*. Boxwood Press, Pacific Grove, California.

Schumacher, E.F. (1974). *Small is Beautiful: a study of economics as if people mattered*. Abacus Books, London.

Shanks, David and Putney, Allen D. (1979). Dominica Forest and Park System Plan. ECNAMP, St. Croix, U.S. Virgin Islands. 155 pp.

*Sharpe, Grant W. (1976). *Interpreting the Environment*. John Wiley and Sons, New York.

Simberloff, D.S. and Abele, L.G. (1976). Island biogeography theory and conservation practice. *Science* 191: 285-286.

Sinclair, A.E.R. and Norton-Griffiths, M. (Eds) (1979). *Serengeti: Dynamics of an Ecosystem*. University of Chicago Press, Chicago.

Soulé, M.E., Wilcox, B.A. and Holtby C. (1979). Benign neglect: a model of faunal collapse in the game reserves of East Africa. *Biological Conservation* 15: 259-272.

*Soulé, M.E. and Wilcox, B.A. (1980). *Conservation Biology*. Sinauer Associates, Sunderland, Massachusetts. 395 pp.

Start, A.N. and Marshall, A.G. (1976). Nectarivorous bats as pollinators of trees in West Malaysia. In: Burley, J. and Styles, B.T. (Eds). *Tropical Trees: Variation, breeding and conservation*. Academi Press, London. Pp. 141-150.

Stein, R.E. and Johnson B. (1979). *Banking on the Biosphere*. Environmental procedures and practice of nine multilateral development agencies. IIED, London.

Sumardja, E.A. (1981). First Five National Parks in Indonesia. *Parks* 8(6): 1-4.

Sumardja, E.A., Harsono, and MacKinnon, J. (1984). Indonesia's Network of Protected Areas. In: McNeely, J.A. and Miller, K.R. (Eds), *National Parks, Conservation, and Development: The Role of Protected Areas in Sustaining Society*. IUCN/Smithsonian Institution Press, Washington, D.C.

Sumardja, E.A., Tarmudji, and Wind, J. (1984). Nature Conservation and Rice Production in the Dumoga Area, North Sulawesi, Indonesia. In: McNeely, J.A. and Miller, K.R. (Eds), *National Parks, Conservation, and Development: The Role of Protected Areas in Sustaining Society*. IUCN Smithsonian Institution Press, Washington, D.C.

Talbot, L. (1979). *The Tip of the Iceberg: A biopolitical perspective on the Endangered Species Act* School of Forestry and Environmental Studies. Yale University, New Haven, Conn.

Terborgh, J. (1974). Preservation of natural diversity: the problem of extinction prone species. *Bioscience* 24: 715-722.

Thorsell, J.W. (1978). Thinking like an Island: Interpretation in Dominica, West Indies. *The Interpreter* X(1).

Thorsell, J.W. (1984a). *Managing Protected Areas in Eastern Africa: A Training Manual*. College of African Wildlife Management, Mweka, Tanzania.

Thorsell, J.W. (1984b). National Parks from the Ground Up: Experience from Dominica, West India. In: McNeely, J.A. and Miller, K.R. (Eds), *National Parks, Conservation, and Development: The Role of Protected Areas in Sustaining Society*. IUCN/Smithsonian Institution Press, Washington, D.C.

Thorsell, J.W. (1985). Parks on the Borderline. *IUCN Bulletin* Vol. 16(10-12).

Thresher, P. (1981). The present value of an Amboseli lion. *World Animal Review* 40: 30-33.

Tilden, Freeman. (1967). *Interpreting our Heritage*. University of North Carolina Press, Chapel Hill.

Turnbull, Colin (1973). *The Mountain People*. Jonathan Cape, London. 253 pp.

Udvardy, M.D.F. (1975). *A Classification of the Biogeographical Provinces of the World*. IUCN Occasional Paper No. 18, Gland, Switzerland. 48 pp.

Udvardy, M.D.F. (1984). A Biogeographical Classification System for Terrestrial Environments. In: McNeely, J.A. and Miller, K.R. (Eds), *National Parks, Conservation, and Development: The Role of Protected Areas in Sustaining Society*. IUCN/Smithsonian Institution Press, Washington, D.C.

Unesco (1972). Convention concerning the protection of the world cultural and natural heritage. General Conference, 17th Session, Paris, 16 November 1972.

Unesco (1974). Criteria and Guidelines for the Choice and Establishment of Biosphere Reserves. MAB Report Series No. 22, Unesco, Paris.

United States Agency For International Development (1979). Environmental and Natural Resources Management in Developing Countries. A Report to Congress. Washington, D.C.

US National Park Service. (1979). Guidelines for the Selection of Biosphere Reserves. Interim Report. Washington, D.C.

*U.S. Peace Corps (1977). *Teaching Conservation in Developing Nations*. U.S. Government Printing Office, Washington, D.C.

Van Lavieren, L.P. (1983). *Wildlife Management in the Tropics with Special Emphasis on South-East Asia: A guidebook for the warden*. Handbook prepared for Ciawi School of Environmental Conservation Management. Bogor, Indonesia. 3 Vols.

Vogl, R.J. (1979). Some Basic Principles of Grassland Fire Management. *Environmental Management* 3(1): 51-57.

von Droste, B. (1984). How Unesco's Man and the Biosphere Reserve Programme is Contributing to Human Welfare. In: McNeely, J.A. and Miller, K.R. (Eds), *National Parks, Conservation, and Development: The Role of Protected Areas in Sustaining Society*. IUCN/Smithsonian Institution Press, Washington, D.C.

Von Richter, W. (1976). Recreational and Subsistence Hunting in a Semi-arid country: Botswana. FAO, Rome. AFO/WL:76/6-3.

Wells, D.R. (1971). Survival of the Malaysian Bird Fauna. *Malay Nature Journal* 24: 248-56.

Western, D. (1984). Amboseli National Park: Human Values and the Conservation of a Savanna Ecosystem. In: McNeely, J.A. and Miller, K.R. (Eds), *National Parks, Conservation, and Development: The Role of Protected Areas in Sustaining Society*. IUCN/Smithsonian Institution Press, Washington, D.C.

Western, D. and Henry, W. (1979). Economics and Conservation in Third World National Parks. *Bioscience* 29(7): 414-418.

Wetterberg, G.B., Prance, G.T. and Lovejoy, T. (1981). Conservation progress in Amazonia: a structural review. *Parks* 6 (2): 5-10.

Wetterberg, G.B. (1984). The Exchange of Wildlands Technology: A Management Agency Perspective. In: McNeely, J.A. and Miller, K.R. (Eds), *National Parks, Conservation, and Development: The Role of Protected Areas in Sustaining Society*. IUCN/Smithsonian Institution Press, Washington, D.C.

Wharton, C. (1968). Man, Fire and Wild Cattle in South East Asia. *Proceedings of the Tall Timber Fire Ecology Conference*, 8: 107-167.

Whitaker, R. (1984). Preliminary Survey of Crocodiles in Sabah, East Malaysia. World Wildlife Fund-Malaysia, Kuala Lumpur.

White, F. (1983). The Vegetation of Africa, a descriptive memoir to accompany the Unesco/AETFAT/UNSO Vegetation Map of Africa. Unesco, Paris.

Wilcox, Bruce A. (1980). Insular Ecology and Conservation. In: Soulé, M.E. and Wilcox, B.A. *Conservation Biology*. Sinauer Associates, Sunderland, Massachusetts. Pp. 95-117

Wilcox, Bruce A. (1984). *In Situ* Conservation of Genetic Resources: Determinants of Minimum Area Requirements. In: McNeely, J.A. and Miller, K.R. (Eds), *National Parks, Conservation, and Development: The Role of Protected Areas in Sustaining Society*. IUCN/Smithsonian Institution Press, Washington, D.C.

Willis, E.O. (1974). Population and local extinction of birds on Barro Colorado Island, Panama. *Ecological Monograph* 44: 153-169.

Wilson, C.C. and Wilson, W.L. (1975). The Influence of Selective Logging on Primates and some other animals in East Kalimantan. *Folia Primatol.* 23: 245-274.

Wilson, E.O. (1982). The Importance of Biological Field Stations. *Bioscience* 32(5): 320.

Winge, E.N. (1978). Involving the Public in Park Planning: USA. *Parks* 3(1).

Wright, R.M., Houseal, B. and de Leon, C. (1985). Kuna Yala: Indigenous Biosphere Reserve in the Making? *Parks*, 10(3): 25-27.

PART E

Appendix

Rangers on parade in Murchison Falls National Park, Uganda. A well-trained and disciplined field staff is an essential basis of

Appendix: Useful addresses of relevant agencies

WWF/IUCN World Conservation Centre Ave du Mont Blanc 1196 Gland Switzerland	See description in Chapter 12
Unesco 7, Place de Fontenoy 75700 Paris, France	See description in Chapter 12
U.S. National Park Service Dept. of the Interior P.O. Box 37127 Washington D.C. 20013-7127 USA.	See description in Chapter 12
CITES rue du Maupas 6 1004 Lausanne 9 Switzerland	See description in Chapter 12
United Nations Environment Programme (UNEP) P.O. Box 30552 Nairobi Kenya	UN agency coordinating global environmental efforts. Write for literature on global environmental issues
Food and Agriculture Organisation of the United Nations (FAO) Via delle Terme di Caracalla 00100 Rome, Italy	Funds and otherwise supports environment related projects with UNDP funding. Contact regional offices for specific information pertinent to the area.
Friends of the Earth 124 Spear Street San Francisco, CA 94105 USA.	Private organisation with members and chapters all over the world. Contact for local chapter/member address. Can provide information on environmental issues.

National Audubon Society
950 Third Ave.
New York, N.Y. 10022
USA.

Private conservation organisation
provides literature, information, and
training for naturalists/interpreters.
Write to the Vice President for Environmental Information and Education

The Nature Conservancy
International Programme
1785 Massachusetts Ave., N.W.
Washington D.C. 20036
USA.

Provides for land acquisition and
supports data centres

National Wildlife Federation
1412 16th Street, N.W.
Washington D.C. 20036, USA.

Conservation education association
develops and distributes conservation
teaching aids and materials

New York Zoological Society
The Zoological Park
Bronx, N.Y. 10460, USA.

Supports international wildlife
conservation projects/establishment of
parks and reserves

Sierra Club
Office of International Affairs
777 United Nations Plaza
New York, N.Y. 10017, USA.

Private conservation organisation
provides information/organises outdoor
activities

Center for International
Environment Information
345 East 46th Street
New York. N.Y. 10017, USA.

Promotes global understanding of
environmental problems.

Fauna & Flora Preservation Society
8-12 Camden High Street
London NW1 0JH
England

Funds wildlife conservation projects
worldwide (particularly when directly
related to endangered species)

Frankfurt Zoological Society
Alfred Brehm Platz 16
6000 Frankfurt am Main
West Germany

Worldwide wildlife conservation
projects

Brot fur die Welt
Stafflenbergstr. 76
7000 Stuttgart
West Germany

A religious foundation that funds
international development projects. Has
funded projects with an environmental
emphasis. Project proposal must contain a strong component of social change

European Economic Community
Rue de la Loi, 200
1049 Brussels
Belgium

Considers protected area components in
larger development aid projects as well
as direct funding of conservation

Peoples Trust for Endangered Species
19 Quarry Street
Surrey, GU1 3EH
England

Funds small environmental projects with
an emphasis on wildlife conservation

International Council for Bird Preservation (ICBP) 219c Huntingdon Road Cambridge CB3 0DL England	Funds small wildlife (bird) conservation projects
International Centre for Conservation Education Greenfield House Guiting Power Cheltenham, Glos. GL54 5T2 England	Prepares audiovisual programmes, runs training courses in use and preparation of audiovisual programmes and other facets of conservation education. Can send advisors/instructors overseas on short assignments

REGIONAL – ASIA AND PACIFIC

South Pacific Regional Environment Programme (SPREP) P.O. Box D5, Noumea Cedex New Caledonia	The regional parks focal point for the South Pacific island countries
FAO Regional Office for Asia and the Far East Maliwan Mansion Phra Athit Road, Bangkok 2 Thailand	News bulletin 'Tigerpaper' information, contacts
Association for the Conservation of Wildlife 4 Old Custom House Lane Bangkok Thailand	'Conservation News – Southeast Asia' information/contacts, association membership
Yayasan Indonesia Hijau (Green Indonesia Foundation) P.O. Box Jakarta Indonesia	Association membership, journal *Suara Alam* (Voice of Nature), booklets, posters, lectures, complete slide presentations with commentary in Indonesian
World Wildlife Fund-India (Nature Clubs) c/o Godrey & Boyce Ltd. Lalbaug, Parel Bombay 400012 India	Information, contacts, possibly teaching aids, funding for small projects
World Wildlife Fund-Malaysia P.O. Box 10769 Kuala Lumpur Malaysia	Information, contacts, possibly teaching aids, funding for small projects

Wildlife Institute of India New Forest Dehra Dun 248006 Uttar Pradesh India	Training and research institution
School of Environmental Conservation Management, CIAWI P.O. Box 109 Bogor Indonesia	Training and research institution

REGIONAL – AFRICA

FAO Regional Office for Africa P.O. Box 1628 Accra Ghana	Literature, contacts
FAO Regional Office for the Near East P.O. Box 2223 Cairo, Egypt	Literature, contacts
African Wildlife Foundation Embassy House, Harambee Avenue P.O. Box 48177 Nairobi Kenya (U.S. address: 1717 Massachusetts Avenue, N.W. Washington D.C. 20036 USA.)	Information, literature, project funding. Publishes 'African Wildlife News'
Elsa Wild Animal Appeal P.O. Box 4572 North Hollywood, CA. 91607 USA.	Funds educational projects affiliated with wildlife clubs in Kenya and elsewhere
East African Wildlife Society P.O. Box 20110 Nairobi Kenya	Information/contacts, publishes *Swara* magazine
Wildlife Clubs of Kenya P.O. Box 40658 Nairobi Kenya	Information, contacts, teaching aids
Wildlife Conservation Society of Zambia P.O. Box 30255 Lusaka Zambia	Information, contacts

College of African Wildlife Management, Mweka P.O. Box 3031 Moshi Tanzania	Regional training centre for anglophone Africa
School for the Formation of Wildlife Specialists P.O. Box 271 Garoua Cameroon	Regional training centre for francophone Africa

REGIONAL – SOUTH AMERICA

FAO Regional Office for Latin America Casilla 10095 Santiago Chile	Information/contacts
Organisation of American States 17th Street, Constitution Ave. N.W., Washington D.C. USA.	Information, legal assistance and policy advice
Caribbean Conservation Association Savannah Lodge The Garrison, St. Michael Barbados West Indies	Technical and financial assistance to conservation efforts
Amigos de la Naturaleza P.O. Box 162 Guadalupe Costa Rica	Information distribution centre assist with project funding
Centro Agronomico Tropical de Investigacion y Enseñanza CATIE Turrialba Costa Rica	Information on wildlands planning, training, and management in Mesoamerica
Asociacion Peruana Para La Conservacion de la Naturaleza Atahualpa 335 Lima 18 Peru	Funds conservation projects in Peru

Index of Protected Areas

General Index